Linux System Administration

White Papers

Olaf Kirch

Lars Wirzenius

President, CEO
Keith Weiskamp

Publisher
Steve Sayre

Acquisitions Editor
Stephanie Wall

Marketing Specialist
Diane Enger

Project Editor
Sharon Sanchez McCarson

Production Coordinator
Jon Gabriel

Cover Design
Jesse Dunn

Layout Design
April Nielsen

Linux System Administration White Papers
This book is covered by the GNU Public License. Please see Appendix B for more information.

The Linux Network Administrators' Guide
The online document was generated using the LaTeX2HTML translator.

Version 1.0 by Olaf Kirch. Copyright Olaf Kirch.

Version 96.1-c (Feb 29, 1996) Copyright © 1993, 1994, 1995, 1996, Nikos Drakos, Computer Based Learning Unit, University of Leeds.

The translation was initiated by Andrew Anderson on Thu Mar 7 23:22:06 EST 1996.

The Linux System Administrators' Guide
Version 0.6.1 by Lars Wirzenius

Copyright 1993–1998 Lars Wirzenius.

Trademarks are owned by their owners.

The Coriolis Group, LLC
14455 North Hayden Road
Suite 220
Scottsdale, Arizona 85260

480/483-0192
FAX 480/483-0193
http://www.coriolis.com

Library of Congress Cataloging-in-Publication Data
Kirch, Olaf
   Linux system administration white papers / by Olaf Kirch and Lars Wirzenius
      p.   cm.
   ISBN 1-57610-474-5
   1. Linux   2. Operating systems (Computers).   I. Wirzenius, Lars.
QA76.76.O63L549   1999
005.4'469 — dc21

99-38872
CIP

Printed in the United States of America
10 9 8 7 6 5 4 3 2 1

14455 North Hayden Road, Suite 220 • Scottsdale, Arizona 85260

Dear Reader:

Coriolis Technology Press was founded to create a very elite group of books: the ones you keep closest to your machine. Sure, everyone would like to have the Library of Congress at arm's reach, but in the real world, you have to choose the books you rely on every day *very* carefully.

To win a place for our books on that coveted shelf beside your PC, we guarantee several important qualities in every book we publish. These qualities are:

- *Technical accuracy*—It's no good if it doesn't work. Every Coriolis Technology Press book is reviewed by technical experts in the topic field, and is sent through several editing and proofreading passes in order to create the piece of work you now hold in your hands.

- *Innovative editorial design*—We've put years of research and refinement into the ways we present information in our books. Our books' editorial approach is uniquely designed to reflect the way people learn new technologies and search for solutions to technology problems.

- *Practical focus*—We put only pertinent information into our books and avoid any fluff. Every fact included between these two covers must serve the mission of the book as a whole.

- *Accessibility*—The information in a book is worthless unless you can find it quickly when you need it. We put a lot of effort into our indexes, and heavily cross-reference our chapters, to make it easy for you to move right to the information you need.

Here at The Coriolis Group we have been publishing and packaging books, technical journals, and training materials since 1989. We're programmers and authors ourselves, and we take an ongoing active role in defining what we publish and how we publish it. We have put a lot of thought into our books; please write to us at **ctp@coriolis.com** and let us know what you think. We hope that you're happy with the book in your hands, and that in the future, when you reach for software development and networking information, you'll turn to one of our books first.

Keith Weiskamp
President and CEO

Jeff Duntemann
VP and Editorial Director

Look For These Other Books From The Coriolis Group:

Contents At A Glance

Table Of Contents

Foreword

By Eric Raymond

Long-established folklore in the computing industry has it that programmers hate writing documentation. Not true, as it turns out—many programmers will cheerfully write documentation for the programs that they truly care about. No better illustration of this could be found than in the book you are about to read.

Linux is a labor of love for the people who develop it. Its astonishing success, taking it from zero visibility to a major contender in three years, demonstrates that love can be more powerful than gold for motivating high-quality creative work. But it takes gold to print books and press CDs, so the Linux world is evolving ways to cooperate with the market and build flourishing distribution industries around their OS. This book is also an illustration of that trend.

The Coriolis Group is exploring ways in which to cooperate with the Linux Documentation Project that will help Linux developers specialize in what they do best (coding and technical-reference documentation), while Coriolis supplies what it does best (editing, production, publication, and marketing). The result should be both nice profits for Coriolis and a better quality of online documentation for the Linux community. All LDP documentation will continue to be distributed under open-content licenses supporting free redistribution, and Coriolis's improvements will be donated back to the community.

This first volume is aimed at Linux system administrators.

Introduction

The *Linux System Administration White Papers* is a printed edition of two online books (out of eight) hosted on the Linux Document Pages (LDP) Web site (**http://metalab.unc.edu/LDP/**). The Coriolis Group is exploring various ways to support Linux and the open source model of developing software. We felt that one way to accomplish this was to publish the LDP in two volumes; this one, and a second one to focus on software development issues, entitled *Linux Programming White Papers*. Please be sure to look at the LDP for additional Linux resources offered. As part of this introduction, you will find the LDP Manifesto. Please read it, as it will provide you with more information on the LDP.

By the grants outlined in the authors' copyrights for this material, we are able to publish it in paper form. This also means that the material contained in this book is freely redistributable as long as the copyright provisions put in place by the authors are upheld. Please refer to Appendix A for the Linux Documentation Project Copying License that clearly states what these copyright provisions are. In addition, please refer to Appendix B for the GNU Public License, the license in which Linux is covered under. If you have additional questions, please refer to the GNU Project Web site at **www.gnu.org**.

While reading this book you will notice that some material is a bit outdated and some examples may be missing. The reason for this is that in respecting the copyright provisions governing use of the LDP, we were not permitted to change the authors' material, even to correct errors and omissions; however, we did mark those places where we found missing or incorrect material. Be sure to refer to the online LDP for updated versions of the documentation in this book.

The Coriolis Group is always looking for ways to further support Linux. If you would like to share an idea with us here on how we can do this, please contact us directly at **ctp@coriolis.com**. We look forward to your comments.

The Coriolis Group

Linux Documentation Project "Manifesto"

Last Revision 21 September 1998, by Michael K. Johnson

This file describes the goals and current status of the Linux Documentation Project, including names of projects, volunteers, FTP sites, and so on.

Overview

The Linux Documentation Project is working on developing good, reliable docs for the Linux operating system. The overall goal of the LDP is to collaborate in taking care of all of the issues of Linux documentation, ranging from online docs (man pages, texinfo docs, and so on) to printed manuals covering topics such as installing, using, and running Linux. The LDP is essentially a loose team of volunteers with little central organization; anyone who is interested in helping is welcome to join in the effort. We feel that working together and agreeing on the direction and scope of Linux documentation is the best way to go, to reduce problems with conflicting efforts—two people writing two books on the same aspect of Linux wastes someone's time along the way.

The LDP is set out to produce the canonical set of Linux online and printed documentation. Because our docs will be freely available (like software licensed under the terms of the GNU GPL) and distributed on the net, we are able to easily update the documentation to stay on top of the many changes in the Linux world. If you are interested in publishing any of the LDP works, see the section "Publishing LDP Manuals," below.

Getting Involved

Send mail to **linux-howto@metalab.unc.edu**.

Of course, you'll also need to get in touch with the coordinator of whatever LDP projects you're interested in working on; see the next section.

Current Projects

For a list of current projects, see the LDP home page at **http://metalab.unc.edu/LDP/**. The best way to get involved with one of these projects is to pick up the current version of the manual and send revisions, editions, or suggestions to the coordinator. You probably want to coordinate with the author before sending revisions so that you know you are working together.

FTP Sites For LDP Works

LDP works can be found on **metalab.unc.edu** in the directory **/pub/Linux/docs**. LDP manuals are found in **/pub/Linux/docs/LDP**, HOWTOs and other documentation found in **/pub/Linux/docs/HOWTO**.

Documentation Conventions

Here are the conventions that are currently used by LDP manuals. If you are interested in writing another manual using different conventions, please let us know of your plans first.

The *man pages*—the Unix standard for online manuals—are created with the Unix standard nroff man (or BSD mdoc) macros.

The *guides*—full books produced by the LDP—have historically been done in LaTeX, as their primary goal has been to be *printed* documentation. However, guide authors have been moving toward SGML with the DocBook DTD, because it allows them to create more different kinds of output, both printed and online. If you use LaTeX, we have a style file you can use to keep your printed look consistent with other LDP documents, and we suggest that you use it.

The *HOWTO* documents are all required to be in SGML format. Currently, they use the *linuxdoc* DTD, which is quite simple. There is a move afoot to switch to the DocBook DTD over time.

LDP documents must be freely redistributable without fees paid to the authors. It is not required that the text be modifiable, but it is encouraged. You can come up with your own license terms that satisfy this constraint, or you can use a previously prepared license. The LDP provides a boilerplate license that you can use, some people like to use the GPL, and others write their own.

The copyright for each manual should be in the name of the head writer or coordinator for the project. "The Linux Documentation Project'" isn't a formal entity and shouldn't be used to copyright the docs.

Copyright And License

Here is a "boilerplate" license you may apply to your work. It has not been reviewed by a lawyer; feel free to have your own lawyer review it (or your modification of it) for its applicability to your own desires. Remember that in order for your document to be part of the LDP, you must allow unlimited reproduction and distribution without fee.

This manual may be reproduced and distributed in whole or in part, without fee, subject to the following conditions:

◆ The copyright notice above and this permission notice must be preserved complete on all complete or partial copies.

◆ Any translation or derived work must be approved by the author in writing before distribution.

◆ If you distribute this work in part, instructions for obtaining the complete version of this manual must be included, and a means for obtaining a complete version provided.

♦ Small portions may be reproduced as illustrations for reviews or quotes in other works without this permission notice if proper citation is given.

Exceptions to these rules may be granted for academic purposes: Write to the author and ask. These restrictions are here to protect us as authors, not to restrict you as learners and educators.

All source code in this document is placed under the GNU General Public License, available via anonymous FTP from **ftp://prep.ai.mit.edu:/pub/gnu/COPYING**.

Publishing LDP Manuals

If you're a publishing company interested in distributing any of the LDP manuals, read on.

By the license requirements given previously, anyone is allowed to publish and distribute verbatim copies of the Linux Documentation Project manuals. You don't need our explicit permission for this. However, if you would like to distribute a translation or derivative work based on any of the LDP manuals, you may need to obtain permission from the author, in writing, before doing so, if the license requires that.

You may, of course, sell the LDP manuals for profit. We encourage you to do so. Keep in mind, however, that because the LDP manuals are freely distributable, anyone may photocopy or distribute printed copies free of charge, if they wish to do so.

We do not require to be paid royalties for any profit earned from selling LDP manuals. However, we would like to suggest that if you do sell LDP manuals for profit, that you either offer the author royalties, or donate a portion of your earnings to the author, the LDP as a whole, or to the Linux development community. You may also wish to send one or more free copies of the LDP manuals that you are distributing to the authors. Your show of support for the LDP and the Linux community will be very much appreciated.

We would like to be informed of any plans to publish or distribute LDP manuals, just so we know how they're becoming available. If you are publishing or planning to publish any LDP manuals, please send mail to **ldp-l@linux.org.au**. It's nice to know who's doing what.

We encourage Linux software distributors to distribute the LDP manuals (such as the Installation And Getting Started Guide) with their software. The LDP manuals are intended to be used as the "official" Linux documentation, and we are glad to see mail-order distributors bundling the LDP manuals with the software. As the LDP manuals mature, hopefully they will fulfill this goal more and more adequately.

Part I

The Linux Network Administrators' Guide

by Olaf Kirch

The Network Administrators' Guide

The online document was generated using the LaTeX2HTML translator.

Version 1.0 by Olaf Kirch. Copyright Olaf Kirch.

Version 96.1-c (Feb 29, 1996) Copyright © 1993, 1994, 1995, 1996, Nikos Drakos, Computer Based Learning Unit, University of Leeds.

The command line arguments were:

```
latex2html toplevel/nag.tex.
```

The translation was initiated by Andrew Anderson on Thu Mar 7 23:22:06 EST 1996.

For Britta

Chapter 1
Introduction To Networking

The idea of networking is probably as old as telecommunications itself. Consider people living in the stone age, where drums may have been used to transmit messages between individuals. Suppose caveman A wants to invite caveman B for a game of hurling rocks at each other, but they live too far apart for B to hear A banging his drum. So what are A's options? He could 1) walk over to B's place, 2) get a bigger drum, or 3) ask C, who lives halfway between them, to forward the message. This last option is called networking.

Of course, we have come a long way from the primitive pursuits and devices of our forebears. Nowadays, we have computers talk to each other over vast assemblages of wires, fiber optics, microwaves, and the like, to make an appointment for Saturday's soccer match. In the following, we will deal with the means and ways by which this is accomplished, but leave out the wires, as well as the soccer part.

We will describe two types of networks in this guide: those based on UUCP, and those based on TCP/IP. These are protocol suites and software packages that supply means to transport data between two computers. In this chapter, we will look at both types of networks, and discuss their underlying principles.

We define a network as a collection of hosts that are able to communicate with each other, often by relying on the services of a number of dedicated hosts that relay data between the participants. Hosts are very often computers, but need not be; one can also think of X-terminals or intelligent printers as hosts. Small agglomerations of hosts are also called sites.

Communication is impossible without some sort of language or code. In computer networks, these languages are collectively referred to as protocols. However, you shouldn't think of written protocols here, but rather of the highly formalized code of behavior observed when heads of state meet, for instance. In a very similar fashion, the protocols used in computer networks are nothing but very strict rules for the exchange of messages between two or more hosts.

UUCP Networks

UUCP is an abbreviation for Unix-to-Unix Copy. It started out as a package of programs to transfer files over serial lines, schedule those transfers, and initiate execution of programs on remote sites. It has undergone major changes since its first implementation in the late seventies, but is still rather Spartan in the services it offers. Its main application is still in wide-area networks based on dial-up telephone links.

UUCP was first developed by Bell Laboratories in 1977 for communication between their Unix development sites. In mid-1978, this network already connected over 80 sites. It was running email as an application, as well as remote printing. However, the system's central use was in distributing new software and bug fixes. Today, UUCP is not confined to the environment anymore. There are both free and commercial ports available for a variety of platforms, including AmigaOS, DOS, Atari's TOS, and so on.

One of the main disadvantages of UUCP networks is their low bandwidth. On one hand, telephone equipment places a tight limit on the maximum transfer rate. On the other hand, UUCP links are rarely permanent connections; instead, hosts dial up each other at regular intervals. Hence, most of the time it takes a mail message to travel a UUCP network it sits idly on some host's disk, awaiting the next time a connection is established.

Despite these limitations, there are still many UUCP networks operating all over the world, run mainly by hobbyists, which offer private users network access at reasonable prices. The main reason for the popularity of UUCP is that it is dirt cheap compared to having your computer connected to The Big Internet Cable. To make your computer a UUCP node, all you need is a modem, a working UUCP implementation, and another UUCP node that is willing to feed you mail and news.

How To Use UUCP

The idea behind UUCP is rather simple: As its name indicates, it basically copies files from one host to another, but it also allows certain actions to be performed on the remote host.

Suppose your machine is allowed to access a hypothetical host named Swim, and have it execute the **lpr** print command for you. Then you could type the following on your command line to have this book printed on Swim:

```
$ uux -r swim!lpr !netguide.dvi
```

This makes **uux**, a command from the UUCP suite, schedule a job for Swim. This job consists of the input file, netguide.dvi, and the request to feed this file to lpr. The -r flag tells **uux** not to call the remote system immediately, but to rather store the job away until a connection is established at a later occasion. This is called spooling.

Another property of UUCP is that it allows to forward jobs and files through several hosts, provided they cooperate. Assume that Swim, from the above examples, has a UUCP link with Groucho, which maintains a large archive of applications. To download the file tripwire-1.0.tar.gz to your site, you might issue

```
$ uucp  -mr  swim!groucho!~/security/tripwire-1.0.tar.gz
trip.tgz
```

The job created will request Swim to fetch the file from Groucho, and send it to your site, where UUCP will store it in trip.tgz and notify you via mail of the file's arrival. This will be done in three steps. First, your site sends the job to Swim. When Swim establishes contact with Groucho the next time, it downloads the file. The final step is the actual transfer from Swim to your host.

The most important services provided by UUCP networks these days are electronic mail and news. We will come back to these later, so we will give only a brief introduction here.

Electronic mail—email for short—allows you to exchange messages with users on remote hosts without actually having to know how to access these hosts. The task of directing a message from your site to the destination site is performed entirely by the mail handling system. In a UUCP environment, mail is usually transported by executing the rmail command on a neighboring host, passing it the recipient address and the mail message. rmail will then forward the message to another host, and so on, until it reaches the destination host. We will look at this in detail in Chapter 12.

News may best be described as sort of a distributed bulletin board system. Most often, this term refers to Usenet news, which is by far the most widely known news exchange network with an estimated number of 120,000 participating sites. The origins of Usenet date back to 1979, when, after the release of UUCP with the new Unix-V7, three graduate students had the idea of a general information exchange within the Unix community. They put together some scripts, which became the first netnews system. In 1980, this network connected Duke, UNC, and PHS, at two universities in North Carolina. Out of this, Usenet eventually grew. Although it originated as a UUCP-based network, it is no longer confined to one single type of network.

The basic unit of information is the article, which may be posted to a hierarchy of newsgroups dedicated to specific topics. Most sites receive only a selection of all newsgroups, which carry an average of 60MB worth of articles a day.

In the UUCP world, news is generally sent across a UUCP link by collecting all articles from the groups requested, and packing them up in a number of batches. These are sent to the receiving site, where they are fed to the rnews command for unpacking and further processing.

Finally, UUCP is also the medium of choice for many dial-up archive sites which offer public access. You can usually access them by dialing them up with UUCP, logging in as a guest user, and download files from a publicly accessible archive area. These guest accounts often have a login name and password of uucp/nuucp or something similar.

TCP/IP Networks

Although UUCP may be a reasonable choice for low-cost dial-up network links, there are many situations in which its store-and-forward technique proves too inflexible, for example in local area networks (LANs). These are usually made up of a small number of machines located in the same building, or even on the same floor, that are interconnected to provide a homogeneous working environment. Typically, you would want to share files between these hosts, or run distributed applications on different machines.

These tasks require a completely different approach to networking. Instead of forwarding entire files along with a job description, all data is broken up in smaller chunks (packets), which are forwarded immediately to the destination host, where they are reassembled. This type of network is called a packet-switched network. Among other things, this allows running interactive applications over the network. The cost of this is, of course, a greatly increased complexity in software.

The solution that systems—and many non-Linux sites—have adopted is known as TCP/IP. In this section, we will have a look at its underlying concepts.

Introduction To TCP/IP Networks

TCP/IP traces its origins to a research project funded by the United States DARPA (Defense Advanced Research Projects Agency) in 1969. This was an experimental network, the ARPANET, which was converted into an operational one in 1975, after it had proven to be a success.

In 1983, the new protocol suite TCP/IP was adopted as a standard, and all hosts on the network were required to use it. When ARPANET finally grew into the Internet (with ARPANET itself passing out of existence in 1990), the use of TCP/IP had spread to networks beyond the Internet itself. Most notable are local area networks, but in the advent of fast digital telephone equipment, such as ISDN, it also has a promising future as a transport for dial-up networks.

For something concrete to look at as we discuss TCP/IP throughout the following sections, we will consider Groucho Marx University (GMU), situated somewhere in Fredland, as an example. Most departments run their own local area networks, while some share one, and others run several of them. They are all interconnected, and are hooked to the Internet through a single high-speed link.

Suppose your box is connected to a LAN of hosts at the Mathematics Department, and its name is Erdos. To access a host at the Physics Department named Quark, you enter the following command:

```
$ rlogin quark.physics
Welcome to the Physics Department at GMU
(ttyq2) login:
```

At the prompt, you enter your login name, Andres, and your password. You are then given a shell on Quark, to which you can type as if you were sitting at the system's console. After you exit the shell, you are returned to your own machine's prompt. You have just used one of the instantaneous, interactive applications that TCP/IP provides: remote login.

While being logged into Quark, you might also want to run an X11-based application, like a function plotting program, or a PostScript previewer. To tell this application that you want to have its windows displayed on your host's screen, you have to set the DISPLAY environment variable:

```
$ export DISPLAY=erdos.maths:0.0
```

If you now start your application, it will contact your X server instead of Quark's, and display all its windows on your screen. Of course, this requires that you have X11 running on Erdos. The point here is that TCP/IP allows Quark and Erdos to send X11 packets back and forth to give you the illusion that you're on a single system. The network is almost transparent here.

Another very important application in TCP/IP networks is NFS, which stands for *Network File System*. It is another form of making the network transparent, because it basically allows you to mount directory hierarchies from other hosts, so that they appear like local file systems. For example, all users' home directories can be on a central server machine, from which all other hosts on the LAN mount the directory. The effect of this is that users can log into any machine, and find themselves in the same home directory. Similarly, it is possible to install applications that require large amounts of disk space (such as TeX) on only one machine, and export these directories to other machines. We will come back to NFS in Chapter 10.

Of course, these are only examples of what you can do over TCP/IP networks. The possibilities are almost limitless.

We will now have a closer look at the way TCP/IP works. You will need this to understand how and why you have to configure your machine. We will start by examining the hardware, and slowly work our way up.

Ethernets

The type of hardware most widely used throughout LANs is what is commonly known as Ethernet. It consists of a single cable with hosts being attached to it through connectors, taps, or transceivers. Simple Ethernets are quite inexpensive to install, which, together with a net transfer rate of 10Mbps, accounts for much of its popularity.

Ethernets come in three flavors, called thick and thin, respectively, and twisted pair. Thin and thick Ethernet each use a coaxial cable, differing in width and the way you may attach a host to this cable. Thin Ethernet uses a T-shaped "BNC" connector, which you insert into the cable, and twist onto a plug on the back of your computer. Thick Ethernet requires that you drill a small hole into the cable, and attach a transceiver using a "vampire tap." One or more hosts can then be connected to the transceiver. Thin and thick Ethernet cable may run for a maximum of 200 and 500 meters, respectively, and are therefore also called 10base-2 and 10base-5. Twisted pair uses a cable made of two copper wires which is also found in ordinary telephone installations, but usually requires additional hardware. It is also known as 10base-T.

Although adding a host to a thick Ethernet is a little hairy, it does not bring down the network. To add a host to a thinnet installation, you have to disrupt network service for at least a few minutes because you have to cut the cable to insert the connector.

Most people prefer thin Ethernet, because it is very cheap: PC cards come for as little as $10, and cable is in the range of a few cents per meter. However, for large-scale installations, thick Ethernet is more appropriate. For example, the Ethernet at GMU's Mathematics Department uses thick Ethernet, so traffic will not be disrupted each time a host is added to the network.

One of the drawbacks of Ethernet technology is its limited cable length, which precludes any use of it other than for LANs. However, several Ethernet segments may be linked to each other using repeaters, bridges, or routers. Repeaters simply copy the signals between two or more segments, so that all segments together will act as if it was one Ethernet.

Ethernet works like a bus system, where a host may send packets (or frames) of up to 1500 bytes to another host on the same Ethernet. A host is addressed by a 6-byte address hard-coded into the firmware of its Ethernet board. These addresses are usually written as a sequence of two-digit hex numbers separated by colons, as in aa:bb:cc:dd:ee:ff.

A frame sent by one station is seen by all attached stations, but only the destination host actually picks it up and processes it. If two stations try to send at the same time, a collision occurs, which is resolved by the two stations aborting the send, and re-attempting it a few moments later.

Other Types Of Hardware

In larger installations, such as Groucho Marx University, Ethernet is usually not the only type of equipment used. At Groucho Marx University, each department's LAN is linked to the campus backbone, which is a fiber optics cable running FDDI (fiber distributed data interface). FDDI uses an entirely different approach to transmitting data, which basically involves sending around a number of tokens, with a station only being allowed to send a frame if it captures a token. The main advantage of FDDI is a speed of up to 100Mbps, and a maximum cable length of up to 200 km.

For long-distance network links, a different type of equipment is frequently used, which is based on a standard named X.25. Many so-called Public Data Networks, like Tymnet in the U.S., or Datex-P in Germany, offer this service. X.25 requires special hardware, namely a packet assembler/disassembler, or PAD. X.25 defines a set of networking protocols of its own right, but is nevertheless frequently used to connect networks running TCP/IP and other protocols. Since IP packets cannot simply be mapped onto X.25 (and vice versa), they are simply encapsulated in X.25 packets and sent over the network.

Frequently, radio amateurs use their equipment to network their computers; this is called packet radio or ham radio. The protocol used by ham radios is called AX.25, which was derived from X.25.

Other techniques involve using slow but cheap serial lines for dial-up access. These require yet another protocol for transmission of packets, such as SLIP or PPP, which will be described below.

The Internet Protocol

Of course, you wouldn't want your networking to be limited to one Ethernet. Ideally, you would want to be able to use a network regardless of what hardware it runs on and how many subunits it is made up of. For example, in larger installations such as Groucho Marx University, you usually have a number of separate Ethernets that have to be connected in some way. At GMU, the Mathematics Department runs two Ethernets: one network of fast machines for professors and graduates, and another one with slow machines for students. Both are linked to the FDDI campus backbone.

This connection is handled by a dedicated host, a so-called gateway, which handles incoming and outgoing packets by copying them between the two Ethernets and the fiber optics cable. For example, if you are at the Math Department, and want to access Quark on the Physics Department's LAN from your box, the networking software cannot send packets to Quark directly, because it is not on the same Ethernet. Therefore, it has to rely on the gateway to act as a forwarder. The gateway (name it Sophus) then forwards these packets to its peer gateway Niels at the Physics Department, using the backbone, with Niels delivering it to the destination machine.

This scheme of directing data to a remote host is called routing, and packets are often referred to as datagrams in this context. To facilitate things, datagram exchange is governed by a single protocol that is independent of the hardware used: IP, or Internet Protocol. In Chapter 2, we will cover IP and the issues of routing in greater detail.

The main benefit of IP is that it turns physically dissimilar networks into one apparently homogeneous network. This is called internetworking, and the resulting "meta-network" is called an internet. Note the subtle difference between an internet and the Internet here. The latter is the official name of one particular global internet.

Of course, IP also requires a hardware-independent addressing scheme. This is achieved by assigning each host a unique 32-bit number, called the IP address. An IP address is usually written as four decimal numbers, one for each 8-bit portion, separated by dots. For example, Quark might have an IP address of 0x954C0C04, which would be written as 149.76.12.4. This format is also called dotted quad notation.

You will notice that we now have three different types of addresses: first there is the host's name, like Quark; then there are IP addresses; and finally, there are hardware addresses, like the 6-byte Ethernet address. All these somehow have to match, so that when you type **rlogin quark**, the networking software can be given Quark's IP address; and when IP delivers any data to the Physics Department's Ethernet, it somehow has to find out what Ethernet address corresponds to the IP address—which is rather confusing.

We will not go into this here, and deal with it in Chapter 2 instead. For now, it's enough to remember that these steps of finding addresses are called hostname resolution, for mapping hostnames onto IP addresses, and address resolution, for mapping the latter to hardware addresses.

IP Over Serial Lines

On serial lines, a "de facto" standard known as SLIP, or *Serial Line IP*, is frequently used. A modification of SLIP is known as CSLIP, or compressed SLIP, and performs compression of IP headers to make better use of the relatively low bandwidth provided by serial links. A different serial protocol is PPP (see Chapter 7), or *Point-to-Point Protocol*. PPP has many more features than SLIP, including a link negotiation phase. Its main advantage over SLIP is, however, that it isn't limited to transporting IP datagrams, but that it was designed to allow for any type of datagrams to be transmitted.

The Transmission Control Protocol

Now, of course, sending datagrams from one host to another is not the whole story. If you log into Quark, you want to have a reliable connection between your rlogin process on Erdos and the shell process on Quark. Thus, the information sent to and fro must be split up into packets by the sender, and reassembled into a character stream by the receiver. Trivial as it seems, this involves a number of hairy tasks.

A very important thing to know about IP is that, by intent, it is not reliable. Assume that ten people on your Ethernet started downloading the latest release of XFree86 from GMU's

FTP server. The amount of traffic generated by this might be too much for the gateway to handle, because it's too slow, and it's tight on memory. Now if you happen to send a packet to Quark, Sophus might just be out of buffer space for a moment and therefore unable to forward it. IP solves this problem by simply discarding it. The packet is irrevocably lost. It is therefore the responsibility of the communicating hosts to check the integrity and completeness of the data, and retransmit it in case of an error.

This is performed by yet another protocol, TCP, or Transmission Control Protocol, which builds a reliable service on top of IP. The essential property of TCP is that it uses IP to give you the illusion of a simple connection between the two processes on your host and the remote machine, so that you don't have to care about how and along which route your data actually travels. A TCP connection works essentially like a two-way pipe that both processes may write to and read from. Think of it as a telephone conversation.

TCP identifies the endpoints of such a connection by the IP addresses of the two hosts involved, and the number of so-called ports on each host. Ports may be viewed as attachment points for network connections. If we are to strain the telephone example a little more, one might compare IP addresses to area codes (numbers map to cities), and port numbers to local codes (numbers map to individual people's telephones).

In the rlogin example, the client application (rlogin) opens a port on Erdos, and connects to port 513 on Quark, which the rlogind server is known to listen to. This establishes a TCP connection. Using this connection, rlogind performs the authorization procedure, and then spawns the shell. The shell's standard input and output are redirected to the TCP connection, so that anything you type to rlogin on your machine will be passed through the TCP stream and be given to the shell as standard input.

The User Datagram Protocol

Of course, TCP isn't the only user protocol in TCP/IP networking. Although suitable for applications like rlogin, the overhead involved is prohibitive for applications like NFS. Instead, it uses a sibling protocol of TCP called UDP, or *User Datagram Protocol*. Just like TCP, UDP also allows an application to contact a service on a certain port on the remote machine, but it doesn't establish a connection for this. Instead, you may use it to send single packets to the destination service—hence its name.

Assume you have mounted the TeX directory hierarchy from the department's central NFS server, Galois, and you want to view a document describing how to use LaTeX. You start your editor, who first reads in the entire file. However, it would take too long to establish a TCP connection with Galois, send the file, and release it again. Instead, a request is made to Galois, who sends the file in a couple of UDP packets, which is much faster. However, UDP was not made to deal with packet loss or corruption. It is up to the application—NFS in this case—to take care of this.

More On Ports

Ports may be viewed as attachment points for network connections. If an application wants to offer a certain service, it attaches itself to a port and waits for clients (this is also called listening on the port). A client that wants to use this service allocates a port on its local host, and connects to the server's port on the remote host.

An important property of ports is that once a connection has been established between the client and the server, another copy of the server may attach to the server port and listen for more clients. This permits, for instance, several concurrent remote logins to the same host, all using the same port 513. TCP is able to tell these connections from each other, because they all come from different ports or hosts. For example, if you twice log into Quark from Erdos, then the first rlogin client will use the local port 1023, and the second one will use port 1022. Both, however, will connect to the same port 513 on Quark.

This example shows the use of ports as rendezvous points, where a client contacts a specific port to obtain a specific service. In order for a client to know the proper port number, an agreement has to be reached between the administrators of both systems on the assignment of these numbers. For services that are widely used, such as rlogin, these numbers have to be administered centrally. This is done by the IETF (or Internet Engineering Task Force), which regularly releases an RFC titled Assigned Numbers. It describes, among other things, the port numbers assigned to well-known services. Linux uses a file mapping service names to numbers, called /etc/services. It is described in Chapter 8.

It is worth noting that although both TCP and UDP connections rely on ports, these numbers do not conflict. This means that TCP port 513, for example, is different from UDP port 513. In fact, these ports serve as access points for two different services, namely rlogin (TCP) and rwho (UDP).

The Socket Library

In operating systems, the software performing all the tasks and protocols described above is usually part of the kernel. The programming interface most common in the world is the Berkeley Socket Library. Its name derives from a popular analogy that views ports as sockets, and connecting to a port as plugging in. It provides the (bind(2)) call to specify a remote host, a transport protocol, and a service which a program can connect or listen to (using connect(2), listen(2), and accept(2)). The socket library is, however, somewhat more general, in that it provides not only a class of TCP/IP-based sockets (the AF_INET sockets), but also a class that handles connections local to the machine (the AF_UNIX class). Some implementations can also handle other classes as well, like the XNS (Xerox Networking System) protocol, or X.25.

In Linux, the socket library is part of the standard libc C-library. Currently, it only supports AF_INET and AF_UNIX sockets, but efforts are made to incorporate support for Novell's networking protocols, so that eventually one or more socket classes for these would be added.

Networking

Being the result of a concerted effort of programmers around the world, Linux wouldn't have been possible without the global network. So it's not surprising that already in early stages of development, several people started to work on providing it with network capabilities. A UUCP implementation was running almost from the very beginning, and work on TCP/IP-based networking started around autumn 1992, when Ross Biro and others created what now has become known as Net-1.

After Ross quit active development in May 1993, Fred van Kempen began to work on a new implementation, rewriting major parts of the code. This ongoing effort is known as Net-2. A first public release, Net-2d, was made in summer 1992 (as part of the 0.99.10 kernel), and has since been maintained and expanded by several people, most notably Alan Cox, as Net-2Debugged. After heavy debugging and numerous improvements to the code, he (Alan Cox) changed its name to Net-3 after 1.0 was released.

Net-3 offers device drivers for a wide variety of Ethernet boards, as well as SLIP (for sending network traffic over serial lines), and PLIP (for parallel lines). Net-3 has a TCP/IP implementation that behaves very well in a local area network environment, showing uptimes that beat some of the commercial PC software makers.

Different Streaks Of Development

In the meanwhile, Fred continued development, going on to Net-2e, which features a much revised design of the networking layer. At the time of writing, Net-2e is still beta software. Most notable about Net-2e is the incorporation of DDI, the *device driver interface*. DDI offers a uniform access and configuration method to all networking devices and protocols.

Yet another implementation of TCP/IP networking comes from Matthias Urlichs, who wrote an ISDN driver for Linux and FreeBSD. For this, he integrated some of the BSD networking code in the kernel.

For the foreseeable future, however, Net-3 seems to be here to stay. Alan currently works on an implementation of the AX.25 protocol used by ham radio amateurs. Doubtlessly, the yet-to-be-developed "module" code for the kernel will also bring new impulses to the networking code. Modules allow you to add drivers to the kernel at run time.

Although these different network implementations all strive to provide the same service, there are major differences between them at the kernel and device level. Therefore, you will not be able to configure a system running a Net-2e kernel with utilities from Net-2d or Net-3, and vice versa. This only applies to commands that deal with kernel internals rather closely; applications and common networking commands such as rlogin or telnet run on either of them.

Nevertheless, all these different network version should not worry you. Unless you are participating in active development, you will not have to worry about which version of the

TCP/IP code you run. The official kernel releases will always be accompanied by a set of networking tools that are compatible with the networking code present in the kernel.

Maintaining Your System

Throughout this book, we will mainly deal with installation and configuration issues. Administration is, however, much more than that. After setting up a service, you have to keep it running, too. For most of them, only little attendance will be necessary, while some, like mail and news, require that you perform routine tasks to keep your system up to date. We will discuss these tasks in later chapters.

The absolute minimum in maintenance is to check system and per-application log files regularly for error conditions and unusual events. Commonly, you will want to do this by writing a couple of administrative shell scripts and run them from cron periodically. The source distribution of some major applications, like smail or C-News, contain such scripts. You only have to tailor them to suit your needs and preferences.

The output from any of your cron jobs should be mailed to an administrative account. By default, many applications will send error reports, usage statistics, or logfile summaries to the root account. This only makes sense if you log in as root frequently; a much better idea is to forward root's mail to your personal account, setting up a mail alias as described in Chapter 13.

However carefully you have configured your site, Murphy's law guarantees that some problem will surface eventually. Therefore, maintaining a system also means being available for complaints. Usually, people expect that the system administrator can at least be reached via email as ROOT, but there are also other addresses that are commonly used to reach the person responsible for a specific aspect of maintenance. For instance, complaints about a malfunctioning mail configuration will usually be addressed to postmaster; and problems with the news system may be reported to newsmaster or Usenet. Mail to hostmaster should be redirected to the person in charge of the host's basic network services, and the DNS name service if you run a name server.

System Security

Another very important aspect of system administration in a network environment is protecting your system and users from intruders. Carelessly managed systems offer malicious people many targets: Attacks range from password guessing to Ethernet snooping, and the damage caused may range from faked mail messages to data loss or violation of your users' privacy. We will mention some particular problems when discussing the context they may occur in, and some common defenses against them.

This section will discuss a few examples and basic techniques in dealing with system security. Of course, the topics covered cannot treat all security issues you may be faced with exhaustively; they merely serve to illustrate the problems that may arise. Therefore, reading a good book on security is an absolute must, especially in a networked system. Simon Garfinkel's *Practical UNIX Security* (O'Reilly) is highly recommendable. You can read about this book at **www.oreilly.com/catalog/puis/**.

System security starts with good system administration. This includes checking the owner-ship and permissions of all vital files and directories, monitoring use of privileged accounts, etc. The COPS program (**www.cert.org/ftp/tools/cops/**), for instance, will check your file system and common configuration files for unusual permissions or other anomalies. It is also wise to use a password suite that enforces certain rules on the users' passwords that make them hard to guess. The shadow password suite, for instance, requires a password to have at least five letters, and contain both upper- and lowercase numbers and digits.

When making a service accessible to the network, make sure to give it "least privilege," meaning that you don't permit it to do things that aren't required for it to work as designed. For example, you should make programs setuid to root or some other privileged account only when they really need this. Also, if you want to use a service for only a very limited application, don't hesitate to configure it as restrictively as your special application allows. For instance, if you want to allow diskless hosts to boot from your machine, you must pro-vide the TFTP (trivial file transfer service) so that they can download basic configuration files from the /boot directory. However, when used unrestricted, TFTP allows any user any-where in the world to download any world-readable file from your system. If this is not what you want, why not restrict TFTP service to the /boot directory?

Along the same line of thought, you might want to restrict certain services to users from certain hosts, say from your local network. In Chapter 8, we introduce TCPD, which does this for a variety of network applications.

Another important point is to avoid "dangerous" software. Of course, any software you use can be dangerous, because software may have bugs that clever people might exploit to gain access to your system. Things like these happen, and there's no complete protection against this. This problem affects free software and commercial products alike. However, programs that require special privilege are inherently more dangerous than others, because any loop-hole can have drastic consequences. If you install a setuid program for network purposes be doubly careful that you don't miss anything from the documentation, so that you don't create a security breach by accident.

You can never rule out that your precautions might fail, regardless of how careful you have been. You should therefore make sure you detect intruders early. Checking the system log files is a good starting point, but the intruder is probably as clever, and will delete any obvious traces he or she left. However, there are tools like Tripwire (**www.cert.org/ftp/tools/tripwire/**) that allow you to check vital system files to see if their contents or permis-sions have been changed. Tripwire computes various strong checksums over these files and stores them in a database. During subsequent runs, the checksums are recomputed and com-pared to the stored ones to detect any modifications.

Outlook On The Following Chapters

The next few chapters will deal with configuring for TCP/IP networking, and with running some major applications. Before getting our hands dirty with file editing and the like, we will examine IP a little closer in Chapter 2. If you already know about the way IP routing works, and how address resolution is performed, you might want to skip this chapter.

Chapter 3 deals with the very basic configuration issues, such as building a kernel and setting up your Ethernet board. The configuration of your serial ports is covered in a separate chapter, because the discussion does not apply to TCP/IP networking only, but is also relevant for UUCP.

Chapter 5 helps you to set up your machine for TCP/IP networking. It contains installation hints for stand-alone hosts with only loopback enabled, and hosts connected to an Ethernet. It will also introduce you to a few useful tools you can use to test and debug your setup. The next chapter discusses how to configure hostname resolution, and explains how to set up a name server.

This is followed by two chapters featuring the configuration and use of SLIP and PPP, respectively. Chapter 6 explains how to establish SLIP connections, and gives a detailed reference of Dip, a tool that allows you to automate most of the necessary steps. Chapter 7 covers PPP and pppd, the PPP daemon you need for this.

Chapter 8 gives a short introduction to setting up some of the most important network applications, such as rlogin, rcp, and so on. Chapter 8 also covers how services are managed by the inetd super, and how you may restrict certain security-relevant services to a set of trusted hosts.

The next two chapters discuss NIS, the Network Information System, and NFS, the Network File System. NIS is a useful tool to distribute administrative information such as user passwords in a local area network. NFS allows you to share file systems between several hosts in your network.

Chapter 11 gives you an extensive introduction to the administration of Taylor UUCP, a free implementation of the UUCP suite.

The remainder of the book is taken up by a detailed tour of electronic mail and Usenet news. Chapter 12 introduces you to the central concepts of electronic mail, like what a mail address looks like, and how the mail handling system manages to get your message to the recipient.

Chapters 13 and 14 each cover the setup of smail and sendmail. This book explains both of them, because smail is easier to install for the beginner, while sendmail is more flexible.

Chapters 15 and 16 explain the way news is managed in Usenet, and how you install and use C-news, a popular software package for managing Usenet news. Chapter 17 briefly covers how to set up an NNTP daemon to provide news reading access for your local network. Chapter 18 finally shows you how to configure and maintain various newsreaders.

Chapter 2
Issues Of TCP/IP Networking

We will now turn to the details you'll come in touch with when connecting your machine to a TCP/IP network including dealing with IP addresses, hostnames, and sometimes routing issues. This chapter gives you the background you need in order to understand what your setup requires, while the next chapters will cover the tools to deal with these.

Networking Interfaces

To hide the diversity of equipment that may be used in a networking environment, TCP/IP defines an abstract interface through which the hardware is accessed. This interface offers a set of operations which is the same for all types of hardware and basically deals with sending and receiving packets.

For each peripheral device you want to use for networking, a corresponding interface has to be present in the kernel. For example, Ethernet interfaces are called eth0 and eth1, and SLIP interfaces come as sl0, sl1, and so on. These interface names are used for configuration purposes when you want to name a particular physical device to the kernel. They have no meaning beyond that.

To be usable for TCP/IP networking, an interface must be assigned an IP address which serves as its identification when communicating with the rest of the world. This address is different from the interface name mentioned above; if you compare an interface to door, then the address is like the name-plate pinned on it.

Of course, there are other device parameters that may be set; one of these is the maximum size of datagrams that can be processed by that particular piece of hardware, also called maximum transfer unit, or MTU. Other attributes will be introduced later.

IP Addresses

As mentioned in the previous chapter, the addresses understood by the IP networking protocol are 32-bit numbers. Every machine must be assigned a number unique to the networking environment. If you are running a local network that does not have TCP/IP traffic with other networks, you may assign these numbers according to your personal preferences. However, for sites on the Internet, numbers are assigned by ICANN, **www.icann.org**.

For easier reading, IP addresses are split up into four 8-bit numbers called octets. For example, **quark.physics.groucho.edu** has an IP address of 0x954C0C04, which is written as 149.76.12.4. This format is often referred to as the dotted quad notation.

Another reason for this notation is that IP addresses are split into a network number, which is contained in the leading octets, and a host number, which is the remainder.

Depending on the size of the network, the host part may need to be smaller or larger. To accommodate different needs, there are several classes of networks, defining different splits of IP addresses (see the bulleted list below).

♦ Class A comprises networks 1.0.0.0 through 127.0.0.0. The network number is contained in the first octet. This provides for a 24-bit host part, allowing roughly 1.6 million hosts.

♦ Class B contains networks 128.0.0.0 through 191.255.0.0; the network number is in the first two octets. This allows for 16,320 nets with 65,024 hosts each.

♦ Class C networks range from 192.0.0.0 through 223.255.255.0, with the network number being contained in the first three octets. This allows for nearly 2 million networks with up to 254 hosts.

♦ Classes D, E, and F addresses falling into the range of 224.0.0.0 through 254.0.0.0 are either experimental, or are reserved for future use and don't specify any network.

If we go back to the example in the previous chapter, we find that 149.76.12.4, the address of Quark, refers to host 12.4 on the class B network 149.76.0.0.

You may have noticed that, in the above list, not all the possible values were allowed for each octet in the host part. This is because host numbers with octets all 0 or all 255 are reserved for special purposes. An address where all host part bits are 0 refers to the network, and one where all bits of the host part are 1 is called a broadcast address. This refers to all hosts on the specified network simultaneously. Thus, 149.76.255.255 is not a valid host address, but refers to all hosts on network 149.76.0.0.

There are also two network addresses that are reserved: 0.0.0.0 and 127.0.0.0. The first is called the default route, the latter the loopback address. The default route has something to do with the way IP routes datagrams, which will be dealt with below.

Network 127.0.0.0 is reserved for IP traffic local to your host. Usually, address 127.0.0.1 will be assigned to a special interface on your host, the so-called loopback interface, which acts like a closed circuit. Any IP packet handed to it from TCP or UDP will be returned to them as if it had just arrived from some network. This allows you to develop and test networking software without ever using a "real" network. Another useful application is when you want to use networking software on a standalone host. This may not be as uncommon as it sounds; for instance, many UUCP sites don't have IP connectivity at all, but still want to run the INN news system nevertheless.

Address Resolution

Now that you've seen how IP addresses are made up, you may be wondering how they are used on an Ethernet to address different hosts. After all, the Ethernet protocol identifies hosts by a six-octet number that has absolutely nothing in common with an IP address, does it?

Right. That's why a mechanism is needed to map IP addresses onto Ethernet addresses. This is the so-called *Address Resolution Protocol*, or ARP. In fact, ARP is not confined to Ethernets at all, but is used on other types of networks such as ham radio as well. The idea underlying ARP is exactly what most people do when they have to find Mr. X. Ample in a throng of 150 people: They go around, calling out his name, confident that he will respond if he's there.

When ARP wants to find out the Ethernet address corresponding to a given IP address, it uses a feature of Ethernet known as "broadcasting," where a datagram is addressed to all stations on the network simultaneously. The broadcast datagram sent by ARP contains a query for the IP address. Each receiving host compares this to its own IP address, and if it matches, returns an ARP reply to the inquiring host. The inquiring host can now extract the sender's Ethernet address from the reply.

Of course you might wonder how a host may know on which of the zillions of Ethernets throughout the world it is to find the desired host, and why this should even be an Ethernet. These questions all involve what is called routing, namely, finding out the physical location of a host in a network. This will be the topic of the following section.

For a moment, let's talk about ARP a little longer. Once a host has discovered an Ethernet address, it stores it in its ARP cache, so that it doesn't have to query for it the next time it wants to send a datagram to the host in question. However, it is unwise to keep this information forever; for instance, the remote host's Ethernet card may be replaced because of technical problems, so the ARP entry becomes invalid. To force another query for the IP address, entries in the ARP cache are therefore discarded after some time.

Sometimes, it is also necessary to find out the IP address associated with a given Ethernet address. This happens when a diskless machine wants to boot from a server on the network, which is quite a common situation on local area networks. A diskless client, however, has virtually no information about itself—except for its Ethernet address! So what it basically does is broadcast a message containing a plea for boot servers to tell it its IP address. There's another protocol for this, named Reverse Address Resolution Protocol, or RARP. Along with the BOOTP protocol, it serves to define a procedure for bootstrapping diskless clients over the network.

IP Routing
IP Networks

When you write a letter to someone, you usually put a complete address on the envelope, specifying the country, state, ZIP code, and so on. After you put it into the letter box, the postal service will deliver it to its destination: It will be sent to the country indicated, whose national service will dispatch it to the proper state and region, and so forth. The advantage of this hierarchical scheme is rather obvious: Wherever you post the letter, the local post-master will know roughly the direction to forward the letter to, but doesn't have to care which way the letter will travel by within the destination country.

IP networks are structured in a similar way. The whole Internet consists of a number of proper networks, called autonomous systems. Each such system performs any routing between its member hosts internally, so that the task of delivering a datagram is reduced to finding a path to the destination host's network. This means, as soon as the datagram is handed to any host that is on that particular network, further processing is done exclusively by the network itself.

Subnetworks

This structure is reflected by splitting IP addresses into a host and network part, as explained above. By default, the destination network is derived from the network part of the IP address. Thus, hosts with identical IP network numbers should be found within the same network, and vice versa. Autonomous systems are slightly more general however. They may comprise more than one IP network.

It makes sense to offer a similar scheme inside the network, too, as it may consist of a collection of hundreds of smaller networks itself, with the smallest units being physical networks like Ethernets. Therefore, IP allows you to subdivide an IP network into several subnets.

A subnet takes over responsibility for delivering datagrams to a certain range of IP addresses from the IP network it is part of. As with classes A, B, or C, it is identified by the network part of the IP addresses. However, the network part is now extended to include some bits from the host part. The number of bits that are interpreted as the subnet number is given by the so-called subnet mask, or netmask. This is a 32-bit number, too, which specifies the bit mask for the network part of the IP address.

The campus network of Groucho Marx University is an example of such a network. It has a class B network number of 149.76.0.0, and its netmask is therefore 255.255.0.0.

Internally, GMU's campus network consists of several smaller networks, such as the LANs of various departments. So the range of IP addresses is broken up into 254 subnets, 149.76.1.0 through 149.76.254.0. For example, the Department of Theoretical Physics has been assigned 149.76.12.0. The campus backbone is a network by its own right, and is given 149.76.1.0. These subnets share the same IP network number, while the third octet is used to distinguish between them. Thus, they will use a subnet mask of 255.255.255.0.

It is worth noting that subnetting (as the technique of generating subnets is called) is only an internal division of the network. Subnets are generated by the network owner (or the administrators). Frequently, subnets are created to reflect existing boundaries, be they physical (between two Ethernets), administrative (between two departments), or geographical, and authority over these subnets is delegated to some contact person. However, this structure affects only the network's internal behavior, and is completely invisible to the outside world.

Gateways

Subnetting is not only an organizational benefit, it is frequently a natural consequence of hardware boundaries. The viewpoint of a host on a given physical network, such as an Ethernet, is a very limited one: The only hosts it is able to talk to directly are those of the network it is on. All other hosts can be accessed only through so-called gateways. A gateway is a host that is connected to two or more physical networks simultaneously and is configured to switch packets between them.

For IP to be able to easily recognize if a host is on a local physical network, different physical networks have to belong to different IP networks. For example the network number 149.76.4.0 is reserved for hosts on the Mathematics LAN. When sending a datagram to Quark, the network software on Erdos immediately sees from the IP address, 149.76.12.4, that the destination host is on a different physical network, and therefore can be reached only through a gateway (Sophus by default).

Sophus itself is connected to two distinct subnets: the Mathematics Department and the campus backbone. It accesses each through a different interface, eth0 and fddi0, respectively. Now, what IP address do we assign it? Should we give it one on subnet 149.76.1.0, or on 149.76.4.0?

The answer is: both. When talking to a host on the Math Department's LAN, Sophus should use an IP address of 149.76.4.1, and when talking to a host on the backbone, it should use 149.76.1.4.

Thus, a gateway is assigned one IP address per network it is on. These addresses—along with the corresponding netmask—are tied to the interface the subnet is accessed through. Thus, the mapping of interfaces and addresses for Sophus would look like Table 2.1.

Table 2.1	Mapping of interfaces and addresses for Sophus.	
Interface	**Address**	**Netmask**
eth0	149.76.4.1	255.255.255.0
fddi0	149.76.1.4	255.255.255.0
lo	127.0.0.1	255.0.0.0

The last entry describes the loopback interface lo, which was introduced above. Notice that the hosts on two subnets at the same time are shown with both addresses.

Generally, you can ignore the subtle difference between attaching an address to a host or its interface. For hosts that are on one network only, like Erdos, you would generally refer of the host as having this-and-that IP address although strictly speaking, it's the Ethernet interface that has this IP address. However, this distinction is only really important when you refer to a gateway.

The Routing Table

We are now focusing our attention on how IP chooses a gateway to use when delivering a datagram to a remote network.

We have seen before that Erdos, when given a datagram for Quark, checks the destination address and finds it is not on the local network. It therefore sends it to the default gateway, Sophus, which is now basically faced with the same task. Sophus recognizes that Quark is not on any of the networks it is connected to directly, so it has to find yet another gateway to forward it through. The correct choice would be Niels, the gateway to the Physics Department. Sophus therefore needs some information to associate a destination network with a suitable gateway.

The routing information IP uses for this is basically a table linking networks to gateways that reach them. A catch-all entry (the default route) must generally be supplied, too; this is the gateway associated with network 0.0.0.0. All packets to an unknown network are sent through the default route. On Sophus, this table might look like Table 2.2.

Table 2.2	Routing information for Sophus.	
Network	**Gateway**	**Interface**
149.76.1.0	...	fddi0
149.76.2.0	149.76.1.2	fddi0
149.76.3.0	149.76.1.3	fddi0
149.76.4.0	...	eth0
149.76.5.0	149.76.1.5	fddi0
...	...	...
0.0.0.0	149.76.1.2	fddi0

Routes to a network that Sophus is directly connected to don't require a gateway; therefore, they show a gateway entry of "-".

Routing tables may be built by various means. For small LANs, it is usually most efficient to construct them by hand and feed them to IP using the route command at boot time (see Chapter 3). For larger networks, they are built and adjusted at run time by routing daemons; these run on central hosts of the network and exchange routing information to compute "optimal" routes between the member networks.

Depending on the size of the network, different routing protocols will be used. For routing inside autonomous systems (such as Groucho Marx campus), the internal routing protocols are used. The most prominent one is RIP, the Routing Information Protocol, which is implemented by the BSD routed daemon. For routing between autonomous systems, external routing protocols like EGP (External Gateway Protocol), or BGP (Border Gateway Protocol) have to be used; these (as well as RIP) have been implemented in Cornell University's gated daemon.

Metric Values

Dynamic routing based on RIP chooses the best route to some destination host or network based on the number of "hops," that is, the gateways a datagram has to pass before reaching it. The shorter a route is, the better RIP rates it. Very long routes are regarded as unusable, and are discarded.

To use RIP to manage routing information internal to your local network, you have to run gated on all hosts. At boot time, gated checks for all active network interfaces. If there is more than one active interface (not counting the loopback interface), it assumes the host is switching packets between several networks, and will actively exchange and broadcast routing information. Otherwise, it will only passively receive any RIP updates and update the local routing table.

When broadcasting the information from the local routing table, gated computes the length of the route from the so-called metric value associated with the routing table entry. This metric value is set by the system administrator when configuring the route and should reflect the actual cost of using this route. Therefore, the metric of a route to a subnet the host is directly connected to should always be zero, while a route going through two gateways should have a metric of two. However, note that you don't have to bother about metrics when you don't use RIP or gated.

The Internet Control Message Protocol

IP has a companion protocol that we haven't talked about yet. This is the Internet Control Message Protocol (ICMP) and is used by the kernel networking code to communicate error messages and the like to other hosts. For instance, assume that you are on Erdos again and want to telnet to port 12345 on Quark, but there's no process listening on that port. When the first TCP packet for this port arrives on Quark, the networking layer will recognize this and immediately return an ICMP message to Erdos stating "Port Unreachable."

There are quite a number of messages ICMP understands, many of which deal with error conditions. However, there is one very interesting message called the Redirect message. It is generated by the routing module when it detects that another host is using it as a gateway, although there is a much shorter route. For example, after booting the routing table of Sophus may be incomplete, containing the routes to the Mathematics network, to the FDDI backbone, and the default route pointing at the Groucho Computing Center's gateway (gcc1). Therefore, any packets for Quark would be sent to gcc1 rather than to Niels, the gateway to the Physics Department. When receiving such a datagram, gcc1 will notice that this is a poor choice of route, and will forward the packet to Niels, at the same time returning an ICMP Redirect message to Sophus telling it of the superior route.

Now, this seems a very clever way to avoid having to set up any but the most basic routes manually. However, be warned that relying on dynamic routing schemes, be it RIP or ICMP Redirect messages, is not always a good idea. ICMP Redirect and RIP offer you little or no choice in verifying that some routing information is indeed authentic. This allows malicious good-for-nothings to disrupt your entire network traffic, or do even worse things. For this reason, there are some versions of the networking code that treat Redirect messages that affect network routes, as if they were only Redirects for host routes.

The Domain Name System
Hostname Resolution

As described above, addressing in TCP/IP networking revolves around 32-bit numbers. However, you will have a hard time remembering more than a few of these. Therefore, hosts are generally known by "ordinary" names such as "gauss" or "strange." It is then the application's duty to find the IP address corresponding to this name. This process is called hostname resolution.

An application that wants to find the IP address of a given hostname does not have to provide its own routines for looking up hosts and IP addresses. Instead, it relies on a number of library functions that do this transparently, called gethostbyname(3) and gethostbyaddr(3). Traditionally, these and a number of related procedures were grouped in a separate library called the resolver library; on Linux, these are part of the standard libc. Colloquially, this collection of functions are therefore referred to as "the resolver."

Now, on a small network like an Ethernet, or even a cluster of them, it is not very difficult to maintain tables mapping hostnames to addresses. This information is usually kept in a file named /etc/hosts. When adding or removing hosts, or reassigning addresses, all you have to do is update the hosts on all hosts. Quite obviously, this will become burdensome with networks that comprise more than a handful of machines.

One solution to this problem is NIS, the Network Information System developed by Sun Microsystems, colloquially called YP, or Yellow Pages. NIS stores the hosts file (and other information) in a database on a master host, from which clients may retrieve it as needed. Still, this approach is only suitable for medium-sized networks such as LANs, because it involves maintaining the entire hosts database centrally, and distributing it to all servers.

On the Internet, address information was initially stored in a single HOSTS.TXT database, too. This file was maintained at the Network Information Center, or NIC, and had to be downloaded and installed by all participating sites. When the network grew, several problems with this scheme arose. Beside the administrative overhead involved in installing HOSTS.TXT regularly, the load on the servers that distributed it became too high. Even more severe was the problem that all names had to be registered with the NIC, which had to make sure that no name was issued twice.

This is why, in 1984, a new name resolution scheme has been adopted, the Domain Name System. DNS was designed by Paul Mockapetris, and addresses both problems simultaneously.

Enter DNS

DNS organizes hostnames in a hierarchy of domains. A domain is a collection of sites that are related in some sense—be it because they form a proper network (e.g., all machines on a campus, or all hosts on BITNET), because they all belong to a certain organization (like the U.S. government), or because they're simply geographically close. For instance, universities are grouped in the .edu domain, with each university or college using a separate subdomain below which their hosts are subsumed. Groucho Marx University might be given the groucho.edu domain, with the LAN of the Mathematics Department being assigned maths.groucho.edu. Hosts on the departmental network would have this domain name tacked onto their hostname; so Erdos would be known as erdos.maths.groucho.edu. This is called the fully qualified domain name, or FQDN, which uniquely identifies this host worldwide.

The entry at the root of this tree, which is denoted by a single dot, is quite appropriately called the root domain, and encompasses all other domains. To indicate that a hostname is a fully qualified domain name, rather than a name relative to some (implicit) local domain, it is sometimes written with a trailing dot. This signifies that the name's last component is the root domain.

Depending on its location in the name hierarchy, a domain may be called top-level, second-level, or third-level. More levels of subdivision occur, but are rare. These are a couple of top-level domains you may see frequently:

- *.edu*—(Mostly U.S.) educational institutions like universities
- *.com*—Commercial organizations, companies
- *.org*—Noncommercial organizations (often private UUCP networks are in this domain)
- *.net*—Gateways and other administrative host on a network
- *.mil*—U.S. military institutions

- *.gov*—U.S. government institutions

- *.uucp*—Officially, all site names formerly used as UUCP names without domain have been moved to this domain

Technically, the first four of these belong to the U.S. part of the Internet, but you may also see non-U.S. sites in these domains. This is especially true of the .net domain. However, .mil and .gov are used exclusively in the U.S.

Outside the U.S., each country generally uses a top-level domain of its own named after the two-letter country code defined in ISO-3166. Finland, for instance, uses the .fi domain, .fr is used by France, .de by Germany, or .au by Australia, and so on. Below this top-level domain, each country's NIC is free to organize hostnames in whatever way they want. Australia, for example, has second-level domain similar to the international top-level domains, named com.au, edu.au, and so on. Others, like Germany, don't use this extra level, but rather have slightly longish names that refer directly to the organizations running a particular domain. For example, it's not uncommon to see hostnames like ftp.informatik. uni-erlangen.de. Chalk that up to German efficiency.

Of course, these national domains do not imply that a host below that domain is actually located in that country; it only signals that the host has been registered with that country's NIC. A Swedish manufacturer might have a branch in Australia, and still have all its hosts registered with the .se top-level domain.

Now, organizing the name space in a hierarchy of domain names nicely solves the problem of name uniqueness; with DNS, a hostname has to be unique only within its domain to give it a name different from all other hosts worldwide. Furthermore, fully qualified names are quite easy to remember. Taken by themselves, these are already very good reasons to split up a large domain into several subdomains.

But DNS does even more for you than this: It allows you to delegate authority over a subdomain to its administrators. For example, the maintainers at the Groucho Computing Center might create a subdomain for each department; we already encountered the math and physics subdomains above. When they find the network at the Physics Department too large and chaotic to manage from outside (after all, physicists are known to be an unruly bunch of people), they may simply pass control over the physics.groucho.edu domain to the administrators of this network. These are then free to use whatever hostnames they like, and assign them IP addresses from their network in whatever fashion the like, without outside interference.

To this end, the name space is split up into zones, each rooted at a domain. Note the subtle difference between a zone and a domain: The domain groucho.edu encompasses all hosts at the Groucho Marx University, while the zone groucho.edu includes only the hosts that are managed by the Computing Center directly, for example those at the Mathematics Department. The hosts at the Physics Department belong to a different zone, namely physics.groucho.edu.

Name Lookups With DNS

At first glance, all this domain and zone fuss seems to make name resolution an awfully complicated business. After all, if no central authority controls what names are assigned to which hosts, then how is a humble application supposed to know?

Now comes the really ingenious part about DNS. If you want to find out the IP address of Erdos, then, DNS says, go ask the people that manage it, and they will tell you.

In fact, DNS is a giant distributed database. It is implemented by means of so-called name servers that supply information on a given domain or set of domains. For each zone, there are at least two, at most a few, name servers that hold all authoritative information on hosts in that zone. To obtain the IP address of Erdos, all you have to do is contact the name server for the groucho.edu zone, which will then return the desired data.

Easier said than done, you might think. So how do I know how to reach the name server at Groucho Marx University? In case your computer isn't equipped with an address-resolving oracle, DNS provides for this, too. When your application wants to look up information on Erdos, it contacts a local name server, which conducts a so-called iterative query for it. It starts off by sending a query to a name server for the root domain, asking for the address of erdos.maths.groucho.edu. The root name server recognizes that this name does not belong to its zone of authority, but rather to one below the .edu domain. Thus, it tells you to contact an .edu zone name server for more information, and encloses a list of all .edu name servers along with their addresses. Your local name server will then go and query one of those, for instance a.isi.edu. In a manner similar to the root name server, a.isi.edu knows that the groucho.edu people run a zone of their own, and point you to their servers. The local name server will then present its query for Erdos to one of these, which will finally recognize the name as belonging to its zone, and return the corresponding IP address.

Now, this looks like a lot of traffic being generated for looking up a measly IP address, but it's really only miniscule compared to the amount of data that would have to be transferred if we were still stuck with HOSTS.TXT. But there's still room for improvement with this scheme.

To improve response time during future queries, the name server will store the information obtained in its local cache. So the next time anyone on your local network wants to look up the address of a host in the groucho.edu domain, your name server will not have to go through the whole process again, but will rather go to the groucho.edu name server directly. If it didn't, then DNS would be about as bad as any other method, because each query would involve the root name servers.

Of course, the name server will not keep this information forever, but rather discard it after some period. This expiry interval is called the time to live, or TTL. Each datum in the DNS database is assigned such a TTL by administrators of the responsible zone.

Domain Name Servers

Name servers that hold all information on hosts within a zone are called authoritative for this zone, and are sometimes referred to as master name servers. Any query for a host within this zone will finally wind down at one of these master name servers.

To provide a coherent picture of a zone, its master servers must be fairly well synchronized. This is achieved by making one of them the primary server, which loads its zone information from data files, and making the others secondary servers who transfer the zone data from the primary server at regular intervals.

One reason to have several name servers is to distribute work load; another is redundancy. When one name server machine fails in a benign way, like crashing or losing its network connection, all queries will fall back to the other servers. Of course, this scheme doesn't protect you from server malfunctions that produce wrong replies to all DNS requests, e.g., from software bugs in the server program itself.

Of course, you can also think of running a name server that is not authoritative for any domain. (Well, almost. A name server at the very least has to provide name service to localhost and reverse lookups of 127.0.0.1.) This type of server is useful, nevertheless, as it is still able to conduct DNS queries for the applications running on the local network, and cache the information. It is therefore called a caching-only server.

The DNS Database

We have seen above that DNS does not only deal with IP addresses of hosts, but also exchanges information on name servers. There are in fact a whole bunch of different types of entries the DNS database may have.

A single piece of information from the DNS database is called a resource record, or RR for short. Each record has a type associated with it, describing the sort of data it represents, and a class specifying the type of network it applies to. The latter accommodates the needs of different addressing schemes, like IP addresses (the IN class), or addresses of Hesiod networks (used at MIT), and a few more. The prototypical resource record type is the A record which associates a fully qualified domain name with an IP address.

Of course, a host may have more than one name. However, one of these names must be identified as the official, or canonical hostname, while the others are simply aliases referring to the former. The difference is that the canonical hostname is the one with an A record associated, while the others only have a record of type CNAME which points to the canonical hostname.

We will not go through all record types here, but save them for a later chapter, and rather give you a brief example here.

Apart from A and CNAME records, you can see a special record at the top of the file, stretching several lines. This is the SOA resource record, signaling the Start of Authority, which holds general information on the zone the server is authoritative for. This comprises, for instance, the default TTL for all records.

Note that all names in the sample file that do not end with a dot should be interpreted relative to the groucho.edu domain. The special name "@" used in the SOA record refers to the domain name by itself.

We have seen above that the name servers for the groucho.edu domain somehow have to know about the physics zone so that they can point queries to their name servers. This is usually achieved by a pair of records: the NS record that gives the server's FQDN, and an A record associating an address with that name. Since these records are what holds the name space together, they are frequently called the glue records. They are the only instances of records where a parent zone actually holds information on hosts in the subordinate zone. The glue records pointing to the name servers for physics.groucho.edu are shown in Listing 2.1.

Reverse Lookups

Listing 2.1   An excerpt from the named.hosts file for the Physics Department.

```
;
; Authoritative Information on physics.groucho.edu
@                       IN    SOA          {
                        niels.physics.groucho.edu.
                        hostmaster.niels.physics.groucho.edu.
                        1034                ; serial no
                        360000              ; refresh
                        3600                ; retry
                        3600000             ; expire
                        3600                ; default ttl
                        }
;
; Name servers
        IN    NS     niels
        IN    NS     gauss.maths.groucho.edu.
gauss.maths.groucho.edu. IN A      149.76.4.23
;
; Theoretical Physics (subnet 12)
niels                   IN    A      149.76.12.1
                        IN    A      149.76.1.12
nameserver              IN    CNAME  niels
otto                    IN    A      149.76.12.2
quark                   IN    A      149.76.12.4
down                    IN    A      149.76.12.5
strange                 IN    A      149.76.12.6
...
; Collider Lab. (subnet 14)
boson                   IN    A      149.76.14.1
```

```
muon                    IN    A       149.76.14.7
bogon                   IN    A       149.76.14.12
...
```

Beside looking up the IP address belonging to a host, it is sometimes desirable to find out the canonical hostname corresponding to an address. This is called reverse mapping and is used by several network services to verify a client's identity. When using a single hosts file, reverse lookups simply involve searching the file for a host that owns the IP address in question. With DNS, an exhaustive search of the name space is out of the question, of course. Instead, a special domain, in-addr.arpa, has been created which contains the IP addresses of all hosts in a reversed dotted-quad notation. For instance, an IP address of 149.76.12.4 corresponds to the name 4.12.76.149.in-addr.arpa. The resource record type linking these names to their canonical hostnames is PTR. This is shown in Listing 2.2.

Listing 2.2   An excerpt from the named.hosts file for GMU.

```
;
; Zone data for the groucho.edu zone.
@                       IN      SOA            {
                        vax12.gcc.groucho.edu.
                        hostmaster.vax12.gcc.groucho.edu.
                        233                    ; serial no
                        360000                 ; refresh
                        3600                   ; retry
                        3600000                ; expire
                        3600                   ; default ttl
                        }
....
;
; Glue records for the physics.groucho.edu zone
physics                 IN      NS             niels.physics.groucho.edu.
                        IN      NS             gauss.maths.groucho.edu.
niels.physics           IN      A              149.76.12.1
gauss.maths             IN      A              149.76.4.23
...
```

Creating a zone of authority usually means that its administrators are given full control over how they assign addresses to names. Since they usually have one or more IP networks or subnets at their hands, there's a one-to-many mapping between DNS zones and IP networks. The Physics Department, for instance, comprises the subnets 149.76.8.0, 149.76.12.0, and 149.76.14.0.

As a consequence, new zones in the in-addr.arpa domain have to be created along with the physics zone and delegated to the network administrators at the department: 8.76.149.in-addr.arpa, 12.76.149.in-addr.arpa, and 14.76.149.in-addr.arpa. Otherwise, installing a new host at the Collider Lab would require them to contact their parent domain to have the new address entered into their in-addr.arpa zone file.

The zone database for subnet 12 is shown in Listing 2.3.

Listing 2.3   An excerpt from the named.rev file for subnet 12.

```
;
; the 12.76.149.in-addr.arpa domain.
@                 IN      SOA    {
                         niels.physics.groucho.edu.
                         hostmaster.niels.physics.groucho.edu.
                         233 360000 3600 3600000 3600
                         }
2                 IN      PTR     otto.physics.groucho.edu.
4                 IN      PTR     quark.physics.groucho.edu.
5                 IN      PTR     down.physics.groucho.edu.
6                 IN      PTR     strange.physics.groucho.edu.
```

The corresponding glue records in the database of their parent zone is shown in Listing 2.4.

Listing 2.4   An excerpt from the named.rev file for network 149.76.

```
;
; the 76.149.in-addr.arpa domain.
@                   IN        SOA            {
                         vax12.gcc.groucho.edu.
                         hostmaster.vax12.gcc.groucho.edu.
                         233 360000 3600 3600000 3600
                         }
...
; subnet 4: Mathematics Dept.
1.4               IN      PTR     sophus.maths.groucho.edu.
17.4              IN      PTR     erdos.maths.groucho.edu.
23.4              IN      PTR     gauss.maths.groucho.edu.
...
; subnet 12: Physics Dept, separate zone
12                IN      NS      niels.physics.groucho.edu.
                  IN      NS      gauss.maths.groucho.edu.
niels.physics.groucho.edu. IN  A 149.76.12.1
gauss.maths.groucho.edu. IN   A   149.76.4.23
...
```

One important consequence of this is that zones can only be created as supersets of IP networks, and, even more severe, that these network's netmasks have to be on byte boundaries. All subnets at Groucho Marx University have a netmask of 255.255.255.0, whence an in-addr.arpa zone could be created for each subnet. However, if the netmask was

255.255.255.128 instead, creating zones for the subnet 149.76.12.128 would be impossible, because there's no way to tell DNS that the 12.76.149.in-addr.arpa domain has been split in two zones of authority, with hostnames ranging from 1 through 127, and 128 through 255, respectively.

Chapter 3
Configuring The Networking Hardware

U p to now, we've been talking quite a bit about network interfaces and general TCP/IP issues, but didn't really cover exactly *what* happens when "the networking code" in the kernel accesses a piece of hardware. For this, we have to talk a little about the concept of interfaces and drivers.

First, of course, there's the hardware itself, for example, an Ethernet board: this is a slice of epoxy, cluttered with lots of tiny chips with silly numbers on them, sitting in a slot of your PC. This is what we generally call a *device*.

For you to be able to use the Ethernet board, special functions have to be present in your kernel that understand the particular way this device is accessed. These are the so-called device drivers. For example, Linux has device drivers for several brands of Ethernet boards that are very similar in function. They are known as the Becker series drivers, named after their author, Donald Becker. A different example is the D-Link driver that handles a D-Link pocket adapter attached to a parallel port.

But what do we mean when we say a driver "handles" a device? Let's go back to that Ethernet board we examined above. The driver has to be able to communicate with the peripheral's on-board logic somehow: It has to send commands and data to the board, while the board should deliver any data received to the driver.

In PCs, this communication takes place through an area of I/O memory that is mapped to on-board registers and the like. All commands and data the kernel sends to the board have to go through these registers. I/O memory is generally described by giving its starting or *base address*. Typical base addresses for Ethernet boards are 0x300, or 0x360.

Usually, you don't have to worry about any hardware issues such as the base address because the kernel makes an attempt at boot time to detect a board's location. This is called *autoprobing*, which means that the kernel reads several memory locations and compares the data read with what it should see if a certain Ethernet board was installed. However, there may be Ethernet boards it cannot detect automatically; this is sometimes the case with cheap Ethernet cards that are not quite clones of standard boards from other manufacturers. Also, the kernel will attempt to detect only one Ethernet device when booting. If you're using more than one board, you have to tell the kernel about this board explicitly.

Another parameter that you might have to tell the kernel about is the *interrupt request channel*. Hardware components usually interrupt the kernel when they need care taken of them, e.g., when data has arrived, or a special condition occurs. In a PC, interrupts may occur on one of 15 interrupt channels numbered 0, 1, and 3 through 15. The interrupt number assigned to a hardware component is called its *interrupt request number*, or IRQ. (IRQs 2 and 9 are the same because the PC has two cascaded interrupt processors with eight IRQs each; the secondary processor is connected to IRQ 2 of the primary one.)

As described in Chapter 1, the kernel accesses a device through a so-called *interface*. Interfaces offer an abstract set of functions that is the same across all types of hardware, such as sending or receiving a datagram.

Interfaces are identified by means of names. These are names defined internally in the kernel, and are not device files in the /dev directory. Typical names are eth0, eth1, and so on, for Ethernet interfaces. The assignment of interfaces to devices usually depends on the order in which devices are configured; for instance, the first Ethernet board installed will become eth0, the next will be eth1, and so on. One exception to this rule are SLIP interfaces, which are assigned dynamically; that is, whenever a SLIP connection is established, an interface is assigned to the serial port. When booting, the kernel displays what devices it detects and what interfaces it installs.

Kernel Configuration

When running a system, you should be familiar with building a kernel. The basics of this are explained in Matt Welsh's "Installation and Getting Started" guide, which is also part of the Documentation Project's series. (This guide has also been published in *The Linux System Programming White Papers* from The Coriolis Group.) In this section, we will therefore discuss only those configuration options that affect networking.

When running **make config**, you will first be asked general configurations, for instance, whether you want kernel math emulation or not, and so on. One of these asks you whether you want TCP/IP networking support. You must answer this with "Y" to get a kernel capable of networking.

Kernel Options In 1.0 And Higher

After the general option part is complete, the configuration will go on to ask you for various features, such as SCSI drivers and so on. The subsequent list questions deal with networking support. The exact set of configuration options is in constant flux because of the ongoing development. A typical list of options offered by most kernel versions around 1.0 and 1.1 looks like this (comments are given in italics):

Despite the macro name displayed in brackets, you must answer this question with "Y" if you want to use *any* type of networking devices, regardless of whether this is Ethernet, SLIP, or PPP. When answering this question with "Y", support for Ethernet-type devices is enabled automatically. Support for other types of network drivers must be enabled separately.

These questions concern the various link layer protocols supported by Linux. SLIP allows you to transport IP datagrams across serial lines. The compressed header option provides support for CSLIP, a technique that compresses TCP/IP headers to as little as three bytes. Note that this kernel option does not turn on CSLIP automatically; it merely provides the necessary kernel functions for it.

PPP is another protocol to send network traffic across serial lines. It is much more flexible than SLIP and is not limited to IP, but also supports IPX. PLIP provides for a way to send IP datagrams across a parallel port connection. It is mostly used to communicate with PCs running DOS.

The following questions deal with Ethernet boards from various vendors. As more drivers are being developed, you are likely to see questions added to this section. If you want to build a kernel you can use on a number of different machines, you can enable more than one driver.

Finally, in the file system section, the configuration script will ask you whether you want support for NFS, the networking file system. NFS lets you export file systems to several hosts, which makes the files appear as if they were on an ordinary hard disk attached to the host.

Kernel Options In 1.1.14 And Higher

Starting with 1.1.14, which added Alpha support for IPX, the configuration procedure changed slightly. The general options section now asks whether you want networking support in general. It is immediately followed by a couple of question on miscellaneous networking options.

To use TCP/IP networking, you must answer this question with "Y". If you answer with "N", however, you will still be able to compile the kernel with IPX support.

You have to enable this option if your system acts as a gateway between two Ethernets, or between and Ethernet and a SLIP link, or so on. Although it doesn't hurt to enable this by default, you may want to disable this to configure a host as a so-called *firewall*. Firewalls are hosts that are connected to two or more networks, but don't route traffic between them. They are commonly used to provide users from a company network with Internet access at a minimal risk to the internal network. Users will be allowed to log into the firewall and use Internet services, but the company's machines will be protected from outside attacks because any incoming connections can't cross the firewall.

This option works around an incompatibility with some versions of PC/TCP, a commercial TCP/IP implementation for DOS-based PCs. If you enable this option, you will still be able to communicate with normal machines, but performance may be hurt over slow links.

This function enables RARP, the Reverse Address Resolution Protocol. RARP is used by diskless clients and X-terminals to inquire their IP address when booting. You should enable RARP only when you plan to serve this sort of clients. The latest package of network utilities (net-0.32d) contains a small utility named **rarp** that allows you to add systems to the RARP cache.

When sending data over TCP, the kernel has to break up the stream into several packets before giving it to IP. For hosts that can be reached over a local network such as an Ethernet, larger packets will be used than for hosts where data has to go through long-distance links. (This is to avoid fragmentation by links that have a very small maximum packet size.) If you don't enable SNARL, the kernel will assume only those networks are local that it actually has an interface to. However, if you look at the class B network at Groucho Marx University, the whole class B network is local, but most hosts interface to only one or two subnets. If you enable SNARL, the kernel will assume *all* subnets are local and use large packets when talking to all hosts on campus.

If you do want to use smaller packet sizes for data sent to specific hosts (because, for instance, the data goes through a SLIP link), you can do so using the mtu option of **route**, which is briefly discussed at the end of this chapter.

Nagle's rule is a heuristic to avoid sending particularly small IP packets, also called *tinygrams*. Tinygrams are usually created by interactive networking tools that transmit single keystrokes, such as telnet or rsh. Tinygrams can become particularly wasteful on low-bandwidth links like SLIP. The Nagle algorithm attempts to avoid them by holding back transmission of TCP data briefly under some circumstances. You might only want to disable Nagle's algorithm if you have severe problems with packets getting dropped.

Starting in the 1.1.16 kernel, Linux supports another driver type, the dummy driver. The following question appears toward the start of the device driver section.

The dummy driver doesn't really do much, but is quite useful on standalone or SLIP hosts. It is basically a masqueraded loopback interface. The reason to have this sort of interface is that on hosts that do SLIP but have no Ethernet, you want to have an interface that bears your IP address all the time. This is discussed in a little more detail in Chapter 5.

A Tour Of Network Devices

The kernel supports a number of hardware drivers for various types of equipment. This section gives a short overview of the driver families available and the interface names used for them.

There are a number of standard names for interfaces in Linux, which are listed below. Most drivers support more than one interface, in which case the interfaces are numbered, as in eth0, eth1, and so on.

- ◆ **lo**—The local loopback interface. It is used for testing purposes, as well as a couple of network applications. It works like a closed circuit in that any datagram written to it will be immediately returned to the host's networking layer. There's always one loopback device present in the kernel, and there's little sense in having fewer or more.
- ◆ **ethn**—The n-th Ethernet card. This is the generic interface name for most Ethernet boards.
- ◆ **dln**—These interfaces access a D-Link DE-600 pocket adapter, another Ethernet device. It is a little special in that the DE-600 is driven through a parallel port.
- ◆ **sln**—The n-th SLIP interface. SLIP interfaces are associated with serial lines in the order in which they are allocated for SLIP; i.e., the first serial line being configured for SLIP becomes sl0, etc. The kernel supports up to four SLIP interfaces.
- ◆ **pppn**—The n-th PPP interface. Just like SLIP interfaces, a PPP interface is associated with a serial line once it is converted to PPP mode. At the moment, up to four interfaces are supported.
- ◆ **plipn**—The n-th PLIP interface. PLIP transports IP datagrams over parallel lines. Up to three PLIP interfaces are supported. They are allocated by the PLIP driver at system boot time and are mapped onto parallel ports.

For other interface drivers that may be added in the future, like ISDN or AX.25, other names will be introduced. Drivers for IPX (Novell's networking protocol) and AX.25 (used by ham radio amateurs) are under development, but are at alpha stage still.

During the following sections, we will discuss the details of using the drivers described above.

Ethernet Installation

The current network code supports various brands of Ethernet cards. Most drivers were written by Donald Becker (**becker@cesdis.gsfc.nasa.gov**), who authored a family of drivers for cards based on the National Semiconductor 8390 chip; these have become known as the Becker series drivers. There are also drivers for a couple of products from D-Link, among them the D-Link pocket adapter that allows you to access an Ethernet through a parallel port. The driver for this was written by Bjørn Ekwall (**bj0rn@blox.se**). The DEPCA driver was written by David C. Davies (**davies@wanton.lkg.dec.com**).

Ethernet Cabling

If you're installing an Ethernet for the first time in your life, a few words about the cabling may be in order here. Ethernet is very picky about proper cabling. The cable must be terminated on both ends with a 50-Ohm resistor, and you must not have any branches (i.e., three cables connected in a star shape). If you are using a thin coaxial cable with T-shaped BNC junctions, these junctions must be twisted on the board's connector directly; you should not insert a cable segment.

If you connect to a thicknet installation, you have to attach your host through a transceiver (sometimes called Ethernet Attachment Unit). You can plug the transceiver into the 15-pin AUI port on your board directly, but may also use a shielded cable.

Supported Boards

Here's a list of the more widely known boards supported by Linux. The actual list in the HOWTO is about three times longer. However, even if you find your board in this list, check the HOWTO first; there are sometimes important details about operating these cards. A case in point is the case of some DMA-based Ethernet boards that use the same DMA channel as the Adaptec 1542 SCSI controller by default. Unless you move either of them to a different DMA channel, you will wind up with the Ethernet board writing packet data to arbitrary locations on your hard disk.

◆ 3Com EtherLink Both 3c503 and 3c503/16 are supported, as are 3c507 and 3c509. The 3c501 is supported, too, but is too slow to be worth buying.

◆ Novell Eagle NE1000 and NE2000, and a variety of clones. NE1500 and NE2100 are supported, too.

◆ Western Digital/SMC WD8003 and WD8013 (same as SMC Elite and SMC Elite Plus) are supported, and also the newer SMC Elite 16 Ultra.

◆ Hewlett Packard HP 27252, HP 27247B, and HP J2405A. D-Link DE-600 pocket adaptor, DE-100, DE-200, and DE-220-T. There's also a patch kit for the DE-650-T, which is a PCMCIA card.(4)

◆ DEC DE200 (32K/64K), DE202, DE100, and DEPCA rev E.

◆ Allied Teliesis AT1500 and AT1700.

To use one of these cards with Linux, you may use a precompiled kernel from one of the major distributions. These generally have drivers for all of them built in. In the long term, however, it's better to roll your own kernel and compile in those drivers you actually need.

Ethernet Autoprobing

At boot time, the Ethernet code will try to locate your board and determine its type. There are two limitations to the autoprobing code. For one, it may not recognize all boards properly. This is especially true for some of the cheaper clones of common boards, but also for some WD80x3 boards. The second problem is that the kernel will not autoprobe for more than one board at the moment. This is a feature, because it is assumed you want to have control about which board is assigned which interface.

If you are using more than one board, or if the autoprobe should fail to detect your board, you have to tell the kernel explicitly about the card's base address and name.

In Net-3, you have can use two different schemes to accomplish this. One way is to change or add information in the drivers/net/Space.c file in the kernel source code that contains all information about drivers. This is recommended only if you are familiar with the networking code. A much better way is to provide the kernel with this information at boot time. If you use **lilo** to boot your system, you can pass parameters to the kernel by specifying them through the append option in lilo.conf. To inform the kernel about an Ethernet device, you can pass the following parameter:

```
ether=irq,base addr,param1,param2,name
```

The first four parameters are numerical, while the last is the device name. All numerical values are optional; if they are omitted or set to zero, the kernel will try to detect the value by probing for it, or use a default value.

The first parameter sets the IRQ assigned to the device. By default, the kernel will try to autodetect the device's IRQ channel. The 3c503 driver has a special feature that selects a free IRQ from the list 5, 9, 3, 4, and configures the board to use this line.

The base_addr parameter gives the I/O base address of the board; a value of zero tells the kernel to probe the addresses listed above.

The remaining two parameters may be used differently by different drivers. For shared-memory boards such as the WD80x3, they specify start and end addresses of the shared memory area. Other cards commonly use param1 to set the level of debugging information that is being displayed. Values of 1 through 7 denote increasing levels of verbosity, while 8 turns them off altogether; 0 denotes the default. The 3c503 driver uses param2 to select the internal transceiver (default) or an external transceiver (a value of 1). The former uses the board's BNC connector; the latter uses its AUI port.

If you have two Ethernet boards, you can have autodetect one board, and pass the second board's parameters with **lilo**. However, you must make sure the driver doesn't accidentally find the second board first, else the other one won't be registered at all. You do this by passing **lilo** a reserve option, which explicitly tells the kernel to avoid probing the I/O space taken up by the second board.

For instance, to make install a second Ethernet board at 0x300 as eth1, you would pass the following parameters to the kernel:

```
reserve=0x300,32 ether=0,0x300,eth1
```

The reserve option makes sure no driver accesses the board's I/O space when probing for some device. You may also use the kernel parameters to override autoprobing for eth0:

```
reserve=0x340,32 ether=0,0x340,eth0
```

To turn off autoprobing altogether, you can specify a base_addr argument of -1:

```
ether=0,-1,eth0
```

The PLIP Driver

PLIP stands for *Parallel Line IP* and is a cheap way to network when you want to connect only two machines. It uses a parallel port and a special cable, achieving speeds of 10Kbps to 20Kbps.

PLIP was originally developed by Crynwr, Inc. Its design is rather ingenious (or, if you prefer, hackish): For a long time, the parallel ports on PCs used to be only unidirectional printer ports; that is, the eight data lines could only be used to send from the PC to the peripheral device, but not the other way round. PLIP works around this by using the port's five status lines for input, which limits it to transferring all data as nibbles (half bytes) only. This mode of operation is called mode zero PLIP. Today, these unidirectional ports don't seem to be used much anymore. Therefore, there is also a PLIP extension called mode 1 that uses the full 8-bit interface.

Currently, Linux only supports mode 0. Unlike earlier versions of the PLIP code, it now attempts to be compatible with the PLIP implementations from Crynwr, as well as the PLIP driver in NCSA Telnet. (NCSA Telnet is a popular program for DOS that runs TCP/IP over Ethernet or PLIP, and supports Telnet and FTP.) To connect two machines using PLIP, you need a special cable sold at some shops as "Null Printer" or "Turbo Laplink" cable. You can, however, make one yourself fairly easily. Chapter 19 shows you how.

The PLIP driver for is the work of almost countless persons. At the time of this writing it is being maintained by Niibe Yutaka. If compiled into the kernel, it sets up a network interface for each of the possible printer ports, with plip0 corresponding to parallel port lp0, plip1 corresponding to lp1, etc.

If you have configured your printer port in a different way, you have to change these values in drivers/net/Space.c in the kernel source and build a new kernel.

This mapping does not mean, however, that you cannot use these parallel ports as usual. They are accessed by the PLIP driver only when the corresponding interface is configured up.

The SLIP And PPP Drivers

SLIP (Serial Line IP) and PPP (Point-to-Point Protocol) are widely used protocols for sending IP packets over a serial link. A number of institutions offer dial-up SLIP and PPP access to machines that are on the Internet, thus providing IP connectivity to private persons (something that's otherwise hardly affordable).

To run SLIP or PPP, no hardware modifications are necessary; you can use any serial port. Since serial port configuration is not specific to TCP/IP networking, a separate chapter has been devoted to this. Please refer to Chapter 4 for more information.

Chapter 4
Setting Up The Serial Hardware

There are rumors that there are some people out there in Netland who only own one PC and don't have the money to spend on a T1 Internet link. To get their daily dose of news and mail nevertheless, they are said to rely on SLIP links, UUCP networks, and bulletin board systems (BBSes) that utilize public telephone networks.

This chapter is intended to help all those people who rely on modems to maintain their link. However, there are many details that this chapter cannot go into (for instance, how to configure your modem for dial-in). All these topics will be covered in the HOWTO located at **www.redhat.com/mirrors/LDP/HOWTO/ Serial-HOWTO.html** (written by David S. Lawyer, **bf347@lanf. org**, and originally by Greg Hankins, **gregh@cc.gatech.edu**).

Communication Software For Modem Links

There are a number of communication packages available for Linux. Many of them are *terminal programs*, which allow a user to dial into another computer as if she were sitting in front of a simple terminal. The traditional terminal program for Linux is called Kermit. It is, however, somewhat Spartan. There are more comfortable programs available that support a dictionary of telephone numbers, script languages for calling and logging into remote computer systems, and so on. One of them is Minicom, which is close to some terminal programs former DOS users might be accustomed to. There are also X-based communications packages, e.g., Seyon.

Also, a number of Linux-based BBS packages are available for people that want to run a bulletin board system. Some of these packages can be found at **sunsite.unc.edu** in **/pub/ Linux/system/Network**.

Apart from terminal programs, there is also software that uses a serial link noninteractively to transport data to or from your computer. The advantage of this technique is that it takes much less time to download a few dozen kilobytes automatically than it might take you to read your mail online. On the other hand, this requires more disk storage because of the loads of useless information you usually get.

The epitome of this sort of communications software is UUCP. It is a program suite that copies files from one host to another, executes programs on a remote host, and so on. It is frequently used to transport mail or news in private networks. Ian Taylor's UUCP package, which also runs under Linux, is described in the following chapter. Other noninteractive communication software is, for example, used throughout Fidonet. Ports of Fidonet applications like *ifmail* are also available.

SLIP, the Serial Line Internet Protocol, is somewhat in between, allowing both interactive and noninteractive use. Many people use SLIP to dial up their campus network or some other sort of public SLIP server to run FTP sessions and so on. SLIP may, however, also be used over permanent or semipermanent connections for LAN-to-LAN coupling, although this is really only interesting with ISDN.

Introduction To Serial Devices

The devices a kernel provides for accessing serial devices are typically called *ttys*. This is an abbreviation for *teletype*, which used to be one of the major manufacturers of terminals in the early days of Unix. The term is used nowadays for any character-based data terminal. Throughout this chapter, we will use the term exclusively to refer to kernel devices.

Linux distinguishes three classes of ttys: (virtual) consoles, pseudo-terminals (similar to a two-way pipe, used by application such as X11), and serial devices. The latter are also counted as ttys because they permit interactive sessions over a serial connection, be it from a hard-wired terminal or a remote computer over a telephone line.

Ttys have a number of configurable parameters which can be set using the ioctl(2) system call. Many of them apply only to serial devices, since they need a great deal more flexibility to handle varying types of connections.

Among the most prominent line parameters are line speed and parity. But there are also flags for the conversion between upper- and lower-case characters, of carriage return into line feed, and so forth. The tty driver may also support various *line disciplines*, which make the device driver behave completely different. For example, the SLIP driver is implemented by means of a special line discipline.

There is a bit of ambiguity about how to measure a line's speed. The correct term is *bit rate*, which is related to the line's transfer speed measured in bits per second (or bps for short). Sometimes, you hear people refer to it as the *baud rate*, which is not quite correct. These two terms are, however, not interchangeable. The baud rate refers to a physical characteristic of some serial device, namely the clock rate at which pulses are transmitted. The bit rate, rather, denotes a current state of an existing serial connection between two points, namely the average number of bits transferred per second. It is important to know that these two values are usually different, as most devices encode more than one bit per electrical pulse.

Accessing Serial Devices

Like all devices in a system, serial ports are accessed through device special files, located in the /dev directory. There are two varieties of device files related to serial drivers, and for each port, there is one device file from each of them. Depending on the file it is accessed by, the device will behave differently.

The first variety is used whenever the port is used for dialing in; it has a major number of 4, and the files are named ttyS0, ttyS1, and so on. The second variety is used when dialing out through a port; the files are called cua0, cua1, and so forth, and have a major number of 5. (Linux devices have a "major" and "minor" numbers. When you do a long directory listing ("ls-l"), the device numbers are listed. An example of this can be seen below in Listing 4.1. The "major" number is 5 and the "minor" numbers are 64–67.)

Minor numbers are identical for both types. If you have your modem on one of the ports COM1 through COM4, its minor number will be the COM port number plus 63. If your setup is different from that, for example when using a board supporting multiple serial lines, please refer to the Serial Howto.

Assume your modem is on COM2. Thus, its minor number will be 65, and its major number will be 5 for dialing out. There should be a device cua1 which has these numbers. List the serial ttys in the /dev directory. Columns 5 and 6 should show major and minor numbers, respectively, as shown in Listing 4.1.

Listing 4.1 Major and minor numbers in device cua1.

```
$ ls -l /dev/cua*
crw-rw-rw-  1 root     root       5,  64 Nov 30 19:31 /dev/cua0
crw-rw-rw-  1 root     root       5,  65 Nov 30 22:08 /dev/cua1
crw-rw-rw-  1 root     root       5,  66 Oct 28 11:56 /dev/cua2
crw-rw-rw-  1 root     root       5,  67 Mar 19  1992 /dev/cua3
```

If there is no such device, you will have to create one: become super-user and type

```
# mknod -m 666 /dev/cua1 c 5 65
# chown root.root /dev/cua1
```

Some people suggest making /dev/modem a symbolic link to your modem device, so that casual users don't have to remember the somewhat unintuitive cua1. However, you cannot use modem in one program, and the real device file name in another. This is because these programs use so-called *lock files* to signal that the device is used. By convention, the lock file name for cua1, for instance, is LCK..cua1. Using different device files for the same port means that programs will fail to recognize each other's lock files and will both use the device at the same time. As a result, both applications will not work at all.

Serial Hardware

Linux currently supports a wide variety of serial boards which use the RS-232 standard. RS-232 is currently the most common standard for serial communications in the PC world. It uses a number of circuits for transmitting single bits as well as for synchronization. Additional lines may be used for signaling the presence of a carrier (used by modems) and handshake.

Although hardware handshake is optional, it is very useful. It allows either of the two stations to signal whether it is ready to receive more data, or if the other station should pause until the receiver is done processing the incoming data. The lines used for this are called "Clear to Send" (CTS) and "Ready to Send" (RTS), respectively, which accounts for the colloquial name of hardware handshake, namely RTS/CTS.

In PCs, the RS-232 interface is usually driven by a UART chip derived from the National Semiconductor 16450 chip, or a newer version thereof, the NSC 16550A. (There was also a NSC 16550, but its FIFO never really worked.) Some brands (most notably internal modems equipped with the Rockwell chipset) also use completely different chips that have been programmed to behave as if they were 16550s.

The main difference between 16450s and 16550s is that the latter have a FIFO buffer of 16 bytes, while the former only have a 1-byte buffer. This makes 16450s suitable for speeds up to 9600 baud, while higher speeds require a 16550-compatible chip. Besides these chips, Linux also supports the 8250 chip, which was the original UART for the PC-AT.

In the default configuration, the kernel checks the four standard serial ports COM1 through COM4. These will be assigned device minor numbers 64 through 67, as described above.

If you want to configure your serial ports properly, you should install Ted Tso's **setserial** command along with the rc.serial script. This script should be invoked from /etc/rc at system boot time. It uses **setserial** to configure the kernel serial devices. A typical rc.serial script looks like this:

```
# /etc/rc.serial - serial line configuration script.
#
# Do wild interrupt detection
/sbin/setserial -W /dev/cua*
```

```
# Configure serial devices
/sbin/setserial /dev/cua0 auto irq skip test autoconfig
/sbin/setserial /dev/cua1 auto irq skip test autoconfig
/sbin/setserial /dev/cua2 auto irq skip test autoconfig
/sbin/setserial /dev/cua3 auto irq skip test autoconfig

# Display serial device configuration
/sbin/setserial -bg /dev/cua*
```

Please refer to the documentation that comes along with **setserial** for an explanation of the parameters.

If your serial card is not detected, or the **setserial -bg** command shows an incorrect setting, you will have to force the configuration by explicitly supplying the correct values. Users with internal modems equipped with the Rockwell chipset are reported to experience this problem. If, for example, the UART chip is reported to be an NSC 16450, although in fact it is NSC 16550-compatible, you have to change the configuration command for the offending port to

```
/sbin/setserial  /dev/cua1  auto irq skip test autoconfig
uart 16550
```

Similar options exist to force COM port, base address, and IRQ setting. Please refer to the setserial(8) manual page.

If your modem supports hardware handshake, you should make sure to enable it. Surprising as it is, most communication programs do not attempt to enable this by default; you have to set it manually instead. This is best performed in the rc.serial script, using the **stty** command:

```
$ stty crtscts < /dev/cua1
```

To check if hardware handshake is in effect, use

```
$ stty -a < /dev/cua1
```

This gives you the status of all flags for that device; a flag shown with a preceding minus, as in -crtscts, means that the flag has been turned off.

Chapter 5
Configuring TCP/IP Networking

In this chapter, we will go through all the steps necessary to setting up TCP/IP networking on your machine. Starting with the assignment of IP addresses, we will slowly work our way through the configuration of TCP/IP network interfaces, and introduce a few tools that come quite handy when hunting down problems with your network installation.

Most of the tasks covered in this chapter you will generally have to do only once. Afterwards, you have to touch most configuration files only when adding a new system to your network, or when you reconfigure your system entirely. Some of the commands used to configure TCP/IP, however, have to be executed each time the system is booted. This is usually done by invoking them from the system /etc/rc scripts.

Note
There are two "major" schools regarding system initialization scripts: BSD-style and SysV init style. Red Hat Linux uses a modified SysV style init process. The reference here to the rc scripts, and the naming convention for the same, is to a BSD-style init process.

Commonly, the network-specific part of this procedure is contained in a script called rc.net or rc.inet. Sometimes, you will also see two scripts named rc.inet1 and rc.inet2, where the former initializes the kernel part of networking, and the latter starts basic networking services and applications. Throughout the following, I will adhere to the latter concept.

Below, I will discuss the actions performed by rc.inet1 and applications will be covered in later chapters. After finishing this chapter, you should have established a sequence of commands that properly configure TCP/IP networking on your computer. You should then replace any sample commands in rc.inet1 with your commands, make sure rc.inet1 is executed at startup time, and reboot your machine. The networking rc scripts that come along with your favorite distribution should give you a good example.

Setting Up The proc Filesystem

Some of the configuration tools of the Net-2 release rely on the proc filesystem for communicating with the kernel. (In kernel version 2.2.x, the networking code is referred to as Net4.) This is an interface that permits access to kernel run-time information through a filesystem-like mechanism. When mounted, you can list its files like any other filesystem, or display their contents. Typical items include the loadavg file, which contains the system load average, or meminfo, which shows current core memory and swap usage.

To this, the networking code adds the net directory. It contains a number of files that show things like the kernel ARP tables, the state of TCP connections, and the routing tables. Most network administration tools get their information from these files.

The proc filesystem (or procfs, as it is also known) is usually mounted on /proc at system boot time. The best method is to add the following line to /etc/fstab:

```
# procfs mont point:
none            /proc           proc    defaults
```

and execute "mount /proc" from your /etc/rc script.

The procfs is nowadays configured into most kernels by default. If the procfs is not in your kernel, you will get a message that reads "mount: fs type procfs not supported by kernel". You will then have to recompile the kernel and answer "Yes" when asked for procfs support.

Installing The Binaries

If you are using one of the prepackaged distributions, it will most probably contain the major networking applications and utilities along with a coherent set of sample files. The only case where you might have to obtain and install new utilities is when you install a new kernel release. As they occasionally involve changes in the kernel networking layer, you will need to update the basic configuration tools. This at least involves recompiling, but sometimes you may also be required to obtain the latest set of binaries. These are usually distributed along with the kernel, packaged in an archive called net-XXX.tar.gz, where XXX is the version number. The release matching -1.0 is 0.32b, the latest kernel as of this writing (1.1.12 and later) require 0.32d.

If you want to compile and install the standard TCP/IP network applications yourself, you can obtain the sources from most FTP servers. These are more or less heavily patched versions of programs from Net-BSD or other sources. Other applications, such as Xmosaic, Xarchie, or Gopher and IRC clients, must be obtained separately. Most of them compile out of the box if you follow the instructions.

Another Example

For the remainder of this book, I will discuss a more practical example that is less complex than the Groucho Marx University example. Consider the Virtual Brewery, a small company that brews virtual beer. To manage their business more efficiently, the virtual brewers want to network their computers, which are all PCs running a bright and shiny 1.0.

On the same floor, just across the hall, there's the Virtual Winery, who works closely with the brewery. They run an Ethernet of their own. Quite naturally, the two companies want to link their networks once they are operational. As a first step, they want to set up a gateway host that forwards datagrams between the two subnets. Later, they want to have a UUCP link to the outside world, through which they exchange mail and news. In the long run, the also want to set up a SLIP connection to connect to the Internet on occasion.

Setting The Hostname

Most, if not all, network applications rely on the local host's name having been set to some reasonable value. This is usually done during the boot procedure by executing the **hostname** command. To set the hostname to name, it is invoked as

```
# hostname name
```

It is common practice to use the unqualified hostname without any domain name for this. For instance, hosts at the Virtual Brewery might be called **vale.vbrew.com**, **vlager.vbrew.com**, and so on. These are their official, fully qualified domain names. Their local hostnames would be only the first component of the name, such as vale. However, as the local hostname is frequently used to look up the host's IP address, you have to make sure that the resolver library is able to look up the host's IP address. This usually means that you have to enter the name in /etc/hosts (see below).

Some people suggest to use the domain name command to set the kernel's idea of a domain name to the remaining part of the FQDN. In this way you could combine the output from hostname and domain name to get the FQDN again. However, this is at best only half correct. Domain name is generally used to set the host's NIS domain, which may be entirely different from the DNS domain your host belongs to. NIS is covered in Chapter 9.

Assigning IP Addresses

If you configure the networking software on your host for standalone operation (for instance, to be able to run the INN netnews software), you can safely skip this section, because you will need an IP address just for the loopback interface, which is always 127.0.0.1.

Things are a little more complicated with real networks like Ethernets. If you want to connect your host to an existing network, you have to ask its administrators to give you an IP address on this network. When setting up the network all by yourself, you have to assign IP addresses yourself, as described below.

Hosts within a local network should usually share addresses from the same logical IP network. Hence, you have to assign an IP network address. If you have several physical networks, you either have to assign them different network numbers or use subnetting to split your IP address range into several subnetworks.

If your network is not connected to the Internet, you are free to choose any (legal) network address. You only have to make sure to choose one from classes A, B, or C, or else things will most likely not work properly. However, if you intend to get on the Internet in the near future, you should obtain an official IP address now. The best way to proceed is to ask your network service provider to help you. If you want to obtain a network number just in case you might get on the Internet someday, request a Network Address Application Form from **hostmaster@internic.net**.

To operate several Ethernets (or other networks, once a driver is available), you have to split your network into subnets. Note that subnetting is required only if you have more than one broadcast network; point-to-point links don't count. For instance, if you have one Ethernet and one or more SLIP links to the outside world, you don't need to subnet your network. The reason for this will be explained in Chapter 6.

To continue our example, the brewery's network manager applies to the NIC for a class B network number and is given 191.72.0.0. To accommodate the two Ethernets, she decides to use eight bits of the host part as additional subnet bits. This leaves another eight bits for the host part, allowing for 254 hosts on each of the subnets. She then assigns subnet number 1 to the brewery, and gives the winery number 2. Their respective network addresses are thus 191.72.1.0 and 191.72.2.0. The subnet mask is 255.255.255.0.

vlager, which is the gateway between the two networks, is assigned a host number of 1 on both of them, which gives it the IP addresses 191.72.1.1 and 191.72.2.1, respectively. The following shows the two subnets and the gateway.

```
#
# Hosts file for Virtual Brewery/Virtual Winery
#
# IP           local      fully qualified domain name
#
```

```
127.0.0.1        localhost
#
191.72.1.1       vlager      vlager.vbrew.com
191.72.1.1       vlager-if1
191.72.1.2       vstout      vstout.vbrew.com
191.72.1.3       vale        vale.vbrew.com
#
191.72.2.1       vlager-if2
191.72.2.2       vbeaujolais vbeaujolais.vbrew.com
191.72.2.3       vbardolino  vbardolino.vbrew.com
191.72.2.4       vchianti    vchianti.vbrew.com
```

Note that in this example I am using a class B network to keep things simple; a class C network would be more realistic. With the new networking code, subnetting is not limited to byte boundaries, so even a class C network may be split into several subnets. For instance, you could use two bits of the host part for the netmask, giving you four possible subnets with 64 hosts on each. (The last number on each subnet is reserved as the broadcast address, so it's in fact 63 hosts per subnet.)

Writing Hosts And Networks Files

After you have subnetted your network, you should prepare for simple hostname resolution using the /etc/hosts file. If you are not going to use DNS or NIS for address resolution, you have to put all hosts in the hosts file.

Even if you want to run DNS or NIS during normal operation, you want to have some subset of all hostnames in /etc/hosts nevertheless. For one, you want to have some sort of name resolution even when no network interfaces are running, for example during boot time. This is not only a matter of convenience but also allows you to use symbolic hostnames in your rc.inet scripts. Thus, when changing IP addresses, you only have to copy an updated hosts file to all machines and reboot, rather than having to edit a large number of rc files separately. Usually, you will put all local hostnames and addresses in hosts, adding those of any gateways and NIS servers if used. (You will need the address of any NIS servers only if you use Peter Eriksson's NYS. Other NIS implementations locate their servers at run-time only by using ypbind.)

Also, during initial testing, you should make sure your resolver only uses information from the hosts file. Your DNS or NIS software may come with sample files that may produce strange results when used. To make all applications use /etc/hosts exclusively when looking up the IP address of a host, you have to edit the /etc/host.conf file. Comment out any lines that begin with the keyword **order** by preceding them with a hash sign, and insert the line

```
order hosts
```

The configuration of the resolver library will be covered in detail later in Chapter 6.

The hosts file contains one entry per line, consisting of an IP address, a hostname, and an optional list of aliases for the hostname. The fields are separated by spaces or tabs, and the address field must begin in column one. Anything following a hash sign (#) is regarded as a comment and is ignored.

Hostnames can be either fully qualified, or relative to the local domain. For vale, you would usually enter the fully qualified name, **vale.vbrew.com**, and vale by itself in the hosts file, so that it is known by both its official name and the shorter local name.

In our same example from above, here is how a hosts file at the Virtual Brewery might look. Two special names are included, vlager-if1 and vlager-if2, that give the addresses for both interfaces used on vlager.

```
#
# Hosts file for Virtual Brewery/Virtual Winery
#
# IP            local       fully qualified domain name
#
127.0.0.1       localhost
#
191.72.1.1      vlager      vlager.vbrew.com
191.72.1.1      vlager-if1
191.72.1.2      vstout      vstout.vbrew.com
191.72.1.3      vale        vale.vbrew.com
#
191.72.2.1      vlager-if2
191.72.2.2      vbeaujolais vbeaujolais.vbrew.com
191.72.2.3      vbardolino  vbardolino.vbrew.com
191.72.2.4      vchianti    vchianti.vbrew.com
```

Just as with a host's IP address, you sometimes would like to use a symbolic name for network numbers, too. Therefore, the hosts file has a companion called /etc/networks that maps network names to network numbers and vice versa.

/etc/networks does not exist in Red Hat Linux.

At the Virtual Brewery, we might install a networks file like this:

```
# /etc/networks for the Virtual Brewery
brew-net        191.72.1.0
wine-net        191.72.2.0
```

Note that names in networks must not collide with hostnames from the hosts file, or else some programs may produce strange results.

Interface Configuration For IP

After setting up your hardware as explained in the previous chapter, you have to make these devices known to the kernel networking software. A couple of commands are used to configure the network interfaces, and initialize the routing table. These tasks are usually performed from the rc.inet1 script each time the system is booted. The basic tools for this are called *ifconfig* (where "if" stands for interface), and *route*.

ifconfig is used to make an interface accessible to the kernel networking layer. This involves the assignment of an IP address and other parameters, and activating the interface, also known as "taking up." Being active here means that the kernel will send and receive IP datagrams through the interface. The simplest way to invoke it is with

```
ifconfig interface ip-address
```

which assigns "ip-address" to the interface and activates it. All other parameters are set to default values. For instance, the default subnet mask is derived from the network class of the IP address, such as 255.255.0.0 for a class B address. (**ifconfig** is described in more detail at the end of this chapter.)

The second tool, **route**, allows you to add or remove routes from the kernel routing table. It can be invoked as

```
route [add|del] target
```

where the **add** and **del** arguments determine whether to add or delete the route to target.

The Loopback Interface

The very first interface to be activated is the loopback interface:

```
# ifconfig lo 127.0.0.1
```

Occasionally, you will also see the dummy hostname localhost being used instead of the IP address. Ifconfig will look up the name in the hosts file where an entry should declare it as the hostname for 127.0.0.1:

```
# Sample /etc/hosts entry for localhost
localhost       127.0.0.1
```

To view the configuration of an interface, you invoke **ifconfig** giving it the interface name as argument:

```
$ ifconfig lo
lo          Link encap Local Loopback
inet addr 127.0.0.1  Bcast [NONE SET]  Mask 255.0.0.0
UP BROADCAST LOOPBACK RUNNING  MTU 2000  Metric 1
RX packets 0 errors 0 dropped 0 overrun 0
TX packets 0 errors 0 dropped 0 overrun 0
```

As you can see, the loopback interface has been assigned a netmask of 255.0.0.0, because 127.0.0.1 is a class A address. As you can see, the interface doesn't have a broadcast address set, which isn't normally very useful for the loopback anyway. However, if you run the **rwhod** daemon on your host, you may have to set the loopback device's broadcast address in order for **rwho** to function properly. Setting the broadcast is explained below.

Now, you can almost start playing with your mini-"network." What is still missing is an entry in the routing table that tells IP that it may use this interface as route to destination 127.0.0.1. This is accomplished by typing

```
# route add 127.0.0.1
```

Again, you can use localhost instead of the IP address.

Next, you should check that everything works fine by using **ping**. **ping** is the networking equivalent of a sonar device and is used to verify that a given address is actually reachable and that a delay occurs when sending a datagram to it and back again. The time required for this is often referred to as the round-trip time.

```
# ping localhost
PING localhost (127.0.0.1): 56 data bytes
64 bytes from 127.0.0.1: icmp seq=0 ttl=32 time=1 ms
64 bytes from 127.0.0.1: icmp seq=1 ttl=32 time=0 ms
64 bytes from 127.0.0.1: icmp seq=2 ttl=32 time=0 ms
^C

- localhost ping statistics -
3 packets transmitted, 3 packets received, 0% packet loss
round-trip min/avg/max = 0/0/1 ms
```

When invoking **ping** as shown here, it will go on emitting packets forever unless interrupted by the user. The ^C above marks the place where we pressed Ctrl+C.

The above example shows that packets for 127.0.0.1 are properly delivered and a reply is returned to ping almost instantaneously. This shows you have succeeded in setting up your first network interface.

If the output you get from **ping** does not resemble that shown above, you are in trouble. Check any error if they indicate some file hasn't been installed properly. Check that the **ifconfig** and **route** binaries you use are compatible with the kernel release you run, and, above all, that the kernel has been compiled with networking enabled (you see this from the presence of the /proc/net directory). If you get an error message saying "Network unreachable," then you probably have got the **route** command wrong. Make sure you use the same address as you gave to **ifconfig**.

The steps described above are enough to use networking applications on a standalone host. After adding the above lines to rc.inet1 and making sure both rc.inet scripts are executed from /etc/rc, you may reboot your machine and try out various applications. For instance, "telnet localhost" should establish a telnet connection to your host, giving you a login prompt.

However, the loopback interface is useful not only as an example in networking books, or as a test-bed during development, but is actually used by some applications during normal operation. For instance, all applications based on RPC use the loopback interface to register themselves with the **portmapper** daemon at startup. Therefore, you always have to configure it, regardless of whether your machine is attached to a network or not.

Ethernet Interfaces

Configuring an Ethernet interface goes pretty much the same as with the loopback interface, it just requires a few more parameters when you are using subnetting.

At the Virtual Brewery, we have subnetted the IP network, which was originally a class B network, into class C subnetworks. To make the interface recognize this, the **ifconfig** incantation would look like this:

```
# ifconfig eth0 vstout netmask 255.255.255.0
```

This assigns the eth0 interface the IP address of vstout (191.72.1.2). If we had omitted the netmask, **ifconfig** would have deduced the the netmask from the IP network class, which would have resulted in a netmask of 255.255.0.0. Now a quick check shows:

```
# ifconfig eth0
eth0      Link encap 10Mps Ethernet HWaddr  00:00:C0:90:B3:42
inet addr 191.72.1.2 Bcast 191.72.1.255 Mask 255.255.255.0
UP BROADCAST RUNNING  MTU 1500  Metric 1
RX packets 0 errors 0 dropped 0 overrun 0
TX packets 0 errors 0 dropped 0 overrun 0
```

You can see that **ifconfig** automatically set the broadcast address (the Bcast field above) to the usual value, which is the hosts network number with the host bits all set. Also, the message transfer unit (the maximum size of Ethernet frames the kernel will generate for this interface) has been set to the maximum value of 1,500 bytes. All these values can be over-ridden with special options that will be described later.

Quite similar to the loopback case, you now have to install a routing entry that informs the kernel about the network that can be reached through eth0. For the Virtual Brewery, you would invoke **route** as

```
# route add -net 191.72.1.0
```

At first, this looks a little like magic, because it's not really clear how **route** detects which interface to route through. However, the trick is rather simple: The kernel checks all interfaces that have been configured so far and compares the destination address (191.72.1.0 in this case) to the network part of the interface address (that is, the bitwise and of the interface address and the netmask). The only interface that matches is eth0.

Now, what's that **-net** option for? This is used because **route** can handle both routes to networks and routes to single hosts (as you have seen above with localhost). When being given an address in dotted quad notation, it attempts to guess whether it is a network or a hostname by looking at the host part bits. If the address's host part is zero, **route** assumes it denotes a network, otherwise it takes it as a host address. Therefore, **route** would think that 191.72.1.0 is a host address rather than a network number, because it cannot know that we use subnetting. We therefore have to tell it explicitly that it denotes a network, giving it the **-net** flag.

Of course, the above **route** command is a little tedious to type, and it's prone to spelling mistakes. A more convenient approach is to use the network names we have defined in /etc/networks above. This makes the command much more readable; even the **-net** flag can now be omitted, because **route** now knows that 191.72.1.0 denotes a network.

```
# route add brew-net
```

Now that you've finished the basic configuration steps, we want to make sure your Ethernet interface is indeed running happily. Choose a host from your Ethernet, for instance vlager, and type

```
# ping vlager
PING vlager: 64 byte packets
64 bytes from 191.72.1.1: icmp seq=0. time=11. ms
64 bytes from 191.72.1.1: icmp seq=1. time=7. ms
64 bytes from 191.72.1.1: icmp seq=2. time=12. ms
64 bytes from 191.72.1.1: icmp seq=3. time=3. ms
^C

—vstout.vbrew.com PING Statistics—
4 packets transmitted, 4 packets received, 0% packet loss
round-trip (ms)  min/avg/max = 3/8/12
```

If you don't see any output similar to this, then something is broken, obviously. If you encounter unusual packet loss rates, this hints at a hardware problem, like bad or missing terminators, and so on. If you don't receive any packets at all, you should check the interface configuration with **netstat**. The packet statistics displayed by **ifconfig** should tell you whether any packets have been sent out on the interface at all. If you have access to the remote host, too, you should go over to that machine and check the interface statistics, too. In this way, you can determine exactly where the packets got dropped. In addition, you should display the routing information with **route** to see if both hosts have the correct routing entry. **route** prints out the complete kernel routing table when invoked without any arguments (the **-n** option only makes it print addresses as dotted quad instead of using the hostname):

```
# route -n
Kernel routing table
Destination    Gateway      Genmask         Flags Metric Ref Use
127.0.0.1      *            255.255.255.255 UH    1      0
191.72.1.0     *            255.255.255.0   U     1      0
```

The detailed meaning of these fields is explained below. The Flag column contains a list of flags set for each interface. U is always set for active interfaces, and H says the destination address denotes a host. If the H flag is set for a route that you meant to be a network route, then you have to specify the **-net** option with the **route** command. To check whether a route you have entered is used at all, check if the Use field in the second-to-last column increases between two invocations of **ping**.

Routing Through A Gateway

In the previous section, I covered only the case of setting up a host on a single Ethernet. Quite frequently, however, one encounters networks connected to one another by gateways. These gateways may simply link two or more Ethernets, but may provide a link to the outside world, the Internet, as well. In order to use the service of a gateway, you have to provide additional routing information to the networking layer.

For instance, the Ethernets of the Virtual Brewery and the Virtual Winery are linked through such a gateway, namely, the host vlager. Assuming that vlager has already been configured, we only have to add another entry to vstout's routing table that tells the kernel it can reach all hosts on the Winery's network through vlager. The appropriate incantation of **route** is shown below; the **gw** keyword tells it that the next argument denotes a gateway.

```
# route add wine-net gw vlager
```

Of course, any host on the Winery network you wish to talk to must have a corresponding routing entry for the Brewery's network, otherwise you would only be able to send data from vstout to vbardolino, but any response returned by the latter would go into the great bit bucket.

This example describes only a gateway that switches packets between two isolated Ethernets. Now assume that vlager also has a connection to the Internet (say, through an additional SLIP link). Then we would want datagrams to any destination network other than the Brewery to be handed to vlager. This can be accomplished by making it the default gateway for vstout:

```
# route add default gw vlager
```

The network name default is a shorthand for 0.0.0.0, which denotes the default route. You do not have to add this name to /etc/networks because it is built into **route**.

When you see high packet loss rates when **ping**ing a host behind one or more gateways, this may hint at a very congested network. Packet loss is not so much due to technical deficiencies as due to temporary excess loads on forwarding hosts, which makes them delay or even drop incoming datagrams.

Configuring A Gateway

Configuring a machine to switch packets between two Ethernets is pretty straightforward. Assume we're back at vlager, which is equipped with two Ethernet boards, each being connected to one of the two networks. All you have to do is configure both interfaces separately, giving them their respective IP address, and that's it.

Note
Packet forwarding by default was turned off in the linux-2.0.x series. Packet forwarded can be enabled at run-time thusly: # echo 1 > /proc/sys/net/ipv4/ip_forward.

It is quite useful to add information on the two interfaces to the hosts file in the way shown below, so we have handy names for them, too:

```
191.72.1.1       vlager       vlager.vbrew.com
191.72.1.1       vlager-if1
191.72.2.1       vlager-if2
```

The sequence of commands to set up the two interfaces is then:

```
# ifconfig eth0 vlager-if1
# ifconfig eth1 vlager-if2
# route add brew-net
# route add wine-net
```

The PLIP Interface

When using a PLIP link to connect two machines, things are a little different from what you have to do when using an Ethernet. The former are so-called point-to-point links, because they involve only two hosts ("points"), as opposed to broadcast networks.

As an example, we consider the laptop computer of some employee at the Virtual Brewery that is connected to vlager via PLIP. The laptop itself is called vlite, and has only one parallel port. At boot time, this port will be registered as plip1. To activate the link, you have to configure the plip1 interface using the following commands:

```
# ifconfig plip1 vlite pointopoint vlager
```

```
# route add default gw vlager
```

Note

Pointopoint is not a typo. It's really spelled like this.

The first command configures the interface, telling the kernel that this is a point-to-point link, with the remote side having the address of vlager. The second installs the default route, using vlager as gateway. On vlager, a similar **ifconfig** command is necessary to activate the link (a **route** invocation is not needed):

```
# ifconfig plip1 vlager pointopoint vlite
```

The interesting point is that the plip1 interface on vlager does not have to have a separate IP address, but may also be given the address 191.72.1.1. Just as a matter of caution, you should, however, configure a PLIP or SLIP link only after you have completely set up the routing table entries for your Ethernets. With some older kernels, your network route might otherwise end up pointing at the point-to-point link.

Now, we have configured routing from the laptop to the Brewery's network; what's still missing is a way to route from any of the Brewery's hosts to vlite. One particularly cumbersome way is to add a specific route to every host's routing table that names vlager as a gateway to vlite:

```
# route add vlite gw vlager
```

A much better option when faced with temporary routes is to use *dynamic routing*. One way to do so is to use gated, a routing daemon, which you would have to install on each host in the network in order to distribute routing information dynamically. The easiest way, however, is to use *proxy ARP*. With proxy ARP, vlager will respond to any ARP query for vlite by sending its own Ethernet address. The effect of this is that all packets for vlite will wind up at vlager, which then forwards them to the laptop. We will come back to proxy ARP in the PLIP section below.

Future Net-3 releases will contain a tool called **plipconfig** which will allow you to set the IRQ of the printer port to use. Later, this may even be replaced by a more general **ifconfig** command.

The SLIP And PPP Interface

Although SLIP and PPP links are only simple point-to-point links like PLIP connections, there is much more to be said about them. Usually, establishing a SLIP connection involves dialing up a remote site through your modem and setting the serial line to SLIP mode. PPP is used in a similar fashion. The tools required for setting up a SLIP or PPP link will be described in Chapter 6 and Chapter 7.

The Dummy Interface

The dummy interface is really a little exotic, but rather useful nevertheless. Its main benefit is with standalone hosts, and machines whose only IP network connection is a dial-up link. In fact, the latter are standalone hosts most of the time, too.

The dilemma with standalone hosts is that they only have a single network device active, the loopback device, which is usually assigned the address 127.0.0.1. On some occasions, however, you need to send data to the "official" IP address of the local host. For instance, consider the laptop vlite, that has been disconnected from any network for the duration of this example. An application on vlite may now want to send some data to another application on the same host. Looking up vlite in /etc/hosts yields an IP address of 191.72.1.65, so the application tries to send to this address. As the loopback interface is currently the only active interface on the machine, the kernel has no idea that this address actually refers to itself! As a consequence, the kernel discards the datagram and returns an error to the application.

This is where the dummy device steps in. It solves the dilemma by simply serving as the alter ego of the loopback interface. In the case of vlite, you would simply give it the address 191.72.1.65 and add a host route pointing to it. Every datagram for 191.72.1.65 would then be delivered locally. The proper invocation is:

```
# ifconfig dummy vlite
# route add vlite
```

All About ifconfig

There are a lot more parameters to **ifconfig** than we have described above. Its normal invocation is this:

```
ifconfig interface [[-net|-host] address [parameters]]
```

"Interface" is the interface name, and "address" is the IP address to be assigned to the interface. This may either be an IP address in dotted quad notation, or a name **ifconfig** will look up in /etc/hosts and /etc/networks. The **-net** and **-host** options force **ifconfig** to treat the address as network number or host address, respectively.

If **ifconfig** is invoked with only the interface name, it displays that interface's configuration. When invoked without any parameters, it displays all interfaces you configured so far; an option of **-a** forces it to show the inactive ones as well. A sample invocation for the Ethernet interface eth0 may look like this:

```
# ifconfig eth0
eth0      Link encap 10Mbps Ethernet  HWaddr 00:00:C0:90:B3:42
          inet addr 191.72.1.2 Bcast 191.72.1.255 Mask 255.255.255.0
UP BROADCAST RUNNING  MTU 1500  Metric 0
RX packets 3136 errors 217 dropped 7 overrun 26
TX packets 1752 errors 25 dropped 0 overrun 0
```

The MTU and Metric fields show the current MTU and metric value for that interface. The metric value is traditionally used by some operating systems to compute the cost of a route.

The RX and TX lines show how many packets have been received or transmitted error-free, how many errors occurred, how many packets were dropped (probably because of low memory), and how many were lost because of an overrun. Receiver overruns usually happen when packets come in faster than the kernel can service the last interrupt. The flag values printed by **ifconfig** correspond more or less to the names of its command line options; they will be explained below.

In Table 5.1 is a list of parameters recognized by **ifconfig** with the corresponding flag names given in brackets. Options that simply turn on a feature also allow it to be turned off again by preceding the option name by a dash (-).

Table 5.1   Parameters recognized by ifconfig.

up	This marks an interface "up," i.e., accessible to the IP layer. This option is implied when an address is given on the command line. It may also be used to re-enable an interface that has been taken down temporarily using the down option. (This option corresponds to the flags **UP RUNNING**.)
down	This marks an interface "down," i.e., inaccessible to the IP layer. This effectively disables any IP traffic through the interface. Note that this does not delete all routing entries that use this interface automatically. If you take the interface down permanently, you should to delete these routing entries and supply alternative routes if possible.
netmask mask	This assigns a subnet mask to be used by the interface. It may be given as either a 32-bit hexadecimal number preceded by 0x, or as a dotted quad of decimal numbers that involve only two hosts. This option is needed to configure, for example, SLIP or PLIP interfaces.

(continued)

Table 5.1 Parameters recognized by ifconfig *(continued).*

pointopoint address	This option is used for point-to-point IP links that involve only two hosts. This option is needed to configure, for example, SLIP or PLIP interfaces. (If a point-to-point address has been set, **ifconfig** displays the **POINTOPOINT** flag.)
broadcast address	The broadcast address is usually made up from the network number by setting all bits of the host part. Some IP implementations use a different scheme; this option is there to adapt to these strange environments. (If a broadcast address has been set, **ifconfig** displays the **BROADCAST** flag.)
metric number	This option may be used to assign a metric value to the routing table entry created for the interface. This metric is used by the Routing Information Protocol (RIP) to build routing tables for the network. The default metric used by ifconfig is a value of zero. If you don't run a RIP daemon, you don't need this option at all; if you do, you will rarely need to change the metric value.
mtu bytes	This sets the Maximum Transmission Unit, which is the maximum number of octets the interface is able to handle in one transaction. For Ethernets, the MTU defaults to 1,500; for SLIP interfaces, this is 296.
arp	This is an option specific to broadcast networks such as Ethernets or packet radio. It enables the use of ARP, the Address Resolution Protocol, to detect the physical addresses of hosts attached to the network. For broadcast networks, is on by default.
-arp	Disables the use of ARP on this interface.
promisc	Puts the interface in promiscuous mode. On a broadcast network, this makes the interface receive all packets, regardless of whether they were destined for another host or not. This allows an analysis of network traffic using packet filters and such, also called Ethernet snooping. Usually, this is a good technique of hunting down network problems that are otherwise hard to come by. On the other hand, this allows attackers to skim the traffic of your network for passwords and do other nasty things. One protection against this type of attack is not to let anyone just plug in their computers in your Ethernet. Another option is to use secure authentication protocols, such as Kerberos, or the SRA login suite. (This option corresponds to the flag **PROMISC**.)
-promisc	Turns off promiscuous mode.
allmulti	Multicast addresses are some sort of broadcast to a group of hosts who don't necessarily have to be on the same subnet. Multicast addresses are not yet supported by the kernel. (This option corresponds to the flag **ALLMULTI**.)
-allmulti	Turns off multicast addresses.

Checking With netstat

Next, I will turn to a useful tool for checking your network configuration and activity. It is called *netstat* and is, in fact, rather a collection of several tools lumped together.

Displaying The Routing Table

When invoking **netstat** with the **-r** flag, it displays the kernel routing table in the way we've been doing this with **route** above. On vstout, it produces:

```
# netstat -nr
Kernel routing table
Destination    Gateway        Genmask        Flags Metric Ref Use
127.0.0.1      *              255.255.255.255 UH   1      0
191.72.1.0     *              255.255.255.0   U    1      0
191.72.2.0     191.72.1.1     255.255.255.0   UGN  1      0
```

The **-n** option makes **netstat** print addresses as dotted quad IP numbers rather than the symbolic host and network names. This is especially useful when you want to avoid address lookups over the network (e.g., to a DNS or NIS server).

The second column of **netstat**'s output shows the gateway the routing entry points to. If no gateway is used, an asterisk is printed instead. Column three shows the "generality" of the route. When given an IP address to find a suitable route for, the kernel goes through all routing table entries, taking the bitwise AND of the address and the genmask before comparing it to the target of the route.

The fourth column displays various flags that describe the route as described in the following bulleted list:

◆ G—The route uses a gateway.

◆ U—The interface to be used is up.

◆ H—Only a single host can be reached through the route. For example, this is the case for the loopback entry 127.0.0.1.

◆ D—This is set if the table entry has been generated by an ICMP redirect message (see Chapter 3).

◆ M—This is set if the table entry was modified by an ICMP redirect message.

The Ref column of **netstat**'s output shows the number of references to this route, that is, how many other routes (e.g., through gateways) rely on the presence of this route. The last two columns show the number of times the routing entry has been used and the interface that datagrams are passed to for delivery.

Displaying Interface Statistics

When invoked with the **-i** flag, **netstat** will display statistics for the network interfaces currently configured. If, in addition, the **-a** option is given, it will print all interfaces present in the kernel, not only those that have been configured currently. On vstout, the output from **netstat** will look like this:

```
$ netstat -i
Kernel Interface table
Iface   MTU Met  RX-OK RX-ERR RX-DRP RX-OVR  TX-OK TX-ERR TX-DRP TX-
lo        0   0   3185      0      0      0   3185      0      0
eth0   1500   0 972633     17     20    120 628711    217      0
```

The MTU and Met fields show the current MTU and metric value for that interface. The RX and TX columns show how many packets have been received or transmitted error-free (RX-OK/TX-OK), damaged (RX-ERR/TX-ERR), how many were dropped (RX-DRP/TX-DRP), and how many were lost because of an overrun (RX-OVR/TX-OVR).

The last column shows the flags that have been set for this interface. These are one-character versions of the long flag names that are printed when you display the interface configuration with **ifconfig**. This is a description of those flags:

- B—A broadcast address has been set.
- L—This interface is a loopback device
- M—All packets are received (promiscuous mode).
- N—Trailers are avoided.
- O—ARP is turned off for this interface.
- P—This is a point-to-point connection.
- R—Interface is running.
- U—Interface is up.

Displaying Connections

netstat supports a set of options to display active or passive sockets. The options **-t**, **-u**, **-w**, and **-x** show active TCP, UDP, RAW, or UNIX socket connections. If you provide the **-a** flag in addition, sockets that are waiting for a connection (i.e., listening) are displayed as well. This will give you a list of all servers that are currently running on your system.

Invoking **netstat -ta** on vlager produces:

```
$ netstat -ta
Active Internet connections
Proto Recv-Q Send-Q Local Address    Foreign Address    (State)
tcp      0      0 *:domain          *:*                LISTEN
tcp      0      0 *:time            *:*                LISTEN
tcp      0      0 *:smtp            *:*                LISTEN
tcp      0      0 vlager:smtp       vstout:1040        ESTABLISHED
tcp      0      0 *:telnet          *:*                LISTEN
tcp      0      0 localhost:1046    vbardolino:telnet  ESTABLISHED
tcp      0      0 *:chargen         *:*                LISTEN
tcp      0      0 *:daytime         *:*                LISTEN
tcp      0      0 *:discard         *:*                LISTEN
tcp      0      0 *:echo            *:*                LISTEN
tcp      0      0 *:shell           *:*                LISTEN
tcp      0      0 *:login           *:*                LISTEN
```

This shows most servers simply waiting for an incoming connection. However, the fourth line shows an incoming SMTP connection from vstout, and the sixth line tells you there is an outgoing telnet connection to vbardolino. Using the **-a** flag all by itself will display all sockets from all families.

Checking The ARP Tables

On some occasions, it is useful to view or even alter the contents of the kernel's ARP tables, for example when you suspect a duplicate Internet address is the cause for some intermittent network problem. The **arp** tool was made for things like these. Its command line options are:

```
arp [-v] [-t hwtype] -a [hostname]
arp [-v] [-t hwtype] -s hostname hwaddr
arp [-v] -d hostname [hostname...]
```

All hostname arguments may be either symbolic hostnames or IP addresses in dotted quad notation.

The first invocation displays the ARP entry for the IP address or host specified, or all hosts known if no hostname is given. For example, invoking **arp** on vlager may yield

```
# arp -a
IP address      HW type              HW address
191.72.1.3      10Mbps Ethernet      00:00:C0:5A:42:C1
191.72.1.2      10Mbps Ethernet      00:00:C0:90:B3:42
191.72.2.4      10Mbps Ethernet      00:00:C0:04:69:AA
```

which shows the Ethernet addresses of vlager, vstout and vale.

Using the **-t** option you can limit the display to the hardware type specified. This may be ether, ax25, or pronet, standing for 10Mbps Ethernet, AMPR-AX.25, and IEEE-802.5 token ring equipment, respectively.

The **-s** option is used to permanently add hostname's Ethernet address to the ARP tables. The **hwaddr** argument specifies the hardware address, which is by default expected to be an Ethernet address, specified as six hexadecimal bytes separated by colons. You may also set the hardware address for other types of hardware, too, using the **-t** option.

One problem which may require you to manually add an IP address to the ARP table is when for some reasons ARP queries for the remote host fail, for instance when its ARP driver is buggy or there is another host in the network that erroneously identifies itself with that host's IP address. Hard-wiring IP addresses in the ARP table is also a (very drastic) measure to protect yourself from hosts on your Ethernet that pose as someone else.

Invoking **arp** using the **-d** switch deletes all ARP entries relating to the given host. This may be used to force the interface to re-attempt to obtain the Ethernet address for the IP address in question. This is useful when a misconfigured system has broadcast wrong ARP information (of course, you have to reconfigure the broken host first).

The **-s** option may also be used to implement proxy ARP. This is a special technique where a host, say, gate, acts as a gateway to another host named fnord, by pretending that both addresses refer to the same host, namely, gate. It does so by publishing an ARP entry for fnord that points to its own Ethernet interface. Now when a host sends out an ARP query for fnord, gate will return a reply containing its own Ethernet address. The querying host will then send all datagrams to gate, which dutifully forwards them to fnord.

These contortions may be necessary, for instance, when you want to access fnord from a DOS machine with a broken TCP implementation that doesn't understand routing too well. When you use proxy ARP, it will appear to the DOS machine as if fnord was on the local subnet, so it doesn't have to know about how to route through a gateway.

Another very useful application of proxy ARP is when one of your hosts acts as a gateway to some other host only temporarily, for instance through a dial-up link. In a previous example, we already encountered the laptop vlite, which was connected to vlager through a PLIP link only from time to time. Of course, this will work only if the address of the host you want to provide proxy ARP for is on the same IP subnet as your gateway. For instance, vstout could proxy ARP for any host on the Brewery subnet (191.72.1.0), but never for a host on the Winery subnet (191.72.2.0).

The proper invocation to provide proxy ARP for fnord is given below; of course, the Ethernet address given must be that of gate.

```
# arp -s fnord 00:00:c0:a1:42:e0 pub
```

The proxy ARP entry may be removed again by invoking:

```
# arp -d fnord
```

The Future

Networking is still evolving. Major changes at the kernel layer will bring a very flexible configuration scheme that will allow you to configure the network devices at run-time. For instance, the **ifconfig** command will take arguments that set the IRQ line and DMA channel.

Another change to come soon is the additional **mtu** flag to the **route** command, which will set the Maximum Transmission Unit for a particular route. This route-specific MTU overrides the MTU specified for the interface. You will typically use this option for routes through a gateway, where the link between the gateway and the destination host requires a very low MTU. For instance, assume host wanderer is connected to vlager through a SLIP link. When sending data from vstout to wanderer, the networking layer on wanderer would would use packets of up to 1,500 bytes, because packets are sent across the Ethernet. The SLIP link, on the other hand, is operated with an MTU of 296, so the network layer on vlager would have to break up the IP packets into smaller fragments that fit into 296 bytes. If instead, you would have configured the route on vstout to use a MTU of 296 right from the start, this relatively expensive fragmentation could be avoided:

```
# route add wanderer gw vlager mtu 296
```

Note that the **mtu** option also allows you to selectively undo the effects of the "Subnets Are Local" Policy (SNARL). This policy is a kernel configuration option and is described in Chapter 3.

Name Service And Resolver Configuraton

As discussed in Chapter 2, TCP/IP networking may rely on different schemes to convert names into addresses. The simplest way, which takes no advantage of the way the name space has been split up into zones, is a host table stored in /etc/hosts. This is useful only for small LANs that are run by one single administrator and otherwise have no IP traffic with the outside world. The format of the hosts file has already been described in Chapter 3.

Alternatively, you may use BIND—the Berkeley Internet Name Domain Service—for resolving hostnames to IP addresses. Configuring BIND may be a real chore, but once you've done it, changes in the network topology are easily made. As on many other Linux systems, name service is provided through a program called **named**. At startup, it loads a set of master files into its cache and waits for queries from remote or local user processes. There are different ways to set up BIND, and not all require you to run a name server on every host.

This chapter can do little more but give a rough sketch of how to operate a name server. If you plan to use BIND in an environment with more than just a small LAN and probably an Internet uplink, you should get a good book on BIND. One good book is Cricket Liu's *DNS and BIND* (O'Reilly), which is now in its third edition and can be found at **www.oreilly.com/catalog/dns3/**. For current information, you may also want to check the release notes contained in the BIND sources. There are also two newsgroups for DNS questions you can refer to: **comp.protocols.dns** and **comp.protocols.dns.bind**.

The Resolver Library

When talking of "the resolver," we do not mean any special application, but rather refer to the resolver library, a collection of functions that can be found in the standard C library. The central routines are gethostbyname(2) and gethostbyaddr(2), which look up all IP addresses belonging to a host and vice versa. They may be configured to simply look up the information in hosts, query a number of name servers, or use the hosts database of NIS (Network Information Service). Other applications, like smail, may include different drivers for any of these, and need special care.

The host.conf File

The central file that controls your resolver setup is host.conf. It resides in /etc and tells the resolver which services to use and in what order.

Options in host.conf must occur on separate lines. Fields may be separated by white space (spaces or tabs). A hash sign (#) introduces a comment that extends to the next new line.

The following options are available:

♦ order—This determines the order in which the resolving services are tried. Valid options are:

 ♦ bind—for querying the name server

 ♦ hosts—for lookups in /etc/hosts

 ♦ nis—for NIS lookups

 Any or all of them may be specified. The order in which they appear on the line determines the order in which the respective services are tried.

♦ multi—Takes on or off as options. This determines if a host in /etc/hosts is allowed to have several IP addresses, which is usually referred to as being "multi-homed." This flag has no effect on DNS or NIS queries.

♦ nospoof—As explained in the previous chapter, DNS allows you to find the hostname belonging to an IP address by using the inaddr.arpa domain. Attempts by name servers to supply a false hostname are called "spoofing." To guard against this, the resolver may be configured to check if the original IP address is in fact associated with the hostname obtained. If not, the name is rejected and an error returned. This behavior is turned on by setting nospoof on.

♦ alert—This option takes on or off as arguments. If it is turned on, any spoof attempts (see above) will cause the resolver to log a message to the syslog facility.

♦ trim—This option takes a domain name as an argument, which will be removed from hostnames before lookup. This is useful for hosts entries, where you might only want to specify hostnames without local domain. A lookup of a host with the local domain name appended will have this removed, thus allowing the lookup in /etc/hosts to succeed. trim options accumulate, making it possible to consider your host as being local to several domains.

A sample file for vlager is shown below:

```
# /etc/host.conf
# We have named running, but no NIS (yet)
order   bind hosts
# Allow multiple addrs
multi   on
# Guard against spoof attempts
nospoof on
# Trim local domain (not really necessary).
trim    vbrew.com.
```

Resolver Environment Variables

The settings from host.conf may be overridden using a number of environment variables. These are

- ◆ RESOLV HOST CONF—This specifies a file to be read instead of /etc/host.conf.

- ◆ RESOLV SERV ORDER—Overrides the order option given in host.conf. Services are given as hosts, bind, and nis, separated by a space, comma, colon, or semicolon.

- ◆ RESOLV SPOOF CHECK—Determines the measures taken against spoofing. It is completely disabled by off. The values warn and warn off enable spoof checking, but turn logging on and off, respectively. A value of * turns on spoof checks, but leaves the logging facility as defined in host.conf.

- ◆ RESOLV MULTI —A value of on or off may be used to override the multi options from tt host.conf.

- ◆ RESOLV OVERRIDE TRIM DOMAINS—This environment specifies a list of trim domains which override those given in host.conf.

- ◆ RESOLV ADD TRIM DOMAINS—This environment specifies a list of trim domains which are added to those given in host.conf.

Configuring Name Server Lookups—resolv.conf

When configuring the resolver library to use the BIND name service for host lookups, you also have to tell it which name servers to use. There is a separate file for this, called resolv.conf. If this file does not exist or is empty, the resolver assumes the name server is on your local host.

If you run a name server on your local host, you have to set it up separately, as will be explained in the following section. If your are on a local network and have the opportunity to use an existing name server, this should always be preferred.

The most important option in resolv.conf is **nameserver**, which gives the IP address of a name server to use. If you specify several name servers by giving the **nameserver** option several times, they are tried in the order given. You should therefore put the most reliable server first. Currently, up to three name servers are supported.

If no **nameserver** option is given, the resolver attempts to connect to the name server on the local host.

Two other options, **domain** and **search**, deal with default domains that are tacked onto a hostname if BIND fails to resolve it with the first query. The **search** option specifies a list of domain names to be tried. The list items are separated by spaces or tabs.

If no **search** option is given, a default search list is constructed from the local domain name by using the domain name itself, plus all parent domains up to the root. The local domain name may be given using the domain statement; if none is given, the resolver obtains it through the getdomainname(2) system call.

If this sounds confusing to you, consider this sample resolv.conf file for the Virtual Brewery:

```
# /etc/resolv.conf
# Our domain
domain          vbrew.com
#
# We use vlager as central nameserver:
nameserver      191.72.1.1
```

When resolving the name vale, the resolver would look up vale, and failing this, vale.vbrew.com, and vale.com.

Resolver Robustness

If you are running a LAN inside a larger network, you definitely should use central name servers if they are available. The advantage of this is that these will develop rich caches, since all queries are forwarded to them. This scheme, however, has a drawback: When a fire recently destroyed the backbone cable at our university, no more work was possible on our department's LAN, because the resolver couldn't reach any of the name servers anymore. There was no logging in on X-terminals anymore, no printing, and so on.

Although it is not very common for campus backbones to go down in flames, one might want to take precautions against cases like these.

One option is to set up a local name server that resolves hostnames from your local domain and forwards all queries for other hostnames to the main servers. Of course, this is applicable only if you are running your own domain.

Alternatively, you can maintain a backup host table for your domain or LAN in /etc/hosts. In /etc/host.conf you would then include "order bind hosts" to make the resolver fall back to the hosts file if the central name server is down.

Running **named**

The program that provides domain name service on most machines is usually called *named* (pronounced name-dee). This is a server program originally developed for BSD providing name service to clients, and possibly to other name servers. The version currently used on most installations seems to be BIND 8.2 (8.x is next major rev from 4.x series; current 4.x is 4.9.7)

This section requires some understanding of the way the Domain Name System works. If the following discussion is all Greek to you, you may want to re-read Chapter 2, which has some more information on the basics of DNS.

named is usually started at system boot time, and runs until the machine goes down again. It takes its information from a configuration file called /etc/named.boot, and various files that contain data mapping domain names to addresses and the like. The latter are called *zone files*. The formats and semantics of these files will be explained in the following section.

To run named, simply enter

```
# /usr/sbin/named
```

at the prompt. **named** will come up, read the named.boot file and any zone files specified therein. It writes its process ID to /var/run/named.pid in ASCII, downloads any zone files from primary servers if necessary, and starts listening on port 53 for DNS queries.

Note

*There are various **named** binaries floating around FTP sites, each configured a little differently. Some have their pid file in /etc, some store it in /tmp or /var/tmp.*

The named.boot File

The named.boot file is generally very small and contains little else but pointers to master files containing zone information and pointers to other name servers. Comments in the boot file start with a semicolon and extend to the next new line. Before we discuss the format of named.boot in more detail, we will take a look at the sample file for vlager:

```
;
; /etc/named.boot file for vlager.vbrew.com
;
```

```
directory       /var/named
;
;               domain                          file
;───────────────────────────────
cache           .                               named.ca
primary         vbrew.com                       named.hosts
primary         0.0.127.in-addr.arpa            named.local
primary         72.191.in-addr.arpa             named.rev
```

The cache and primary commands shown in this example load information into **named**. This information is taken from the master files specified in the second argument. They contain textual representations of DNS resource records, which we will look at below.

In this example, we configured **named** as the primary name server for three domains, as indicated by the primary statements at the end of the file. The first of these lines, for instance, instructs **named** to act as a primary server for vbrew.com, taking the zone data from the file named.hosts. The **directory** keyword tells it that all zone files are located in /var/named.

The cache entry is very special and should be present on virtually all machines running a name server. Its function is twofold: It instructs named to enable its cache, and to load the root name server hints from the cache file specified (named.ca in our example). We will come back to the name server hints below.

Here's a list of the most important options you can use in named.boot:

♦ **directory**—This specifies a directory in which zone files reside. Names of files may be given relative to this directory. Several directories may be specified by repeatedly using directory. According to the Linux filesystem standard, this should be /var/named.

♦ **primary** —This takes a domain name and a file name as an argument, declaring the local server authoritative for the named domain. As a primary server, **named** loads the zone information from the given master file. Generally, there will always be at least one primary entry in every boot file, namely for reverse mapping of network 127.0.0.0, which is the local loopback network.

♦ **secondary**—This statement takes a domain name, an address list, and a file name as an argument. It declares the local server a secondary master server for the domain specified. A secondary server holds authoritative data on the domain, too, but it doesn't gather it from files, but tries to download it from the primary server. The IP address of at least one primary server must thus be given to named in the address list. The local server will contact each of them in turn until it successfully transfers the zone database, which is then stored in the backup file given as the third argument. If none of the primary servers responds, the zone data is retrieved from the backup file instead. **named** will then attempt to refresh the zone data at regular intervals. This is explained below, in connection with the SOA resource record type.

- **cache**—This takes a domain and a file name as arguments. This file contains the root server hints, that is a list of records pointing to the root name servers. Only NS and A records will be recognized. The domain argument is generally the root domain name ".". This information is absolutely crucial to **named**: If the cache statement does not occur in the boot file, **named** will not develop a local cache at all. This will severely degrade performance and increase network load if the next server queried is not on the local net. Moreover, **named** will not be able to reach any root name servers, and thus it won't resolve any addresses except those it is authoritative for. An exception from this rule is when using forwarding servers (cf. the forwarders option below).

- **forwarders**—This statement takes an address list as an argument. The IP addresses in this list specify a list of name servers that **named** may query if it fails to resolve a query from its local cache. They are tried in order until one of them responds to the query.

- **slave**—This statement makes the name server a slave server. That is, it will never perform recursive queries itself, but only forwards them to servers specified with the forwarders statement.

There are two options which we will not describe here, **sortlist** and **domain**. Additionally, there are two directives that may be used inside the zone database files. These are $INCLUDE and $ORIGIN. Since they are rarely needed, we will not describe them here, either.

The DNS Database Files

Master files included by **named**, like named.hosts, always have a domain associated with them, which is called the *origin*. This is the domain name specified with the cache and primary commands. Within a master file, you are allowed to specify domain and hostnames relative to this domain. A name given in a configuration file is considered absolute if it ends in a single dot, otherwise it is considered relative to the origin. The origin all by itself may be referred to using "@".

All data contained in a master file is split up in *resource records*, or RRs for short. They make up the smallest unit of information available through DNS. Each resource record has a type. A records, for instance, map a hostname to an IP address, and a CNAME record associates an alias for a host with its official hostname. As an example, take a look at Listing 5.1 (on page 30), which shows the named.hosts master file for the virtual brewery.

Resource record representations in master files share a common format, which is

```
[domain] [ttl] [class] type rdata
```

Fields are separated by spaces or tabs. An entry may be continued across several lines if an opening brace occurs before the first new line, and the last field is followed by a closing brace. Anything between a semicolon and a new line is ignored.

- domain—This is the domain name to which the entry applies. If no domain name is given, the RR is assumed to apply to the domain of the previous RR.

♦ ttl—In order to force resolvers to discard information after a certain time, each RR is associated a "time to live," or ttl for short. The ttl field specifies the time in seconds the information is valid after it has been retrieved from the server. It is a decimal number with at most eight digits. If no ttl value is given, it defaults to the value of the minimum field of the preceding SOA record.

♦ class—This is an address class, like IN for IP addresses, or HS for objects in the Hesiod class. For TCP/IP networking, you have to make this IN. If no class field is given, the class of the preceding RR is assumed.

♦ type—This describes the type of the RR. The most common types are A, OA, PTR, and NS. The following sections describe the various types of RRs.

♦ rdata—This holds the data associated with the RR. The format of this field depends on the type of the RR. Below, it will be described for each RR separately.

The following is an incomplete list of RRs to be used in DNS master files. There are a couple more of them, which we will not explain. They are experimental and of little use generally.

♦ SOA—This describes a zone of authority (SOA means "start of authority"). It signals that the records following the SOA RR contain authoritative information for the domain. Every master file included by a primary statement must contain an SOA record for this zone. The resource data contains the following fields:

♦ origin—This is the canonical hostname of the primary name server for this domain. It is usually given as an absolute name.

♦ contact—This is the email address of the person responsible for maintaining the domain, with the "@" character replaced by a dot. For instance, if the responsible person at the Virtual Brewery is janet, then this field would contain janet.vbrew.com.

♦ serial—This is the version number of the zone file, expressed as a single decimal number. Whenever data is changed in the zone file, this number should be incremented. The serial number is used by secondary name servers to recognize when zone information has changed. To stay up to date, secondary servers request the primary server's SOA record at certain intervals, and compare the serial number to that of the cached SOA record. If the number has changed, the secondary servers transfers the whole zone database from the primary server.

♦ refresh—This specifies the interval in seconds that the secondary servers should wait between checking the SOA record of the primary server. Again, this is a decimal number with at most eight digits. Generally, the network topology doesn't change too often, so that this number should specify an interval of roughly a day for larger networks, and even more for smaller ones.

♦ retry—This number determines the intervals at which a secondary server should retry contacting the primary server if a request or a zone refresh fails. It must not be too low, or else a temporary failure of the server or a network problem may cause the secondary server to waste network resources. One hour, or perhaps one half-hour, might be a good choice.

♦ expire—This specifies the time in seconds after which the server should finally discard all zone data if it hasn't been able to contact the primary server. It should normally be very large. Craig Hunt ([GETST "hunt-tcpip"]) recommends 42 days.

♦ minimum—This is the default ttl value for resource records that do not explicitly specify one. This requires other name servers to discard the RR after a certain amount of time. It has however nothing to do with the time after which a secondary server tries to update the zone information. Minimum should be a large value, especially for LANs where the network topology almost never changes. A value of around a week or a month is probably a good choice. In the case that single RRs may change more frequently, you can still assign them different ttls.

♦ A—This associates an IP address with a hostname. The resource data field contains the address in dotted quad notation. For each host, there must be only one A record. The hostname used in this A record is considered the official or canonical hostname. All other hostnames are aliases and must be mapped onto the canonical hostname using a CNAME record.

♦ NS—This points to a master name server of a subordinate zone. For an explanation why one has to have NS records, see Chapter 3. The resource data field contains the hostname of the name server. To resolve the hostname, an additional A record is needed, the so-called glue record that gives the name server's IP address.

♦ CNAME—This associates an alias for a host with its canonical hostname. The canonical hostname is the one the master file provides an A record for; aliases are simply linked to that name by a CNAME record, but don't have any other records of their own.

♦ PTR—This type of record is used to associate names in the inaddr.arpa domain with hostnames. This is used for reverse mapping of IP addresses to hostnames. The hostname given must be the canonical hostname.

♦ MX—This RR announces a mail exchanger for a domain. The reasons to have mail exchangers are discussed in Chapter 14. The syntax of an MX record is

```
[domain] [ttl] [class] MX preference host
```

where host names the mail exchanger for domain. Every mail exchanger has an integer preference associated with it. A mail transport agent who desires to deliver mail to domain will try all hosts who have an MX record for this domain until it succeeds. The one with the lowest preference value is tried first, then the others in order of increasing preference value.

♦ HINFO—This record provides information on the system's hardware and software. Its syntax is

```
[domain] [ttl] [class] HINFO hardware software
```

The hardware field identifies the hardware used by this host. There are special conventions to specify this. A list of valid names is given in the "Assigned Numbers" (RFC 1340). If the field contains any blanks, it must be enclosed in double quotes. The software field names the operating system software used by the system. Again, a valid name from the "Assigned Numbers" RFC should be chosen.

Writing The Master Files

Listings 5.1, 5.2, 5.3, and 5.4 give sample files for a name server at the brewery, located on vlager. Owing to the nature of the network discussed (a single LAN), the example is pretty straightforward. If your requirements are more complex, and you can't get **named** going, get *DNS and BIND* by Cricket Liu and Paul Albitz.

The named.ca cache file shown in Figure 5.1 shows sample hint records for a root name server. A typical cache file usually describes about a dozen name servers or so. You can obtain the current list of name servers for the root domain using the **nslookup** tool described toward the end of this chapter.

Note

*You can't query your name server for the root servers if you don't have any root server hints installed: catch-22! To escape this dilemma, you can either make **nslookup** use a different name server, or you can use the sample file in Listing 5.1 as a starting point, and then obtain the full list of valid servers.*

Listing 5.1   The named.ca file.

```
;
; /var/named/named.ca           Cache file for the brewery.
;                   We're not on the Internet, so we don't need
;                   any root servers. To activate these
;                   records, remove the semicolons.
;
; .                99999999   IN   NS   NS.NIC.DDN.MIL
; NS.NIC.DDN.MIL   99999999   IN   A    26.3.0.103
; .                99999999   IN   NS   NS.NASA.GOV
; NS.NASA.GOV      99999999   IN   A    128.102.16.10
```

Listing 5.2   The named.hosts file.

```
;
; /var/named/named.hosts        Local hosts at the brewery
;                               Origin is vbrew.com
;
@                      IN   SOA   vlager.vbrew.com. (
```

```
                              janet.vbrew.com.
                              16          ; serial
                              86400       ; refresh: once per day
                              3600        ; retry:   one hour
                              3600000     ; expire:  42 days
                              604800      ; minimum: 1 week
                              )
                   IN  NS    vlager.vbrew.com.
;
; local mail is distributed on vlager
                   IN  MX    10 vlager
;
; loopback address
localhost.         IN  A     127.0.0.1
; brewery Ethernet
vlager             IN  A     191.72.1.1
vlager-if1         IN  CNAME vlager
; vlager is also news server
news               IN  CNAME vlager
vstout             IN  A     191.72.1.2
vale               IN  A     191.72.1.3
; winery Ethernet
vlager-if2         IN  A     191.72.2.1
vbardolino         IN  A     191.72.2.2
vchianti           IN  A     191.72.2.3
vbeaujolais        IN  A     191.72.2.4
```

Listing 5.3 The named.local file.

```
;
; /var/named/named.local       Reverse mapping of 127.0.0
;                                Origin is 0.0.127.in-addr.arpa.
;
@                  IN  SOA   vlager.vbrew.com. (
                              joe.vbrew.com.
                              1           ; serial
                              360000      ; refresh: 100 hrs
                              3600        ; retry:   one hour
                              3600000     ; expire:  42 days
                              360000      ; minimum: 100 hrs
                              )
                   IN  NS    vlager.vbrew.com.
1                  IN  PTR   localhost.
```

Listing 5.4 The named.rev file.

```
;
; /var/named/named.rev        Reverse mapping of our IP addresses
;                             Origin is 72.191.in-addr.arpa.
;
@                IN  SOA    vlager.vbrew.com. (
                           joe.vbrew.com.
                           16          ; serial
                           86400       ; refresh: once per day
                           3600        ; retry:   one hour
                           3600000     ; expire:  42 days
                           604800      ; minimum: 1 week
                           )
                 IN  NS     vlager.vbrew.com.
; brewery
1.1              IN  PTR    vlager.vbrew.com.
2.1              IN  PTR    vstout.vbrew.com.
3.1              IN  PTR    vale.vbrew.com.
; winery
1.2              IN  PTR    vlager-if1.vbrew.com.
2.2              IN  PTR    vbardolino.vbrew.com.
3.2              IN  PTR    vchianti.vbrew.com.
4.2              IN  PTR    vbeaujolais.vbrew.com.
```

Verifying The Name Server Setup

There's a fine tool for checking the operation of your name server setup. It is called **nslookup**, and may be used both interactively and from the command line. In the latter case, you simply invoke it as

```
nslookup hostname
```

and it will query the name server specified in resolv.conf for hostname. (If this file names more than one server, **nslookup** will choose one at random.)

The interactive mode, however, is much more exciting. Besides looking up individual hosts, you may query for any type of DNS record and transfer the entire zone information for a domain.

When invoked without argument, **nslookup** will display the name server it uses and enter interactive mode. At the **>** prompt, you may type any domain name it should query for. By default, it asks for class A records, those containing the IP address relating to the domain name.

You may change this type by issuing "set type=*type*", where *type* is one of the resource record names described above, or ANY.

For example, you might have the following dialogue with it:

```
$ nslookup
Default Name Server:  rs10.hrz.th-darmstadt.de
Address:  130.83.56.60

 sunsite.unc.edu
Name Server:  rs10.hrz.th-darmstadt.de
Address:  130.83.56.60

Non-authoritative answer:
Name:    sunsite.unc.edu
Address:  152.2.22.81
```

If you try to query for a name that has no IP address associated, but other records were found in the DNS database, **nslookup** will come back with an error message saying "No type A records found." However, you can make it query for records other than type A by issuing the **set type** command. For example, to get the SOA record of unc.edu, you would issue:

```
 unc.edu
*** No address (A) records available for unc.edu
Name Server:  rs10.hrz.th-darmstadt.de
Address:  130.83.56.60

 set type=SOA
 unc.edu
Name Server:  rs10.hrz.th-darmstadt.de
Address:  130.83.56.60

Non-authoritative answer:
unc.edu
        origin = ns.unc.edu
        mail addr = shava.ns.unc.edu
        serial = 930408
        refresh = 28800 (8 hours)
        retry   = 3600 (1 hour)
        expire  = 1209600 (14 days)
        minimum ttl = 86400 (1 day)

Authoritative answers can be found from:
UNC.EDU nameserver = SAMBA.ACS.UNC.EDU
SAMBA.ACS.UNC.EDU       internet address = 128.109.157.30
```

In a similar fashion you can query for MX records, and so forth. Using a type of ANY returns all resource records associated with a given name.

```
 set type=MX
 unc.edu
Non-authoritative answer:
unc.edu preference = 10, mail exchanger = lambada.oit.unc.edu
lambada.oit.unc.edu     internet address = 152.2.22.80

Authoritative answers can be found from:
UNC.EDU nameserver = SAMBA.ACS.UNC.EDU
SAMBA.ACS.UNC.EDU      internet address = 128.109.157.30
```

A practical application of **nslookup** beside debugging is to obtain the current list of root
name servers for the named.ca file. You can do this by querying for all type NS records
associated with the root domain:

```
 set typ=NS

Name Server:  fb0430.mathematik.th-darmstadt.de
Address:   130.83.2.30

Non-authoritative answer:
(root)   nameserver = NS.INTERNIC.NET
(root)   nameserver = AOS.ARL.ARMY.MIL
(root)   nameserver = C.NYSER.NET
(root)   nameserver = TERP.UMD.EDU
(root)   nameserver = NS.NASA.GOV
(root)   nameserver = NIC.NORDU.NET
(root)   nameserver = NS.NIC.DDN.MIL

Authoritative answers can be found from:
(root)   nameserver = NS.INTERNIC.NET
(root)   nameserver = AOS.ARL.ARMY.MIL
(root)   nameserver = C.NYSER.NET
(root)   nameserver = TERP.UMD.EDU
(root)   nameserver = NS.NASA.GOV
(root)   nameserver = NIC.NORDU.NET
(root)   nameserver = NS.NIC.DDN.MIL
NS.INTERNIC.NET internet address = 198.41.0.4
AOS.ARL.ARMY.MIL       internet address = 128.63.4.82
AOS.ARL.ARMY.MIL       internet address = 192.5.25.82
AOS.ARL.ARMY.MIL       internet address = 26.3.0.29
C.NYSER.NET     internet address = 192.33.4.12
TERP.UMD.EDU    internet address = 128.8.10.90
NS.NASA.GOV     internet address = 128.102.16.10
NS.NASA.GOV     internet address = 192.52.195.10
NS.NASA.GOV     internet address = 45.13.10.121
NIC.NORDU.NET   internet address = 192.36.148.17
NS.NIC.DDN.MIL  internet address = 192.112.36.4
```

The complete set of commands available with **nslookup** may be obtained by the **help** command from within **nslookup**.

Other Useful Tools

There are a few tools that can help you with your tasks as a BIND administrator. I will briefly describe two of them here. Please refer to the documentation that comes with these tools for information on how to use them.

hostcvt is a tool that helps you with your initial BIND configuration by converting your /etc/ hosts file into master files for named. It generates both the forward (A) and reverse mapping (PTR) entries, and takes care of aliases and the like. Of course, it won't do the whole job for you, as you may still want to tune the timeout values in the SOA record, for instance, or add MX records and the like. Still, it may help you save a few aspirins. **hostcvt** is part of the BIND source, but can also be found as a standalone package on a few FTP servers.

After setting up your name server, you may want to test your configuration. The ideal (and, to my knowledge) only tool for this is **dnswalk**, a perl-based package that walks your DNS database, looking for common mistakes and verifying that the informaiton is consistent. **dnswalk** has been released on **comp.sources.misc** recently, and should be available on all FTP sites that archive this group (**ftp.uu.net** should be a safe bet if you don't know of any such site near you).

Chapter 6
Serial Line IP

The serial line protocols, SLIP and PPP, provide the Internet connectivity for the poor. Apart from a modem and a serial board equipped with a FIFO buffer, no hardware is needed. Using it is not much more complicated than a mailbox, and an increasing number of private organizations offer dial-up IP at an affordable cost to everyone.

There are both SLIP and PPP drivers available. SLIP has been there for quite a while and works fairly reliably. A PPP driver has been developed recently by Michael Callahan and Al Longyear. It will be described in the next chapter.

General Requirements

To use SLIP or PPP, you have to configure some basic networking features as described in the previous chapters. At the least, you have to set up the loopback interface and provide for name resolution. When connecting to the Internet, you will of course want to use DNS. The simplest option is to put the address of some name server into your resolv.conf file; this server will be queried as soon as the SLIP link is activated. The closer this name server is to the point where you dial in, the better.

However, this solution is not optimal, because all name lookups will still go through your SLIP/PPP link. If you worry about the bandwidth this consumes, you can also set up a caching-only name server. It doesn't really serve a domain, but only acts as a relay for all DNS queries produced on your host. The advantage of this scheme is that it builds up a cache, so that most queries have to be sent over the serial line only once. A named.boot file for a caching-only server looks like this:

```
; named.boot file for caching-only server
directory                            /var/named

primary        0.0.127.in-addr.arpa   db.127.0.0  ; loopback net
cache          .                      db.cache    ; root servers
```

In addition to this name.boot file, you also have to set up the db.cache file with a valid list of root name servers.

SLIP Operation

Dial-up IP servers frequently offer SLIP service through special user accounts. After logging into such an account, you are not dropped into the common shell; instead, a program or shell script is executed that enables the server's SLIP driver for the serial line and configures the appropriate network interface. Then you have to do the same at your end of the link.

On some operating systems, the SLIP driver is a user-space program; under Linux, it is part of the kernel, which makes it a lot faster. This requires, however, that the serial line be converted to SLIP mode explicitly. This is done by means of a special tty line discipline, SLIPDISC. While the tty is in normal line discipline (DISC0), it will exchange data only with user processes, using the normal read(2) and write(2) calls, and the SLIP driver is unable to write to or read from the tty. In SLIPDISC, the roles are reversed: Now any user-space processes are blocked from writing to or reading from the tty, while all data coming in on the serial port will be passed directly to the SLIP driver.

The SLIP driver itself understands a number of variations on the SLIP protocol. Apart from ordinary SLIP, it also understands CSLIP, which performs the so-called Van Jacobson header compression on outgoing IP packets. (Van Jacobson header compression is described in RFC-1441.) This improves throughput for interactive sessions noticeably. Additionally, there are six-bit versions for each of these protocols.

A simple way to convert a serial line to SLIP mode is by using the **slattach** tool. Assume you have your modem on /dev/cua3, and have logged into the SLIP server successfully. You will then execute:

```
# slattach /dev/cua3 &
```

This will switch the line discipline of cua3 to SLIPDISC, and attach it to one of the SLIP network interfaces. If this is your first active SLIP link, the line will be attached to sl0; the second would be attached to sl1, and so on. The current kernels support up to eight simultaneous SLIP links.

The default encapsulation chosen by **slattach** is CSLIP. You may choose any other mode using the **-p** switch. To use normal SLIP (no compression), you would use

```
# slattach -p slip /dev/cua3 &
```

Other modes are cslip, slip6, cslip6 (for the six-bit version of SLIP), and adaptive for adaptive SLIP. The latter leaves it to the kernel to find out which type of SLIP encapsulation the remote end uses.

Note that you must use the same encapsulation as your peer does. For example, if cowslip uses CSLIP, you have to do so, too. The symptoms of a mismatch will be that a **ping** to the remote host will not receive any packets back. If the other host **ping**s you, you may also see messages like "Can't build ICMP header" on your console. One way to avoid these difficulties is to use adaptive SLIP.

In fact, **slattach** does not only allow you to enable SLIP but also other protocols that use the serial line as well, like PPP or KISS (another protocol used by ham radio people). For details, please refer to the **slattach** manual page.

After turning over the line to the SLIP driver, you have to configure the network interface. Again, we do this using the standard **ifconfig** and **route** commands. Assume that from vlager, we have dialed up a server named cowslip. You would then execute

```
# ifconfig sl0 vlager pointopoint cowslip
# route add cowslip
   # route add default gw cowslip
```

The first command configures the interface as a point-to-point link to cowslip, while the second and third add the route to cowslip and the default route using cowslip as a gateway.

When taking down the SLIP link, you first have to remove all routes through cowslip using **route** with the **del** option, take the interface down, and send **slattach** the hangup signal. Afterward you have to hang up the modem using your terminal program again:

```
# route del default
# route del cowslip
# ifconfig sl0 down
# kill -HUP 516
```

Using **dip**

Now, that was rather simple. Nevertheless, you might want to automate the above steps so that you only have to invoke a simple command that performs all steps shown above. This is what **dip** is for. (*dip* means Dialup IP and it was written by Fred van Kempen.) The current release as of this writing is version 3.3.7. It has been patched very heavily by a number of people, so that you can't speak of the **dip** program anymore. These different strains of development will hopefully be merged in a future release.

dip provides an interpreter for a simple scripting language that can handle the modem for you, convert the line to SLIP mode, and configure the interfaces. This is rather primitive and restrictive, but sufficient for most cases. A new release of **dip** may feature a more versatile language one day.

To be able to configure the SLIP interface, **dip** requires root privilege. It would now be tempting to make **dip** setuid to root, so that all users can dial up some SLIP server without having to give them root access. This is very dangerous, because setting up bogus interfaces and default routes with **dip** may disrupt routing on your network badly. Even worse, this will give your users the power to connect to any SLIP server and launch dangerous attacks on your network. So if you want to allow your users to fire up a SLIP connection, write small wrapper programs for each prospective SLIP server, and have these wrappers invoke **dip** with the specific script that establishes the connection. These programs can then safely be made setuid root. (diplogin can and must be run setuid, too. See the section at the end of this chapter.) Listing 6.1 contains a sample **dip** script.

Listing 6.1   A sample **dip** script.

```
# Sample dip script for dialing up cowslip
# Set local and remote name and address
get $local vlager
get $remote cowslip


port cua3                # choose a serial port
speed 38400              # set speed to max
modem HAYES              # set modem type
reset                    # reset modem and tty
flush                    # flush out modem response


# Prepare for dialing.
send ATQ0V1E1X1\r
wait OK 2
if $errlvl != 0 goto error
dial 0123456789
if $errlvl != 0 goto error
wait CONNECT 60
if $errlvl != 0 goto error


# Okay, we're connected now
sleep 3
send \r\n\r\n
```

```
wait ogin: 10
if $errlvl != 0 goto error
send Cvlager\r
wait ssword: 5
if $errlvl != 0 goto error
#better not leave your password in ascii (thanx noud)
password
wait running 30
if $errlvl != 0 goto error
#to set up your remote and local IP
get $remote remote
print remote = $remote
if $errlvl != 0 goto error
wait to 3
get $local remote
print local = $local
if $errlvl != 0 goto error


# We have logged in, and the remote side is firing up CSLIP.
print Connected to $remote with address $rmtip
default                    # Make this link our default route
mode CSLIP                 # We go to CSLIP mode, too
# fall through in case of error
error:
print CSLIP to $remote failed.
```

A sample script is produced in the above listing. It can be used to connect to cowslip by invoking **dip** with the script name as argument:

```
# dip cowslip.dip
DIP: Dialup IP Protocol Driver version 3.3.7 (12/13/93)
Written by Fred N. van Kempen, MicroWalt Corporation.

connected to cowslip.moo.com with addr 193.174.7.129
#
```

After connecting to cowslip and enabling CSLIP, **dip** will detach from the terminal and go to the background. You can then start using the normal networking services on the CSLIP link. To terminate the connection, simply invoke **dip** with the **-k** option. This sends a hangup signal to dip process, using the process ID **dip** records in /etc/dip.pid: (See the **newsgroup alt.tla** for more palindromic fun with three-letter acronyms.)

```
# kill -k
```

In **dip**'s scripting language, keywords prefixed with a dollar symbol denote variable names. **dip** has a predefined set of variables, which will be listed below. $remote and $local, for instance, contain the hostnames of the local and remote host involved in the SLIP link.

The first two statements in the sample script are **get** commands, which is **dip**'s way to set a variable. Here, the local and remote hostname are set to vlager and cowslip, respectively.

The next five statements set up the terminal line and the modem. The reset sends a reset string to the modem; for Hayes-compatible modems, this is the **ATZ** command. The next statement flushes out the modem response, so that the login chat in the next few lines will work properly. This chat is pretty straightforward: It simply dials 41988, the phone number of cowslip, and logs into the account "Svlager" using the password "hey-jude." The **wait** command makes **dip** wait for the string given as its first argument; the number given as second argument make the wait time out after that many seconds if no such string is received. The **if** commands interspersed in the login procedure check that no error has occurred while executing the command.

The final commands executed after logging in are **default**, which makes the SLIP link the default route to all hosts, and **mode**, which enables SLIP mode on the line and configures the interface and routing table for you.

A **dip** Reference

Although widely used, **dip** hasn't been very well documented yet. In this section, we will therefore give a reference for most of **dip**'s commands. You can get an overview of all commands it provides by invoking **dip** in test mode, and entering the **help** command. To find out about the syntax of a command, you may enter it without any arguments; of course this does not work with commands that take no arguments.

```
DIP help
DIP knows about the following commands:

databits default  dial     echo     flush
get      goto     help     if       init
mode     modem    parity   print    port
reset    send     sleep    speed    stopbits
term     wait

DIP echo
Usage: echo on|off
DIP
```

Throughout the following, examples that display the DIP> prompt show how to enter a command in test mode, and what output it produces. Examples lacking this prompt should be taken as script excerpts.

The Modem Commands

There is a number of commands **dip** provides to configure your serial line and modem. Some of these are obvious, such as **port**, which selects a serial port, and **speed**, **databits**, **stopbits**, and **parity**, which set the common line parameters.

The **modem** command selects a modem type. Currently, the only type supported is HAYES (capitalization required). You have to provide **dip** with a modem type, or else it will refuse to execute the **dial** and **reset** commands. The **reset** command sends a reset string to the modem; the string used depends on the modem type selected. For Hayes-compatible modems, this is **ATZ**.

The flush code can be used to flush out all responses the modem has sent so far. Otherwise a chat script following the reset might be confused, because it reads the OK responses from earlier commands.

The **init** command selects an initialization string to be passed to the modem before dialing. The default for Hayes modems is "ATE0 Q0 V1 X1", which turns on echoing of commands and long result codes and selects blind dialing (no checking of dial tone).

The **dial** command finally sends the initialization string to the modem and dials up the remote system. The default **dial** command for Hayes modems is **ATD**.

echo And term

The **echo** command serves as a debugging aid, in that using Echo On makes **dip** echo to the console everything sends to the serial device. This can be turned off again by calling Echo Off.

dip also allows you to leave script mode temporarily and enter terminal mode. In this mode, you can use **dip** just like any ordinary terminal program, writing to the serial line and reading from it. To leave this mode, enter Ctrl+].

The get Command

The **get** command is **dip**'s way of setting a variable. The simplest form is to set a variable to a constant, as used throughout the above example. You may, however, also prompt the user for input by specifying the keyword ask instead of a value:

```
DIP get $local ask
Enter the value for $local:
```

A third method is to try to obtain the value from the remote host. Bizarre as it seems first, this is very useful in some cases: Some SLIP servers will not allow you to use your own IP address on the SLIP link, but will rather assign you one from a pool of addresses whenever you dial in, printing some message that informs you about the address you have been assigned. If the message looks something like this "Your address: 193.174.7.202," then the following piece of **dip** code would let you pick up the address:

```
wait address: 10
get $locip remote
```

The **print** Command

This is the command to echo text to the console dip was started from. Any of **dip**'s variables may be used in **print** commands, such as

```
DIP print Using port $port at speed $speed
Using port cua3 at speed 38400
```

Variable Names

Dip only understands a predefined set of variables. A variable name always begins with a dollar symbol and must be written in lowercase letters.

The $local and $locip variables contain the local host's name and IP address. Setting the hostname makes **dip** store the canonical hostname in $local, at the same time assigning $locip the corresponding IP address. The analogous thing happens when setting the $locip.

The $remote and $rmtip variables do the same for the remote host's name and address. $mtu contains the MTU value for the connection.

These five variables are the only ones that may be assigned values directly using the **get** command. A host of other variables can only be set through corresponding commands, but may be used as print statements; these are $modem, $port, and $speed.

$errlvl is the variable through which you can access the result of the last command executed. An error level of 0 indicates success, while a nonzero value denotes an error.

The **if** And **goto** Commands

The **if** command is rather a conditional branch than what one usually calls an if. Its syntax is

```
if var op number goto label
```

where the expression must be a simple comparison between one of the variables $errlvl, $locip, and $rmtip. The second operand must be an integer number; the operator op may be one of ==, !=, <, >, <=, and >=.

The **goto** command makes the execution of the script continue at the line following that bearing the label. A label must occur as the very first token on the line, and must be followed immediately by a colon.

send, wait, And **sleep**

These commands help implement simple chat scripts in **dip. send** outputs its arguments to the serial line. It does not support variables, but understands all C-style backslash character sequences, such as n and b. The tilde character (~) is used as an abbreviation for carriage return/new line.

wait takes a word as an argument, and scans all input on the serial line until it recognizes this word. The word itself may not contain any blanks. Optionally, you may give **wait** a timeout value as second argument; if the expected word is not received within that many seconds, the command will return with an $errlvl value of 1.

The **sleep** statement may be used to wait for a certain amount of time, for instance, to patiently wait for any login sequence to complete. Again, the interval is specified in seconds.

mode And default

These commands are used to flip the serial line to SLIP mode and configure the interface.

The **mode** command is the last command executed by **dip** before gong into daemon mode. Unless an error occurs, the command does not return.

mode takes a protocol name as argument. **dip** currently recognizes SLIP and CSLIP as valid names. The current version of **dip** does not understand adaptive SLIP, however.

After enabling SLIP mode on the serial line, **dip** executes **ifconfig** to configure the interface as a point-to-point link, and invokes **route** to set the route to the remote host.

If, in addition, the script executes the default command before **mode**, **dip** will also make the default route point to the SLIP link.

Running In Server Mode

Setting up your SLIP client was the hard part. Doing the opposite, namely, configuring your host to act as a SLIP server, is much easier.

One way to do this is to use **dip** in server mode, which can be achieved by invoking it as **diplogin**. Its main configuration file is /etc/diphosts, which associates login names with the address this host is assigned. Alternatively, you can also use **sliplogin**, a BSD-derived tool that features a more flexible configuration scheme that lets you execute shell scripts whenever a host connects and disconnects. It is currently at beta.

Both programs require that you set up one login account per SLIP client. For instance, assume you provide SLIP service to Arthur Dent at dent.beta.com, you might create an account named "dent" by adding the following line to your passwd file:

```
dent:*:501:60:Arthur Dent's SLIP account:/tmp:/usr/sbin/diplogin
```

Afterward, you would set dent's password using the **passwd** utility.

Now, when dent logs in, **dip** will start up as a server. To find out if he is indeed permitted to use SLIP, it will look up the username in /etc/diphosts. This file details the access rights and connection parameter for each SLIP user. A sample entry for dent could look like this:

```
dent::dent.beta.com:Arthur Dent:SLIP,296
```

The first of the colon-separated fields is the name the user must log in as. The second field may contain an additional password (see below). The third is the hostname or IP address of the calling host. Next comes an informational field without any special meaning (yet). The last field describes the connection parameters. This is a comma-separated list specifying the protocol (currently one of SLIP or CSLIP), followed by the MTU.

When dent logs in, **diplogin** extracts the information on him from the diphosts file, and, if the second field is not empty, prompts for an "external security password." The string entered by the user is compared to the (unencrypted) password from diphosts. If they do not match, the login attempt is rejected.

Otherwise, diplogin proceeds by flipping the serial line to CSLIP or SLIP mode, and sets up the interface and route. This connection remains established until the user disconnects and the modem drops the line. **diplogin** will then return the line to normal line discipline, and exit.

diplogin requires super-user privilege. If you don't have **dip** running setuid root, you should make **diplogin** a separate copy of **dip** instead of a simple link. **diplogin** can then safely be made setuid, without affecting the status of **dip** itself.

Chapter 7
The Point-To-Point Protocol

J ust like SLIP, PPP is a protocol to send datagrams across a serial connection, but addresses a couple of deficiencies of the former. It lets the communicating sides negotiate options such as the IP address and the maximum datagram size at startup time and provides for client authorization. For each of these capabilities, PPP has a separate protocol. Below, we will briefly cover these basic building blocks of PPP. This discussion is far from complete; if you want to know more about PPP, you are urged to read its specification in RFC-1548, as well as the dozen or so companion RFCs.

At the very bottom of PPP is the *High-Level Data Link Control Protocol*, abbreviated HDLC. HDLC defines the boundaries around the individual PPP frames, and provides a 16-bit checksum. As opposed to the more primitive SLIP encapsulation, a PPP frame is capable of holding packets from other protocols than IP, such as Novell's IPX, or AppleTalk. PPP achieves this by adding a protocol field to the basic HDLC frame that identifies the type of packet is carried by the frame.

LCP, the *Link Control Protocol*, is used on top of HDLC to negotiate options pertaining to the data link, such as the *Maximum Receive Unit* (MRU), that states the maximum datagram size one side of the link agrees to receive.

An important step at the configuration stage of a PPP link is client authorization. Although it is not mandatory, it is really a must for dial-up lines. Usually, the called host (the server) asks the client to authorize itself by proving it knows some secret key. If the caller fails to produce the correct secret, the connection is terminated. With PPP, authorization works both ways; that is, the caller may also ask the server to authenticate itself. These authentication procedures are totally independent of each other. There are two protocols for different types of authorization, which we will discuss further below. They are named *Password Authentication Protocol*, or PAP, and *Challenge Handshake Authentication Protocol*, or CHAP.

Each network protocol that is routed across the data link, like IP, AppleTalk, and so forth, is configured dynamically using a corresponding *Network Control Protocol* (NCP). For instance, to send IP datagrams across the link, both PPPs must first negotiate which IP address each of them uses. The control protocol used for this is IPCP, the *Internet Protocol Control Protocol*.

Beside sending standard IP datagrams across the link, PPP also supports Van Jacobson header compression of IP datagrams. This is a technique to shrink the headers of TCP packets to as little as three bytes. It is also used in CSLIP, and is more colloquially referred to as *VJ-header compression*. The use of compression may be negotiated at startup time through IPCP as well.

PPP On

On Linux, PPP functionality is split up in two parts: a low-level HDLC driver located in the kernel, and the user space pppd daemon that handles the various control protocols. At the time of this writing, the current release of PPP is for linux-ppp-1.0.0, and contains the kernel PPP module, **pppd**, and a program named "chat" used to dial up the remote system.

Note

*Currently ppp protocol support is in the kernel proper, support programs like the pppd daemon can be found at **metalab.unc.edu/pub/Linux/system/network/serial/ppp/** (current is ppp-2.3.4)*

The PPP kernel driver was written by Michael Callahan. **pppd** was derived from a free PPP implementation for Sun and 386BSD machines, which was written by Drew Perkins and others, and is maintained by Paul Mackerras. It was ported to Linux by Al Longyear.

Just like SLIP, PPP is implemented by means of a special line discipline. To use some serial line as a PPP link, you first establish the connection over your modem as usual, and subsequently convert the line to PPP mode. In this mode, all incoming data is passed to the PPP driver, which checks the incoming HDLC frames for validity (each HDLC frame carries a 16-bit checksum), and unwraps and dispatches them. Currently, it is able to handle IP datagrams, optionally using Van Jacobson header compression. As soon as supports IPX, the PPP driver will be extended to handle IPX packets, too.

The kernel driver is aided by **pppd**, the PPP daemon, which performs the entire initialization and authentication phase that is necessary before actual network traffic can be sent across the link. **pppd**'s behavior may be fine-tuned using a number of options. As PPP is rather complex, it is impossible to explain all of them in a single chapter. This book therefore cannot cover all aspects of **pppd**, but only give you an introduction. For more information, refer to the manual pages and READMEs in the **pppd** source distribution, which should help you sort out most questions this chapter fails to discuss. If your problems persist even after reading all documentation, you should turn to **comp.protocols.ppp** or **linux.dev.ppp** for help, which is the place where you will reach most of the people involved in the development of **pppd**.

Running pppd

When you want to connect to the Internet through a PPP link, you have to set up basic networking capabilities, such as the loopback device and the resolver. Both have been covered in the previous chapters. There are some things to be said about using DNS over a serial link; please refer to the SLIP chapter for a discussion of this.

As an introductory example of how to establish a PPP connection with **pppd**, assume you are at vlager again. You have already dialed up the PPP server, c3po, and logged into the ppp account. C3po has already fired up its PPP driver. After exiting the communications program you used for dialing, you execute the following command:

```
# pppd /dev/cua3 38400 crtscts defaultroute
```

This will flip the serial line cua3 to PPP mode and establish an IP link to c3po. The transfer speed used on the serial port will be 38400bps. The **crtscts** option turns on hardware handshake on the port, which is an absolute must at speeds above 9600bps.

The first thing **pppd** does after starting up is to negotiate several link characteristics with the remote end, using LCP. Usually, the default set of options **pppd** tries to negotiate will work, so we won't go into this here. We will return to LCP in more detail in some later section.

For the time being, we also assume that c3po doesn't require any authentication from us, so that the configuration phase is completed successfully.

pppd will then negotiate the IP parameters with its peer using IPCP, the IP control protocol. Since we didn't specify any particular IP address to **pppd** above, it will try to use the address obtained by having the resolver look up the local hostname. Both will then announce their address to each other.

Usually, there's nothing wrong with these defaults. Even if your machine is on an Ethernet, you can use the same IP address for both the Ethernet and the PPP interface. Nevertheless, **pppd** allows you to use a different address, or even to ask your peer to use some specific address. These options are discussed in a later section.

After going through the IPCP setup phase, **pppd** will prepare your host's networking layer to use the PPP link. It first configures the PPP network interface as a point-to-point link, using ppp0 for the first PPP link that is active, ppp1 for the second, and so on. Next, it will set up a routing table entry that points to the host at the other end of the link. In the example shown above, **pppd** will make the default network route point to c3po, because we gave it the **defaultroute** option. (The default network route is only installed if none is present yet.) This causes all datagrams to hosts not on your local network to be sent to c3po. There are a number of different routing schemes **pppd** supports, which we will cover in detail later in this chapter.

Using Options Files

Before **pppd** parses its command line arguments, it scans several files for default options. These files may contain any valid command line arguments, spread out across an arbitrary number of lines. Comments are introduced by hash signs.

The first options file is /etc/ppp/options, which is always scanned when **pppd** starts up. Using it to set some global defaults is a good idea, because it allows you to keep your users from doing several things that may compromise security. For instance, to make **pppd** require some kind of authentication (either PAP or CHAP) from the peer, you would add the auth option to this file. This option cannot be overridden by the user, so that it becomes impossible to establish a PPP connection with any system that is not in our authentication databases.

The other option file, which is read after /etc/ppp/options, is .ppprc in the user's home directory. It allows each user to specify his or her own set of default options.

A sample /etc/ppp/options file might look like this:

```
# Global options for pppd running on vlager.vbrew.com
auth                # require authentication
usehostname         # use local hostname for CHAP
lock                # use UUCP-style device locking
domain vbrew.com    # our domain name
```

The first two of these options apply to authentication and will be explained below. The lock keyword makes **pppd** comply to the standard UUCP method of device locking. With this convention, each process that accesses a serial device, say, /dev/cua3, creates a lock file named LCK..cua3 in the UUCP spool directory to signal that the device is in use. This is necessary to prevent any other programs, such as minicom or uucico, to open the serial device while used by PPP.

The reason to provide these options in the global configuration file is that options such as those shown above cannot be overridden, and so provide for a reasonable level of security. Note, however, that some options can be overridden later; one such example is the connect string.

Dialing Out With chat

One of the things that may have struck you as inconvenient in the above example is that you had to establish the connection manually before you could fire up **pppd**. Unlike **dip**, **pppd** does not have its own scripting language for dialing the remote system and logging in, but rather relies on some external program or shell script to do this. The command to be executed can be given to **pppd** with the connect command line option. **pppd** will redirect the command's standard input and output to the serial line. One useful program for this is Expect, written by Don Libes. It has a very powerful language based on Tcl, and was designed exactly for this sort of application.

The **pppd** package comes along with a similar program called *chat*, which lets you specify a UUCP-style chat script. Basically, a chat script consists of an alternating sequence of strings that we expect to receive from the remote system, and the answers we are to send. We will call the expect and send strings, respectively. This is a typical excerpt from a chat script:

```
ogin: b1ff ssword: s3kr3t
```

This tells chat to wait for the remote system to send the login prompt, and return the login name b1ff. We only wait for ogin: so that it doesn't matter if the login prompt starts with an uppercase or lowercase l, or if it arrives garbled. The following string is an expect-string again that makes chat wait for the password prompt and send our password in response.

This is basically all that chat scripts are about. A complete script to dial up a PPP server would, of course, also have to include the appropriate modem commands. Assume your modem understands the Hayes command set, and the server's telephone number was 318714. The complete chat invocation to establish a connection with c3po would then be

```
$ chat -v '' ATZ OK ATDT318714 CONNECT '' ogin: ppp word: GaGariN
```

By definition, the first string must be an expect string, but as the modem won't say anything before we have kicked it, we make chat skip the first expect by specifying an empty string. We go on and send **ATZ**, the reset command for Hayes-compatible modems, and wait for its response (OK). The next string sends the **dial** command along with the phone number to chat, and expects the CONNECT message in response. This is followed by an empty string again, because we don't want to send anything now, but rather wait for the login prompt. The remainder of the chat script works exactly as described above.

The **-v** option makes chat log all activities to the syslog daemon's local2 facility. (If you edit syslog.conf to redirect these log messages to a file, make sure this file isn't world-readable, as chat also logs the entire chat script by default—including passwords and all.)

Specifying the chat script on the command line bears a certain risk, because users can view a process's command line with the **ps** command. You can avoid this by putting the chat script in a file, for example, dial-c3po. You make chat read the script from the file instead of the command line by giving it the **-f** option, followed by the file name. The complete **pppd** incantation would now look like this:

```
# pppd connect "chat -f dial-c3po" /dev/cua3 38400 -detach \crtscts modem
defaultroute
```

Beside the connect option that specifies the dial-up script, we have added two more options to the command line: nodetach, which tells **pppd** not to detach from the console and become a background process. The modem keyword makes it perform some modem-specific actions on the serial device, like hanging up the line before and after the call. If you don't use this keyword, **pppd** will not monitor the port's DCD line, and will therefore not detect if the remote end hangs up unexpectedly.

The examples shown above were rather simple; chat allows for much more complex chat scripts. One very useful feature is the ability to specify strings on which to abort the chat with an error. Typical abort strings are messages like BUSY, or NO CARRIER, that your modem usually generates when the called number is busy, or doesn't pick up the phone. To make chat recognize these immediately, rather than timing out, you can specify them at the beginning of the script using the ABORT keyword:

```
$ chat -v ABORT BUSY ABORT 'NO CARRIER' '' ATZ OK ...
```

In a similar fashion, you may change the timeout value for parts of the chat scripts by inserting TIMEOUT options. For details, please check the chat manual page.

Sometimes, you'd also want to have some sort of conditional execution of parts of the chat script. For instance, when you don't receive the remote end's login prompt, you might want to send a BREAK, or a carriage return. You can achieve this by appending a subscript to an expect string. It consists of a sequence of send- and expect-strings, just like the overall script itself, which are separated by hyphens. The subscript is executed whenever the expected string they are appended to is not received in time. In the example above, we would modify the chat script as follows:

```
ogin:-BREAK-ogin: ppp ssword: GaGariN
```

Now, when chat doesn't see the remote system send the login prompt, the subscript is executed by first sending a BREAK, and then waiting for the login prompt again. If the prompt now appears, the script continues as usual, otherwise it will terminate with an error.

Debugging Your PPP Setup

By default, **pppd** will log any warnings and error messages to syslog's daemon facility. You have to add an entry to syslog.conf that redirects this to a file, or even the console, otherwise syslog simply discards these messages. The following entry sends all messages to /var/log/ppp-log:

```
daemon.*                    /var/log/ppp-log
```

If your PPP setup doesn't work at once, looking into this log file should give you a first hint of what goes wrong. If this doesn't help, you can also turn on extra debugging output using the debug option. This makes **pppd** log the contents of all control packets sent or received to syslog. All messages will go to the daemon facility.

Finally, the most drastic feature is to enable kernel-level debugging by invoking **pppd** with the **kdebug** option. It is followed by a numeric argument that is the bitwise OR of the following values: 1 for general debug messages, 2 for printing the contents of all incoming HDLC frames, and 4 to make the driver print all outgoing HDLC frames. To capture kernel debugging messages, you must either run a syslogd daemon that reads the /proc/kmsg file, or the klogd daemon. Either of them directs kernel debugging to syslog's kernel facility.

IP Configuration Options

IPCP is used to negotiate a couple of IP parameters at link configuration time. Usually, each peer may send an IPCP Configuration Request packet, indicating which values it wants to change from the defaults, and to what value. Upon receipt, the remote end inspects each option in turn, and either acknowledges or rejects it.

pppd gives you a lot of control about which IPCP options it will try to negotiate. You can tune this through various command line options we will discuss below.

Choosing IP Addresses

In the example above, we had **pppd** dial up c3po and establish an IP link. No provisions were taken to choose a particular IP address on either end of the link. Instead, we picked vlager's address as the local IP address, and let c3po provide its own. Sometimes, however, it is useful to have control over what address is used on one or the other end of the link. **pppd** supports several variations of this.

To ask for particular addresses, you generally provide **pppd** with the following option:

```
local addr:remote addr
```

where local_addr and remote_addr may be specified either in dotted quad notation or as hostnames. (Using hostnames in this option has consequences on CHAP authentication. Please refer to the section on CHAP below.) This makes **pppd** attempt to use the first address as its own IP address and the second as the peer's. If the peer rejects either of them during IPCP negotiation, no IP link will be established. (You can allow the peer PPP to override your ideas of IP addresses by giving **pppd** the ipcp-accept-local and ipcp-accept-remote options. Please refer to the manual page for details.)

If you want to set only the local address, but accept any address the peer uses, you simply leave out the remote_addr part. For instance, to make vlager use the IP address 130.83.4.27 instead of its own, you would give it 130.83.4.27: on the command line. Similarly, to set the remote address only, you would leave the local_addr field blank. By default, **pppd** will then use the address associated with your hostname.

Some PPP servers that handle a lot of client sites assign addresses dynamically: Addresses are assigned to systems only when calling in, and are claimed after they have logged off again. When dialing up such a server, you must make sure that **pppd** doesn't request any particular IP-address from the server, but rather accepts the address the server asks you to use. This means that you mustn't specify a local_addr argument. In addition, you have to use the noipdefault option, which makes **pppd** wait for the peer to provide the IP address instead of using the local host's address.

Routing Through A PPP Link

After setting up the network interface, **pppd** will usually set up a host route to its peer only. If the remote host is on a LAN, you certainly want to be able to connect to hosts "behind" your peer as well; that is, a network route must be set up.

We have already seen above that **pppd** can be asked to set the default route using the defaultroute option. This option is very useful if the PPP server you dialed up will act as your Internet gateway.

The reverse case, where your system acts as a gateway for a single host, is also relatively easy to accomplish. For example, take some employee at the Virtual Brewery whose home machine is called Loner. When connecting to vlager through PPP, he uses an address on the Brewery's subnet. At vlager, we can now give **pppd** the proxyarp option, which will install a proxy ARP entry for Loner. This will automatically make Loner accessible from all hosts at the Brewery and the Winery.

However, things aren't always as easy as that, for instance, when linking two local area networks. This usually requires adding a specific network route, because these networks may have their own default routes. Besides, having both peers use the PPP link as the default route would generate a loop, where packets to unknown destinations would ping-pong between the peers until their time-to-live expired.

As an example, suppose the Virtual Brewery opens a branch in some other city. The subsidiary runs an Ethernet of their own using the IP network number 191.72.3.0, which is subnet 3 of the Brewery's class B network. They want to connect to the Brewery's main Ethernet via PPP to update customer databases, and so on. Again, vlager acts as the gateway; its peer is called sub-etha and has an IP address of 191.72.3.1.

When sub-etha connects to vlager, it will make the default route point to vlager as usual. On vlager, however, we will have to install a network route for subnet 3 that goes through sub-etha. For this, we use a feature of **pppd** not discussed so far—the **ip-up** command. This is a shell script or program located in /etc/ppp that is executed after the PPP interface has been configured. When present, it is invoked with the following parameters:

```
ip-up iface device speed local addr remote addr
```

where iface names the network interface used, device is the pathname of the serial device file used (/dev/tty if stdin/stdout are used), and speed is the device's speed. Local_addr and remote_addr give the IP addresses used at both ends of the link in dotted quad notation. In our case, the **ip-up** script may contain the following code fragment:

```
#!/bin/sh
case $5 in
191.72.3.1)                 # this is sub-etha
        route add -net 191.72.3.0 gw 191.72.3.1;;
esac
exit 0
```

In a similar fashion, /etc/ppp/ip-down is used to undo all actions of **ip-up** after the PPP link has been taken down again.

However, the routing scheme is not yet complete. We have set up routing table entries on both PPP hosts, but so far, all other hosts on both networks don't know anything about the PPP link. This is not a big problem if all hosts at the subsidiary have their default route pointing at sub-etha, and all Brewery hosts route to vlager by default. If this is not the case, your only option will usually be to use a routing daemon like **gated**. After creating the network route on vlager, the routing daemon would broadcast the new route to all hosts on the attached subnets.

Link Control Options

Above, we already encountered LCP, the Link Control Protocol, which is used to negotiate link characteristics and to test the link.

The two most important options that may be negotiated by LCP are the maximum receive unit, and the Asynchronous Control Character Map. There are a number of other LCP configuration options, but they are far too specialized to discuss here. Please refer to RFC-1548 for a description of those.

The Asynchronous Control Character Map, colloquially called the async map, is used on asynchronous links such as telephone lines to identify control characters that must be escaped (replaced by a specific two-character sequence). For instance, you may want to avoid the XON and XOFF characters used for software handshake, because some misconfigured modem might choke upon receipt of an XOFF. Other candidates include Ctrl+] (the Telnet escape character). PPP allows you to escape any of the characters with ASCII codes 0 through 31 by specifying them in the async map.

The async map is a bitmap 32 bits wide, with the least significant bit corresponding to the ASCII NUL character, and the most significant bit corresponding to ASCII 31. If a bit is set, it signals that the corresponding character must be escaped before sending it across the link. Initially, the async map is set to 0xffffffff, that is, all control characters will be escaped.

To tell your peer that it doesn't have to escape all control characters but only a few of them, you can specify a new asyncmap to **pppd** using the asyncmap option. For instance, if only ^S and ^Q (ASCII 17 and 19, commonly used for XON and XOFF) must be escaped, use the following option:

```
asyncmap 0x000A0000
```

The Maximum Receive Unit, or MRU, signals to the peer the maximum size of HDLC frames we want to receive. Although this may remind you of the MTU value (Maximum Transfer Unit), these two have little in common. The MTU is a parameter of the kernel networking device, and describes the maximum frame size the interface is able to handle. The MRU is more of an advice to the remote end not to generate any frames larger than the MRU; the interface must nevertheless be able to receive frames of up to 1,500 bytes.

Choosing an MRU is therefore not so much a question of what the link is capable of transferring, but of what gives you the best throughput. If you intend to run interactive applications over the link, setting the MRU to values as low as 296 is a good idea, so that an occasional larger packet (say, from an FTP session) doesn't make your cursor "jump." To tell **pppd** to request an MRU of 296, you would give it the option mru 296. Small MRUs, however, only make sense if you don't have VJ header compression disabled (it is enabled by default).

pppd understands also a couple of LCP options that configure the overall behavior of the negotiation process, such as the maximum number of configuration requests that may be exchanged before the link is terminated. Unless you know exactly what you are doing, you should leave these alone.

Finally, there are two options that apply to LCP echo messages. PPP defines two messages, Echo Request and Echo Response. **pppd** uses this feature to check if a link is still operating. You can enable this by using the lcp-echo-interval option together with a time in seconds. If no frames are received from the remote host within this interval, **pppd** generates an Echo Request, and expects the peer to return an Echo Response. If the peer does not produce a response, the link is terminated after a certain number of requests sent. This number can be set using the lcp-echo-failure option. By default, this feature is disabled altogether.

General Security Considerations

A misconfigured PPP daemon can be a devastating security breach. It can be as bad as letting anyone plug in their machine into your Ethernet (and that is very bad). In this section, we will discuss a few measures that should make your PPP configuration safe.

One problem with **pppd** is that to configure the network device and the routing table, it requires root privilege. You will usually solve this by running it setuid root. However, **pppd** allows users to set various security-relevant options. To protect against any attacks a user may launch by manipulating these options, it is suggested you set a couple of default values in the global /etc/ppp/options file, like those shown in the sample file. Some of them, such as the authentication options, cannot be overridden by the user, and so provide a reasonable protection against manipulations.

Of course, you have to protect yourself from the systems you speak PPP with, too. To fend off hosts posing as someone else, you should always some sort of authentication from your peer. Additionally, you should not allow foreign hosts to use any IP address they choose, but restrict them to at least a few. The following section will deal with these topics.

Authentication With PPP
CHAP Versus PAP

With PPP, each system may require its peer to authenticate itself using one of two authentication protocols. These are the Password Authentication Protocol (PAP) and the Challenge Handshake Authentication Protocol (CHAP). When a connection is established, each end can request the other to authenticate itself, regardless of whether it is the caller or the callee. Below I will loosely talk of "client" and "server" when I want to distinguish between the authenticating system and the authenticator. A PPP daemon can ask its peer for authentication by sending yet another LCP configuration request identifying the desired authentication protocol.

PAP works basically the same way as the normal login procedure. The client authenticates itself by sending a username and an (optionally encrypted) password to the server, which the server compares to its secrets database. This technique is vulnerable to eavesdroppers who may try to obtain the password by listening in on the serial line and to repeated trial and error attacks.

CHAP does not have these deficiencies. With CHAP, the authenticator (i.e., the server) sends a randomly generated "challenge" string to the client, along with its hostname. The client uses the hostname to look up the appropriate secret, combines it with the challenge, and encrypts the string using a one-way hashing function. The result is returned to the server along with the client's hostname. The server now performs the same computation, and acknowledges the client if it arrives at the same result.

Another feature of CHAP is that it doesn't only require the client to authenticate itself at startup time, but sends challenges at regular intervals to make sure the client hasn't been replaced by an intruder, for instance by just switching phone lines.

pppd keeps the secret keys for CHAP and PAP in two separate files, called /etc/ppp/chap-secrets and pap-secrets, respectively. By entering a remote host in one or the other file, you have a fine control over whether CHAP or PAP is used to authenticate ourselves with our peer and vice versa.

By default, **pppd** doesn't require authentication from the remote, but will agree to authenticate itself when requested by the remote. As CHAP is so much stronger than PAP, **pppd** tries to use the former whenever possible. If the peer does not support it, or if **pppd** can't find a CHAP secret for the remote system in its chap-secrets file, it reverts to PAP. If it doesn't have a PAP secret for its peer either, it will refuse to authenticate altogether. As a consequence, the connection is closed down.

This behavior can be modified in several ways. For instance, when given the auth keyword, **pppd** will require the peer to authenticate itself. **pppd** will agree to use either CHAP or PAP for this, as long as it has a secret for the peer in its CHAP or PAP database, respectively. There are other options to turn a particular authentication protocol on or off, but I won't describe them here. Please refer to the **pppd** manual page for details.

If all systems you talk PPP with agree to authenticate themselves with you, you should put the auth option in the global /etc/ppp/options file and define passwords for each system in the chap-secrets file. If a system doesn't support CHAP, add an entry for it to the pap-secrets file. In this way, you can make sure no unauthenticated system connects to your host.

The next two sections discuss the two PPP secrets files, pap-secrets and chap-secrets. They are located in /etc/ppp and contain triples of clients, servers, and passwords, optionally followed by a list of IP addresses. The interpretation of the client and server fields is different for CHAP and PAP, and also depends on whether we authenticate ourselves with the peer, or whether we require the server to authenticate itself with us.

The CHAP Secrets File

When it has to authenticate itself with some server using CHAP, **pppd** searches the pap-secrets file for an entry with the client field equal to the local hostname, and the server field equal to the remote hostname sent in the CHAP challenge. When requiring the peer to authenticate itself, the roles are simply reversed: **pppd** will then look for an entry with the client field equal to the remote hostname (sent in the client's CHAP response), and the server field equal to the local hostname.

The following is a sample chap-secrets file for vlager (the double quotes are not part of the password, they merely serve to protect the white space within the password):

```
# CHAP secrets for vlager.vbrew.com
#
# client          server           secret               addrs
#-------------------------------------------
vlager.vbrew.com  c3po.lucas.com   "Use The Source Luke" vlager.vbr
c3po.lucas.com    vlager.vbrew.com "riverrun, pasteve"   c3po.lucas
*                 vlager.vbrew.com "VeryStupidPassword"  pub.vbrew.
```

When establishing a PPP connection with c3po, c3po asks vlager to authenticate itself using CHAP by sending a CHAP challenge. **pppd** then scans chap-secrets for an entry with the client field equal to vlager.vbrew.com and the server field equal to c3po.lucas.com (this hostname is taken from the CHAP challenge) and finds the first line shown above. It then produces the CHAP response from the challenge string and the secret (Use The Source Luke), and sends it off to c3po.

At the same time, **pppd** composes a CHAP challenge for c3po, containing a unique challenge string, and its fully qualified hostname, vlager.vbrew.com. C3po constructs a CHAP response in the manner we just discussed, and returns it to vlager. pppd now extracts the client hostname (c3po.vbrew.com) from the response, and searches the chap-secrets file for a line matching c3po as a client, and vlager as the server. The second line does this, so pppd combines the CHAP challenge and the secret riverrun, pasteve, encrypts them, and compares the result to c3po's CHAP response.

The optional fourth field lists the IP addresses that are acceptable for the clients named in the first field. The addresses may be given in dotted quad notation or as hostnames that are looked up with the resolver. For instance, if c3po requests to use an IP address during IPCP negotiation that is not in this list, the request will be rejected, and IPCP will be shut down. In the sample file shown above, c3po is therefore limited to using its own IP address. If the address field is empty, any addresses will be allowed; a value of - prevents the use of IP with that client altogether.

The third line of the sample chap-secrets file allows any host to establish a PPP link with vlager because a client or server field of * matches any hostname. The only requirement is that it knows the secret and uses the address of pub.vbrew.com. Entries with wildcard hostnames may appear anywhere in the secrets file, because **pppd** will always use the most specific entry that applies to a server/client pair.

There are some words to be said about the way **pppd** arrives at the hostnames it looks up in the secrets file. As explained before, the remote hostname is always provided by the peer in the CHAP challenge or response packet. The local hostname will be derived by calling the gethostname(2) function by default. If you have set the system name to your unqualified hostname, you have to provide **pppd** with the domain name in addition using the domain option:

```
# pppd ...domain vbrew.com
```

This will append the Brewery's domain name to vlager for all authentication-related activities. Other options that modify **progpppd**'s idea of the local hostname are usehostname and name. When you give the local IP address on the command line using "local:varremote," and local is a name instead of a dotted quad, **pppd** will use this as the local hostname. For details, please refer to the **pppd** manual page.

The PAP Secrets File

The PAP secrets file is very similar to that used by CHAP. The first two fields always contain a username and a server name; the third holds the PAP secret. When the remote sends an authenticate request, **pppd** uses the entry that has a server field equal to the local hostname, and a user field equal to the user name sent in the request. When authenticating itself with the peer, **pppd** picks the secret to be sent from the line with the user field equal to the local user name, and the server field equal to the remote hostname.

A sample PAP secrets file might look like this:

```
# /etc/ppp/pap-secrets
#
# user          server         secret          addrs
vlager-pap      c3po           cresspahl       vlager.vbrew.com
c3po            vlager         DonaldGNUth     c3po.lucas.com
```

The first line is used to authenticate ourselves when talking to c3po. The second line describes how a user named c3po has to authenticate itself with us.

The name vlager-pap in column one is the username we send to c3po. By default, **pppd** will pick the local hostname as the user name, but you can also specify a different name by giving the user option, followed by that name.

When picking an entry from the pap-secrets file for authentication with the peer, **pppd** has to know the remote host's name. As it has no way of finding that out, you have to specify it on the command line using the remotename keyword, followed by the peer's hostname. For instance, to use the above entry for authentication with c3po, we have to add the following option to **pppd**'s command line:

```
# pppd ...domain vbrew.com
```

In the fourth field (and all fields following), you may specify what IP addresses are allowed for that particular host, just as in the CHAP secrets file. The peer may then only request addresses from that list. In the sample file, we require c3po to use its real IP address.

Note that PAP is a rather weak authentication method, and it is suggested you use CHAP instead whenever possible. We will therefore not cover PAP in greater detail here; if you are interested in using PAP, you will find some more PAP features in the **pppd** manual page.

Configuring A PPP Server

Running **pppd** as a server is just a matter of adding the appropriate options to the command line. Ideally, you would create a special account, say ppp, and give it a script or program as login shell that invokes **pppd** with these options. For instance, you would add the following line to /etc/passwd:

```
ppp:*:500:200:Public PPP Account:/tmp:/etc/ppp/ppplogin
```

Of course, you may want to use different uids and gids than those shown above. You would also have to set the password for the above account using the **passwd** command.

The ppplogin script might then look like this:

```
#!/bin/sh
# ppplogin - script to fire up pppd on login
mesg n
stty -echo
exec pppd -detach silent modem crtscts
```

The **mesg** command disables other users to write to the tty using, for instance, the write command. The **stty** command turns off character echoing. The is necessary, because otherwise everything the peer sends would be echoed back to it. The most important **pppd** option given above is -detach, because it prevents **pppd** from detaching from the controlling tty. If we didn't specify this option, it would go to the background, making the shell script exit. This would in turn would cause the serial line to be hung up and the connection to be dropped. The silent option causes **pppd** to wait until it receives a packet from the calling system before it starts sending. This prevents transmit timeouts to occur when the calling system is slow in firing up its PPP client. The modem makes **pppd** watch the DTR line to see if the peer has dropped the connection, and crtscts turns on hardware handshake.

Beside these options, you might want to force some sort of authentication, for example by specifying auth on **pppd**'s command line or in the global options file. The manual page also discusses more specific options for turning individual authentication protocols on and off.

Chapter 8
Various Network Applications

After successfully setting up IP and the resolver, you have to turn to the services you want to provide over the network. This chapter covers the configuration of a few simple network applications, including the inetd server, and the programs from the rlogin family. The Remote Procedure Call interface that services like the Network File System (NFS) and the Network Information System (NIS) are based on will be dealt with briefly, too. The configuration of NFS and NIS, however, takes up more room, and will be described in separate chapters. This applies to electronic mail and netnews as well.

Of course, we can't cover all network applications in this book. If you want to install one that's not discussed here, instead please refer to its manual pages for details.

The inetd Super-Server

Frequently, services are performed by so-called *daemons*. A daemon is a program that opens a certain port and waits for incoming connections. If one occurs, it creates a child process which accepts the connection, while the parent continues to listen for further requests. This concept has the drawback that for every service offered, a daemon has to run that listens on the port for a connection to occur, which generally means a waste of system resources like swap space.

Thus, almost all installations run a "super-server" that creates sockets for a number of services, and listens on all of them simultaneously using the select(2) system call. When a remote host requests one of the services, the super-server notices this and spawns the server specified for this port.

The super-server commonly used is inetd, the *Internet Daemon*. It is started at system boot time, and takes the list of services it is to manage from a startup file named /etc/inetd.conf. In addition to those servers invoked, there are a number of trivial services that are performed by inetd itself called internal services. They include "chargen" which simply generates a string of characters, and "daytime" which returns the system's idea of the time of day.

An entry in this file consists of a single line made up of the following fields:

```
service type protocol wait user server cmdline
```

The meaning of each field is outlined in Table 8.1.

Table 8.1   Field definitions.

service	Gives the service name. The service name has to be translated to a port number by looking it up in the /etc/services file. This file will be described in Chapter 10.
type	Specifies a socket type, either stream (for connection-oriented protocols) or dgram (for datagram protocols). TCP-based services should therefore always use stream, while UDP-based services should always use dgram.
protocol	Names the transport protocol used by the service. This must be a valid protocol name found in the protocols file, also explained below.
wait	This option applies only to dgram sockets. It may be either wait or nowait. If wait is specified, inetd will only execute one server for the specified port at any time. Otherwise, it will immediately continue to listen on the port after executing the server. This is useful for "single-threaded" servers that read all incoming datagrams until no more arrive, and then exit. Most RPC servers are of this type and should therefore specify wait. The opposite type, "multi-threaded" servers, allow an unlimited number of instances to run concurrently; this is only rarely used. These servers should specify nowait. Stream sockets should always use nowait.
user	This is the login ID of the user the process is executed under. This will frequently be the root user, but some services may use different accounts. It is a very good idea to apply the principle of least privilege here, which states that you shouldn't run a command under a privileged account if the program doesn't require this for proper functioning. For example, the NNTP news server will run as news, while services that may pose a security risk (such as **tftp** or **finger**) are often run as nobody.
server	Gives the full path name of the server program to be executed. Internal services are marked by the keyword internal.
cmdline	This is the command line to be passed to the server. This includes argument 0, that is, the command name. Usually, this will be the program name of the server, unless the program behaves differently when invoked by a different name. This field is empty for internal services.

The following listing is a sample /etc/inetd.conf file.

Listing 8.1 A sample /etc/inetd.conf file.

```
#
# inetd services
ftp       stream tcp nowait root    /usr/sbin/ftpd     in.ftpd -l
telnet    stream tcp nowait root    /usr/sbin/telnetd in.telnetd -b/etc/issue
#finger   stream tcp nowait bin     /usr/sbin/fingerd in.fingerd
#tftp     dgram  udp wait    nobody /usr/sbin/tftpd    in.tftpd
#tftp     dgram  udp wait    nobody /usr/sbin/tftpd    in.tftpd /boot/diskless
login     stream tcp nowait root    /usr/sbin/rlogind in.rlogind
shell     stream tcp nowait root    /usr/sbin/rshd     in.rshd
exec      stream tcp nowait root    /usr/sbin/rexecd   in.rexecd
#
#         inetd internal services
#
daytime   stream tcp nowait root internal
daytime   dgram  udp nowait root internal
time      stream tcp nowait root internal
time      dgram  udp nowait root internal
echo      stream tcp nowait root internal
echo      dgram  udp nowait root internal
discard   stream tcp nowait root internal
discard   dgram  udp nowait root internal
chargen   stream tcp nowait root internal
chargen   dgram  udp nowait root internal
```

The **finger** service is commented out, so that it is not available. This is often done for security reasons, because may be used by attackers to obtain names of users on your system.

The **tftp** is shown commented out as well. **tftp** implements the Primitive File Transfer Protocol that allows to transfer any world-readable files from your system without password checking and so on. This is especially harmful with the /etc/passwd file, even more so when you don't use shadow password.

tftp is commonly used by diskless clients and X-terminals to download their code from a boot server. If you need to run **tftpd** for this reason, make sure to limit its scope to those directories clients will retrieve files from by adding those directory names to **tftpd**'s command line. This is shown in the second **tftp** line in Listing 8.1.

The tcpd Access Control Facility

Because opening a computer to network access involves many security risks, applications are designed to guard against several types of attacks. Some of these, however, may be flawed (most drastically demonstrated by the RTM Internet worm), or do not distinguish between secure hosts from which requests for a particular service will be accepted and insecure hosts whose requests should be rejected. We already briefly discussed the **finger** and **tftp** services above. Thus, one would want to limit access to these services to "trusted hosts" only, which is impossible with the usual setup, where inetd either provides this service to all clients, or not at all.

A useful tool for this is *tcpd* (written by Wietse Venema, **wietse@wzv.win.tue.nl**), a so-called daemon wrapper. For TCP services you want to monitor or protect, it is invoked instead of the server program. **tcpd** logs the request to the syslog daemon, ckecks if the remote host is allowed to use that service, and only if this succeeds will it executes the real server program. Note that this does not work with UDP-based services.

For example, to wrap the finger daemon, you have to change the corresponding line in inetd.conf to

```
# wrap finger daemon
finger  stream  tcp     nowait  root     /usr/sbin/tcpdin.fingerd
```

Without adding any access control, this will appear to the client just as a usual **finger** setup, except that any requests are logged to syslog's auth facility.

Access control is implemented by means of two files called /etc/hosts.allow and /etc/hosts.deny. They contain entries allowing and denying access, respectively, to certain services and hosts. When **tcpd** handles a request for a service such as **finger** from a client host named biff.foobar.com, it scans hosts.allow and hosts.deny (in this order) for an entry matching both the service and client host. If a matching entry is found in hosts.allow, access is granted, regardless of any entry in hosts.deny. If a match is found in hosts.deny, the request is rejected by closing down the connection. If no match is found at all, the request is accepted.

Entries in the access files look like this:

```
servicelist: hostlist [:shellcmd]
```

Servicelist and hotlist are defined in Table 8.2.

Table 8.2 Servicelist and hotlist.

servicelist	This is a list of service names from /etc/services, or the keyword ALL. To match all services except **finger** and **tftp**, use "ALL EXCEPT finger, tftp."
hostlist	This is a list of hostnames or IP addresses, or the keywords ALL, LOCAL, or UNKNOWN. ALL matches any host, while LOCAL matches hostnames not containing a dot. (Usually only local hostnames obtained from lookups in /etc/hosts contain no dots.) UNKNOWN matches any hosts whose name or address lookup failed. A name starting with a dot matches all hosts whose domain is equal to this name. For example, .foobar.com matches biff.foobar.com. There are also provisions for IP network addresses and subnet numbers. Please refer to the hosts_access manual page for details.

To deny access to the **finger** and **tftp** services to all but the local hosts, put the following in /etc/hosts.deny, and leave /etc/hosts.allow empty:

```
in.tftpd, in.fingerd: ALL EXCEPT LOCAL, .your.domain
```

The optional shellcmd field may contain a shell command to be invoked when the entry is matched. This is useful to set up traps that may expose potential attackers:

```
in.ftpd: ALL EXCEPT LOCAL, .vbrew.com :
echo "request from %d@%h"  /var/log/finger.log;
if [ %h != "vlager.vbrew.com" ]; then
    finger -l @%h  /var/log/finger.log
fi
```

The %h and %d arguments are expanded by **tcpd** to the client hostname and service name, respectively. Please refer to the hosts_access manual page for details.

The Services And Protocols Files

The port numbers on which certain "standard" services are offered are defined in the "Assigned Numbers" RFC. To enable server and client programs to convert service names to these numbers, at least a part of the list is kept on each host; it is stored in a file called /etc/services. An entry is made up like this:

```
service port/protocol   [aliases]
```

Here, service specifies the service name, port defines the port the service is offered on, and protocol defines which transport protocol is used. Commonly, this is either udp or tcp. It is possible for a service to be offered for more than one protocol, as well as offering different services on the same port, as long as the protocols are different. The aliases field allows to specify alternative names for the same service.

Usually, you don't have to change the services file that comes along with the network software on your system. Nevertheless, we give a small excerpt from that file below.

```
# The services file:
#
# well-known services
echo          7/tcp                   # Echo
echo          7/udp                   #
discard       9/tcp    sink null      # Discard
discard       9/udp    sink null      #
daytime      13/tcp                   # Daytime
daytime      13/udp                   #
```

```
chargen      19/tcp   ttytst source   # Character Generator
chargen      19/udp   ttytst source   #
ftp-data     20/tcp                    # File Transfer Protocol (Data)
ftp          21/tcp                    # File Transfer Protocol (Contr
telnet       23/tcp                    # Virtual Terminal Protocol
smtp         25/tcp                    # Simple Mail Transfer Protocol
nntp         119/tcp  readnews         # Network News Transfer Protoco
#
# UNIX services
exec         512/tcp                   # BSD rexecd
biff         512/udp  comsat           # mail notification
login        513/tcp                   # remote login
who          513/udp  whod             # remote who and uptime
shell        514/tcp  cmd              # remote command, no passwd use
syslog       514/udp                   # remote system logging
printer      515/tcp  spooler          # remote print spooling
route        520/udp  router routed    # routing information protocol
```

Note that, for example, the echo service is offered on port 7 for both TCP and UDP, and that port 512 is used for two different services, namely the COMSAT daemon (which notifies users of newly arrived mail, see xbiff(1x)), over UDP, and for remote execution (rexec(1)), using TCP.

Similar to the services file, the networking library needs a way to translate protocol names—for example, those used in the services file—to protocol numbers understood by the IP layer on other hosts. This is done by looking up the name in the /etc/protocols file. It contains one entry per line, each containing a protocol name, and the associated number. Having to touch this file is even more unlikely than having to meddle with /etc/services. A sample file is given below:

```
ip    0    IP     # internet protocol, pseudo protocol number
icmp  1    ICMP   # internet control message protocol
igmp  2    IGMP   # internet group multicast protocol
tcp   6    TCP    # transmission control protocol
pup   12   PUP    # PARC universal packet protocol
udp   17   UDP    # user datagram protocol
idp   22   IDP    # WhatThis?
raw   255  RAW    # RAW IP interface
```

Remote Procedure Call

A very general mechanism for client-server applications is provided by RPC, the *Remote Procedure Call* package. RPC was developed by Sun Microsystems and is a collection of tools and library functions. Important applications built on top of RPC are NFS, the Network Filesystem, and NIS, the Network Information System, both of which will be introduced in later chapters.

An RPC server consists of a collection of procedures that clients may call by sending an RPC request to the server, along with the procedure parameters. The server will invoke the indicated procedure on behalf of the client, handing back the return value, if there is any. In order to be machine-independent, all data exchanged between client and server is converted to a so-called External Data Representation format (XDR) by the sender, and converted back to the machine-local representation by the receiver.

Sometimes, improvements to an RPC application introduce incompatible changes in the procedure call interface. Of course, simply changing the server would crash all application that still expect the original behavior. Therefore, RPC programs have version numbers assigned to them, usually starting with 1, and with each new version of the RPC interface this counter will be bumped. Often, a server may offer several versions simultaneously; clients then indicate by the version number in their requests which implementation of the service they want to use.

The network communication between RPC servers and clients is somewhat peculiar. An RPC server offers one or more collections of procedures; each set is called a program, and is uniquely identified by a program number. A list of the mapping service names to their respective program numbers is usually kept in /etc/rpc, an excerpt of which is reproduced here:

```
#ident      "@(#) rpc       1.11         95/07/14 SMI"      /* SVr4.0 1.2
*/
#
#       rpc
#
rpcbind             100000    portmap sunrpc rpcbind
rstatd              100001    rstat rup perfmeter
rusersd             100002    rusers
nfs                 100003    nfsprog
ypserv              100004    ypprog
mountd              100005    mount showmount
ypbind              100007
walld               100008    rwall shutdown
yppasswdd           100009    yppasswd
etherstatd          100010    etherstat
rquotad             100011    rquotaprog quota rquota
sprayd              100012    spray
3270_mapper         100013
rje_mapper          100014
selection_svc       100015    selnsvc
database_svc        100016
rexd                100017    rex
alis                100018
sched               100019
llockmgr            100020
```

```
nlockmgr          100021
x25.inr           100022
statmon           100023
status            100024
ypupdated         100028     ypupdate
keyserv           100029     keyserver
bootparam         100026
sunlink_mapper    100033
tfsd              100037
nsed              100038
nsemntd           100039
showfhd           100043     showfh
ioadmd            100055     rpc.ioadmd
NETlicense        100062
sunisamd          100065
debug_svc         100066     dbsrv
ypxfrd            100069     rpc.ypxfrd
bugtraqd          100071
kerbd             100078
event             100101     na.event      # SunNet Manager
logger            100102     na.logger     # SunNet Manager
sync              100104     na.sync
hostperf          100107     na.hostperf
activity          100109     na.activity   # SunNet Manager
hostmem           100112     na.hostmem
sample            100113     na.sample
x25               100114     na.x25
ping              100115     na.ping
rpcnfs            100116     na.rpcnfs
hostif            100117     na.hostif
etherif           100118     na.etherif
iproutes          100120     na.iproutes
layers            100121     na.layers
snmp              100122     na.snmp snmp-cmc snmp-synoptics snmp-unisys snmp-
utk
traffic           100123     na.traffic
nfs_acl           100227
sadmind           100232
nisd              100300     rpc.nisd
nispasswd         100303     rpc.nispasswdd
ufsd              100233     ufsd
pcnfsd            150001
amd               300019     amq
bwnfsd            545580417
fypxfrd           600100069   freebsd-ypxfrd
```

In TCP/IP networks, the authors of RPC were faced with the problem of mapping program numbers to generic network services. They chose to have each server provide both a TCP and a UDP port for each program and each version. Generally, RPC applications will use UDP when sending data, and only fall back to TCP when the data to be transferred doesn't fit into a single UDP datagram.

Of course, client programs have to have a way to find out which port a program number maps to. Using a configuration file for this would be too inflexible; because RPC applications don't use reserved ports, there's no guarantee that a port originally meant to be used by our database application hasn't been taken by some other process. Therefore, RPC applications pick any port they can get, and register it with the so-called portmapper daemon. The latter acts as a service broker for all RPC servers running on its machine: A client that wishes to contact a service with a given program number will first query the portmapper on the server's host, which returns the TCP and UDP port numbers the service can be reached at.

This method has the particular drawback that it introduces a single point of failure, much like the inetd daemon does for the standard Berkeley services. However, this case is even a little worse, because when the portmapper dies, all RPC port information is lost; this usually means you have to restart all RPC servers manually or reboot the entire machine.

The portmapper is called rpc.portmap and resides in /usr/sbin.

Note

For Red Hat 6, the portmapper resides in /sbin/portmap.

Configuring The r Commands

There are a number of commands for executing commands on remote hosts. These are **rlogin**, **rsh**, **rcp** and **rcmd**. They all spawn a shell on the remote host and allow the user to execute commands. Of course, the client needs to have an account on the host where the command is to be executed. Thus, all these commands perform an authorization procedure. Usually, the client will tell the user's login name to the server, which in turn requests a password that is validated in the usual way.

```
#
# /etc/rpc - miscellaneous RPC-based services
#
portmapper     100000   portmap sunrpc
rstatd         100001   rstat rstat svc rup perfmeter
rusersd        100002   rusers
nfs            100003   nfsprog
ypserv         100004   ypprog
mountd         100005   mount showmount
ypbind         100007
```

```
walld              100008   rwall shutdown
yppasswdd          100009   yppasswd
bootparam          100026
ypupdated          100028   ypupdate
```

Sometimes, however, it is desirable to relax authorization checks for certain users. For instance, if you frequently have to log into other machines on your LAN, you might want to be admitted without having to type your password every time.

Disabling authorization is advisable only on a small number of hosts whose password databases are synchronized, or for a small number of privileged users who need to access many machines for administrative reasons. Whenever you want to allow people to log into your host without having to specify a login ID or password, make sure that you don't accidentally grant access to anybody else.

There are two ways to disable authorization checks for the r commands. One is for the super-user to allow certain or all users on certain or all hosts (the latter definitely being a bad idea) to log in without being asked for a password. This access is controlled by a file called /etc/hosts.equiv. It contains a list of host-and usernames that are considered equivalent to users on the local host. An alternative option is for a user to grant other users on certain hosts access to his or her account. These may be listed in the file .rhosts in the user's home directory. For security reasons, this file must be owned by the user or the super-user, and must not be a symbolic link, otherwise it will be ignored. (In an NFS environment, you may need to give it a protection of 444, because the super-user is often very restricted in accessing files on disks mounted via NFS.)

When a client requests an r service, the host and username are searched in the /etc/hosts.equiv file, and then in the .rhosts file of the user he or she wants to log in as. As an example, assume Janet is working on Gauss and tries to log into Joe's account on Euler. Throughout the following, we will refer to Janet as the client user and to Joe as the local user. Now, when Janet types

```
$ rlogin -l joe euler
```

on Gauss, the server will first check hosts.equiv (note that the hosts.equiv file is not searched when someone attempts to log in as root) if Janet should be granted free access, and if this fails, it will try to look her up in .rhosts in Joe's home directory.

The hosts.equiv file on Euler looks like this:

```
gauss
euler
-public
quark.physics.groucho.edu       andres
```

An entry consists of a hostname, optionally followed by a username. If a hostname appears all by itself, all users from that host will be admitted to their local accounts without any checks. In the above example, Janet would be allowed to log into her account "janet" when coming from Gauss, and the same applies to any other user except root. However, if Janet wants to log in as Joe, she will be prompted for a password as usual.

If a hostname is followed by a username, as in the last line of the above sample file, this user is given password-free access to all accounts except the root account.

The hostname may also be preceded by a minus sign, as in the entry "-public". This requires authorization for all accounts on public, regardless of what rights individual users grant in their .rhosts file.

The format of the .rhosts file is identical to that of hosts.equiv, but its meaning is a little different. Consider Joe's .rhosts file on Euler:

```
chomp.cs.groucho.edu
gauss        janet
```

The first entry grants Joe free access when logging in from chomp.cs.groucho.edu, but does not affect the rights of any other account on Euler or Chomp. The second entry is a slight variation of this, in that it grants Janet free access to Joe's account when logging in from Gauss.

Note that the client's hostname is obtained by reverse mapping the caller's address to a name, so that this feature will fail with hosts unknown to the resolver. The client's hostname is considered to match the name in the hosts files in one of the following cases:

♦ The client's canonical hostname (not an alias) literally matches the hostname in the file.

♦ If the client's hostname is a fully qualified domain name (such as returned by the resolver when you have DNS running), and it doesn't literally match the hostname in the hosts file, it is compared to that hostname expanded with the local domain name.

Note

The r commands are an incredibly bad idea to enable. SSH does strong encryption and user authentication, and should almost always be used instead. Unfortunately, because of U.S. government crypto policy, U.S. Linux distributions can't include software like SSH on their CDs.

Chapter 9
The Network Information System

W hen you are running a local area network, your overall goal is usually to provide an environment to your users that makes the network transparent. An important stepping stone to this end is to keep vital data such as user account information synchronized between all hosts. We have seen before that for hostname resolution, a powerful and sophisticated service exists, being DNS. For others tasks, there is no such specialized service. Moreover, if you manage only a small LAN with no Internet connectivity, setting up DNS may not seem worth the trouble for many administrators.

This is why Sun developed NIS, the *Network Information System*. NIS provides generic database access facilities that can be used to distribute information, such as that contained in the passwd and groups files to all hosts on your network. This makes the network appear just as a single system, with the same accounts on all hosts. In a similar fashion, you can use NIS to distribute the hostname information from /etc/hosts to all machines on the network.

NIS is based on RPC, and comprises a server, a client-side library, and several administrative tools. Originally, NIS was called Yellow Pages, or YP, which is still widely used to informally refer this service. On the other hand, Yellow Pages is a trademark of British Telecom, which required Sun to drop that name. As things go, some names stick with people, and so YP lives on as a prefix to the names of most NIS-related commands such as ypserv, ypbind, and so forth.

Today there are free implementations of NIS available. One is from the BSD Net-2 release, and has been derived from a public domain reference implementation donated by Sun. The library client code from this release has been in the GNU libc for a long time, while the administrative programs have only recently been ported by Swen Thümmler. (He can be reached at **swen@uni-paderborn.de**. The NIS clients are available as yp-linux.tar.gz from **sunsite.unc.edu** in **system/Network**.) An NIS server is missing from the reference implementation. Tobias Reber has written another NIS package including all tools and a server; it is called *yps*. (The current version [as of this writing] is yps-0.21 and can be obtained from **ftp.lysator.liu.se** in the **/pub/NYS** directory.)

Currently, a complete rewrite of the NIS code called NYS is being done by Peter Eriksson (**pen@lysator.liu.se**), and supports both plain NIS and Sun's much revised NIS+. NYS not only provides a set of NIS tools and a server but also adds a whole new set of library functions, which will most probably make it into the standard libc eventually. This includes a new configuration scheme for hostname resolution that replaces the current scheme using host.conf. The features of these functions will be discussed below.

This chapter will focus on NYS rather than the other two packages, to which I will refer as the "traditional" NIS code. If you do want to run any of these packages, the instructions in this chapter may or may not be enough. To obtain additional information, please get a standard book on NIS, such as Hal Stern's *NFS and NIS*, or check out the howto at **www.suse.de/~kukuk/linux/HOWTO/NIS-HOWTO.html**.

For the time being, NYS is still under development, and therefore standard utilities such as the network programs or the login program are not yet aware of the NYS configuration scheme. Until NYS is merged into the mainstream libc, you therefore have to recompile all these binaries if you want to make them use NYS. In any of these applications' Makefiles, specify -lnsl as the last option before libc to the linker. This links in the relevant functions from libnsl, the NYS library, instead of the standard C-library.

Getting Acquainted With NIS

NIS keeps database information in its so-called maps containing key-value pairs. Maps are stored on a central host running the NIS server, from which clients may retrieve the information through various RPC calls. Quite frequently, maps are stored in DBM files. (DBM is a simple database management library that uses hashing techniques to speed up search operations. There's a free DBM implementation from the GNU project called gdbm, which is part of most distributions.)

The maps themselves are usually generated from master text files such as /etc/hosts or /etc/passwd. For some files, several maps are created, one for each search key type. For instance, you may search the hosts file for a hostname as well as for an IP address. Accordingly, two NIS maps are derived from it, called hosts.byname and hosts.byaddr, respectively.

There are other files and maps you may find support for in some NIS package or other. These may contain information for applications not discussed in this book, such as the bootparams map that may used by some BOOTP servers, or which currently don't have any function (like the ethers.byname and ethers.byaddr maps).

For some maps, people commonly use nicknames, which are shorter and therefore easier to type. To obtain a full list of nicknames understood by your NIS tools (for Red Hat version 6), run the following command:

```
$ cat /var/yp/nicknames
```

The NIS server is traditionally called *ypserv*. For an average network, a single server usually suffices; large networks may choose to run several of these on different machines and different segments of the network to relieve the load on the server machines and routers. These servers are synchronized by making one of them the master server, and the others slave servers. Maps will be created only on the master server's host. From there, they are distributed to all slaves.

You will have noticed that we have been talking about "networks" very vaguely all the time; of course, there's a distinctive concept in NIS that refers to such a network, that is, the collection of all hosts that share part of their system configuration data through NIS: the NIS domain. Unfortunately, NIS domains have absolutely nothing in common with the domains we encountered in DNS. To avoid any ambiguity throughout this chapter, I will therefore always specify which type of domain I mean.

NIS domains have a purely administrative function only. They are mostly invisible to users, except for the sharing of passwords between all machines in the domain. Therefore, the name given to a NIS domain is relevant only to the administrators. Usually, any name will do, as long as it is different from any other NIS domain name on your local network. For instance, the administrator at the Virtual Brewery may choose to create two NIS domains, one for the Brewery itself, and one for the Winery, which she names brewery and winery, respectively. Another quite common scheme is to simply use the DNS domain name for NIS as well. To set and display the NIS domain name of your host, you can use the **domainname** command. When invoked without any argument, it prints the current NIS domain name; to set the domain name, you must become super-user and type:

```
# domainname <YOURNISDOMAIN>
```

NIS domains determine which NIS server an application will query. For instance, the login program on a host at the Winery should, of course, only query the Winery's NIS server (or one of them, if there were several) for a user's password information; an application on a Brewery host should stick with the Brewery's server.

One mystery now remains to be solved, namely, how a client finds out which server to connect to. The simplest approach would be to have a configuration file that names the host on which to find the server. However, this approach is rather inflexible, because it doesn't allow clients to use different servers (from the same domain, of course), depending on their availability. Therefore, traditional NIS implementations rely on a special daemon called *ypbind* to detect a suitable NIS server in their NIS domain. Before being able to perform any NIS queries, any application first finds out from ypbind which server to use.

ypbind probes for servers by broadcasting to the local IP network; the first to respond is assumed to be the potentially fastest one and will be used in all subsequent NIS queries. After a certain interval has elapsed, or if the server becomes unavailable, ypbind will probe for active servers again.

Now, the arguable point about dynamic binding is that you rarely need it and that it introduces a security problem: ypbind blindly believes whoever answers, which could be a humble NIS server as well as a malicious intruder. Needless to say this becomes especially troublesome if you manage your password databases over NIS. To guard against this, NYS does not use ypbind by default, but rather picks up the server hostname from a configuration file.

NIS Versus NIS+

NIS and NIS+ share little more than their name and a common goal. NIS+ is structured in an entirely different way. Instead of a flat name space with disjoint NIS domains, it uses a hierarchical name space similar to that of DNS. Instead of maps, so-called tables are used that are made up of rows and columns, where each row represents an object in the NIS+ database, while the columns cover those properties of the objects that NIS+ knows and cares about. Each table for a given NIS+ domain comprises those of its parent domains. In addition, an entry in a table may contain a link to another table. These features make it possible to structure information in many ways.

Traditional NIS has an RPC version number of 2, while NIS+ is version 3.

NIS+ does not seem to be very widely used yet, and I don't really know that much about it (well, almost nothing). For this reason, we will not deal with it here. If you are interested in learning more about it, please refer to the current howto at **www.suse.de/~kukuk/linux/HOWTO/NIS-HOWTO.html**.

The Client Side Of NIS

If you are familiar with writing or porting network applications, you will notice that most NIS maps listed above correspond to library functions in the C-library. For instance, to obtain passwd information, you generally use the getpwnam(3) and getpwuid(3) functions, which return the account information associated with the given username or numerical user ID, respectively. Under normal circumstances, these functions will perform the requested lookup on the standard file, such as /etc/passwd.

A NIS-aware implementation of these functions, however, will modify this behavior and place an RPC call to have the NIS server look up the username or ID. This happens completely transparent to the application. The function may either "append" the NIS map to or "replace" the original file with it. Of course, this does not refer to a real modification of the file, it only means that it appears to the application as if the file had been replaced or appended to.

For traditional NIS implementations, there used to be certain conventions as to which maps replaced and which were appended to the original information. Some, like the passwd maps, required kludgy modifications of the passwd file, which, when done wrong, would open up security holes. To avoid these pitfalls, NYS uses a general configuration scheme that determines whether a particular set of client functions uses the original files, NIS, or NIS+, and in which order. It will be described in a later section of this chapter.

Running An NIS Server

After so much theoretical techno-babble, it's time to get our hands dirty with actual configuration work. In this section, we will cover the configuration of a NIS server. If there's already a NIS server running on your network, you won't have to set up your own server; in this case, you may safely skip this section.

Note

If you are just going to experiment with the server, make sure you don't set it up for a NIS domain name that is already in use on your network. This may disrupt the entire network service and make a lot of people very unhappy and very angry.

There are currently two NIS servers freely available for Linux, one contained in Tobias Reber's yps package, and the other in Peter Eriksson's ypserv package. It shouldn't matter which one you run, regardless of whether you use NYS or the standard NIS client code that is in libc currently. At the time of this writing, the code for the handling of NIS slave servers seems to be more complete in yps. So if you have to deal with slave servers, yps might be a better choice.

The next section explains how to configure the NIS client code. If your setup doesn't work, you should try to find out whether any requests arrive at your server or not. If you specify the -D command line flag to the NYS server, it prints debugging messages to the console about all incoming NIS queries, and the results returned. These should give you a hint as to where the problem lies.

Setting Up An NIS Client With NYS

Throughout the remainder of this chapter, we will cover the configuration of an NIS client.

Your first step should be to tell NYS which server to use for NIS service, setting it in the /etc/yp.conf configuration file. A very simple sample file for a host on the Winery's network may look like this:

```
# /etc/yp.conf - ypbind configuration file
# Valid entries are
#
#domain NISDOMAIN server HOSTNAME
```

```
#           Use server HOSTNAME for the domain NISDOMAIN.
#
#domain NISDOMAIN broadcast
#           Use broadcast on the local net for domain NISDOMAIN
#
#ypserver HOSTNAME
#           Use server HOSTNAME for the local domain.
#           The IP-address of server must be listed in /etc/hosts.
```

The first statement tells all NIS clients that they belong to the winery NIS domain. If you omit this line, NYS will use the domain name you assigned your system through the **domainname** command. The server statement names the NIS server to use. Of course, the IP address corresponding to vbardolino must be set in the hosts file; alternatively, you may use the IP address itself with the server statement.

In the form shown above, the **server** command tells NYS to use the named server whatever the current NIS domain may be. If, however, you are moving your machine between different NIS domains frequently, you may want to keep information for several domains in the yp.conf file. You can have information on the servers for various NIS domains in yp.conf by adding the NIS domain name to the server statement.

After creating this basic configuration file and making sure it is world-readable, you should run your first test to check if you can connect to your server. Make sure to choose any map your server distributes, like hosts.byname, and try to retrieve it by using the ypcat utility. ypcat, like all other administrative NIS tools, should live in /usr/sbin.

The output you get should look something like that shown above. If you get an error message instead that says "Can't bind to server which serves domain" or something similar, then either the NIS domain name you've set doesn't have a matching server defined in yp.conf, or the server is unreachable for some reason. In the latter case, make sure that a **ping** to the host yields a positive result, and that it is indeed running an NIS server. You can verify the latter by using rpcinfo, which should produce the output found in Table 9.1.

Table 9.1   Output verifying NIS configuration.

Program	Vers	Proto	Port	
100000	4	tcp	111	rpcbind
100000	3	tcp	111	rpcbind
100000	2	tcp	111	rpcbind
100000	4	udp	111	rpcbind
100000	3	udp	111	rpcbind
100000	2	udp	111	rpcbind
100024	1	udp	32772	status
100024	1	tcp	32771	status
100133	1	udp	32772	

(continued)

Table 9.1   Output verifying NIS configuration *(continued)*.

Program	Vers	Proto	Port	
100133	1	tcp	32771	
100021	1	udp	4045	nlockmgr
100021	2	udp	4045	nlockmgr
100021	3	udp	4045	nlockmgr
100021	4	udp	4045	nlockmgr
100012	1	udp	32773	sprayd
100001	2	udp	32774	rstatd
100001	3	udp	32774	rstatd
100001	4	udp	32774	rstatd
100221	1	tcp	32772	
100235	1	tcp	32773	
100068	2	udp	32775	
100068	3	udp	32775	
100068	4	udp	32775	
100068	5	udp	32775	
100083	1	tcp	32774	
100021	1	tcp	4045	nlockmgr
100021	2	tcp	4045	nlockmgr
100021	3	tcp	4045	nlockmgr
100021	4	tcp	4045	nlockmgr
805502976	2	tcp	911	
805502976	1	tcp	912	
300598	1	udp	32796	
300598	1	tcp	32782	
805306368	1	udp	32796	
805306368	1	tcp	32782	
100249	1	udp	32799	
100249	1	tcp	32783	

Choosing The Right Maps

Having made sure you can reach the NIS server, you have to decide which configuration files to replace or augment with NIS maps. Commonly, you will want use NIS maps for the host and password lookup functions. The former is especially useful if you do not run BIND. The latter permits all users to log into their account from any system in the NIS domain; this usually requires sharing a central /home directory between all hosts via NFS. It is explained later in this chapter. Other maps, like services.byname, aren't such a dramatic gain, but save you some editing work if you install any network applications that use a service name that's not in the standard services file.

Generally, you want to have some freedom of choice when a lookup function uses the local files and when it queries the NIS server. NYS allows you to configure the order in which a function accesses these services. This is controlled through the /etc/nsswitch.conf file, which stands for Name Service Switch, but of course isn't limited to the name service. For any of the data lookup functions supported by NYS, it contains a line naming the services to use.

The right order of services depends on the type of data. It is unlikely that the services.byname map will contain entries differing from those in the local services file; it may only contain more. So a good choice may be to query the local files first, and check NIS only if the service name wasn't found. Hostname information, on the other hand, may change very frequently, so that DNS or the NIS server should always have the most accurate account, while the local hosts file is only kept as a backup if DNS and NIS should fail. In this case, you would want to check the local file last.

Currently, NYS supports the following nsswitch.conf entries: hosts, networks, passwd, group, shadow, gshadow, services, protocols, rpc, and ethers. More entries are likely to be added.

Listing 9.1 shows a more complete example which introduces another feature of nsswitch.conf: The [NOTFOUND=return] keyword in the hosts entry tells NYS to return if the desired item couldn't be found in the NIS or DNS database. That is, NYS will continue and search the local files only if calls to the NIS and DNS servers failed for some other reason. The local files will then only be used at boot time and as a backup when the NIS server is down.

Listing 9.1   Example of a Name Service Switch config file.

```
#
# /etc/nsswitch.conf
#
# An example Name Service Switch config file. This file should be
# sorted with the most-used services at the beginning.
#
#The entry '[NOTFOUND=return]' means that the search for an
#entry should stop if the search in the previous entry turned
#up nothing. Note that if the search failed due to some other reason
#(like no NIS server responding) then the search continues with the
#next entry.
#
#Legal entries are:
#
#       nisplus or nis+ Use NIS+ (NIS version 3)
#       nis or yp Use NIS (NIS version 2), also called YP
#       dns Use DNS (Domain Name Service)
#       files Use the local files
#       [NOTFOUND=return] Stop searching if not found so far
#
```

```
passwd:      files nisplus nis
shadow:      files nisplus nis
group:       files nisplus nis

hosts:       files nisplus nis dns

services:    nisplus [NOTFOUND=return] files
networks:    nisplus [NOTFOUND=return] files
protocols:   nisplus [NOTFOUND=return] files
rpc:         nisplus [NOTFOUND=return] files
ethers:      nisplus [NOTFOUND=return] files
netmasks:    nisplus [NOTFOUND=return] files
bootparams:  nisplus [NOTFOUND=return] files

netgroup:    nisplus

publickey:   nisplus

automount:   files nisplus
aliases:     files nisplus
```

Using The passwd And group Maps

One of the major applications of NIS is in synchronizing user and account information on all hosts in a NIS domain. To this end, you usually keep only a small local /etc/passwd file, to which the site-wide information from the NIS maps is appended. However, simply enabling NIS lookups for this service in nsswitch.conf is not nearly enough.

When relying on the password information distributed by NIS, you first have to make sure that the numeric user IDs of any users you have in your local passwd file match the NIS server's idea of user IDs. You will want this for other purposes as well, like mounting NFS volumes from other hosts in your network.

If any of the numeric IDs in /etc/passwd or /etc/group deviate from those in the maps, you have to adjust file ownerships for all files that belong to that user. First you should change all uids and gids in passwd and group to the new values; then find all files that belong to the users just changed, and finally change their ownership. Assume news used to have a user ID of 9, and okir had a user ID of 103, which were changed to some other value; you could then issue the following commands:

```
# find / -uid 9 -exec chown news {} \;
followed by a
# find / -uid 103 -exec chown okir {} \;
```

Explaining the first command: find everything from the root directory down, owned by numeric user 9, and on each file or directory you find, change ownership to the "news" user (whose uid was just updated in the password file). The reason we need to do a **find** is that the usernames and group names are strictly speaking only for human consumption; all files and directories are owned by numeric user ID (uid) and group ID (gid). When the numbers for uid or gid for a particular user change in the password file or group file, the files on disk are still owned by the uid/gid of the previous numeric uid/gid pair. To reclaim ownership of the files, we have to recurse through the file system and "chown" the files to the new uid/gid. The reason why I can get away with saying "chown news" is that chown will look in the password file for the uid that "news" corresponds to. The final "\;" terminates the **find** command; the backslash escapes the semicolon from the shell, which would interpret it as a command separator.

It is important that you execute these commands with the new passwd file installed, and that you collect all file names before you change the ownership of any of them. To update the group ownerships of files, you will use a similar command.

Having done this, the numerical uids and gids on your system will agree with those on all other hosts in your NIS domain. The next step will be to add configuration lines to nsswitch.conf that enables NIS lookups for user and group information. (Refer to Listing 9.1 above. Particularly look at the lines for "passwrd", "shadow", and "group".)

This makes the **login** command and all its friends first query the NIS maps when a user tries to log in, and if this lookup fails, fall back to the local files. Usually, you will remove almost all users from your local files, and only leave entries for root and generic accounts like mail in it. This is because some vital system tasks may require to map uids to user names or vice versa. For example, administrative cron jobs may execute the **su** command to temporarily become news, or the UUCP subsystem may mail a status report. If news and uucp don't have entries in the local passwd file, these jobs will fail miserably during an NIS brownout.

There are two big caveats in order here: On one hand, the setup as described up to here only works for login suites that don't use shadow password, like those included in the util-linux package. The intricacies of using shadow passwords with NIS will be covered below. On the other hand, the login commands are not the only ones that access the passwd file—look at the **ls** command, which most people use almost constantly. Whenever doing a long listing, **ls** will display the symbolic names for user and group owners of a file; that is, for each uid and gid it encounters, it will have to query the NIS server once. This will slow things down rather badly if your local network is clogged, or, even worse, when the NIS server is not on the same physical network, so that datagrams have to pass through a router.

Still, this is not the whole story yet. Imagine what happens if a user wants to change her password. Usually, she will invoke **passwd**, which reads the new password and updates the local passwd file. This is impossible with NIS, since that file isn't available locally anymore, but having users log into the NIS server whenever they want to change their password is not an option either. Therefore, NIS provides a drop-in replacement for **passwd** called **yppasswd**, which does the analogous thing in the presence of NIS. To change the password on the server host, it contacts the yppasswdd daemon on that host via RPC, and provides it with the updated password information. Usually, you install yppasswd over the normal program by doing something like this:

```
# cd /usr/bin
# mv passwd passwd.local
# ln yppasswd passwd
```

This "replaces" the **passwd** command with the **yppasswd** command.

At the same time you have to install rpc.yppasswdd on the server and start it from rc.inet2. This will effectively hide any of the contortions of NIS from your users.

Using NIS With Shadow Support

John F. Haugh, the author of the shadow suite, recently released a version of the shadow library functions covered by the GNU Library GPL to **comp.sources.misc**. It already has some support for NIS, but it isn't complete, and the files haven't been added to the standard C library yet. On the other hand, publishing the information from /etc/shadow via NIS kind of defeats the purpose of the shadow suite.

Although the NYS password lookup functions don't use a shadow.byname map or anything likewise, NYS supports using a local /etc/shadow file transparently. When the NYS implementation of getpwnam is called to look up information related to a given login name, the facilities specified by the passwd entry in nsswitch.conf are queried. The NIS service will simply look up the name in the passwd.byname map on the NIS server. The files service, however, will check if /etc/shadow is present, and if so, try to open it. If none is present, or if the user doesn't have root privilege, if reverts to the traditional behavior of looking up the user information in /etc/passwd only. However, if the shadow file exists and can be opened, NYS will extract the user password from shadow. The getpwuid function is implemented accordingly. In this fashion, binaries compiled with NYS will deal with a local the shadow suite installation transparently.

Using The Traditional NIS Code

If you are using the client code that is in the standard libc currently, configuring a NIS client is a little different. On one hand, it uses a ypbind daemon to broadcast for active servers rather than gathering this information from a configuration file. You therefore have to make sure to start ypbind at boot time. It must be invoked after the NIS domain has been set and the RPC portmapper has been started. Invoking ypcat to test the server should then work as shown above.

Recently, there have been numerous bug reports that NIS fails with an error message saying "clntudp_create: RPC: portmapper failure - RPC: unable to receive". These are due to an incompatible change in the way ypbind communicates the binding information to the library functions. Obtaining the latest sources for the NIS utilities and recompiling them should cure this problem. (The source for yp-linux can be gotten from **ftp.uni-paderborn.de** in directory **/pub/Linux/LOCAL**.)

Also, the way traditional NIS decides if and how to merge NIS information with that from the local files deviates from that used by NYS. For instance, to use the NIS password maps, you have to include the following line somewhere in your /etc/passwd map:

```
+::::::
```

This marks the place where the password lookup functions "insert" the NIS maps. Inserting a similar line (minus the last two colons) into /etc/group does the same for the group.* maps. To use the hosts.* maps distributed by NIS, change the order line in the host.conf file. For instance, if you want to use NIS, DNS, and the /etc/hosts file (in that order), you need to change the line to:

```
order nis,bind,hosts
```

The traditional NIS implementation does not support any other maps at the moment.

Chapter 10
The Network File System

N FS, the network file system, is probably the most prominent network services using RPC. It allows to access files on remote hosts in exactly the same way as a user would access any local files. This is made possible by a mixture of kernel functionality on the client side (that uses the remote file system) and an NFS server on the server side (that provides the file data). This file access is completely transparent to the client and works across a variety of server and host architectures.

NFS offers a number of advantages:

♦ Data accessed by all users can be kept on a central host, with clients mounting this directory at boot time. For example, you can keep all user accounts on one host, and have all hosts on your network mount /home from that host. If installed alongside with NIS, users can then log into any system and still work on one set of files.

♦ Data consuming large amounts of disk space may be kept on a single host. For example, all files and programs relating to LaTeX and METAFONT could be kept and maintained in one place.

♦ Administrative data may be kept on a single host. No need to use rcp anymore to install the same stupid file on 20 different machines.

NFS is largely the work of Rick Sladkey (**jrs@world.std.com**), who wrote the Linux implementation of the NFS kernel code and large parts of the NFS server. The latter is derived from the unfsd user space NFS server originally written by Mark Shand, and the hnfs Harris NFS server written by Donald Becker.

Let's have a look now at how NFS works: A client may request to mount a directory from a remote host on a local directory just the same way it can mount a physical device. However, the syntax used to specify the remote directory is different. For example, to mount /home from host vlager to /users on vale, the administrator would issue the following command on vale (note that you can omit the -t nfs argument, because **mount** sees from the colon that this specifies an NFS volume):

```
# mount vlager:/home /users
```

mount will then try to connect to the mountd mount daemon on vlager via RPC. The server will check if vale is permitted to mount the directory in question, and if so, return it a file handle. This file handle will be used in all subsequent requests to files below /users.

When someone accesses a file over NFS, the kernel places an RPC call to nfsd (the NFS daemon) on the server machine. This call takes the file handle, the name of the file to be accessed, and the user's user and group ID as parameters. These are used in determining access rights to the specified file. In order to prevent unauthorized users from reading or modifying files, user and group IDs must be the same on both hosts.

On most implementations, the NFS functionality of both client and server are implemented as kernel-level daemons that are started from user space at system boot. These are the NFS daemon (nfsd) on the server host, and the Block I/O Daemon (biod) running on the client host. To improve throughput, biod performs asynchronous I/O using read-ahead and write-behind; also, several nfsd daemons are usually run concurrently.

The NFS implementation of is a little different in that the client code is tightly integrated in the virtual file system (VFS) layer of the kernel and doesn't require additional control through biod. On the other hand, the server code runs entirely in user space, so that running several copies of the server at the same time is almost impossible because of the synchronization issues this would involve. (Please note that there is a kernel version of NFS under development.) NFS currently also lacks read-ahead and write-behind, but Rick Sladkey plans to add this someday. (The problem with write-behind is that the kernel buffer cache is indexed by device/inode pairs, and therefore can't be used for NFS-mounted file systems.)

The biggest problem with the NFS code is that the kernel as of version 1 is not able to allocate memory in chunks bigger than 4K; as a consequence, the networking code cannot handle datagrams bigger than roughly 3,500 bytes after subtracting header sizes and so forth. This means that transfers to and from NFS daemons running on systems that use large UDP datagrams by default (e.g., 8K on SunOS) need to be downsized artificially. This hurts performance badly under some circumstances. (As explained to me by Alan Cox: The NFS specification requires the server to flush each write to disk before it returns an acknowledgment. As BSD kernels are only capable of page-sized writes [4K], writing four chunks of 1K each to a BSD-based NFS server results in four write operations of 4K each.) This limit is gone in late 1.1 kernels, and the client code has been modified to take advantage of this.

Preparing NFS

Before you can use NFS, be it as server or client, you must make sure your kernel has NFS support compiled in. Newer kernels have a simple interface on the proc file system for this, the /proc/filesystems file, which you can display using **cat**:

```
$ cat /proc/filesystems
minix
ext2
msdos
nodev    proc
nodev    nfs
```

If nfs is missing from this list, then you have to compile your own kernel with NFS enabled. Configuring the kernel network options is explained in the section called "Kernel Configuration" in Chapter 3.

For older kernels prior to 1.1, the easiest way to find out whether your kernel has NFS support enabled is to actually try to mount an NFS file system. For this, you could create a directory below /tmp, and try to mount a local directory on it:

```
# mkdir /tmp/test
# mount localhost:/etc /tmp/test
```

If this mount attempt fails with an error message saying "fs type nfs no supported by kernel," you must make a new kernel with NFS enabled. Any other error messages are completely harmless, as you haven't configured the NFS daemons on your host yet.

Mounting An NFS Volume

NFS volumes (one doesn't say file system, because these are not proper file systems) are mounted very much the way usual file systems are mounted. You invoke **mount** using the following syntax:

```
# mount -t nfs nfs volume local dir options
```

nfs_volume is given as remote_host:remote_dir. Since this notation is unique to NFS file systems, you can leave out the -t nfs option.

There are a number of additional options that you may specify to **mount** upon mounting an NFS volume. These may either be given following the -o switch on the command line, or in the options field of the /etc/fstab entry for the volume. In both cases, multiple options are separated from each other by commas. Options specified on the command line always override those given in the fstab file.

A sample entry in /etc/fstab might be

```
# volume                 mount point        type   options
news:/usr/spool/news    /usr/spool/news     nfs    timeo=14,intr
```

This volume may then be mounted using

```
# mount news:/user/spool/news
```

In the absence of a fstab entry, NFS mount invocations look a lot uglier. For instance, suppose you mount your users' home directories from a machine named Moonshot, which uses a default block size of 4K for read/write operations. You might decrease block size to 2K to suit Linux's datagram size limit by issuing

```
# mount moonshot:/home /home -o rsize=2048,wsize=2048
```

The list of all valid options is described in its entirety in the nfs manual page that comes with Rick Sladkey's NFS-aware **mount** tool, which can be found in Rik Faith's util-linux package. Table 10.1 provides an incomplete list of those you would probably want to use.

Except for rsize and wsize, all of these options apply to the client's behavior if the server should become inaccessible temporarily. They play together in the following way: Whenever the client sends a request to the NFS server, it expects the operation to have finished after a given interval (specified in the timeout option). If no confirmation is received within this time, a so-called minor timeout occurs, and the operation is retried with the timeout interval doubled. After reaching a maximum timeout of 60 seconds, a major timeout occurs.

By default, a major timeout will cause the client to print a message to the console and start all over again, this time with an initial timeout interval twice that of the previous cascade. Potentially, this may go on forever. Volumes that stubbornly retry an operation until the server becomes available again are called hard-mounted. The opposite variety, soft-mounted volumes generates an I/O error for the calling process whenever a major timeout occurs. Because of the write-behind introduced by the buffer cache, this error condition is not propagated

Table 10.1   Some mounting options.

Option	Description
rsize=n and wsize=n	These specify the datagram size used by the NFS clients on read and write requests, respectively. They currently default to 1,024 bytes, due to the limit on UDP datagram size described above.
timeo=n	This sets the time (in tenths of a second) the NFS client will wait for a request to complete. The default values is 0.7 seconds.
Hard	Explicitly mark this volume as hard-mounted. This is on by default.
Soft	Soft-mount the driver (as opposed to hard-mount).
Intr	Allow signals to interrupt an NFS call. Useful for aborting when the server doesn't respond.

to the process itself before it calls the write(2) function the next time, so a program can never be sure that a write operation to a soft-mounted volume has succeeded at all.

Whether you hard- or soft-mount a volume is not simply a question of taste but also has to do with what sort of information you want to access from this volume. For example, if you mount your X-programs by NFS, you certainly would not want your X-session to go berserk just because someone brought the network to a grinding halt by firing up seven copies of xv at the same time or by pulling the Ethernet plug for a moment. By hard-mounting these, you make sure that your computer will wait until it is able to reestablish contact with your NFS server. On the other hand, noncritical data such as NFS-mounted news partitions or FTP archives may as well be soft-mounted, so it doesn't hang your session in case the remote machine should be temporarily unreachable, or down. If your network connection to the server is flaky or goes through a loaded router, you may either increase the initial timeout using the timeo option, or hard-mount the volumes, but allow for signals interrupting the NFS call so that you may still abort any hanging file access.

Usually, the mountd daemon will in some way or other keep track of which directories have been mounted by what hosts. This information can be displayed using the showmount program, which is also included in the NFS server package. The mountd, however, does not do this yet.

The NFS Daemons

If you want to provide NFS service to other hosts, you have to run the nfsd and mountd daemons on your machine. As RPC-based programs, they are not managed by inetd, but are started up at boot time, and register themselves with the portmapper. Therefore, you have to make sure to start them only after rpc.portmap is running. Usually, you include the following two lines in your rc.inet2 script:

```
if [ -x /usr/sbin/rpc.mountd ]; then
      /usr/sbin/rpc.mountd; echo -n " mountd"
fi
if [ -x /usr/sbin/rpc.nfsd ]; then
      /usr/sbin/rpc.nfsd; echo -n " nfsd"
fi
```

The ownership information of files a NFS daemon provides to its clients usually contains only numerical user and group IDs. If both client and server associate the same user and group names with these numerical IDs, they are said to share the same uid/gid space. For example, this is the case when you use NIS to distribute the passwd information to all hosts on your LAN.

On some occasions, however, they do not match. Rather than updating the uids and gids of the client to match those of the server, you can use the ugidd mapping daemon to work

around this. Using the map_daemon option explained below, you can tell nfsd to map the
server's uid/gid space to the client's uid/gid space with the aid of the ugidd on the client.

Ugidd is an RPC-based server, and is started from rc.inet2 just like nfsd and mountd.

```
if [ -x /usr/sbin/rpc.ugidd ]; then
        /usr/sbin/rpc.ugidd; echo -n " ugidd"
fi
```

Note

*While I found it useful to include this information, this reference to rc.inet2 could be
seen as a deprecated startup method by some. Instead, a script for each service you
wish to run can be found in the etc/rc.d/* hierarchy.*

The Exports File

While the above options applied to the client's NFS configuration, there is a different set of
options on the server side that configure its per-client behavior. These options must be set
in the /etc/exports file.

By default, mountd will not allow anyone to mount directories from the local host, which is
a rather sensible attitude. To permit one or more hosts to NFS-mount a directory, it must
exported, that is, must be specified in the exports file. A sample file may look like this:

```
# exports file for vlager
/home           vale(rw) vstout(rw) vlight(rw)
/usr/X386       vale(ro) vstout(ro) vlight(ro)
/usr/TeX        vale(ro) vstout(ro) vlight(ro)
/               vale(rw,no root squash)
/home/ftp       (ro)
```

Each line defines a directory, and the hosts allowed to mount it. A hostname is usually a
fully qualified domain name, but may additionally contain the * and ? wildcards, which act
the way they do with the Bourne shell. For instance, lab*.foo.com matches lab01.foo.com
as well as laber.foo.com. If no hostname is given, as with the /home/ftp directory in the
example above, any host is allowed to mount this directory.

When checking a client host against the exports file, mountd will look up the client's
hostname using the gethostbyaddr(2) call. With DNS, this call returns the client's canonical hostname, so you must make sure not to use aliases in exports. Without using DNS, the
returned name is the first hostname found in the hosts file that matches the client's address.

The hostname is followed by an optional, comma-separated list of flags, enclosed in brackets. Table 10.2 shows some flags and their values.

Table 10.2   **Some flags and their values.**

Flag	Value
nsecure	Permit nonauthenticated access from this machine.
unix-rpc	Require UNIX-domain RPC authentication from this machine. This simply requires that requests originate from a reserved internet port (i.e., the port number has to be less than 1024). This option is on by default.
secure-rpc	Require secure RPC authentication from this machine. This has not been implemented yet. See Sun's documentation on Secure RPC.
kerberos	Require Kerberos authentication on accesses from this machine. This has not been implemented yet. See the MIT documentation on the Kerberos authentication system.
root squash	This is a security feature that denies the super-user on the specified hosts any special access rights by mapping requests from uid 0 on the client to uid 65534 (-2) on the server. This uid should be associated with the user nobody.
no root squash	Don't map requests from uid 0. This option is on by default.
ro	Mount file hierarchy read-only. This option is on by default.
rw	Mount file hierarchy read-write.
link relative	Convert absolute symbolic links (where the link contents start with a slash) into relative links by prepending the necessary number of ../'s to get from the directory containing the link to the root on the server. This option only makes sense when a host's entire file system is mounted, else some of the links might point to nowhere, or even worse, files they were never meant to point to. This option is on by default.
link absolute	Leave all symbolic links as they are (the normal behavior for Sun-supplied NFS servers).
map daemon	This option tells the NFS server to assume that client and server do not share the same uid/gid space. nfsd will then build a list mapping IDs between client and server by querying the client's ugidd daemon.

An error parsing the exports file is reported to syslogd's daemon facility at level notice whenever nfsd or mountd is started up.

Note that hostnames are obtained from the client's IP address by reverse mapping, so you have to have the resolver configured properly. If you use BIND and are very security-conscious, you should enable spoof checking in your host.conf file.

The Automounter

Sometimes, it is wasteful to mount all NFS volumes users might possibly want to access; either because of the sheer number of volumes to be mounted, or because of the time this would take at startup. A viable alternative to this is a so-called *automounter*. This is a daemon that automatically and transparently mounts any NFS volume as needed, and unmounts them after they have not been used for some time. One of the clever things about an automounter is that it is able to mount a certain volume from alternative places. For instance, you may keep copies of your X-programs and support files on two or three hosts, and have all other hosts mount them via NFS. Using an automounter, you may specify all three of them to be mounted on /usr/X386; the automounter will then try to mount any of these until one of the mount attempts succeeds.

The automounter commonly used with Linux is called *amd*. It was originally written by Jan-Simon Pendry and has been ported to by Rick Sladkey. The current version is amd-5.3.

Explaining amd is beyond the scope of this chapter; for a good manual please refer to the sources; they contain a texinfo file with very detailed information.

Chapter 11
Managing Taylor UUCP

U UCP was designed in the late 1970s by Mike Lesk at AT&T Bell Laboratories to provide a simple dial-up network over public telephone lines. Since most people that want to have email and Usenet news on their home machine still communicate through modems, UUCP has remained very popular. Although there are many implementations running on a wide variety of hardware platforms and operating systems, they are compatible to a high degree.

However, as with most software that has somehow become "standard" over the years, there is no UUCP which one would call *the* UUCP. It has undergone a steady process of evolution since the first version, which was implemented in 1976. Currently, there are two major species, which differ mainly in their support of hardware and their configuration. Of these, various implementations exist, each varying slightly from its siblings.

One species is the so-called "Version 2 UUCP," which dates back to a 1977 implementation by Mike Lesk, David A. Novitz, and Greg Chesson. Although it is fairly old, it is still in frequent use. Recent implementations of Version 2 provide much of the comfort of the newer UUCP species.

The second species was developed in 1983, and is commonly referred to as BNU (Basic Networking Utilities), HoneyDanBer UUCP, or HDB for short. The name is derived from the authors' names: P. Honeyman, D. A. Novitz, and B. E. Redman. HDB was conceived to eliminate some of Version 2 UUCP's deficiencies. For example, new transfer protocols were added, and the spool directory was split so that now there is one directory for each site you have UUCP traffic with.

The implementation of UUCP currently distributed with is Taylor UUCP 1.04 (written and copyrighted by Ian Taylor, 1993), which is the version this chapter is based on. Taylor UUCP Version 1.04 was released in February 1993. Apart from traditional configuration files, Taylor UUCP may also be compiled to understand the new-style—a.k.a. "Taylor"—configuration files.

At the time of this writing, version 1.05 is the latest version and will soon make its way into most distributions. The differences between these versions mostly affect features you will never use, so you should be able to configure Taylor UUCP 1.05 using the information from this book.

As included in most distributions, Taylor UUCP is usually compiled for BNU compatibility, the Taylor configuration scheme, or both. As the latter is much more flexible, and probably easier to understand than the often rather obscure BNU configuration files, I will describe the Taylor scheme below.

The purpose of this chapter is not to give you an exhaustive description of what the command line options for the UUCP commands are and what they do, but to give you an introduction on how to set up a working UUCP node. The first section gives a hopefully gentle introduction about how UUCP implements remote execution and file transfers.

We will, however, assume that you are familiar with the user programs of the UUCP suite. These are *uucp* and *uux*. For a description, please refer to the online manual pages.

Besides the publicly accessible programs, uucp and uux, the UUCP suite contains a number of commands used for administrative purposes only. They are used to monitor UUCP traffic across your node, remove old log files, or compile statistics. None of these will be described here, because they're peripheral to the main tasks of UUCP. Besides, they're well documented and fairly easy to understand. However, there is a third category, which comprises the actual UUCP "work horses." They are called *uucico* (where cico stands for copy-in copy-out), and *uuxqt*, which executes jobs sent from remote systems.

More Information On UUCP

Those who don't find everything they need in this chapter should read the documentation that comes along with the package. This is a set of texinfo files that describe the setup using the Taylor configuration scheme. Texinfo can be converted to DVI and to GNU info files using tex and makeinfo, respectively.

If you want to use BNU or even (shudder!) Version 2 configuration files, there is a very good book, *Managing UUCP and Usenet*. I find it very useful. Another good source for information about UUCP on Linux is Guylhem Aznar (**guylhem.@.oeil.qc.ca**) UUCP-HOWTO, which is posted regularly to **comp.os.linux.announce**.

There's also a newsgroup for the discussion of UUCP, called **comp.mail.uucp**. If you have questions specific to Taylor UUCP, you may be better off asking them there, rather than on the **comp.os.linux** groups.

Introduction

Layout Of UUCP Transfers And Remote Execution

Vital to the understanding of UUCP is the concept of *jobs*. Every transfer a user initiates with uucp or uux is called a job. It is made up of a command to be executed on a remote system, and a collection of files to be transferred between sites. One of these parts may be missing.

UUCP does not generally call the remote system immediately to execute a job (or else you could make do with kermit). Instead, it temporarily stores the job description away. This is called *spooling*. The directory tree under which jobs are stored is therefore called the *spool directory* and is generally located in /var/spool/uucp. In our example, the job description would contain information about the remote command to be executed (**lpr**), the user who requested the execution, and a couple of other items. In addition to the job description, UUCP has to store the input file, netguide.ps.

The exact location and naming of spool files may vary, depending on some compile-time options. HDB-compatible UUCPs generally store spool files in a directory named /var/spool/uucp/site, where *site* is the name of the remote site. When compiled for Taylor configuration, UUCP will create subdirectories below the site-specific spool directory for different types of spool files.

At regular intervals, UUCP dials up the remote system. When a connection to the remote machine is established, UUCP transfers the files describing the job, plus any input files. The incoming jobs will not be executed immediately, but only after the connection terminates. This is done by uuxqt, which also takes care of forwarding any jobs if they are designated for another site.

To distinguish between important and less important jobs, UUCP associates a grade with each job. This is a single letter, ranging from 0 through 9, A though Z, and a through z, in decreasing precedence. Mail is customarily spooled with grade B or C, while news is spooled with grade N. Jobs with higher grade are transferred earlier. Grades may be assigned using the -g flag when invoking uucp or uux.

You can also disallow the transfer of jobs below a given grade at certain times. This is also called the maximum spool grade allowed during a conversation and defaults to -z. Note the terminological ambiguity here: A file is transferred only if it is equal *or* above the maximum spool grade.

The Inner Workings Of uucico

To understand why uucico needs to know certain things, a quick description of how it actually connects to a remote system might be in order here.

When you execute uucico -s system from the command line, it first has to connect physically. The actions taken depend on the type of connection to open—e.g., when using telephone line, it has to find a modem, and dial out. Over TCP, it has to call gethostbyname(3) to convert the name to a network address, find out which port to open, and bind the address to the corresponding socket.

After this connection has been established, an authorization procedure has to be passed. It generally consists of the remote system asking for a login name and possibly a password. This is commonly called the *login chat*. The authorization procedure is performed either by the usual getty/login suite, or—on TCP sockets—by uucico itself. If authorization succeeds, the remote end fires up uucico. The local copy of uucico which initiated the connection is referred to as master, the remote copy as slave.

Next follows the handshake phase: The master now sends its hostname, plus several flags. The slave checks this hostname for permission to log in, send and receive files, and so on. The flags describe (among other things) the maximum grade of spool files to transfer. If enabled, a conversation count, or call sequence number check takes place here. With this feature, both sites maintain a count of successful connections, which are compared. If they do not match, the handshake fails. This is useful to protect yourself against impostors.

Finally, the two uucico's try to agree on a common transfer protocol. This protocol governs the way data is transferred, checked for consistency, and retransmitted in case of an error. There is a need for different protocols because of the differing types of connections supported. For example, telephone lines require a "safe" protocol, which is pessimistic about errors, while TCP transmission is inherently reliable and can use a more efficient protocol that forgoes most extra error checking.

After the handshake is complete, the actual transmission phase begins. Both ends turn on the selected protocol driver. The drivers possibly perform a protocol-specific initialization sequence.

First, the master sends all files queued for the remote system whose spool grade is high enough. When it has finished, it informs the slave that it is done, and that the slave may now hang up. The slave now can either agree to hang up, or take over the conversation. This is a change of roles: Now the remote system becomes master, and the local one becomes slave. The new master now sends its files. When done, both uucico's exchange termination messages, and close the connection.

We will not go into this in greater detail. Please refer to either the sources or any good book on UUCP for this. There is also a really antique article floating around the net, written by David A. Novitz, which gives a detailed description of the UUCP protocol. The Taylor UUCP FAQ also discusses some details of the way UUCP is implemented. It is posted to **comp.mail.uucp** regularly.

uucico Command Line Options

This section describes the most important command line options for uucico. For a complete list, please refer to the uucico manual page.

UUCP Configuration Files

In contrast to simpler file transfer programs, UUCP was designed to be able to handle all transfers automatically. Once it is set up properly, interference by the administrator should not be necessary on a day-to-day basis. The information required for this is kept in a couple of configuration files that reside in the directory /usr/lib/uucp. Most of these files are used only when dialing out.

> **Note**
> *In this chapter you will see multiple instances in which the referred example is not available. We've left the text reference, but please refer to the LDP for the examples when they become available.*

A Gentle Introduction To Taylor UUCP

To say that UUCP configuration is hard would be an understatement. It is really a hairy subject, and the sometimes terse format of the configuration files doesn't make things easier (although the Taylor format is almost easy reading compared to the older formats in HDB or Version 2).

To give you a feel of how all these files interact, we will introduce you to the most important ones, and have a look at sample entries of these files. We won't explain everything in detail now; a more accurate account is given in separate sections below. If you want to set up your machine for UUCP, you had best start with some sample files and adapt them gradually. You can pick either those shown below, or those included in your favorite distribution.

All files described in this section are kept in /usr/lib/uucp or a subdirectory thereof. Some distributions contain UUCP binaries that have support for both HDB and Taylor configuration enabled, and use different subdirectories for each configuration file set. There will usually be a README file in /usr/lib/uucp.

For UUCP to work properly, these files must be owned by the uucp user. Some of them contain passwords and telephone numbers, and therefore should have permissions of 600.

> **Note**
> *Although most UUCP commands must be setuid to uucp, you must make sure the uuchk program is not. Otherwise, users will be able to display passwords even though they have mode 600.*

The central UUCP configuration file is /usr/lib/uucp/config, and is used to set general parameters. The most important of them (and for now, the only one), is your host's UUCP name.

The next important configuration file is the sys file. It contains all system-specific information of sites you are linked to. This includes the site's name, and information on the link itself, such as the telephone number when using a modem link.

The port names a port to be used, and time specifies the times at which it may be called. Chat describes the login chat scripts—the sequence of strings that must be exchanged between to allow uucico to log into Pablo. We will get back to chat scripts later. The **port** command does not name a device special file such as /dev/cua1, but rather names an entry in the port file. You can assign these names as you like as long as they refer to a valid entry in port.

The port file holds information specific to the link itself. For modem links, it describes the device special file to be used, the range of speeds supported, and the type of dialing equipment connected to the port. The entry below describes /dev/cua1 (a.k.a. COM 2), to which a NakWell modem is connected that is capable of running at speeds up to 38,400bps. The entry's name was chosen to match the port name given in the sys file.

The information pertaining to the dialers itself is kept in yet another file, called—you guessed it—dial. For each dialer type, it basically contains the sequence of commands to be issued to dial up a remote site, given the telephone number. Again, this is specified as a chat script.

The line starting with chat specifies the modem chat, which is the sequence of commands sent to and received from the modem to initialize it and make it dial the desired number. The "T" sequence will be replaced with the phone number by uucico.

The first thing uucico does is look up Pablo in the sys file. From the sys file entry for Pablo, it sees that it should use the serial1 port to establish the connection. The port file tells it that this is a modem port, and that it has a NakWell modem attached.

Uucico now searches dial for the entry describing the NakWell modem, and having found one, opens the serial port /dev/cua1 and executes the dialer chat. That is, it sends "ATZ", waits for the "OK" response, and so on. When encountering the string "T", it substitutes the phone number (123-4567) extracted from the sys file.

After the modem returns CONNECT, the connection has been established, and the modem chat is complete. Uucico now returns to the sys file and executes the login chat. In our example, it would wait for the "login:" prompt, then send its username (Neruda), wait for the "password:" prompt, and send its password, "lorca".

After completing authorization, the remote end is assumed to fire up its own uucico. The two will then enter the handshake phase described in the previous section.

What UUCP Needs To Know

Before you start writing the UUCP configuration files, you have to gather some information it needs to know.

First, you will have to figure out what serial device your modem is attached to. Usually, the (DOS) ports COM1 through COM4 map to the device special files /dev/cua0 through /dev/cua3. Most distributions, such as Slackware, create a link /dev/modem as a link to the appropriate cua* device file, and configure kermit, seyon, and so on, to use this generic file. In this case, you should either use /dev/modem in your UUCP configuration, too.

The reason for this is that all dial-out programs use so-called lock files to signal when a serial port is in use. The names of these lock files are a concatenation of the string LCK.. and the device file name, for instance LCK..cua1. If programs use different names for the same device, they will fail to recognize each other's lock files. As a consequence, they will disrupt each other's session when started at the same time. This is not an unlikely event when you schedule your UUCP calls using a crontab entry. For details of setting up your serial ports, please refer to Chapter 4.

Next, you must find out at what speed your modem will communicate. You will have to set this to the maximum effective transfer rate you expect to get. The effective transfer rate may be much higher than the raw physical transfer rate your modem is capable of. For instance, many modems send and receive data at 2,400bps (bits per second). Using compression protocols such as V.42bis, the actual transfer rate may climb up to 9,600bps.

Of course, if UUCP is to do anything, you will need the phone number of a system to call. Also, you will need a valid login ID and possibly a password for the remote machine.

Tip

If you're just going to try out UUCP, get the number of an archive site near you. Write down the login and password—they're public to make anonymous downloads possible. In most cases, they're something like uucp/uucp or nuucp/uucp.

You will also have to know exactly how to log into the system. E.g., do you have to press the Break key before the login prompt appears? Does it display "login:" or "user:"? This is necessary for composing the chat script, which is a recipe telling uucico how to log in. If you don't know, or if the usual chat script fails, try to call the system with a terminal program like kermit or minicom, and write down exactly what you have to do.

Site Naming

As with TCP/IP-based networking, your host has to have a name for UUCP networking. As long as you simply want to use UUCP for file transfers to or from sites you dial up directly, or on a local network, this name does not have to meet any standards. The only limitation is that it shouldn't be longer than seven characters, so as to not confuse hosts with file systems that impose a narrow limit on file names.

However, if you use UUCP for a mail or news link, you should think about having the name registered with the UUCP Mapping Project. The UUCP Mapping Project is described in Chapter 12. Even if you participate in a domain, you might consider having an official UUCP name for your site.

Frequently, people choose their UUCP name to match the first component of their fully qualified domain name. Suppose your site's domain address is swim.twobirds.com, then your UUCP hostname would be Swim. Think of UUCP sites as knowing each other on a first-name basis. Of course, you can also use a UUCP name completely unrelated to your fully qualified domain name.

However, make sure not to use the unqualified site name in mail addresses unless you have registered it as your official UUCP name. (The UUCP Mapping Project registers all UUCP hostnames worldwide and makes sure they are unique. To register your UUCP name, ask the maintainers of the site that handles your mail; they will be able to help you with it.) At the very best, mail to an unregistered UUCP host will vanish in some big black bit bucket. If you use a name already held by some other site, this mail will be routed to that site, and cause its postmaster no end of headaches.

By default, the UUCP suite uses the name set by hostname as the site's UUCP name. This name is commonly set in the /etc/rc.local script. If your UUCP name is different from what you set your hostname to, you have to use the hostname option in the config file to tell uucico about your UUCP name. This is described below.

Taylor Configuration Files

We now return to the configuration files.

Taylor configuration files are generally made up of lines containing keyword-value pairs. A hash sign introduces a comment that indents to the end of the line. To use a hash sign by itself, you may escape it with a backslash.

There are quite a number of options you can tune with these configuration files. We can't go into all parameters here, but will only cover the most important ones. They you should be able to configure a modem-based UUCP link. Additional sections will describe the modifications necessary if you want to use UUCP over TCP/IP or over a direct serial line. A complete reference is given in the Texinfo documents that accompany the Taylor UUCP sources.

When you think you have configured your UUCP system completely, you can check your configuration using the uuchk tool (located in /usr/lib/uucp). uuchk reads your configuration files, and prints out a detailed report of the configuration values used for each system.

General Configuration Options: The config File

You won't generally use this file to describe much besides your UUCP hostname. By default, UUCP will use the name you set with the **hostname** command, but it is generally a good idea to set the UUCP name explicitly.

Of course, there are a number of miscellaneous parameters that may be set here, too, such as the name of the spool directory, or access rights for anonymous UUCP. The latter will be described in a later section.

How To Tell UUCP About Other Systems: The sys File

The sys file describes the systems your machine knows about. An entry is introduced by the system keyword; the subsequent lines up to the next system directive detail the parameters specific to that site. Commonly, a system entry will define parameters such as the telephone number and the login chat.

Parameters before the very first system line set default values used for all systems. Usually, you will set protocol parameters and the like in the defaults section.

Below, the most prominent fields are discussed in some detail.

System Name

The **system** command names the remote system. You must specify the correct name of the remote system, not an alias you invented, because uucico will check it against what the remote system says it is called when you log on. (Older Version 2 UUCPs don't broadcast their name when being called; however, newer implementations often do, and so does Taylor UUCP.)

Each system name may appear only once. If you want to use several sets of configurations for the same system (such as different telephone numbers uucico should try in turn), you can specify alternates. Alternates are described below.

Telephone Number

If the remote system is to be reached over a telephone line, the phone field specifies the number the modem should dial. It may contain several tokens interpreted by uucico's dialing procedure. An equal sign means to wait for a secondary dial tone, and a dash generates a one-second pause. For instance, some telephone installations will choke when you don't pause between dialing the prefix code and telephone number. (Don't know the proper English term for this—you know, something like a company's private internal installation where you have to dial a 0 or 9 to get a line to the outside.)

Any embedded alphabetic string may be used to hide site-dependent information like area codes. Any such string is translated to a dialcode using the dialcode file.

With these translations, you can use a phone number such as Bogoham7732 in the sys file, which makes things probably a little more legible.

Port And Speed

The port and speed options are used to select the device used for calling the remote system, and the maximum speed to which the device should be set. (The baud rate of the tty must be at least as high as the maximum transfer speed.) A system entry may use either option alone, or both options in conjunction. When looking up a suitable device in the port file, only those ports are selected that have a matching port name and/or speed range.

Generally, using the speed option should suffice. If you have only one serial device defined in port, uucico will always pick the right one anyway, so you only have to give it the desired speed. If you have several modems attached to your systems, you still often don't want to name a particular port, because if uucico finds that there are several matches, it tries each device in turn until it finds an unused one.

The Login Chat

Above, we already encountered the login chat script, which tells uucico how to log into the remote system. It consists of a list of tokens, specifying strings expected and sent by the local uucico process. The intention is to make uucico wait until the remote machine sends a login prompt, then return the login name, wait for the remote system to send the password prompt, and send the password. Expect and send strings are given in alternation. uucico automatically appends a carriage return character (r) to any send string.

uucico also allows for some sort of conditional execution, for example, in the case that the remote machine's getty needs to be reset before sending a prompt. For this, you can attach a subchat to an expect string, offset by a dash. The subchat is executed only if the main expect fails, i.e., a timeout occurs. One way to use this feature is to send a BREAK if the remote site doesn't display a login prompt. The following example gives an all-around chat script that should also work in case you have to hit Return before the login appears. Linux tells UUCP to not wait for anything and continue with the next send string immediately.

Alternates

Sometimes it is desirable to have multiple entries for a single system, for instance, if the system can be reached on different modem lines. With Taylor UUCP, you can do this by defining a so-called alternate.

An alternate entry retains all settings from the main system entry, and specifies only those values that should be overridden in the default system entry or added to it. An alternate is offset from the system entry by a line containing the keyword alternate.

When calling Pablo, uucico will now first dial 123-456, and if this fails, try the alternate. The alternate entry retains all settings from the main system entry, and overrides only the telephone number.

Restricting Call Times

Taylor UUCP provides a number of ways you may restrict the times when calls can be placed to a remote system. You might do this either because of limitations the remote host places on its services during business hours, or simply to avoid times with high call rates. Note that it is always possible to override call time restrictions by giving uucico the -S or -f option.

By default, Taylor UUCP will disallow connections at any time, so you have to use some sort of time specification in the sys file. If you don't care about call time restrictions, you can specify the time option with a value of Any in your sys file.

The simplest way to restrict call time is the time entry, which is followed by a string made up of a day and a time subfield. Day may be any of Mo, Tu, We, Th, Fr, Sa, Su combined, or Any, Never, or Wk for weekdays. The time consists of two 24-hour clock values, separated by a dash. They specify the range during which calls may be placed. The combination of these tokens is written without white space in between. Any number of day and time specifications may be grouped together with commas.

The special time strings Any and Never mean what they say: Calls may be placed at any or no time, respectively.

The **time** command takes an optional second argument that describes a retry time in minutes. When an attempt to establish a connection fails, uucico will not allow another attempt to dial up the remote host within a certain interval. By default, uucico uses an exponential backoff scheme, where the retry interval increases with each repeated failure. For instance, when you specify a retry time of 5 minutes, uucico will refuse to call the remote system within 5 minutes after the last failure.

The **timegrade** command allows you to attach a maximum spool grade to a schedule. This allows jobs with a spoolgrade of C or higher (usually, mail is queued with grade B or C) to be transferred whenever a call is established, while news (usually queued with grade N) will be transferred only during the night and at weekends.

Just like **time**, the **timegrade** command takes a retry interval in minutes as an optional third argument.

However, a caveat about spool grades is in order here: First, the timegrade option applies only to what your systems sends; the remote system may still transfer anything it likes. You can use the call-timegrade option to explicitly request it to send only jobs above some given spool grade; but there's no guarantee it will obey this request. (If the remote system runs Taylor UUCP, it will obey.)

Similarly, the timegrade field is not checked when a remote system calls in, so any jobs queued for the calling system will be sent. However, the remote system can explicitly request your uucico to restrict itself to a certain spool grade.

What Devices There Are: The port File

The port file tells uucico about the available ports. These may be modem ports, but other types such as direct serial lines and TCP sockets are supported as well.

Like the sys file, port consists of separate entries starting with the keyword port, followed by the port name. This name may be used by in the sys file's port statement. The name need not be unique; if there are several ports with the same name, uucico will try each in turn until it finds one that is not currently being used.

The **port** command should be immediately followed by the type statement that describes what type of port is described. Valid types are modem, direct for direct connections, and tcp for TCP sockets. If the **port** command is missing, the port type defaults to modem.

In this section, we will cover only modem ports; TCP ports and direct lines are discussed in a later section.

For modem and direct ports, you have to specify the device for calling out using the device directive. Usually, this is the name of a device special file in the /dev directory, like /dev/cua1.

Note

Some people use the ttyS* devices instead, which are intended for dial-in only.

In the case of a modem device, the port entry also determines what type of modem is connected to the port. Different types of modems have to be configured differently. Even modems that claim to be Hayes-compatible needn't be really compatible with each other. Therefore, you have to tell uucico how to initialize the modem and how to make it dial the desired number. Taylor UUCP keeps the descriptions of all dialers in a file named dial. To use any of these, you have to specify the dialer's name using the **dialer** command.

Sometimes, you will want to use a modem in different ways, depending on which system you call. For instance, some older modems don't understand when a high-speed modem attempts to connect at 14,400bps; they simply drop the line instead of negotiating a connect at, say, 9,600bps. When you know site drop uses such a dumb modem, you have to set up your modem differently when calling them. For this, you need an additional port entry in the port file that specifies a different dialer. Now you can give the new port a different name, such as serial1-slow, and use the port directive in drop system entry in sys.

A better way is to distinguish the ports by the speeds they support. The system entry for site drop would now give serial1 as port name, but request to use it at 9,600bps only. uucico will then automatically use the second port entry. All remaining sites that have a speed of 38,400bps in the system entry will be called using the first port entry.

How To Dial A Number: The dial File

The dial file describes the way various dialers are used. Traditionally, UUCP talks of dialers rather than modems, because in earlier times, it was usual practice to have one (expensive) automatic dialing device serve a whole bank of modems. Today, most modems have dialing support built in, so this distinction gets a little blurred.

Nevertheless, different dialers or modems may require a different configuration. You can describe each of them in the dial file. Entries in dial start with the **dialer** command, which gives the dialer's name.

The most important entry beside this is the modem chat, specified by the **chat** command. Similar to the login chat, it consists of a sequence of strings uucico sends to the dialer and the responses it expects in return. It is commonly used to reset the modem to some known state, and dial the number.

The modem chat begins with uucico, the empty expect string. uucico will therefore send the first command (**ATZ**) right away. **ATZ** is the Hayes command to reset the modem. It then waits until the modem has sent OK, and sends the next command, which turns off local echo, and the like. After the modem returns OK again, uucico sends the dialing command (**ATDT**). The escape sequence T in this string is replaced with the phone number taken from the system entry sys file. uucico then waits for the modem to return the string CONNECT, which signals that a connection with the remote modem has been established successfully.

Often, the modem fails to connect to the remote system, for instance, if the other system is talking to someone else and the line is busy. In this case, the modem will return some error message indicating the reason. Modem chats are not able to detect such messages; uucico will continue to wait for the expected string until it times out. The UUCP log file will therefore only show a bland "timed out in chat script" instead of the true reason.

However, Taylor UUCP allows you to tell uucico about these error messages using the **chat-fail** command as shown above. When uucico detects a chat-fail string while executing the modem chat, it aborts the call, and logs the error message in the UUCP log file.

The last command in the example shown above tells UUCP to toggle the DTR line before starting the modem chat. Most modems can be configured to go on-hook when detecting a change on the DTR line, and enter command mode.

Note
You can also configure some modems to reset themselves when detecting a transition on DTR. Some of them, however, don't seem to like this, and occasionally get hung.

UUCP Over TCP

Absurd as it may sound at the first moment, using UUCP to transfer data over TCP is not that bad an idea, especially when transferring large amount of data such as Usenet news. On TCP-based links, news is generally exchanged using the NNTP protocol, where articles are requested and sent individually, without compression or any other optimization. Although adequate for large sites with several concurrent newsfeeds, this technique is very unfavorable for small sites that receive their news over a slow connection, such as ISDN. These sites will usually want to combine the qualities of TCP with the advantages of sending news in large batches, which can be compressed and thus transferred with very low overhead. A standard way to transfer these batches is to use UUCP over TCP.

Using A Direct Connection

Assume you use a direct line connecting your system vstout to tiny. Very much like in the modem case, you have to write a system entry in the sys file. The **port** command identifies the serial port tiny is hooked up to.

In the port file, you have to describe the serial port for the direct connection. A dialer entry is not needed, because there's no need for dialing.

The Do's And Don'ts Of UUCP: Tuning Permissions
Command Execution

UUCP's task is to copy files from one system to another and to request execution of certain commands on remote hosts. Of course, you as an administrator would want to control what rights you grant other systems—allowing them to execute any command on your system is definitely not a good idea.

By default, the only commands Taylor UUCP allows other systems to execute on your machine are **rmail** and **rnews**, which are commonly used to exchange email and Usenet news over UUCP. The default search path used by uuxqt is a compile-time option, but should usually contain /bin, /usr/bin, and /usr/local/bin. To change the set of commands for a particular system, you can use the commands' keyword in the sys file. Similarly, the search path can be changed with the command-path statement. For instance, you may want to allow system Pablo to execute the **rsmtp** command in addition to **rmail** and **rnews** (**rsmtp** is used to deliver mail with batched SMTP; this is described in the mail chapters)

File Transfers

Taylor UUCP also allows you to fine-tune file transfers in great detail. At one extreme, you can disable transfers to and from a particular system. Just set request to No, and the remote system will not be able to either retrieve files from your system or send it any files. Similarly, you can prohibit your users from transferring files to or from a system by setting transfer to No. By default, users on both the local and the remote system are allowed to up- and download files.

In addition, you can configure the directories to and from which files may be copied. Usually, you will want to restrict access from remote systems to a single directory hierarchy, but still allow your users to send files from their home directory. Commonly, remote users will be allowed to receive files only from the public UUCP directory, /var/spool/uucppublic. This is the traditional place to make files publicly available; very much like FTP servers on the Internet. It is commonly referred to using the tilde (~) character.

Therefore, Taylor UUCP provides four different commands to configure the directories for sending and receiving files. They are **local-send**, which specifies the list of directories a user may ask UUCP to send files from; **local-receive**, which gives the list of directories a user may ask to receive files to; and **remote-send** and **remote-receive**, which do the analogous for requests from a foreign system.

The **local-send** command allows users on your host to send any files below /home and from the public UUCP directory to Pablo. The **local-receive** command allows them to receive files either to the world-writable receive directory in the uucppublic, or any world-writable directory below /home. The **remote-send** directive allows Pablo to request files from /var/spool/uucppublic, except for files below the incoming and receive directories. This is signaled to uucico by preceding the directory names with exclamation marks. Finally, the last line allows Pablo to upload any files to incoming.

One of the biggest problems with file transfers using UUCP is that will only receive files to directories that are world-writable. This may tempt some users to set up traps for other users, and so on. However, there's no way escaping this problem except disabling UUCP file transfers altogether.

Forwarding

UUCP provides a mechanism to have other systems execute file transfers on your behalf. For instance, this allows you to make seci retrieve a file from uchile for you, and send it to your system.

This technique of passing a job through several systems is called *forwarding*. In the above example, the reason to use forwarding may be that seci has UUCP access to uchile, but your host doesn't. However, if you run a UUCP system, you would want to limit the forwarding service to a few hosts you trust not to run up a horrendous phone bill by making you download the latest X11R6 source release for them.

By default, Taylor UUCP disallows forwarding altogether. To enable forwarding for a particular system, you can use the **forward** command. This command specifies a list of sites the system may request you to forward jobs to and from.

The forward-to entry for uchile is necessary so that any files returned by it are actually passed on to Pablo. Otherwise UUCP would drop them. This entry uses a variation of the **forward** command that permits uchile only to send files to Pablo through seci; not the other way around.

To permit forwarding to any system, use the special keyword ANY (capital letters required).

Setting Up Your System For Dialing In

If you want to set up your site for dialing in, you have to permit logins on your serial port, and customize some system files to provide UUCP accounts. This will be the topic of the current section.

Setting Up getty

If you want to use a serial line as a dial-in port, you have to enable a getty process on this port. However, some getty implementations aren't really suitable for this, because you usually want to use a serial port for dialing in and out. You therefore have to make sure to use a getty that is able to share the line with other programs, like uucico or minicom. One program that does this is uugetty from the getty_ps package. Most distributions have it; check for uugetty in your /sbin directory. Another program I am aware of is Gert Doering's mgetty, which also supports reception of facsimiles. You can also obtain the latest versions of these from **sunsite.unc.edu** as either binary or source.

Explaining the differences in the way uugetty and mgetty handle logins is beyond the scope of this little section; for more information, please refer to the Serial HOWTO by Greg Hankins, as well as the documentation that comes along with getty_ps and mgetty.

Providing UUCP Accounts

Next, you have to set up user accounts that let remote sites log into your system and establish a UUCP connection. Generally, you will provide a separate login name to each system that polls you. When setting up an account for system Pablo, you would probably give it Upablo as the username.

For systems that dial in through the serial port, you usually have to add these accounts to the system password file, /etc/passwd. A good practice is to put all UUCP logins in a special group such as uuguest. The account's home directory should be set to the public spool directory /var/spool/uucppublic; its login shell must be uucico.

If you have the shadow password suite installed, you can do this with the **useradd** command:

```
# useradd -d /var/spool/uucppublic -G uuguest -s /usr/lib/uucp/uucic
```

If you don't use the shadow password suite, you probably have to edit /etc/passwd by hand, adding a line like that shown below, where 5000 and 150 are the numerical uid and gid assigned to user Upablo and group uuguest, respectively.

```
Upablo:x:5000:150:UUCP Account:/var/spool/uucppublic:/usr/lib/uucp/u
```

After installing the account, you have to activate it by setting its password with the **passwd** command.

To serve UUCP systems that connect to your site over TCP, you have to set up inetd to handle incoming connections on the uucp port. You do this by adding the following line to /etc/inetd.conf:

```
uucp    stream  tcp   nowait  root  /usr/sbin/tcpd  /usr/lib/uucp/uuc
```

Note

Usually, tcpd has mode 700, so that you must invoke it as user root, not uucp as you would usually do.

The -l option makes uucico perform its own login authorization. It will prompt for a login name and a password just like the standard login program, but will rely on its private password database instead of /etc/passwd. This private password file is named /usr/lib/uucp/passwd and contains pairs of login names and passwords:

```
Upablo   IslaNegra
Ulorca   co'rdoba
```

Of course, this file must be owned by uucp and have permissions of 600.

If this database sounds like such a good idea you would like to use on normal serial logins, too, you will be disappointed to hear that this isn't possible at the moment without major contortions. First off, you need Taylor UUCP 1.05 for this, because it allows getty to pass the login name of the calling user to uucico using the -u option. (The -u option is present in 1.04, too, but is only a no-op.) Then, you have to trick the getty you are using into invoking uucico instead of the usual /bin/login. With getty_ps, you can do this by setting the LOGIN option in the configuration file. However, this disables interactive logins altogether. mgetty, on the other hand, has a nice feature that allows you to invoke different login commands based on the name the user provided. For instance, you can tell mgetty to use uucico for all users that provide a login name beginning with a capital U, but let everyone else be handled by the standard login command.

To protect your UUCP users from callers giving a false system name and snarfing all their mail, you should add **called-login** commands to each system entry in the sys file. This is described above.

Protecting Yourself Against Swindlers

One of the biggest problems about UUCP is that the calling system can lie about its name; it announces its name to the called system after logging in, but the server doesn't have a way to check this. Thus, an attacker could log into his or her own UUCP account, pretend to be someone else, and pick up that other site's mail. This is particularly troublesome if you offer login via anonymous UUCP, where the password is made public.

Unless you know you can trust all sites that call your system to be honest, you must guard against this sort of impostor. The cure against this disease is to require each system to use a particular login name by specifying a **called-login** in sys.

The upshot of this is that whenever a system logs in and pretends it is Pablo, uucico will check whether it has logged in as Upablo. If it hasn't, the calling system will be turned down, and the connection is dropped. You should make it a habit to add the **called-login** command to every system entry you add to your sys file. It is important that you do this for all systems, regardless of whether they will ever call your site or not. For those sites that never call you, you should probably set **called-login** to some totally bogus username, such as neverlogsin.

Be Paranoid: Call Sequence Checks

Another way to fend off and detect impostors is to use call sequence checks. Call sequence checks help you protect against intruders that somehow managed to find out the password you log into your UUCP system with.

When using call sequence checks, both machines keep track of the number of connections established so far. It is incremented with each connection. After logging in, the caller sends its call sequence number, and the callee checks it against its own number. If they don't match, the connection attempt will be rejected. If the initial number is chosen at random, attackers will have a hard time guessing the correct call sequence number.

But call sequence checks do more for you than this: Even if some very clever person should detect your call sequence number as well as your password, you will find this out. When the attacker call your UUCP feed and steals your mail, this will increase the feeds call sequence number by one. The next time you call your feed and try to log in, the remote uucico will refuse you, because the numbers don't match anymore!

If you have enabled call sequence checks, you should check your log files regularly for error messages that hint at possible attacks. If your system rejects the call sequence number the calling system offers it, uucico will put a message into the log file saying something like "Out of sequence call rejected." If your system is rejected by its feed because the sequence numbers are out of sync, it will put a message in the log file saying "Handshake failed (RBADSEQ)."

Next, you have to create the file containing the sequence number itself. Taylor UUCP keeps the sequence number is in a file called .Sequence in the remote site's spool directory. It must be owned by uucp, and must be mode 600 (i.e., readable and writable only by uucp). It is best to initialize this file with an arbitrary, agreed-upon start value. Otherwise, an attacker might manage to guess the number by trying out all values smaller than, say, 60.

Of course, the remote site has to enable call sequence checks as well, and start by using exactly the same sequence number as you.

Anonymous UUCP

If you want to provide anonymous UUCP access to your system, you first have to set up a special account for it as described above. A common practice is to give it a login name and a password of uucp.

In addition, you have to set a few of the security options for unknown systems. For instance, you may want to prohibit them from executing any commands on your system. However, you cannot set these parameters in a sys file entry, because the **system** command requires the system's name, which you don't have. Taylor UUCP solves this dilemma through the **unknown** command. **unknown** can be used in the config file to specify any command that can usually appear in a system entry.

This will restrict unknown systems to downloading files from below the pub directory and uploading files to the incoming directory below /var/spool/uucppublic. The next line will make uucico ignore any requests from the remote system to turn on debugging locally. The last two lines permit unknown systems to execute **rmail**; but the command path specified makes uucico look for the **rmail** command in a private directory named anon-bin only. This allows you to provide some special **rmail** that, for instance, forwards all mail to the super-user for examination. This allows anonymous users to reach the maintainer of the system, but prevents them at the same time from injecting any mail to other sites.

To enable anonymous UUCP, you must specify at least one unknown statement in config. Otherwise uucico will reject any unknown systems.

UUCP Low-Level Protocols

To negotiate session control and file transfers with the remote end, uucico uses a set of standardized messages. This is often referred to as the high-level protocol. During the initialization phase and the hangup phase these are simply sent across as strings. However, during the real transfer phase, an additional low-level protocol is employed that is mostly transparent to the higher levels. This is to make error checks possible when using unreliable lines, for instance.

Protocol Overview

As UUCP is used over different types of connections, such as serial lines or TCP, or even X.25, specific low-level protocols are needed. In addition, several implementations of UUCP have introduced different protocols that do roughly the same thing.

Protocols can be divided into two categories: *streaming* and *packet-oriented* protocols. Protocols of the latter variety transfer a file as a whole, possibly computing a checksum over it. This is nearly free of any overhead, but requires a reliable connection, because any error will cause the whole file to be retransmitted. These protocols are commonly used over TCP connections, but are not suitable for use over telephone lines. Although modern modems do quite a good job at error correction, they are not perfect, nor is there any error detection between your computer and the modem.

On the other hand, packet protocols split up the file into several chunks of equal size. Each packet is sent and received separately, a checksum is computed, and an acknowledgment is returned to the sender. To make this more efficient, sliding-window protocols were invented, which allow for a limited number (a window) of outstanding acknowledgments at any time. This greatly reduces the amount of time uucico has to wait during a transmission. Still, the relatively large overhead compared to a streaming protocol make packet protocols inefficient for use over TCP.

The width of the data path also makes a difference. Sometimes, sending eight-bit characters over a serial connection is impossible, for instance, if the connection goes through a stupid terminal server. In this case, characters with the eighth bit set have to be quoted on transmission. When you transmit eight-bit characters over a seven-bit connection, they have to be under worst-case assumptions; this doubles the amount of data to be transmitted, although compression done by the hardware may compensate for this. Lines that can transmit arbitrary eight-bit characters are usually called *eight-bit clean*. This is the case for all TCP connections, as well as for most modem connections.

Tuning The Transmission Protocol

All protocols allow for some variation in packet sizes, timeouts, and the like. Usually, the defaults provided work well under standard circumstances, but may not be optimal for your situation. The g protocol, for instance, uses window sizes from 1 to 7, and packet sizes in powers of 2 ranging from 64 through 4,096. (Most binaries included in distributions default to a window size of 7 and 128-byte packets.) If your telephone line is usually so noisy that it drops more than 5 percent of all packets, you should probably lower the packet size and shrink the window. On the other hand, on very good telephone lines the protocol overhead of sending ACKs for every 128 bytes may prove wasteful, so that you might increase the packet size to 512 or even 1,024.

Taylor UUCP provides a mechanism to suit your needs by tuning these parameters with the **protocol-parameter** command in the sys file.

The tunable parameters and their names vary from protocol to protocol. For a complete list of them please refer to the documentation enclosed in the Taylor UUCP source.

Selecting Specific Protocols

Not every implementation of uucico speaks and understand each protocol, so during the initial handshake phase, both processes have to agree on a common protocol. The master uucico offers the slave a list of supported protocols by sending Pprotlist, from which the slave may pick one.

Based on the type of port used (modem, TCP, or direct), uucico will compose a default list of protocols. For modem and direct connections, this list usually comprises i, a, g, G, and j. For TCP connections, the list is t, e, i, a, g, G, j, and f. You can override this default list with the **protocols** command, which may be specified in a system entry as well as a port entry.

This will require any incoming or outgoing connection through this port to use i, g, or G. If the remote system does not support any of these, the conversation will fail.

Troubleshooting

This section describes what may go wrong with your UUCP connection, and makes suggestions where to look for the error. However, the questions were compiled off the top of my head. There's much more that can go wrong.

In any case, enable debugging with -xall, and take a look at the output in Debug in the spool directory. It should help you quickly recognize where the problem lies. Also, I have always found it helpful to turn on my modem's speaker when it didn't connect. With Hayes-compatible modems, this is accomplished by adding "ATL1M1 OK" to the modem chat in the dial file.

The first check always should be whether all file permissions are set correctly. uucico should be setuid uucp, and all files in /usr/lib/uucp, /var/spool/uucp, and /var/spool/uucppublic should be owned by uucp. There are also some hidden files (that is, files whose name begins with a dot; such files aren't normally displayed by the **ls** command) in the spool directory which must be owned by uucp as well.

uucico keeps saying "Wrong time to call": This probably means that in the system entry in sys, you didn't specify a **time** command that details when the remote system may be called, or you gave one which actually forbids calling at the current time. If no call schedule is given, uucico assumes that the system may never be called.

uucico complains that the site is already locked: This means that uucico detected a lock file for the remote system in /var/spool/uucp. The lock file may be from an earlier call to the system that crashed or was killed. However, it's also likely that there's another uucico process sitting around that is trying to dial the remote system and got stuck in a chat script, or so on. If this uucico process doesn't succeed in connecting to the remote system, kill it with a hangup signal, and remove any lock files it left lying around.

I can connect to the remote site, but the chat script fails: Look at the text you receive from the remote site. If it's garbled, this might be a speed-related problem. Otherwise, confirm if it really agrees with what your chat script expects. Remember, the chat script starts with an expect string. If you receive the login prompt, then send your name, but never get the password prompt, insert some delays before sending it, or even in between the letters. You might be too fast for your modem.

My modem does not dial: If your modem doesn't indicate that the DTR line has been raised when uucico calls out, you possibly haven't given the right device to uucico. If your modem recognizes DTR, check with a terminal program that you can write to it. If this works, turn on echoing with E at the start of the modem chat. If it doesn't echo your commands during the modem chat, check if your line speed is too high or low for your modem. If you see the echo, check if you have disabled modem responses, or set them to number codes. Verify that the chat script itself is correct. Remember that you have to write two backslashes to send one to the modem.

My modem tries to dial, but doesn't get out: Insert a delay into the phone number. This is especially useful when dialing out from a company's internal telephone net. For people in Europe, who usually dial pulse-tone, try touch-tone. In some countries, postal services have been upgrading their nets recently. Touch-tone sometimes helps.

Log file says I have extremely high packet loss rates: This looks like a speed problem. Maybe the link between computer and modem is too slow (remember to adapt it to the highest effective rate possible)? Or is it your hardware that is too slow to service interrupts in time? With a NSC-16550A chipset on your serial port, 38Kbps are said to work reasonably well; however, without FIFOs (like 16450 chips), 9,600bps is the limit. Also, you should make sure hardware handshake is enabled on the serial line.

Another likely cause is that hardware handshake isn't enabled on the port. Taylor UUCP 1.04 has no provisions for turning on RTS/CTS handshake.

I can log in, but handshake fails: Well, there can be a number of problems. The output in the log file should tell you a lot. Look at what protocols the remote site offers (it sends a string Pprotlist during the handshake). Maybe they don't have any in common (did you select any protocols in sys or port?).

If the remote system sends RLCK, there is a stale lockfile for you on the remote system. If it's not because you're already connected to the remote system on a different line, ask to have it removed.

If it sends RBADSEQ, the other site has conversation count checks enabled for you, but numbers didn't match. If it sends RLOGIN, you were not permitted to login under this ID.

Log Files

When compiling the UUCP suite to use Taylor-style logging, you have only three global log files, all of which reside in the spool directory. The main log file is named Log and contains all information about connections established and files transferred.

The next important log file is Stats, which lists file transfer statistics.

The third file if Debug. This is the place where debugging information is written. If you use debugging, you should make sure that this file has a protection mode of 600. Depending on the debug mode you selected, it may contain the login and password you use to connect to the remote system.

Some UUCP binaries included in distributions have been compiled to use HDB-style logging. HDB UUCP uses a whole bunch of log files stored below /var/spool/uucp/.Log. This directory contains three more directories, named uucico, uuxqt, and uux. They contain the logging output generated by each of the corresponding commands, sorted into different files for each site. Thus, output from uucico when calling site Pablo will go into .Log/uucico/pablo, while the subsequent uuxqt run will write to .Log/uuxqt/pablo. The lines written to the various logfiles are, however, the same as with Taylor logging.

When you enable debugging output with HDB-style logging compiled in, it will go to the .Admin directory below /var/spool/uucp. During outgoing calls, debugging information will be sent to .Admin/audit.local, while the output from uucico when someone calls in will go to .Admin/audit.

Chapter 12
Electronic Mail

One of the most prominent uses of networking, since the first networks were devised, has been electronic mail. It started as a simple service that copied a file from one machine to another, and appended it to the recipient's mailbox file. Basically, this is still what email is all about, although an ever-growing net with its complex routing requirements and its ever-increasing load of messages has made a more elaborate scheme necessary.

Various standards of mail exchange have been devised. Sites on the Internet adhere to one laid out in RFC-822, augmented by some RFCs that describe a machine-independent way of transferring special characters, and the like. Much thought has also been given recently to "multimedia mail," which deals with including pictures and sound in mail messages. Another standard, X.400, has been defined by CCITT.

Quite a number of mail transport programs have been implemented for systems. One of the best known is the University of Berkeley's sendmail, which is used on a number of platforms. The original author was Eric Allman, who is now actively working on the sendmail team again. There are two ports of sendmail 5.56c available, one of which will be described in Chapter 14. The sendmail version currently being developed is 8.9.3. For more information, see **http://send.mail/org** and **http://sendmail.com/**.

The mail agent most commonly used with Linux is smail 3.1.28, written and copyrighted by Curt Landon Noll and Ronald S. Karr. This is the one included in most distributions. In the following, we will refer to it simply as smail, although there are other versions of it which are entirely different, and which we don't describe here.

Compared to sendmail, smail is rather young. When handling mail for a small site without complicated routing requirements, their capabilities are pretty close. For large sites, however, sendmail always wins, because its configuration scheme is much more flexible.

Both smail and sendmail support a set of configuration files that have to be customized. Apart from the information that is required to make the mail subsystem run (such as the local hostname), there are many more parameters that may be tuned. sendmail's main configuration file is very hard to understand at first. It looks as if your cat had taken a nap on your keyboard with the Shift key pressed. smail configuration files are more structured and easier to understand than sendmail's, but don't give the user as much power in tuning the mailer's behavior. However, for small UUCP or Internet sites, the work required in setting up any of them is roughly the same.

In this chapter, we will deal with what email is and what issues you as an administrator will have to deal with. Chapters 13 and 14 will give instructions on setting up smail and sendmail for the first time. The information provided there should suffice to get smaller sites operational, but there are many more options, and you can spend many happy hours in front of your computer configuring the fanciest features.

Toward the end of the current chapter we will briefly cover setting up elm, a very common mail user agent on many Linuxish systems.

For more information about issues specific to electronic mail on Linux, please refer to the Linux Electronic Mail HOWTO by Guylhem Aznar (**guylhem@oeil.qc.ca**) at **http:// metalab.unc.edu/LDP/HOWTO/Mail-HOWTO.html**. The source distributions of elm, smail, and sendmail also contain very extensive documentation that should answer most of your questions on setting them up. If you are looking for information on email in general, there's a number of RFCs that deal with this topic. They are listed in the bibliography at the end of the book.

What Is A Mail Message?

A mail message generally consists of a message body, which is the text the sender wrote, and special data specifying recipients, transport medium, and so on, very much like what you see when you look at a letter's envelope.

This administrative data falls into two categories; in the first category is any data that is specific to the transport medium, like the address of sender and recipient. It is therefore called the envelope. It may be transformed by the transport software as the message is passed along.

The second variety is any data necessary for handling the mail message, which is not particular to any transport mechanism, such as the message's subject line, a list of all recipients, and the date the message was sent. In many networks, it has become standard to prepend this data to the mail message, forming the so-called *mail header*. It is offset from the mail body by an empty line. (It is customary to append a signature or .sig to a mail message, usually containing information on the author, along with a joke or a motto. It is offset from the mail message by a line containing "-".)

Most mail transport software in the world uses a header format outlined in RFC-822. Its original purpose was to specify a standard for use on the ARPANET, but since it was designed to be independent from any environment, it has been easily adapted to other networks, including many UUCP-based networks.

RFC-822, however, is only the greatest common denominator. More recent standards have been conceived to cope with such growing needs as, for example, data encryption, international character set support, and multipurpose Internet mail extensions (MIME).

In all these standards, the header consists of several lines, separated by newline characters. A line is made up of a field name, beginning in column one, and the field itself, offset by a colon and white space. The format and semantics of each field vary depending on the field name. A header field may be continued across a new line, if the next line begins with a tab. Fields can appear in any order.

A typical mail header may look like this:

```
From brewhq.swb.de!ora.com!andyo Wed Apr 13 00:17:03 1994
Return-Path: <brewhq.swb.de!ora.com!andyo
Received: from brewhq.swb.de by monad.swb.de with uucp
        (Smail3.1.28.1 #6) id m0pqqlT-00023aB; Wed, 13 Apr 94 00:17
Received: from ora.com (ruby.ora.com) by brewhq.swb.de with smtp
        (Smail3.1.28.1 #28.6) id <m0pqoQr-0008qhC>; Tue, 12 Apr 94 2
Received: by ruby.ora.com (8.6.8/8.6.4) id RAA26438; Tue, 12 Apr 94
Date: Tue, 12 Apr 1994 15:56:49 -0400
Message-Id: <199404121956.PAA07787@ruby
From: andyo@ora.com (Andy Oram)
To: okir@monad.swb.de
Subject: Re: Your RPC section
```

Usually, all necessary header fields are generated by the mailer interface you use, like elm, pine, mush, or mailx. Some, however, are optional, and may be added by the user. elm, for example, allows you to edit part of the message header. Others are added by the mail transport software. A list of common header fields and their meanings are given in Table 12.1.

Table 12.1   Common header fields and their meanings.

From	This contains the sender's email address, and possibly the "real name." A complete zoo of formats is used here.
To	This is the recipient's email address.
Subject	Describes the content of the mail in a few words. At least that's what it should do.

(continued)

Table 12.1   Common header fields and their meanings *(continued)*.

Date	The date the mail was sent.
Reply-To	Specifies the address the sender wants the recipient's reply directed to. This may be useful if you have several accounts, but want to receive the bulk of mail only on the one you use most frequently. This field is optional.
Organization	The organization that owns the machine from which the mail originates. If your machine is owned by you privately, either leave this out, or insert "private" or some complete nonsense. This field is optional.
Message-ID	A string generated by mail transport on the originating system. It is unique to this message.
Received	Every site that processes your mail (including the machines of sender and recipient) inserts such a field into the header, giving its site name, a message ID, time and date it received the message, which site it is from, and which transport software was used. This is so that you can trace which route the message took, and can complain to the person responsible if something went wrong.
X-anything	No mail-related programs should complain about any header which starts with X-. It is used to implement additional features that have not yet made it into an RFC, or never will. This is used by the Linux Activists mailing list, for example, where the channel is selected by the X-Mn-Key: header field.

The one exception to this structure is the very first line. It starts with the keyword "From," which is followed by a blank instead of a colon. To distinguish it from the ordinary From: field, it is frequently referred to as From_. It contains the route the message has taken in UUCP bang-path style (explained below), time and date when it was received by the last machine having processed it, and an optional part specifying which host it was received from. Since this field is regenerated by every system that processes the message, it is sometimes subsumed under the envelope data.

The From_ field is there for backward compatibility with some older mailers, but is not used very much anymore, except by mail user interfaces that rely on it to mark the beginning of a message in the user's mailbox. To avoid potential trouble with lines in the message body that begin with "From", too, it has become standard procedure to escape any such occurrence by preceding it with ">".

How Is Mail Delivered?

Generally, you will compose mail using a mailer interface like mail or mailx; or more sophisticated ones like elm, mush, or pine. These programs are called *mail user agents*, or MUAs for short. If you send a mail message, the interface program will in most cases hand it to another program for delivery. This is called the *mail transport agent*, or MTA. On some systems, there are different mail transport agents for local and remote delivery; on others, there is only one. The command for remote delivery is usually called **rmail**, the other is called **lmail** (if it exists).

Local delivery of mail is, of course, more than just appending the incoming message to the recipient's mailbox. Usually, the local MTA will understand aliasing (setting up local recipient addresses pointing to other addresses) and forwarding (redirecting a user's mail to some other destination). Also, messages that cannot be delivered must usually be bounced, that is, returned to the sender along with some error message.

For remote delivery, the transport software used depends on the nature of the link. If the mail must be delivered over a network using TCP/IP, SMTP is commonly used. SMTP stands for Simple Mail Transfer Protocol, and is defined in RFC-788 and RFC-821. SMTP usually connects to the recipient's machine directly, negotiating the message transfer with the remote side's SMTP daemon.

In UUCP networks, mail will usually not be delivered directly, but rather be forwarded to the destination host by a number of intermediate systems. To send a message over a UUCP link, the sending MTA will usually execute **rmail** on the forwarding system using uux, and feed it the message on standard input.

Because this is done for each message separately, it may produce a considerable work load on a major mail hub, as well as clutter the UUCP spool queues with hundreds of small files taking up an unproportional amount of disk space. (This is because disk space is usually allocated in blocks of 1,024 bytes. So even a message of at most 400 bytes will eat a full kilobyte.) Some MTAs therefore allow you to collect several messages for a remote system in a single batch file. The batch file contains the SMTP commands that the local host would normally issue if a direct SMTP connection was used. This is called BSMTP, or batched SMTP. The batch is then fed to the rsmtp or bsmtp program on the remote system, which will process the input as if a normal SMTP connection had occurred.

Email Addresses

For electronic mail, an address is made up of at least the name of a machine handling the person's mail, and a user identification recognized by this system. This may be the recipient's login name, but may also be anything else. Other mail addressing schemes, like X.400, use a more general set of "attributes," which are used to look up the recipient's host in an X.500 directory server.

The way a machine name is interpreted, i.e., at which site your message will finally wind up, and how to combine this name with the recipient's user name greatly depends on the network you are on.

Internet sites adhere to the RFC-822 standard, which requires a notation of **user@ host.domain**, where host.domain is the host's fully qualified domain name. The middle thing is called an "at" sign. Because this notation does not involve a route to the destination host but gives the (unique) hostname instead, this is called an absolute address.

In the original UUCP environment, the prevalent form was path!host!user, where path described a sequence of hosts the message had to travel before reaching the destination host. This construct is called the bang path notation, because an exclamation mark is loosely called a "bang." Today, many UUCP-based networks have adopted RFC-822, and will understand this type of address.

Now, these two types of addressing don't mix too well. Assume an address of **hostA! user@hostB**. It is not clear whether the "@" sign takes precedence over the path, or vice versa: Do we have to send the message to hostB, which mails it to hostA!user, or should it be sent to hostA, which forwards it to user@hostB?

Addresses that mix different types of address operators are called *hybrid addresses*. Most notorious is the above example. It is usually resolved by giving the "@" sign precedence over the path. In the above example, this means sending the message to hostB first.

However, there is a way to specify routes in RFC-822-conformant ways: <@hostA,@hostB: user@hostC> denotes the address of user on hostC, where hostC is to be reached through hostA and hostB (in that order). This type of address is frequently called a route-addr address.

Then, there is the "%" address operator: **user%hostB@hostA** will first be sent to hostA, which expands the rightmost (in this case, only) percent sign to an "@" sign. The address is now **user@hostB**, and the mailer will happily forward your message to hostB, which delivers it to user. This type of address is sometimes referred to as "Ye Olde ARPANET Kludge," and its use is discouraged. Nevertheless, many mail transport agents generate this type of address.

Other networks have still different means of addressing. DECnet-based networks, for example, use two colons as an address separator, yielding an address of host::user. (When trying to reach a DECnet address from an RFC-822 environment, you may use "host::user"@relay, where relay is the name of a known Internet-DECnet relay.) Last, the X.400 standard uses an entirely different scheme, by describing a recipient by a set of attribute-value pairs, like country and organization.

On FidoNet, each user is identified by a code like 2:320/204.9, consisting of four numbers denoting zone (2 is for Europe), net (320 being Paris and Banlieue), node (the local hub), and point (the individual user's PC). Fidonet addresses can be mapped to RFC-822; the above would be written as **Thomas.Quinot@p9.f204.n320.z2.fidonet.org**. Now didn't I say domain names are easy to remember?

There are some implications to using these different types of addressing, which will be described throughout the following sections. In a RFC-822 environment, however, you will rarely use anything else than absolute addresses like **user@host.domain**.

How Does Mail Routing Work?

The process of directing a message to the recipient's host is called *routing*. Apart from finding a path from the sending site to the destination, it involves error checking as well as speed and cost optimization.

There is a big difference between the way a UUCP site handles routing and the way an Internet site does. On the Internet, the main job of directing data to the recipient host (once it is known by its IP address) is done by the IP networking layer, while in the UUCP zone, the route has to be supplied by the user or generated by the mail transfer agent.

Mail Routing On The Internet

On the Internet, it depends entirely on the destination host whether any specific mail routing is performed at all. The default is to deliver the message to the destination host directly by looking up its IP address, and leave the actual routing of the data to the IP transport layer.

Most sites will usually want to direct all in-bound mail to a highly available mail server that is capable of handling all this traffic, and have it distribute this mail locally. To announce this service, the site publishes a so-called MX record for their local domain in the DNS database. MX stands for Mail Exchanger and basically states that the server host is willing to act as a mail forwarder for all machines in this domain. MX records may also be used to handle traffic for hosts that are not connected to the Internet themselves, like UUCP networks or company networks with hosts carrying confidential information.

MX records also have a preference associated with them. This is a positive integer. If several mail exchangers exist for one host, the mail transport agent will try to transfer the message to the exchanger with the lowest preference value, and only if this fails will it try a host with a higher value. If the local host is itself a mail exchanger for the destination address, it must not forward messages to any MX hosts with a higher preference than its own; this is a safe way of avoiding mail loops.

Suppose that an organization, say Foobar Inc., want all their mail handled by their machine called mailhub. They will then have an MX record like this in the DNS database:

```
foobar.com        IN   MX     5    mailhub.foobar.com
```

This announces mailhub.foobar.com as a mail exchanger for foobar.com with a preference value of 5. A host that wishes to deliver a message to **joe@greenhouse.foobar.com** will check DNS for foobar.com, and finds the MX record pointing at mailhub. If there's no MX with a preference smaller than 5, the message will be delivered to mailhub, which then dispatches it to greenhouse.

The above is really only a sketch of how MX records work. For more information on the mail routing on the Internet, please refer to RFC-974.

Mail Routing In The UUCP World

Mail routing on UUCP networks is much more complicated than on the Internet, because the transport software does not perform any routing itself. In earlier times, all mail had to be addressed using bang paths. Bang paths specified a list of hosts through which to forward the message, separated by exclamation marks, and followed by the user's name. To address a letter to Janet User on a machine named Moria, you would have used the path eek!swim!moria!janet. This would have sent the mail from your host to Eek, from there on to Swim and finally to Moria.

The obvious drawback of this technique is that it requires you to remember much about the network topology, fast links, and so on. Much worse than that, changes in the network topology—like links being deleted or hosts being removed—may cause messages to fail simply because you weren't aware of the change. And finally, in case you move to a different place, you will most likely have to update all these routes.

One thing, however, that made the use of source routing necessary was the presence of ambiguous hostnames. For instance, assume there are two sites named Moria, one in the United States, and one in France. Which site now does moria!janet refer to? This can be made clear by specifying what path to reach Moria through.

The first step in disambiguating hostnames was the founding of the UUCP Mapping Project. It is located at Rutgers University and registers all official UUCP hostnames, along with information on their UUCP neighbors and their geographic location, making sure no hostname is used twice. The information gathered by the Mapping Project is published as the Usenet Maps, which are distributed regularly through Usenet. (Maps for sites registered with the UUCP Mapping Project are distributed through the newsgroup **comp.mail.maps**; other organizations may publish separate maps for their network.) A typical system entry in a map (after removing the comments) looks like this.

```
moria
        bert(DAILY/2),
        swim(WEEKLY)
```

This entry says that Moria has a link to Bert, which it calls twice a day, and Swim, which it calls weekly. We will come back to the Map file format in more detail below.

Using the connectivity information provided in the maps, you can automatically generate the full paths from your host to any destination site. This information is usually stored in the paths file, also called pathalias database sometimes. Assume the maps state that you can reach Bert through Ernie, then a pathalias entry for Moria generated from the map snippet above may look like this:

```
moria           ernie!bert!moria!%s
```

If you now give a destination address of **janet@moria.uucp**, your MTA will pick the route shown above, and send the message to Ernie with an envelope address of bert!moria!janet.

Building a paths file from the full Usenet maps is, however, not a very good idea. The information provided in them is usually rather distorted and occasionally out of date. Therefore, only a number of major hosts use the complete UUCP world maps to build their paths file. Most sites only maintain routing information for sites in their neighborhood, and send any mail to sites they don't find in their databases to a smarter host with more complete routing information. This scheme is called *smart-host routing*. Hosts that have only one UUCP mail link (so-called *leaf sites*) don't do any routing of their own; they rely entirely on their smart host.

Mixing UUCP And RFC-822

The best cure against the problems of mail routing in UUCP networks so far is the adoption of the domain name system in UUCP networks. Of course, you can't query a name server over UUCP. Nevertheless, many UUCP sites have formed small domains that coordinate their routing internally. In the maps, these domains announce one or two host as their mail gateways, so that there doesn't have to be a map entry for each host in the domain. The gateways handle all mail that flows into and out of the domain. The routing scheme inside the domain is completely invisible to the outside world.

This works very well with the smart-host routing scheme described above. Global routing information is maintained by the gateways only; minor hosts within a domain will get along with only a small handwritten paths file that lists the routes inside their domain, and the route to the mail hub. Even the mail gateways do not have to have routing information for every single UUCP host in the world anymore. Beside the complete routing information for the domain they serve, they only need to have routes to entire domains in their databases now. For instance, the pathalias entry shown below will route all mail for sites in the sub.org domain to Smurf:

```
.sub.org        swim!smurf!%s
```

Any mail addressed to **claire@jones.sub.org** will be sent to swim with an envelope address of smurf!jones!claire.

The hierarchical organization of the domain name space allows mail servers to mix more specific routes with less specific ones. For instance, a system in France may have specific routes for subdomains of "fr," but route any mail for hosts in the "us" domain toward some system in the United States. In this way, *domain-based routing* (as this technique is called) greatly reduces the size of routing databases as well as the administrative overhead needed.

The main benefit of using domain names in a UUCP environment, however, is that compliance with RFC-822 permits easy gatewaying between UUCP networks and the Internet.

Many UUCP domains nowadays have a link with an Internet gateway that acts as their smart host. Sending messages across the Internet is faster, and routing information is much more reliable because Internet hosts can use DNS instead of the Usenet maps.

In order to be reachable from the Internet, UUCP-based domains usually have their Internet gateway announce an MX record for them (MX records were described above). For instance, assume that Moria belongs to the orcnet.org domain. Gcc2.groucho.edu acts as their Internet gateway. Moria would therefore use gcc2 as its smart host, so that all mail for foreign domains is delivered across the Internet. On the other hand, gcc2 would announce an MX record for orcnet.org, and deliver all incoming mail for orcnet sites to Moria.

The only remaining problem is that the UUCP transport programs can't deal with fully qualified domain names. Most UUCP suites were designed to cope with site names of up to eight characters, some even less, and using non-alphanumeric characters such as dots is completely out of the question for most.

Therefore, some mapping between RFC-822 names and UUCP hostnames is needed. The way this mapping is done is completely implementation-dependent. One common way of mapping FQDNs to UUCP names is to use the pathalias file for this:

```
moria.orcnet.org   ernie!bert!moria!%s
```

This will produce a pure UUCP-style bang path from an address that specifies a fully qualified domain name. Some mailers provide a special files for this; sendmail, for instance, uses the uucpxtable for this.

The reverse transformation (colloquially called *domainizing*) is sometimes required when sending mail from a UUCP network to the Internet. As long as the mail sender uses the fully qualified domain name in the destination address, this problem can be avoided by not removing the domain name from the envelope address when forwarding the message to the smart-host. However, there are still some UUCP sites that are not part of any domain. They are usually domainized by appending the pseudo-domain uucp.

Pathalias And Map File Format

The pathalias database provides the main routing information in UUCP-based networks. A typical entry looks like this (site name and path are separated by tabs):

```
moria.orcnet.org   ernie!bert!moria!%s
moria              ernie!bert!moria!%s
```

This makes any message to Moria be delivered via Ernie and Bert. Both Moria's fully qualified name and its UUCP name have to be given if the mailer does not have a separate way to map between these name spaces.

If you want to direct all messages to hosts inside some domain to its mail relay, you may also specify a path in the pathalias database, giving the domain name as target, preceded by a dot. For example, if all hosts in the sub.org may be reached through swim!smurf, the pathalias entry might look like this:

```
\&.sub.org        swim!smurf!%s
```

Writing a pathalias file is acceptable only when you are running a site that does not have to do much routing. If you have to do routing for a large number of hosts, a better way is to use the **pathalias** command to create the file from map files. Maps can be maintained much easier, because you may simply add or remove a system by editing the system's map entry, and re-create the map file. Although the maps published by the Usenet Mapping Project aren't used for routing very much anymore, smaller UUCP networks may provide routing information in their own set of maps.

A map file mainly consists of a list of sites, listing the sites each system polls or is polled by. The system name begins in column one, and is followed by a comma-separated list of links. The list may be continued across new lines if the next line begins with a tab. Each link consists of the name of the site, followed by a cost given in brackets. The cost is an arithmetic expression, made up of numbers and symbolic costs. Lines beginning with a hash sign are ignored.

As an example, consider Moria, which polls swim.twobirds.com twice a day, and bert.sesame.com once per week. Moreover, the link to bert only uses a slow 2,400bps modem. Moria's would publish the following maps entry:

```
moria.orcnet.org
        bert.sesame.com(DAILY/2),
        swim.twobirds.com(WEEKLY+LOW)

moria.orcnet.org = moria
```

The last line would make it known under its UUCP name, too. Note that it must be DAILY/ 2, because calling twice a day actually halves the cost for this link.

Using the information from such map files, **pathalias** is able to calculate optimal routes to any destination site listed in the paths file, and produce a pathalias database from this which can then be used for routing to these sites.

pathalias provides a couple of other features like site-hiding (i.e., making sites accessible only through a gateway), and so on. See the manual page for **pathalias** for details, as well as a complete list of link costs.

Comments in the map file generally contain additional information on the sites described in it. There is a rigid format in which to specify this, so that it can be retrieved from the maps. For instance, a program called uuwho uses a database created from the map files to display this information in a nicely formatted way.

When you register your site with an organization that distributes map files to its members, you generally have to fill out such a map entry.

Below is a sample map entry (in fact, it's the one for my site):

```
#N      monad, monad.swb.de, monad.swb.sub.org
#S      AT 486DX50; Linux 0.99
#O      private
#C      Olaf Kirch
#E      okir@monad.swb.de
#P      Kattreinstr. 38, D-64295 Darmstadt, FRG
#L      49 52 03 N / 08 38 40 E
#U      brewhq
#W      okir@monad.swb.de (Olaf Kirch); Sun Jul 25 16:59:32 MET DST
#
monad   brewhq(DAILY/2)
# Domains
monad = monad.swb.de
monad = monad.swb.sub.org
```

The white space after the first two characters is a tab. The meaning of most of the fields is pretty obvious; you will receive a detailed description from whichever domain you register with. The L field is the most fun to find out: It gives your geographical position in latitude/longitude and is used to draw the PostScript maps that show all sites for each country, as well as worldwide. (They are posted regularly in **news.lists.ps-maps**. Beware. They're *huge*.)

Configuring elm

elm stands for "electronic mail" and is one of the more reasonably named tools. It provides a full-screen interface with a good help feature. We won't discuss here how to use elm, but only dwell on its configuration options.

Theoretically, you can run elm unconfigured, and everything works well—if you are lucky. But there are a few options that must be set, although only required on occasion.

When it starts, elm reads a set of configuration variables from the elm.rc file in /usr/lib/elm. Then, it will attempt to read the file .elm/elmrc in your home directory. You don't usually write this file yourself. It is created when you choose Save Options from elm's Options menu.

The set of options for the private elmrc file is also available in the global elm.rc file. Most settings in your private elmrc file override those of the global file.

Global elm Options

In the global elm.rc file, you must set the options that pertain to your host's name. For example, at the Virtual Brewery, the file for vlager would contain the following:

```
#
# The local hostname
hostname = vlager
#
# Domain name
hostdomain = .vbrew.com
#
# Fully qualified domain name
hostfullname = vlager.vbrew.com
```

These options set elm's idea of the local hostname. Although this information is rarely used, you should set these options nevertheless. Note that these options only take effect when giving them in the global configuration file; when found in your private elmrc, they will be ignored.

National Character Sets

Recently, there have been proposals to amend the RFC-822 standard to support various types of messages, such as plain text, binary data, PostScript files, and so on. The set of standards and RFCs covering these aspects are commonly referred to as MIME, or Multipurpose Internet Mail Extensions. Among other things, this also lets the recipient know if a character set other than standard ASCII has been used when writing the message, for example, using French accents or German umlauts. This is supported by elm to some extent.

The character set used by Linux internally to represent characters is usually referred to as ISO 8859-1, which is the name of the standard it conforms to. It is also known as Latin 1. Any message using characters from this character set should have the following line in its header:

```
Content-Type: text/plain; charset=iso-8859-1
```

The receiving system should recognize this field and take appropriate measures when displaying the message. The default for text/plain messages is a charset value of us-ascii.

To be able to display messages with character sets other than ASCII, elm must know how to print these characters. By default, when elm receives a message with a charset field other than us-ASCII (or a content type other than text/plain, for that matter), it tries to display the message using a command called **metamail**. Messages that require **metamail** to be displayed are shown with an "M" in the very first column in the overview screen.

Since Linux's native character set is ISO-8859-1, calling **metamail** is not necessary to display messages using this character set. If elm is told that the display understands ISO 8859-1, it will not use **metamail** but will display the message directly instead. This can be done by setting the following option in the global elm.rc:

```
displaycharset = iso-8859-1
```

Note that you should set this options even when you are never going to send or receive any messages that actually contain characters other than ASCII. This is because people who do send such messages usually configure their mailer to put the proper Content-Type: field into the mail header by default, whether or not they are sending ASCII-only messages.

However, setting this option in elm.rc is not enough. The problem is that when displaying the message with its built-in pager, elm calls a library function for each character to determine whether it is printable or not. By default, this function will only recognize ASCII characters as printable, and display all other characters as "?". You may overcome this by setting the environment variable LC_CTYPE to ISO 8859-1, which tells the library to accept Latin-1 characters as printable. Support for this and other features is available since libc-4.5.8.

When sending messages that contain special characters from ISO 8859-1, you should make sure to set two more variables in the elm.rc file:

```
charset = iso-8859-1
textencoding = 8bit
```

This makes elm report the character set as ISO 8859-1 in the mail header, and send it as an eight-bit value (the default is to strip all characters to seven bit).

Of course, any of these options can also be set in the private elmrc file instead of the global one.

Chapter 13
Getting smail Up And Running

This chapter will give you a quick introduction to setting up smail and an overview of the functionality it provides. Although smail is largely compatible with sendmail in its behavior, their configuration files are completely different.

The main configuration file is the /usr/lib/smail/config. You always have to edit this file to reflect values specific to your site. If you are only a UUCP leaf site, you will have relatively little else to do, ever. Other files that configure routing and transport options may also be used; they will be dealt with briefly, too.

By default, smail processes and delivers all incoming mail immediately. If you have relatively high traffic, you may instead have smail collect all messages in the so-called queue and process it at regular intervals only.

When handling mail within a TCP/IP network, smail is frequently run in daemon mode: At system boot time, it is invoked from rc.inet2, and puts itself in the background where it waits for incoming TCP connections on the SMTP port (usually port-25). This is very beneficial whenever you expect to have a significant amount of traffic, because smail isn't started up separately for every incoming connection. The alternative would be to have inetd manage the SMTP port and have it spawn smail whenever there is a connection on this port.

smail has a lot a flags that control its behavior; describing them in detail here wouldn't help you much. Fortunately, smail supports a number of standard modes of operation that are enabled when you invoke it by a special command name, like **rmail**, or **smtpd**.

Usually, these aliases are symbolic links to the smail binary itself. We will encounter most of them when discussing the various features of smail.

There are two links to smail you should have under all circumstances: namely, /usr/bin/rmail and /usr/sbin/sendmail. (This is the new standard location of sendmail according to the File System Standard. Another common location is /usr/lib.) When you compose and send a mail message with a user agent like elm, the message will be piped into **rmail** for delivery, with the recipient list given to it on the command line. The same happens with mail coming in via UUCP. Some versions of elm, however, invoke /usr/sbin/sendmail instead of **rmail**, so you need both of them. For example, if you keep smail in /usr/local/bin, type the following at the shell prompt:

```
# ln -s /usr/local/bin/smail /usr/bin/rmail
# ln -s /usr/local/bin/smail /usr/sbin/sendmail
```

If you want to dig further into the details of configuring smail, please refer to the manual pages smail(1) and smail(5). If it isn't included in your favorite distribution, you can get it from the source to smail.

UUCP Setup

To use smail in a UUCP-only environment, the basic installation is rather simple. First, you must make sure you have the two symbolic links to **rmail** and **sendmail** mentioned above. If you expect to receive SMTP batches from other sites, you also have to make **rsmtp** a link to smail.

In Vince Skahan's smail distribution, you will find a sample configuration file. It is named config.sample and resides in /usr/lib/smail. You have to copy it to config and edit it to reflect values specific to your site.

Assume your site is named swim.twobirds.com, and is registered in the UUCP maps as swim. Your smart host is Ulysses. Then your config file should look like this:

```
#
# Our domain names
visible domain=two.birds:uucp
#
# Our name on outgoing mails
visible name=swim.twobirds.com
#
# Use this as uucp-name as well
uucp name=swim.twobirds.com
#
# Our smarthost
        smart host=ulysses
```

The first statement tells smail about the domains your site belongs to. Insert their names here, separated by colons. If your site name is registered in the UUCP maps, you should also add uucp. When being handed a mail message, smail determines your host's name using the hostname(2) system call, and checks the recipient's address against this hostname, tacking on all names from this list in turn. If the address matches any of these names or the unqualified hostname, the recipient is considered local, and smail attempts to deliver the message to a user or alias on the local host. Otherwise, the recipient is considered remote, and delivery to the destination host is attempted.

visible_name should contain a single, fully qualified domain name of your site that you want to use on outgoing mail. This name is used when generating the sender's address on all outgoing mail. You must make sure to use a name that smail recognizes as referring to the local host (i.e., the hostname with one of the domains listed in the visible_domain attribute). Otherwise, replies to your mail will bounce off your site.

The last statement sets the path used for smart-host routing. With this sample setup, smail will forward any mail for remote addresses to the smart host. The path specified in the smart_path attribute will be used as a route to the smart host. Since messages will be delivered via UUCP, the attribute must specify a system known to your UUCP software. Please refer to Chapter 11 on making a site known to UUCP.

There's one option used in the above file that we haven't explained yet; this is uucp_name. The reason to use the option is this: By default, smail uses the value returned by hostname(2) for UUCP-specific things, such as the return path given in the From_ header line. If your hostname is not registered with the UUCP mapping project, you should tell smail to use your fully qualified domain name instead. (The reason is this: Assume your hostname is Monad, but is not registered in the maps. However, there is a site in the maps called Monad, so every mail to monad!root, even sent from a direct UUCP neighbor of yours, will wind up on the other Monad. This is a nuisance for everybody.) This can be done by adding the uucp_name option to the config file.

There is another file in /usr/lib/smail, called paths.sample. It is an example of what a paths file might look like. However, you will not need one unless you have mail links to more than one site. If you do, however, you will have to write one yourself, or generate one from the Usenet maps. The paths file will be described later in this chapter.

Setup For A LAN

If you are running a site with two or more hosts connected by a LAN, you will have to designate one host that handles your UUCP connection with the outside world. Between the hosts on your LAN, you will most probably want to exchange mail with SMTP over TCP/IP. Assume we're back at the Virtual Brewery again, and vstout is set up as the UUCP gateway.

In a networked environment, it is best to keep all user mailboxes on a single file system, which is NFS-mounted on all other hosts. This allows users to move from machine to machine, without having to move their mail around (or even worse, check some three or four machines for newly arrived mail each morning). Therefore, you also want to make sender addresses independent from the machine the mail was written on. It is common practice to use the domain name all by itself in the sender address, instead of a hostname. Janet User, for example, would specify **janet@vbrew.com** instead of **janet@vale.vbrew.com**. We will explain below how to make the server recognize the domain name as a valid name for your site.

A different way of keeping all mailboxes on a central host is to use POP or IMAP. POP stands for Post Office Protocol and lets users access their mailboxes over a simple TCP/IP connection. IMAP, the Interactive Mail Access Protocol, is similar to POP, but more general. Both clients and servers for IMAP and POP have been ported to Linux, and are available from **sunsite.unc.edu** below **/pub/Linux/system/Network**.

Writing The Configuration Files

The configuration for the Brewery works as follows: all hosts except the mail server vstout itself route all outgoing mail to the server, using smart-host routing. vstout itself sends all outgoing mail to the real smart host that routes all of the Brewery's mail; this host is called Moria.

The standard config file for all hosts other than vstout looks like this:

```
#
# Our domain:
visible domain=vbrew.com
#
# What we name ourselves
visible name=vbrew.com
#
# Smart-host routing: via SMTP to vstout
smart path=vstout
smart transport=smtp
```

This is very similar to what we used for a UUCP-only site. The main difference is that the transport used to send mail to the smart host is, of course, SMTP. The visible_domain attribute makes smail use the domain name instead of the local hostname on all outgoing mail.

On the UUCP mail gateway vstout, the config file looks a little different:

```
# Our hostnames:
hostnames=vbrew.com:vstout.vbrew.com:vstout
#
# What we name ourselves
visible name=vbrew.com
#
# in the uucp world, we're known as vbrew.com
```

```
uucp name=vbrew.com
#
# Smart transport: via uucp to moria
smart path=moria
smart transport=uux
#
# we're authoritative for our domain
auth domains=vbrew.com
```

This config file uses a different scheme to tell smail what the local host is called. Instead of giving it a list of domains and letting it find the hostname with a system call, it specifies a list explicitly. The above list contains both the fully qualified and the unqualified hostname and the domain name all by itself. This makes smail recognize **janet@vbrew.com** as a local address and deliver the message to Janet.

The auth_domains variable names the domains for which vstout is considered to be authoritative. That is, if smail receives any mail addressed to host.vbrew.com where host does not name an existing local machine, it rejects the message and returns it to the sender. If this entry isn't present, any such message will be sent to the smart host, who will return it to vstout, and so on until it is discarded for exceeding the maximum hop count.

Running smail

First, you have to decide whether to run smail as a separate daemon, or whether to have inetd manage the SMTP port and invoke smail only whenever an SMTP connection is requested from some client. Usually, you will prefer daemon operation on the mail server, because this loads the machine far less than spawning smail over and over again for each single connection. As the mail server also delivers most incoming mail directly to the users, you will choose inetd operation on most other hosts.

Whatever mode of operation you choose for each individual host, you have to make sure you have the following entry in your /etc/services file:

```
smtp            25/tcp          # Simple Mail Transfer Protocol
```

This defines the TCP port number that smail should use for SMTP conversations. Twenty-five is the standard defined by the Assigned Numbers RFC.

When run in daemon mode, smail will put itself in the background and wait for a connection to occur on the SMTP port. When a connection occurs, it forks and conducts an SMTP conversation with the peer process. The smail daemon is usually started by invoking it from the rc.inet2 script using the following command:

```
/usr/local/bin/smail -bd -q15m
```

The **-bd** flag turns on daemon mode, and **-q15m** makes it process whatever messages have accumulated in the message queue every 15 minutes.

If you want to use inetd instead, your /etc/inetd.conf file should contain a line like this:

```
smtp    stream tcp nowait  root  /usr/sbin/smtpd smtpd
```

smtpd should be a symbolic link to the smail binary. Remember you have to make inetd re-read inetd.conf by sending it a HUP signal after making these changes.

Daemon mode and inetd mode are mutually exclusive. If you run smail in daemon mode, you should make sure to comment out any line in inetd.conf for the smtp service. Equivalently, when having inetd manage smail, make sure that rc.inet2 does not start the smail daemon.

If You Don't Get Through...

If something goes wrong with your installation, there are a number of features that may help you find what's at the root of the problem. The first place to check are smail's log files. They are kept in /var/spool/smail/log, and are named logfile and paniclog, respectively. The former lists all transactions, while the latter is only for error messages related to configuration errors and the like.

A typical entry in logfile looks like this:

```
04/24/94 07:12:04: [m0puwU8-00023UB] received
|            from: root
|         program: sendmail
|            size: 1468 bytes
04/24/94 07:12:04: [m0puwU8-00023UB] delivered
|             via: vstout.vbrew.com
|              to: root@vstout.vbrew.com
|         orig-to: root@vstout.vbrew.com
|          router: smart host
|       transport: smtp
```

This shows that a message from root to root@vstout.vbrew.com has been properly delivered to host vstout over SMTP.

Messages smail could not deliver generate a similar entry in the log file, but with an error message instead of the delivered part:

```
04/24/94 07:12:04: [m0puwU8-00023UB] received
|            from: root
|         program: sendmail
|            size: 1468 bytes
```

```
04/24/94 07:12:04: [mOpuwU8-00023UB] root@vstout.vbrew.com ... defer
  (ERR 148) transport smtp: connect: Connection refused
```

The above error is typical for a situation in which smail properly recognizes that the message should be delivered to vstout, but was not able to connect to the SMTP service on vstout. If this happens, you either have a configuration problem, or TCP support is missing from your smail binaries.

This problem is not as uncommon as one might think. There have been precompiled smail binaries around, even in some distributions, without support for TCP/IP networking. If this is the case for you, you have to compile smail yourself. Having installed smail, you can check if it has TCP networking support by telnetting to the SMTP port on your machine. A successful connect to the SMTP server is shown below (your input is marked like this):

```
telnet localhost smtp
Trying 127.0.0.1...
Connected to localhost.
Escape character is '^]'.
220 monad.swb.de Smail3.1.28.1 #6 ready at Sun, 23 Jan 94
19:26 MET
QUIT
221 monad.swb.de closing connection
```

If this test doesn't produce the SMTP banner (the line starting with the 220 code), first make sure that your configuration is really correct before you go through compiling smail yourself, which is described below.

If you encounter a problem with smail that you are unable to locate from the error message smail generates, you may want to turn on debugging messages. You can do this using the **-d** flag, optionally followed by a number specifying the level of verbosity (you may not have any space between the flag and the numerical argument). smail will then print a report of its operation to the screen, which may give you more hints about what is going wrong.

If nothing else helps, you may want to invoke smail in Rogue mode by giving the **-bR** option on the command line. The manpage says on this option: "Enter the hostile domain of giant mail messages, and RFC standard scrolls. Attempt to make it down to protocol level 26 and back." Although this option won't solve your problems, it may provide you some comfort and consolation.

Compiling smail

If you know for sure that smail is lacking TCP network support, you have to get the source. It is probably included in your distribution, if you got it via CD-ROM, otherwise you may get it from the net via FTP at **ftp://ftp.planix.com/pub/Smail/**.

When compiling smail, you had best start with the set of configuration files from Vince Skahan's newspak distribution. To compile in the TCP networking driver, you have to set the DRIVER_CONFIGURATION macro in the conf/EDITME file to either bsd-network or arpa-network. The former is suitable for LAN installations, but the Internet requires arpa-network. The difference between these two is that the latter has a special driver for BIND service that is able to recognize MX records, which the former doesn't.

Mail Delivery Modes

As noted above, smail is able to deliver messages immediately or queue them for later processing. If you choose to queue messages, smail will store away all mail in the messages directory below /var/spool/smail. It will not process them until explicitly told so (this is also called "running the queue").

You can select one of three delivery modes by setting the delivery_mode attribute in the config file to either of foreground, background, or queued. These select delivery in the foreground (immediate processing of incoming messages), in the background (message is delivered by a child of the receiving process, with the parent process exiting immediately after forking), and queued. Incoming mail will always be queued regardless of this option if the Boolean variable queue_only is set in the config file.

If you turn on queuing, you have to make sure the queues are checked regularly; probably every 10 or 15 minutes. If you run smail in daemon mode, you have to add the option **-q10m** on the command line to process the queue every 10 minutes. Alternatively, you can invoke **runq** from **cron** at these intervals. **runq** should be a link to smail.

You can display the current mail queue by invoking smail with the **-bp** option. Equivalently, you can make **mailq** a link to smail, and invoke **mailq**:

```
$ mailq -v
m0pvB1r-00023UB From: root   (in /var/spool/smail/input)
                Date: Sun, 24 Apr 94 07:12 MET DST
                Args: -oem -oMP sendmail root@vstout.vbrew.com
Log of transactions:
 Xdefer: <root@vstout.vbrew.com reason: (ERR 148) transport smtp:
 connect: Connection refused
```

This shows a single message sitting in the message queue. The transaction log (which is only displayed if you give **mailq** the **-v** option) may give an additional reason why it is still waiting for delivery. If no attempt has been made yet to deliver the message, no transaction log will be displayed.

Even when you don't use queuing, smail will occasionally put messages into the queue when it finds immediate delivery fails for a transient reason. For SMTP connections, this may be an unreachable host; but messages may also be deferred when the file system is found to be full. You should therefore put in a queue run every hour or so (using **runq**), else any deferred message will stick around the queue forever.

Miscellaneous config Options

There are quite a number of options you may set in the config file, which, although useful, are not essential to running smail and which we will not discuss here. Instead, we will only mention a few that you might find a reason to use:

♦ **error copy postmaster**—If this Boolean variable is set, any error will generate a message to the postmaster. Usually, this is only done for errors that are due to a faulty configuration. The variable can be turned on by putting it in the config file, preceded by a plus (+).

♦ **max hop count**—If the hop count for a message (i.e., the number of hosts already traversed) equals or exceeds this number, attempts at remote delivery will result in an error message being returned to the sender. This is used to prevent messages from looping forever. The hop count is generally computed from the number of Received: fields in the mail header, but may also be set manually using the **-h** option on the command line. This variable defaults to 20.

♦ **postmaster**—The postmaster's address. If the address postmaster cannot be resolved to a valid local address, then this is used as the last resort. The default is root.

Message Routing And Delivery

smail splits up mail delivery into three different tasks: the router, director, and transport modules.

The router module resolves all remote addresses, determining to which host the message should be sent to next and which transport must be used. Depending on the nature of the link, different transports such as UUCP or SMTP may be used.

Local addresses are given to the director task which resolves any forwarding or aliasing. For example, the address might be an alias or a mailing list, or the user might want to forward her mail to another address. If the resulting address is remote, it is handed to the router module for additional routing, otherwise it is assigned a transport for local delivery. By far the most common case will be delivery to a mailbox, but messages may also be piped into a command or appended to some arbitrary file.

The transport module, finally, is responsible for whatever method of delivery has been chosen. It tries to deliver the message, and in case of failure either generates a bounce message or defers it for a later retry.

With smail, you have much freedom in configuring these tasks. For each of them, a number of drivers are available, from which you can choose those you need. You describe them to smail in a couple of files, namely routers, directors, and transports, located in /usr/lib/smail.

If these files do not exist, reasonable defaults are assumed that should be suitable for many sites that either use SMTP or UUCP for transport. If you want to change smail's routing policy or modify a transport, you should get the sample files from the smail source distribution (the default configuration files can be found in samples/generic below the source directory), copy the sample files to /usr/lib/smail, and modify them according to your needs. Sample configuration files are also given in the Appendix.

Routing Messages

When given a message, smail first checks if the destination is the local host or a remote site. If the target host address is one of the local hostnames configured in config, the message is handed to the director module. Otherwise, smail hands the destination address to a number of router drivers to find out which host to forward a message to. They can be described in the routers file; if this file does not exist, a set of default routers are used.

The destination host is passed to all routers in turn, and the one finding the most specific route is selected. Consider a message addressed to **joe@foo.bar.com**. Then, one router might know a default route for all hosts in the bar.com domain, while another one has information for foo.bar.com itself. Since the latter is more specific, it is chosen over the former. If there are two routers that provide a "best match," the one coming first in the routers file is chosen.

This router now specifies the transport to be used, for instance, UUCP, and generates a new destination address. The new address is passed to the transport along with the host to forward the message to. In the above example, smail might find out that foo.bar.com is to be reached via UUCP using the path ernie!bert. It will then generate a new target of bert!foo.bar.com!user, and have the UUCP transport use this as the envelope address to be passed to ernie.

When using the default setup, the following routers are available:

♦ If the destination host address can be resolved using the gethostbyname(3) or gethostbyaddr(3) library call, the message will be delivered via SMTP. The only exception is if the address is found to refer to the local host, it is handed to the director module, too.

  smail also recognizes IP addresses written as dotted quad as a legal hostname, as long as they can be resolved through a gethostbyaddr(3) call. For example, **scrooge@ [149.76.12.4]** would be a valid although highly unusual mail address for scrooge on quark.physics.groucho.edu.

♦ If your machine is on the Internet, these routers are not what you are looking for, because they do not support MX records. See below for what to do in this case.

♦ If /usr/lib/smail/paths, the pathalias database, exists, smail will try to look up the target host (minus any trailing .uucp) in this file. Mail to an address matched by this router will be delivered using UUCP, using the path found in the database.

♦ The host address (minus any trailing .uucp) will be compared to the output of the **uuname** command to check if the target host is in fact a UUCP neighbor. If this is the case, the message will be delivered using the UUCP transport.

♦ If the address has not been matched by any of the above routers, it will be delivered to the smart host. The path to the smart host as well as the transport to be used are set in the config file.

These defaults work for many simple setups, but fail if routing requirements get a little more complicated. If you are faced with any of the problems discussed below, you will have to install your own routers file to override the defaults. A sample routers file you might start with is given in the Appendix. Some distributions also come with a set of configuration files that are tailored to work around these difficulties.

Probably the worst problems arise when your host lives in a dual universe with both dial-up IP and UUCP links. You will then have hostnames in your hosts file that you only talk occasionally to through your SLIP link, so smail will attempt to deliver any mail for these hosts via SMTP. This is usually not what you want, because even if the SLIP link is activated regularly, SMTP is much slower than sending the mail over UUCP. With the default setup, there's no way of escaping smail.

You can avoid this problem by having smail check the paths file before querying the resolver, and put all hosts you want to force UUCP delivery to into the paths file. If you don't want to send any messages over SMTP ever, you can also comment out the resolver-based routers altogether.

Another problem is that the default setup doesn't provide for true Internet mail routing, because the resolver-based router does not evaluate MX records. To enable full support for Internet mail routing, comment out this router, and uncomment the one that used BIND instead. There are, however, smail binaries included in some distributions that don't have BIND support compiled in. If you enable BIND, but get a message in the paniclog file saying "router inet_hosts: driver bind not found," then you have to get the sources and recompile smail.

Finally, it is not generally a good idea to use the uuname driver. For one, it will generate a configuration error when you don't have UUCP installed, because no **uuname** command will be found. The second is when you have more sites listed in your UUCP Systems file than you actually have mail links with. These may be sites you only exchange news with, or sites you occasionally download files from via anonymous UUCP, but have no traffic with otherwise.

To work around the first problem, you can substitute a shell script for uuname which does a simple exit 0. The more general solution is, however, to edit the routers file and remove this driver altogether.

The Paths Database

smail expects to find the pathalias database in the paths file below /usr/lib/smail. This file is optional, so if you don't want to perform any pathalias routing at all, simply remove any existing paths file.

Paths must be a sorted ASCII file that contains entries which map destination site names to UUCP bang paths. The file has to be sorted because smail uses a binary search for looking up a site. Comments are not allowed in this file, and the site name must be separated from the path using a tab. Pathalias databases are discussed in somewhat greater detail in Chapter 12.

If you generate this file by hand, you should make sure to include all legal names for a site. For example, if a site is known by both a plain UUCP name and a fully qualified domain name, you have to add an entry for each of them. The file can be sorted by piping it through the **sort(1)** command.

If your site is only a leaf site, however, then no paths file should be necessary at all: Just set up the smart host attributes in your config file, and leave all routing to your mail feed.

Delivering Messages To Local Addresses

Most commonly, a local address is just a user's login name, in which case the message is delivered to her mailbox, /var/spool/mail/user. Other cases include aliases and mailing list names and mail forwarding by the user. In these cases, the local address expands to a new list of addresses, which may be either local or remote.

Apart from these "normal" addresses, smail can handle other types of local message destinations, like file names and pipe commands. These are not addresses in their own right, so you can't send mail to, say, **/etc/passwd@vbrew.com**; they are only valid if they have been taken from forwarding or alias files.

A file name is anything that begins with a slash (/) or a tilde (~). The latter refers to the user's home directory, and is possible only if the file name was taken from a .forward file or a forwarding entry in the mailbox (see below). When delivering to a file, smail appends the messages to the file, creating it if necessary.

A pipe command may be any command preceded by the pipe symbol (|). This causes smail to hand the command to the shell along with its arguments, but without the leading "|". The message itself is fed to this command on standard input.

For example, to gate a mailing list into a local newsgroup, you might use a shell script named gateit, and set up a local alias which delivers all messages from this mailing list to the script using " | gateit".

If the invocation contains white space, it has to be enclosed in double quotes. Due to the security issues involved, care is taken not to execute the command if the address has been obtained in a somewhat dubious way (for example, if the alias file from which the address was taken was writable by everyone).

Local Users

The most common case for a local address is to denote a user's mailbox. This mailbox is located in /var/spool/mail and has the name of the user. It is owned by her, with a group of mail, and has mode 660. If it does not exist, it is created by smail.

Note that although /var/spool/mail is currently the standard place to put the mailbox files, some mail software may have different paths compiled in, for example, /usr/spool/mail. If delivery to users on your machine fails consistently, you should try if it helps to make this a symbolic link to /var/spool/mail.

There are two addresses smail requires to exist: MAILER-DAEMON and postmaster. When generating a bounce message for an undeliverable mail, a carbon copy is sent to the postmaster account for examination (in case this might be due to a configuration problem). The MAILER-DAEMON is used as the sender's address on the bounce message.

If these addresses do not name valid accounts on your system, smail implicitly maps MAILER-DAEMON to postmaster, and postmaster to root, respectively. You should usually override this by aliasing the postmaster account to whoever is responsible for maintaining the mail software.

Forwarding

A user may redirect her mail by having it forwarded to an alternative address using one of two methods supported by smail. One option is to put

```
Forward to recipient,...
```

in the first line of her mailbox file. This will send all incoming mail to the specified list of recipients. Alternatively, she might create a .forward file in her home directory, which contains the comma-separated list of recipients. With this variety of forwarding, all lines of the file are read and interpreted.

Note that any type of address may be used. Thus, a practical example of a .forward file for vacations might be

```
janet, "|vacation"
```

The first address delivers the incoming message to Janet's mailbox nevertheless, while the **vacation** command returns a short notification to the sender.

Alias Files

smail is able to handle alias files compatible with those known by Berkeley's sendmail. Entries in the alias file may have the form

```
alias: recipients
```

Recipients is a comma-separated list of addresses that will be substituted for the alias. The recipient list may be continued across new lines if the next line begins with a tab.

There is a special feature that allows smail to handle mailing lists from the alias file: If you specify ":include:filename" as recipient, smail will read the file specified and substitute its contents as a list of recipients.

The main aliases file is /usr/lib/aliases. If you choose to make this file world-writable, smail will not deliver any messages to shell commands given in this file. A sample file is shown below:

```
# vbrew.com /usr/lib/aliases file
hostmaster: janet
postmaster: janet
usenet: phil
# The development mailing list.
development: joe, sue, mark, biff
        /var/mail/log/development
owner-development: joe
# Announcements of general interest are mailed to all
# of the staff
announce: :include: /usr/lib/smail/staff,
          /var/mail/log/announce
owner-announce: root
# gate the foobar mailing list to a local newsgroup
ppp-list: "|/usr/local/lib/gateit local.lists.ppp"
```

If an error occurs while delivering to an address generated from the aliases file, smail will attempt to send a copy of the error message to the "alias owner." For example, if delivery to biff fails when delivering a message to the development mailing list, a copy of the error message will be mailed to the sender, as well as to postmaster and owner-development. If the owner address does not exist, no additional error message will be generated.

When delivering to files or when invoking programs given in the aliases file, smail will become the nobody user to avoid any security hassles. Especially when delivering to files, this can be a real nuisance. In the file given above, for instance, the log files must be owned and writable by nobody, or delivery to them will fail.

Mailing Lists

Instead of using the aliases file, mailing lists may also be managed by means of files in the /usr/lib/smail/lists directory. A mailing list named nag-bugs is described by the file lists/nag-bugs, which should contain the members' addresses, separated by commas. The list may be given on multiple lines, with comments being introduced by a hash sign.

For each mailing list, a user (or alias) named owner-listname should exist; any errors occurring when resolving an address are reported to this user. This address is also used as the sender's address on all outgoing messages in the Sender: header field.

UUCP-Based Transports

There are a number of transports compiled into smail that utilize the UUCP suite. In a UUCP environment, messages are usually passed on by invoking rmail on the next host, giving it the message on standard input and the envelope address on the command line. On your host, **rmail** should be a link to the smail command.

When handing a message to the UUCP transport, smail converts the target address to a UUCP bang path. For example, **user@host** will be transformed to **host!user**. Any occurrence of the "%" address operator is preserved, so **user%host@gateway** will become **gateway!user%host**. However, smail will never generate such addresses itself.

Alternatively, smail can send and receive BSMTP batches via UUCP. With BSMTP, one or more messages are wrapped up in a single batch that contains the commands the local mailer would issue if a real SMTP connection had be established. BSMTP is frequently used in store-and-forward (e.g., UUCP-based) networks to save disk space. The sample transports file in the Appendix contains a transport dubbed bsmtp that generates partial BSMTP batches in a queue directory. They must be combined into the final batches later, using a shell script that adds the appropriate **HELO** and **QUIT** command.

To enable the bsmtp transport for specific UUCP links you have to use so-called method files (please refer to the smail(5) manual page for details). If you have only one UUCP link and use the smart host router, you enable sending SMTP batches by setting the smart_transport configuration variable to bsmtp instead of uux.

To receive SMTP batches over UUCP, you must make sure that you have the un-batching command the remote site sends its batches to. If the remote site uses smail, too, you need to make **rsmtp** a link to smail. If the remote site runs sendmail, you should additionally install a shell script named /usr/bin/bsmtp that does a simple "exec rsmtp" (a symbolic link won't work).

SMTP-Based Transports

smail currently supports an SMTP driver to deliver mail over TCP connections. (The authors call this support "simple." For a future version of smail, they advertise a complete back end which will handle this more efficiently.) It is capable of delivering a message to any number of addresses on one single host, with the hostname being specified as either a fully qualified domain name that can be resolved by the networking software, or in dotted quad notation enclosed in square brackets. Generally, addresses resolved by any of the BIND, gethostbyname(3), or gethostbyaddr(3) router drivers will be delivered to the SMTP transport.

The SMTP driver will attempt to connect to the remote host immediately through the smtp port as listed in /etc/services. If it cannot be reached, or the connection times out, delivery will be re-attempted at a later time.

Delivery on the Internet requires that routes to the destination host be specified in the route-addr format described in Chapter 12, rather than as a bang path. (However, the use of routes in the Internet is discouraged altogether. Fully qualified domain names should be used instead.) smail will therefore transform **user%host@gateway**, where gateway is reached via host1!host2!host3, into the source-route address <@host2,@host3:user%host@gateway> which will be sent as the message's envelope address to host1. To enable these transformation (along with the built-in BIND driver), you have to edit the entry for the smtp driver in the transports file. A sample transports file is given in the Appendix.

Hostname Qualification

Sometimes it is desirable to catch unqualified hostnames (i.e., those that don't have a domain name) specified in sender or recipient addresses, for example, when gatewaying between two networks, where one requires fully qualified domain names. On an Internet-UUCP relay, unqualified hostnames should be mapped to the uucp domain by default. Other address modifications than these are questionable.

The /usr/lib/smail/qualify file tells smail which domain names to tack onto which hostnames. Entries in the qualify file consists of a hostname beginning in column one, followed by domain name. Lines containing a hash sign as its first nonwhite character are considered comments. Entries are searched in the order they appear in.

If no qualify file exists, no hostname qualification is performed at all.

A special hostname of * matches any hostnames, thus enabling you to map all hosts not mentioned before into a default domain. It should be used only as the last entry.

At the Virtual Brewery, all hosts have been set up to use fully qualified domain names in the sender's addresses. Unqualified recipient addresses are considered to be in the uucp domain, so only a single entry in the qualify file is needed.

```
# /usr/lib/smail/qualify, last changed Feb 12, 1994 by janet
#
*           uucp
```

Chapter 14
Introduction To Sendmail+IDA

I t's been said that you aren't a real Unix system administrator until you've edited a sendmail.cf file. It's also been said that you're crazy if you've attempted to do so twice.

sendmail is an incredibly powerful program. It's also incredibly difficult to learn and understand for most people. Any program whose definitive reference (*Sendmail*, published by O'Reilly and Associates) is 792 pages long quite justifiably scares most people off.

Sendmail+IDA is different.

Note
*Please refer to **http://send.mail/com/** or **http://send.mail/org/** for the current Sendmail version.*

It removes the need to edit the always cryptic sendmail.cf file and allows the administrator to define the site-specific routing and addressing configuration through relatively easy-to-understand support files called tables. Switching to Sendmail+IDA can save you many hours of work and stress.

Compared to the other major mail transport agents, there is probably nothing that can't be done faster and simpler with Sendmail+IDA. Typical things that are needed to run a normal UUCP or Internet site become simple to accomplish. Configurations that normally are extremely difficult are simple to create and maintain.

At this writing, the current version of Sendmail5.67b+IDA1.5 is available via anonymous FTP from **vixen.cso.uiuc.edu**. It compiles without any patching required under Linux.

All the configuration files required to get sendmail+IDA sources to compile, install, and run under are included in newspak-2.2.tar.gz, which is available via anonymous FTP on **sunsite.unc.edu** in the directory **/pub/Linux/system/Mail**.

Configuration Files: Overview

Traditional sendmail is set up through a system configuration file (typically /etc/sendmail.cf or /usr/lib/sendmail.cf) that is not anything close to any language you've seen before. Editing the sendmail.cf file to provide customized behavior can be a humbling experience.

Sendmail+IDA makes such pain essentially a thing of the past by having all configuration options table-driven with rather easy-to-understand syntax. These options are configured by running m4 (a macro processor) or dbm (a database processor) on a number of data files via Makefiles supplied with the sources.

The sendmail.cf file defines only the default behavior of the system. Virtually all special customization is done through a number of optional tables rather than by directly editing the sendmail.cf file. Here is a list of recent sendmail files:

```
/etc/aliases        raw data for alias names
/etc/aliases.db     data base of alias names
/etc/sendmail.cf    configuration file
/etc/sendmail.hf    help file
/var/log/sendmail.st  collected statistics
/var/spool/mqueue/*   temp files
/var/run/sendmail.pid   The process id of the daemon
```

The sendmail.cf File

The sendmail.cf file for Sendmail+IDA is not edited directly, but is generated from an m4 configuration file provided by the local system administrator. In the following, we will refer to it as sendmail.m4.

This file contains a few definitions and otherwise merely points to the tables where the real work gets done. In general, it is only necessary to specify:

♦ the path names and file names used on the local system.

♦ the name(s) the site is known by for email purposes.

♦ which default mailer (and perhaps smart relay host) is desired.

There is a large variety of parameters that can be defined to establish the behavior of the local site or to override compiled-in configuration items. These configuration options are identified in the file ida/cf/OPTIONS in the source directory.

A sendmail.m4 file for a minimal configuration (UUCP or SMTP with all nonlocal mail being relayed to a directly connected smart host) can be as short as 10 or 15 lines excluding comments.

Typically Used sendmail.m4 Parameters

A few of the items in the sendmail.m4 file are required all the time; others can be ignored if you can get away with defaults. The following sections describe each of the items in the example sendmail.m4 file in more detail.

Items That Define Paths

LIBDIR defines the directory where Sendmail+IDA expects to find configuration files, the various dbm tables, and special local definitions. In a typical binary distribution, this is compiled into the sendmail binary and does not need to be explicitly set in the sendmail.m4 file.

Defining The Local Mailer

Most operating systems provide a program to handle local delivery of mail. Typical programs for many of the major variants of Unix are already built into the sendmail binary.

In Linux, it is necessary to explicitly define the appropriate local mailer since a local delivery program is not necessarily present in the distribution you've installed. This is done by specifying LOCAL_MAILER_DEF in the sendmail.m4 file.

For example, to have the commonly used deliver program provide this service, you would set LOCAL_MAILER_DEF to mailers.linux.

Note

*Deliver was written by Chip Salzenberg (**chip%tct@ateng.com**). It is part of several distributions and can be found in the usual anonymous FTP archives such as **ftp.uu.net**.*

Dealing With Bounced Mail

Many sites find that it is important to ensure that mail is sent and received with close to a 100 percent success rate. While examining syslogd(8) logs is helpful, the local mail administrator generally needs to see the headers on bounced mail in order to determine if the mail was undeliverable because of user error or a configuration error on one of the systems involved.

Defining POSTMASTERBOUNCE results in a copy of each bounced message being set to the person defined as Postmaster for the system.

Unfortunately, setting this parameter also results in the text of the message being sent to the Postmaster, which potentially has related privacy concerns for people using mail on the system.

Site postmasters should in general attempt to discipline themselves (or do so via technical means through shell scripts that delete the text of the bounce messages they receive) from reading mail not addressed to them.

Domain Name Service Related Items

There are several well-known networks that are commonly referenced in mail addresses for historical reasons but that are not valid for DNS purposes. Defining PSEUDODOMAINS prevents needless DNS lookup attempts that will always fail.

Defining Names The Local System Is Known By

Frequently, systems wish to hide their true identity, serve as mail gateways, or receive and process mail addressed to "old" names by which they used to be known.

PSEUDONYMS specifies the list of all hostnames for which the local system will accept mail.

DEFAULT_HOST specifies the hostname that will appear in messages originating on the local host. It is important that this parameter be set to a valid value or all return mail will be undeliverable.

UUCP-Related Items

Frequently, systems are known by one name for DNS purposes and another for UUCP purposes. UUCPNAME permits you to define a different hostname that appears in the headers of outgoing UUCP mail.

UUCPNODES defines the commands that return a list of hostnames for the systems we are connected directly to via UUCP connections.

BANGIMPLIESUUCP and BANGONLYUUCP ensure that mail addressed with UUCP "bang" syntax is treated according to UUCP behavior rather than the more current Domain Name Service behavior used today on Internet.

Relay Systems And Mailers

Many system administrators do not want to be bothered with the work needed to ensure that their system is able to reach all the networks (and therefore systems) on all networks worldwide. Instead of doing so, they would rather relay all outgoing mail to another system that is known to be indeed "smart."

RELAY_HOST defines the UUCP hostname of such a smart neighboring system.

RELAY_MAILER defines the mailer used to relay the messages there.

It is important to note that setting these parameters results in your outgoing mail being forwarded to this remote system, which will affect the load of their system. Be certain to get explicit agreement from the remote Postmaster before you configure your system to use another system as a general-purpose relay host.

The Various Configuration Tables

With these macros, you can change the location where Sendmail+IDA looks for the various dbm tables that define the system's "real" behavior. It is generally wise to leave them in LIBDIR.

The Master sendmail.mc File

The authors of Sendmail+IDA provide the sendmail.mc file, which contains the true "guts" of what becomes the sendmail.cf file. Periodically, new versions are released to fix bugs or add functionality without requiring a full release and recompilation of sendmail from sources.

It is important not to edit this file.

So Which Entries Are Really Required?

When not using any of the optional dbm tables, Sendmail+IDA delivers mail via the DEFAULT_MAILER (and possibly RELAY_HOST and RELAY_MAILER) defined in the sendmail.m4 file used to generate sendmail.cf. It is easily possible to override this behavior through entries in the domaintable or uucpxtable.

A generic site that is on Internet and speaks Domain Name Service, or one that is UUCP-only and forwards all mail via UUCP through a smart RELAY_HOST, probably does not need any specific table entries at all.

Virtually all systems should set the DEFAULT_HOST and PSEUDONYMS macros, which define the canonical site name and aliases it is known by, and DEFAULT_MAILER. If all you have is a relay host and relay mailer, you don't need to set these defaults since it works automatically.

UUCP hosts will probably also need to set UUCPNAME to their official UUCP name. They will also probably set RELAY_MAILER, and RELAY_HOST, which enable smart-host routing through a mail relay. The mail transport to be used is defined in RELAY_MAILER and should usually be UUCP-A for UUCP sites.

If your site is SMTP-only and talks Domain Name Service, you would change the DEFAULT_MAILER to TCP-A and probably delete the RELAY_MAILER and RELAY_HOST lines.

A Tour Of Sendmail+IDA Tables

Sendmail+IDA provides a number of tables that allow you to override the default behavior of sendmail (specified in the sendmail.m4 file) and define special behavior for unique situations, remote systems, and networks. These tables are post-processed with dbm using the Makefile provided with the distribution.

Most sites will need few, if any, of these tables. If your site does not require these tables, the easiest thing is probably to make them zero-length files (with the **touch** command) and use the default Makefile in LIBDIR rather than editing the Makefile itself.

mailertable

The mailertable defines special treatment for specific hosts or domains based on the remote host or network name. It is frequently used on Internet sites to select an intermediate mail relay host or gateway to reach a remote network through, and to specify a particular protocol (UUCP or SMTP) to be used. UUCP sites will generally not need to use this file.

Order is important. sendmail reads the file top-down and processes the message according to the first rule it matches. So it is generally wise to place the most explicit rules at the top of the file and the more generic rules below.

There are a number of possible mailers. The differences are generally in how they treat addresses. Typical mailers are TCP-A (TCP/IP with Internet-style addresses), TCP-U (TCP/IP with UUCP-style addresses), and UUCP-A (UUCP with Internet-style addresses).

The character that separates the mailer from the host portion on the left-hand side of a mailertable line defines how the address is modified by the mailertable. The important thing to realize is that this only rewrites the envelope (to get the mail into the remote system). Rewriting anything other than the envelope is generally frowned upon due to the high probability of breaking the mail configuration.

uucpxtable

Usually, mail to hosts with fully qualified domain names is delivered via Internet-style (SMTP) delivery using Domain Name Service (DNS) or via the relay host. The uucpxtable forces delivery via UUCP routing by converting the domainized name into a UUCP-style un-domainized remote hostname.

It is frequently used when you're a mail forwarder for a site or domain or when you wish to send mail via a direct and reliable UUCP link rather than potentially multiple hops through the default mailer and any intermediate systems and networks.

UUCP sites that talk to UUCP neighbors who use domainized mail headers would use this file to force delivery of the mail through the direct UUCP point-to-point link between the two systems rather than using the less direct route through the RELAY_MAILER and RELAY_HOST or through the DEFAULT_MAILER.

Internet sites who do not talk UUCP probably would not use the uucpxtable.

Suppose you provide mail forwarding service to a system called sesame.com in DNS and sesame in the UUCP maps. You would need the following uucpxtable entry to force mail for their host to go through your direct UUCP connection.

pathtable

The pathtable is used to define explicit routing to remote hosts or networks. The pathtable file should be in pathalias-style syntax, sorted alphabetically. The two fields on each line must be separated by a real tab, else dbm might complain.

Most systems will not need any pathtable entries.

domaintable

The domaintable is generally used to force certain behavior after a DNS lookup has occurred. It permits the administrator to make shorthand names available for commonly referenced systems or domains by replacing the shorthand name with the proper one automatically. It can also be used to replace incorrect host or domain names with the "correct" information.

Most sites will not need any domaintable entries.

Aliases

Aliases permit a number of things to happen:

♦ They provide a shorthand or well-known name for mail to be addressed to in order to go to one or more persons.

♦ They invoke a program with the mail message as the input to the program.

♦ They send mail to a file.

All systems require aliases for Postmaster and MAILER-DAEMON to be RFC-compliant.

Always be extremely aware of security when defining aliases that invoke programs or write to programs since sendmail generally runs setuid-root.

Details concerning mail aliases may be found in the aliases manual page.

Installing sendmail

In this section, we'll take a look at how to install a typical binary distribution of Sendmail+IDA, and walk through what needs to be done to make it localized and functional.

The current binary distribution of sendmail+IDA for can be gotten from **sunsite.unc.edu** in **/pub/Linux/system/Mail**. Even if you have an earlier version of sendmail, I strongly recommend you go to the sendmail5.67b+IDA1.5 version since all required Linux-specific patches are now in the vanilla sources and several significant security holes have been plugged that were in versions prior to about December 1, 1993.

If you are building sendmail from the sources, you should follow the instructions in the READMEs included in the source distribution. The current Sendmail+IDA source is available from **vixen.cso.uiuc.edu**. To build Sendmail+IDA on , you also need the Linux-specific configuration files from newspak-2.2.tar.gz, which is available on **sunsite.unc.edu** in the **/pub/Linux/system/Mail** directory.

If you have previously installed smail or another mail delivery agent, you'll probably want to remove (or rename) all the files from smail to be safe.

Building sendmail.cf

To build a sendmail.cf file customized for your site, you have to write a sendmail.m4 file, and process it with m4. In /usr/local/lib/mail/CF, you find a sample file called sample.m4. Copy it to yourhostname.m4, and edit it to reflect the situation of your site.

The sample file is set up for a UUCP-only site that has domainized headers and talks to a smart host. Sites like this only need to edit a few items.

Testing The sendmail.cf file

To put sendmail into "test" mode, you invoke it with the -bt flag. The default configuration file is the sendmail.cf file that is installed on the system. You can test an alternate file by using the -Cfilename option.

Putting It All Together: Integration Testing sendmail.cf And The Tables

At this point, you've verified that mail will have the desired default behavior and that you'll be able to both send and received validly addressed mail. To complete the installation, it may be necessary to create the appropriate dbm tables to get the desired final results.

After creating the table(s) that are required for your site, you must process them through dbm by typing make in the directory containing the tables.

If you are UUCP-only, you do not need to create any of the tables mentioned in the README.linux file. You'll just have to touch the files so that the Makefile works.

If you're UUCP-only and you talk to sites in addition to your smart host, you'll need to add uucpxtable entries for each (or mail to them will also go through the smart host) and run dbm against the revised uucpxtable.

First, you need to make certain that mail through your RELAY_HOST is sent to them via the RELAY_MAILER.

If you have UUCP neighbors other than your RELAY_HOST, you need to ensure that mail to them has the proper behavior. Mail addressed with UUCP-style syntax to a host you talk UUCP with should go directly to them (unless you explicitly prevent it with a domaintable entry).

If you have uucpxtable entries to force UUCP delivery to certain UUCP neighbors who send their mail with Internet-style domainized headers, that also needs to be tested.

Administrivia And Stupid Mail Tricks

Now that we've discussed the theory of configuring, installing, and testing a Sendmail+IDA system, lets take a few moments to look into things that do happen routinely in the life of a mail administrator.

Remote systems sometimes break. Modems or phone lines fail, DNS definitions are set incorrectly due to human error. Networks go down unexpectedly. In such cases, mail administrators need to know how to react quickly, effectively, and safely to keep mail flowing through alternate routes until the remote systems or service providers can restore normal services.

The rest of this chapter is intended to provide you with the solutions to the most frequently encountered "electronic mail emergencies."

Forwarding Mail To A Relay Host

To forward mail for a particular host or domain to a designated relay system, you generally use the mailertable.

Forcing Mail Into Misconfigured Remote Sites

Frequently, Internet hosts will have trouble getting mail into misconfigured remote sites. There are several variants of this problem, but the general symptom is that mail is bounced by the remote system or never gets there at all.

These problems can put the local system administrator in a bad position because your users generally don't care that you don't personally administer every system worldwide (or know how to get the remote administrator to fix the problem). They just know that their mail didn't get through to the desired recipient on the other end and that you're a likely person to complain to.

A remote site's configuration is their problem, not yours. In all cases, be certain to not break your site in order to communicate with a misconfigured remote site. If you can't get in touch with the Postmaster at the remote site to get them to fix their configuration in a timely manner, you have two options.

♦ It is generally possible to force mail into the remote system successfully, although since the remote system is misconfigured, replies on the remote end might not work...but then that's the remote administrator's problem.

You can fix the bad headers in the envelope on your outgoing messages only by using a domaintable entry for their host/domain that results in the invalid information being corrected in mail originating from your site:

♦ Frequently, misconfigured sites "bounce" mail back to the sending system and effectively say "that mail isn't for this site" because they do not have their PSEUDONYMNS or equivalent set properly in their configuration. It is possible to totally strip off all hostname and domain information from the envelope of messages going from your site to them.

Forcing Mail To Be Transferred Via UUCP

In an ideal world (from the Internet perspective), all hosts have records in the Domain Name Service (DNS) and will send mail with fully qualified domain names.

If you happen to talk via UUCP to such a site, you can force mail to go through the point-to-point UUCP connection rather than through your default mailer by essentially "undomainizing" their hostname through the uucpxtable.

Preventing Mail From Being Delivered Via UUCP

The opposite condition also occurs. Frequently, systems may have a number of direct UUCP connections that are used infrequently or that are not as reliable and always available as the default mailer or relay host.

For example, in the Seattle area there are a number of systems that exchange the various distributions via anonymous UUCP when the distributions are released. These systems talk UUCP only when necessary, so it is generally faster and more reliable to send mail through multiple very reliable hops and common (and always available) relay hosts.

Running The sendmail Queue On Demand

To process queued messages immediately, merely type "/usr/lib/runq". This invokes sendmail with the appropriate options to cause sendmail to run through the queue of pending jobs immediately rather than waiting for the next scheduled run.

Reporting Mail Statistics

Many site administrators (and the persons they work for) are interested in the volume of mail passing to, from, and through the local site. There are a number of ways to quantify mail traffic.

♦ sendmail comes with a utility called mailstats that reads a file called /usr/local/lib/mail/sendmail.st and reports the number of messages and number of bytes transferred by each of the mailers used in the sendmail.cf file. This file must be created by the local administrator manually for sendmail logging to occur. The running totals are cleared by removing and re-creating the sendmail.st file.

♦ Probably the best way to do quality reporting regarding who uses mail and how much volume passes to, from, and through the local system is to turn on mail debugging with syslogd(8). Generally, this means running the /etc/syslogd daemon from your system startup file (which you should be doing anyway), and adding a line to /etc/syslog.conf(5).

If you use mail.debug and get any medium to high mail volume, the syslog output can get quite large. Output files from syslogd generally need to be rotated or purged on a routine basis from crond(8).

There are a number of commonly available utilities that can summarize the output of mail logging from syslogd. One of the more well-known utilities is syslog-stat.pl, a Perl script that is distributed with the Sendmail+IDA sources.

Mixing And Matching Binary Distributions

There is no true standard configuration of electronic mail transport and delivery agents and there is no "one true directory structure."

Accordingly, it is necessary to ensure that all the various pieces of the system (USENET news, mail, TCP/IP) agree on the location of the local mail delivery program (lmail, deliver, and so on), remote mail delivery program (rmail), and the mail transport program (sendmail or smail). Such assumptions are not generally documented, although use of the strings command can help determine what files and directories are expected. The following are some problems we've seen in the past with some of the commonly available binary distributions and sources.

- Some versions of the Net-2 distribution of TCP/IP have services defined for a program called umail rather than sendmail.
- There are various ports of elm and mailx that look for a delivery agent of /usr/bin/smail rather than sendmail.
- Sendmail+IDA has a built-in local mailer for deliver, but expects it to be located in /bin rather than the more typical location of /usr/bin.

Rather than go through the trouble of building all the mail clients from sources, we generally fake it with the appropriate soft links.

Where To Get More Information

There are many places you can look for more information on sendmail. For a list, see the MAIL Howto posted regularly to **comp.answers**. It is also available for anonymous FTP on **rtfm.mit.edu**. However, the definitive place is in the Sendmail+IDA sources. Look in the directory ida/cf below the source directory for the files DBM-GUIDE, OPTIONS, and sendmail.mc.

Chapter 15
Netnews

The idea of network news was born in 1979 when two graduate students, Tom Truscott and Jim Ellis, thought of using UUCP to connect machines for the purpose of information exchange among users. They set up a small network of three machines in North Carolina.

Initially, traffic was handled by a number of shell scripts (later rewritten in C), but they were never released to the public. They were quickly replaced by "A" news, the first public release of news software.

"A" news was not designed to handle more than a few articles per group and day. When the volume continued to grow, it was re-written by Mark Horton and Matt Glickman, who called it the "B" release (a.k.a. Bnews). The first public release of Bnews was version 2.1 in 1982. It was expanded continuously, with several new features being added. Its current version is Bnews 2.11. It is slowly becoming obsolete, with its last official maintainer having switched to INN.

Another rewrite was done and released in 1987 by Geoff Collyer and Henry Spencer; this is release "C," or C-News. In the time following there have been a number of patches to C-News, the most prominent being the C-News Performance Release. On sites that carry a large number of groups, the overhead involved in frequently invoking relaynews, which is responsible for dispatching incoming articles to other hosts, is significant. The Performance Release adds an option to relaynews that allows to run it in daemon mode, in which the program puts itself in the background.

The Performance Release is the C-News version currently included in most releases.

All news releases up to "C" are primarily targeted for UUCP networks, although they may be used in other environments as well. Efficient news transfer over networks like TCP/IP, DECNet, or related requires a new scheme. This was the reason why, in 1986, the *Network News Transfer Protocol*, NNTP, was introduced. It is based on network connections, and specifies a number of commands to interactively transfer and retrieve articles.

There are a number of NNTP-based applications available from the Net. One of them is the nntpd package by Brian Barber and Phil Lapsley, which you can use, among other things, to provides newsreading service to a number of hosts inside a local network. Nntpd was designed to complement news packages such as Bnews or C-News to give them NNTP features.

A different NNTP package is INN, or Internet News. It is not merely a front end, but a news system by its own right. It comprises a sophisticated news relay daemon that is capable of maintaining several concurrent NNTP links efficiently, and is therefore the news server of choice for many Internet sites.

What Is Usenet, Anyway?

One of the most astounding facts about Usenet is that it isn't part of any organization, or has any sort of centralized network management authority. In fact, it's part of Usenet lore that except for a technical description, you cannot define what it is, you can only say what it isn't. If you have Brendan Kehoe's excellent "Zen and the Art of the Internet" (available online at **www.cs.indiana.edu/docproject/zen/zen-1.0_toc/html**; or take a look at the author's home page at **www.zen.org/~brendan/**) at hand, you will find an amusing list of Usenet's nonproperties.

At the risk of sounding stupid, one might define Usenet as a collaboration of separate sites who exchange Usenet news. To be a Usenet site, all you have to do is find another site Usenet site, and strike an agreement with its owners and maintainers to exchange news with you. Providing another site with news is also called feeding it, whence another common axiom of Usenet philosophy originates: "Get a feed and you're on it."

The basic unit of Usenet news is the article. This is a message a user writes and "posts" to the net. In order to enable news systems to deal with it, it is prepended with administrative information, the so-called *article header*. It is very similar to the mail header format laid down in the Internet mail standard RFC-822, in that it consists of several lines of text, each beginning with a field name terminated by a colon, which is followed by the field's value.

Note

The format of Usenet news messages is specified in RFC-1036, "Standard For Interchange Of USENET Messages."

Articles are submitted to one or more newsgroups. One may consider a newsgroup a forum for articles relating to a common topic. All newsgroups are organized in a hierarchy, with each group's name indicating its place in the hierarchy. This often makes it easy to see what a group is all about. For example, anybody can see from the newsgroup name that **comp.os.linux.announce** is used for announcements concerning a computer operating system named Linux.

These articles are then exchanged between all Usenet sites that are willing to carry news from this group. When two sites agree to exchange news, they are free to exchange whatever newsgroups they like to, and may even add their own local news hierarchies. For example, groucho.edu might have a news link to barnyard.edu, which is a major news feed, and several links to minor sites which it feeds news. Now, Barnyard College might receive all Usenet groups, while GMU only wants to carry a few major hierarchies like sci, comp, rec, and so on. Some of the downstream sites, say a UUCP site called brewhq, will want to carry even fewer groups, because they don't have the network or hardware resources. On the other hand, brewhq might want to receive newsgroups from the fj hierarchy, which GMU doesn't carry. It therefore maintains another link with gargleblaster.com, who carries all fj groups, and feed them to brewhq.

How Does Usenet Handle News?

Today, Usenet has grown to enormous proportions. Sites that carry the whole of netnews, they typically transfer something along the lines of 3–5GB per day. Of course this requires much more than pushing around files. So let's take a look at the way most systems handle Usenet news.

> **Note**
>
> *If you would like to read about the most recent Usenix conference where they cover some highly interesting topics, be sure to check out **www.infosys.tuwien.ac.at/staff/pooh/papers/NewsCacheHP/**.*

News is distributed through the net by various transports. The historical medium used to be UUCP, but today the main traffic is carried by Internet sites. The routing algorithm used is called *flooding*: Each site maintains a number of links (news feeds) to other sites. Any article generated or received by the local news system is forwarded to them, unless it has already been seen at that site, in which case it is discarded. A site may find out about all other sites the article has already traversed by looking at the Path: header field. This header contains a list of all systems the article has been forwarded by in bang path notation.

To distinguish articles and recognize duplicates, Usenet articles have to carry a message ID (specified in the Message-Id: header field), which combines the posting site's name and a serial number into "<serial@site>". For each article processed, the news system logs this ID into a history file against which all newly arrived articles are checked.

The flow between any two sites may be limited by two criteria: For one, an article is assigned a distribution (in the Distribution: header field), which may be used to confine it to a certain group of sites. On the other hand, the newsgroups exchanged may be limited by both the sending or receiving system. The set of newsgroups and distributions allowed for transmission to a site are usually kept in the sys file.

The sheer number of articles usually requires that improvements be made to the above scheme. On UUCP networks, the natural thing to do is to collect articles over a period of time, and combine them into a single file, which is compressed and sent to the remote site. This is called *batching*. (The golden rule of netnews, according to Geoff Collyer: "Thou shalt batch thine articles.")

An alternative technique is the ihave/sendme protocol that prevents duplicate articles from being transferred in the first place, thus saving net bandwidth. Instead of putting all articles in batch files and sending them along, only the message IDs of articles are combined into a giant "ihave" message and sent to the remote site. It reads this message, compares it to its history file, and returns the list of articles it wants in a "sendme" message. Only these articles are then sent.

Of course, ihave/sendme only makes sense if it involves two big sites that receive news from several independent feeds each, and who poll each other often enough for an efficient flow of news.

Sites that are on the Internet generally rely on TCP/IP-based software that uses the Network News Transfer Protocol, NNTP. (Described in RFC-977.) It transfers news between feeds and provides Usenet access to single users on remote hosts.

NNTP knows three different ways to transfer news. One is a real-time version of ihave/sendme, also referred to as *pushing* news. The second technique is called *pulling* news, in which the client requests a list of articles in a given newsgroup or hierarchy that have arrived at the server's site after a specified date, and chooses those it cannot find in its history file. The third mode is for interactive newsreading, and allows you or your newsreader to retrieve articles from specified newsgroups, as well as post articles with incomplete header information.

At each site, news are kept in a directory hierarchy below /var/spool/news, each article in a separate file and each newsgroup in a separate directory. The directory name is made up of the newsgroup name, with the components being the path components. Thus, **comp.os.linux.misc** articles are kept in /var/spool/news/comp/os/linux/misc. The articles in a newsgroup are assigned numbers in the order they arrive. This number serves as the file's name. The range of numbers of articles currently online is kept in a file called active, which at the same time serves as a list of newsgroups known at your site. Since disk space is a finite resource, one has to start throwing away articles after some time. This is called *expiring*. Usually, articles from certain groups and hierarchies are expired at a fixed number of days after they arrive. This may be overridden by the poster by specifying a date of expiration in the Expires: field of the article header.

Chapter 16
C-News

One of the most popular software packages for Netnews is C-News. You can download it from **ftp://ftp.cs.toronto.edu/pub/c-news/c-news.tar.Z**. It was designed for sites that carry news over UUCP links. This chapter will discuss the central concepts of C-News and the basic installation and maintenance tasks.

C-News stores its configuration files in /usr/lib/news, and most of its binaries are in the /usr/lib/news/bin directory. Articles are kept below /var/spool/news. You should make sure virtually all files in these directories are owned by user news, group news. Most problems arise from files being inaccessible to C-News. Make it a rule for you to become user news using su before you touch anything in there. The only exception is setnewsids, which is used to set the real user ID of some news programs. It must be owned by root and must have the setuid bit set.

In the following, we describe all C-News configuration files in detail and show you what you have to do to keep your site running.

Delivering News

Articles may be fed to C-News in several ways. When a local user posts an article, the newsreader usually hands it to the **inews** command, which completes the header information. News from remote sites, be it a single article or a whole batch, is given to the **rnews** command, which stores it in the /var/spool/newsin.coming directory, from where it will be picked up at a later time by newsrun. With any of these two techniques, however, the article will eventually be handed to the **relaynews** command.

For each article, the **relaynews** command first checks if the article has already been seen at the local site by looking up the message ID in the history file. Duplicate articles will be dropped. Then, **relaynews** looks at the Newsgroups: header line to find out if the local site requests articles from any of these groups. If it does, and the newsgroup is listed in the active file, **relaynews** tries to store the article in the corresponding directory in the news spool area. If this directory does not exist, it is created. The article's message ID will then be logged to the history file. Otherwise, **relaynews** drops the article.

If **relaynews** fails to store an incoming article because a group it has been posted to is not listed in your active file, the article will be moved to the junk group. (There may be a difference between the groups that exist at your site, and those that your site is willing to receive. For example, the subscription list may specify comp.all, which means all newsgroups below the comp hierarchy, but at your site, only a number of comp groups are listed in active. Articles posted to those groups will be moved to junk.) **relaynews** will also check for stale or misdated articles and reject them. Incoming batches that fail for any other reason are moved to /var/spool/news/in.coming/bad, and an error message is logged.

After this, the article will be relayed to all other sites that request news from these groups, using the transport specified for each particular site. To make sure it isn't sent to a site that already has seen it, each destination site is checked against the article's Path: header field, which contains the list of sites the article has traversed so far, written in bang path style. Only if the destination site's name does not appear in this list will the article be sent to it.

C-News is commonly used to relay news between UUCP sites, although it is also possible to use it in a NNTP environment. To deliver news to a remote UUCP site—either single articles or whole batches—uux is used to execute the **rnews** command on the remote site and feed the article or batch to it on standard input.

When batching is enabled for a given site, C-News does not send any incoming article immediately, but appends its path name to a file, usually out.going/site/togo. Periodically, a batcher program is executed from a crontab entry (note that this should be the crontab of news, in order not to mangle file permissions), which puts the articles in one or more files, optionally compresses them, and sends them to **rnews** at the remote site.

Installation

To install C-News, untar the files into their proper places if you haven't done so yet, and edit the configuration files listed below in the following bulleted list. (They are all located in /usr/lib/news.) Their formats will be described in the following sections.

Note

*Here is some information on how news flows through **relaynews**:*

1. *There may be a difference between the groups that exist at your site, and those that your site is willing to receive. For example, the subscription list may specify*

comp.all, which means all newsgroups below the comp hierarchy, but at your site, only a number of comp groups are listed in active. Articles posted to those groups will be moved to junk.

2. *Note that this should be the crontab of news, in order not to mangle file permissions.*

♦ **sys**—You probably have to modify the ME line that describes your system, although using all/all is always a safe bet. You also have to add a line for each site you feed news to. If you are a leaf site, you only need a line that sends all locally generated articles to your feed. Assume your feed is moria, then your sys file should look like this:

```
ME:all/all::
moria/moria.orcnet.org:all/all,!local:f:
```

♦ **organization**—Your organization's name. For example, "Virtual Brewery, Inc." On your home machine, enter "private site," or anything else you like. Most people will not call your site properly configured if you haven't customized this file.

♦ **mailname**—Your site's mail name, e.g., vbrew.com.

♦ **whoami**—Your site's name for news purposes. Quite often, the UUCP site name is used, for example, vbrew.

♦ **explist**—You should probably edit this file to reflect your preferred expiry times for some special newsgroups. Disk space may play an important role in it. To create an initial hierarchy of newsgroups, obtain an active and a newsgroups file from the site that feeds you, and install them in /usr/lib/news, making sure they are owned by news and have a mode of 644. Remove all to.* groups from the active file, and add to.mysite and to.feedsite, as well as junk and control. The to.* groups are normally used for exchanging ihave/sendme messages, but you should create them regardless of whether you plan to use ihave/sendme or not. Next, replace all article numbers in the second and third field of active using the following command:

```
# cp active active.old
# sed 's/ [0-9]* [0-9]* / 0000000000 00001 /' active.old  active
# rm active.old
```

The second command is an invocation of **sed(1)**, one of my favorite commands. This invocation replaces two strings of digits with a string of zeroes and the string 000001, respectively.

Finally, create the news spool directory and the subdirectories used for incoming and outgoing news:

```
# cd /var/spool
# mkdir news news/in.coming news/out.going
# chown -R news.news news
# chmod -R 755 news
```

If you're using a later release of C-News, you may also have to create the out.master directory in the news spool directory.

If you're using newsreaders from a different distribution than the C-News you have running, you may find that some expect the news spool on /usr/spool/news rather than in /var/spool/news. If your newsreader doesn't seem to find any articles, create a symbolic from /usr/spool/news to /var/spool/news.

Now, you are ready to receive news. Note that you don't have to create any directories other than those shown above, because each time C-News receives an article from a group for which there's no spool directory yet, it will create it.

In particular, this happens to all groups an article has been cross-posted to. So, after a while, you will find your news spool cluttered with directories for newsgroups you have never subscribed to, like alt.lang.teco. You may prevent this by either removing all unwanted groups from active, or by regularly running a shell script which removes all empty directories below /var/spool/news (except out.going and in.coming, of course).

C-News needs a user to send error messages and status reports to. By default, this is usenet. If you use the default, you have to set up an alias for it which forwards all of its mail to one or more responsible persons. (Chapters 13 and 14 explain how to do so for smail and sendmail.) You may also override this behavior by setting the environment variable NEWSMASTER to the appropriate name. You have to do so in news' crontab file, as well as every time you invoke an administrative tool manually, so installing an alias is probably easier.

While you're hacking /etc/passwd, make sure that every user has her real name in the pw_gecos field of the password file (this is the fourth field). It is a question of Usenet netiquette that the sender's real name appears in the From: field of the article. Of course, you will want to do so anyway when you use mail.

The sys File

The sys file, located in /usr/lib/news, controls which hierarchies you receive and forward to other sites. Although there are maintenance tools named addfeed and delfeed, I think it's better to maintain this file by hand.

The sys file contains entries for each site you forward news to, as well as a description of the groups you will accept. An entry looks like

```
site[/exclusions]:grouplist[/distlist][:flags[:cmds]]
```

Entries may be continued across newlines using a backslash (\ ). A hash sign (#) denotes a comment. The following are definitions of the sys entry:

♦ **site**—This is the name of the site the entry applies to. One usually chooses the site's UUCP name for this. There has to be an entry for your site in the sys file, too, or else you will not receive any articles yourself.

The special site name ME denotes your site. The ME entry defines all groups you are willing to store locally. Articles that aren't matched by the ME line will go to the junk group.

Because C-News checks site against the site names in the Path: header field, you have to make sure they really match. Some sites use their fully qualified domain name in this field or an alias like news.site.domain. To prevent any articles from being returned to these sites, you have to add these to the exclusion list, separated by commas.

For the entry applying to site moria, for instance, the site field would contain moria/moria.orcnet.org.

♦ **grouplist**—This is a comma-separated subscription list of groups and hierarchies for that particular site. A hierarchy may be specified by giving the hierarchy's prefix (such as comp.os for all groups whose name starts with this prefix), optionally followed by the keyword all (e.g., comp.os.all).

A hierarchy or group is excluded from forwarding by preceding it with an exclamation mark. If a newsgroup is checked against the list, the longest match applies. For example, if grouplist contains

```
!comp,comp.os.linux,comp.folklore.computers
```

no groups from the comp hierarchy except comp.folklore.computers and all groups below comp.os.linux will be fed to that site.

If the site requests to be forwarded all news you receive yourself, enter all as grouplist.

♦ **distlist**—is offset from the grouplist by a slash, and contains a list of distributions to be forwarded. Again, you may exclude certain distributions by preceding them with an exclamation mark. All distributions are denoted by all. Omitting distlist implies a list of all.

For example, you may use a distribution list of all,!local to prevent news for local use only from being sent to remote sites.

There are usually at least two distributions: world, which is often the default distribution used when none is specified by the user, and local. There may be other distributions that apply to a certain region, state, country, and so on. Finally, there are two distributions used by C-News only; these are sendme and ihave, and are used for the sendme/ihave protocol.

The use of distributions is a subject of debate. For one, some newsreaders create bogus distributions by simply using the top-level hierarchy, for example comp when posting to comp.os.linux. Distributions that apply to regions are often questionable, too, because news may travel outside of your region when sent across the Internet. Distributions applying to an organization, however, are very meaningful, for example, to prevent confidential information from leaving the company network. This purpose, however, is generally served better by creating a separate newsgroup or hierarchy.

- **flags**—This describes certain parameters for the feed. It may be empty, or a combination of the following:

  - **F**—This flag enables batching.

  - **f**—This is almost identical to the F flag, but allows C-News to calculate the size of outgoing batches more precisely.

  - **I**—This flag makes C-News produce an article list suitable for use by ihave/sendme. Additional modifications to the sys and the batchparms file are required to enable ihave/sendme.

- **n**—This creates batch files for active NNTP transfer clients like nntpxmit (see Chapter 19). The batch files contain the article's file name along with its message ID.

- **I**—This flag makes C-News produce an article list suitable for use by ihave/sendme. Additional modifications to the sys and the batchparms file are required to enable ihave/ sendme.

- **n**—This creates batch files for active NNTP transfer clients like nntpxmit (see Chapter 19). The batch files contain the article's file name along with its message ID.

- **L**—This tells C-News to transmit only articles posted at your site. This flag may be followed by a decimal number n, which makes C-News only transfer articles posted within n hops from your site. C-News determines the number of hops from the Path: field.

- **u**—Tells C-News to batch only articles from unmoderated groups.

- **m**—Tells C-News to batch only articles from moderated groups. You may use at most one of F, f, I, or n.

- **cmds**—This field contains a command to be executed for each article, unless batching is enabled. The article will be fed to the command on standard input. This should only be used for very small feeds; otherwise the load on both systems will be too high.

  The default command is

```
uux - -r -z system!rnews
```

which invokes **rnews** on the remote system, feeding it the article on standard input. The default search path for commands given in this field is /bin:/usr/bin:/usr/lib/news/bin/ batch. The latter directory contains a number of shell scripts whose name starts with via; they are briefly described later in this chapter.

If batching is enabled using either of the F or f, I or n flags, C News expects to find a file name in this field rather than a command. If the file name does not begin with a slash (/), it is assumed to be relative to /var/spool/news/out.going. If the field is empty, it defaults to system/togo.

When setting up C-News, you will most probably have to write your own sys file. To help you with it, we give a sample file for vbrew.com below, from which you might copy what you need.

```
# We take whatever they give us.
ME:all/all::

# We send everything we receive to moria, except for local and
# brewery-related articles. We use batching.

moria/moria.orcnet.org:all,!to,to.moria/all,!local,!brewery:f:

# We mail comp.risks to jack@ponderosa.uucp
ponderosa:comp.risks/all::rmail jack@ponderosa.uucp

# swim gets a minor feed
swim/swim.twobirds.com:comp.os.linux,rec.humor.oracle/all,!local:f:

# Log mail map articles for later processing
usenet-maps:comp.mail.maps/all:F:/var/spool/uumaps/work/batch
```

The active File

The active file is located in /usr/lib/news and lists all groups known at your site, and the articles currently online. You will rarely have to touch it, but we explain it nevertheless for sake of completeness. Entries take the following form:

```
newsgroup high low perm
```

Newsgroup is, of course, the group's name. low and high are the lowest and highest numbers of articles currently available. If none are available at the moment, low is equal to high+1.

At least, that's what the low field is meant to do. However, for efficiency reasons, C-News doesn't update this field. This wouldn't be such a big loss if there weren't some newsreaders that depend on it. For instance, trn checks this field to see if it can purge any articles from its thread database. To update the low field, you therefore have to run the **updatemin** command regularly (or, in earlier version of C-News, the upact script).

Perm is a parameter detailing the access users are granted to the group. It takes one of the following values:

♦ **y**—Users are allowed to post to this group.

♦ **n**—Users are not allowed to post to this group. However, the group may still be read.

♦ **x**—This group has been disabled locally. This happens sometimes when news administrators (or their superiors) take offense to articles posted to certain groups.

Articles received for this group are not stored locally, although they are forwarded to the sites that request them.

♦ **m**—This denotes a moderated group. When a user tries to post to this group, an intelligent newsreader will notify her of this, and send the article to the moderator instead. The moderator's address is taken from the moderators file in /usr/lib/news.

♦ **=real-group**—This marks newsgroup as being a local alias for another group, namely real-group. All articles posted to newsgroup will be redirected to it.

In C-News, you will generally not have to access this file directly. Groups may be added or deleted locally using **addgroup** and **delgroup** (see below). When groups are added or deleted for the whole of Usenet, this is usually done by sending a newgroup or rmgroup control message, respectively. Never send such a message yourself! For instructions on how to create a newsgroup, read the monthly postings in news.announce.newusers.

A file closely related to active is active.times. Whenever a group is created, C-News logs a message to this file, containing the name of the group created, the date of creation, whether it was done by a newgroup control message or locally, and who did it. This is for the convenience of newsreaders who may notify the user of any recently created groups. It is also used by the **NEWGROUPS** command of NNTP.

Article Batching

News batches follow a particular format which is the same for Bnews, C-News, and INN. Each article is preceded by a line like this:

```
#! rnews count
```

where count is the number of bytes in the article. When batch compression is used, the resulting file is compressed as a whole, and preceded by another line, indicated by the message to be used for unpacking. The standard compression tool is compress, which is marked by

```
#! Cunbatch
```

Sometimes, when having to send batches via mail software that removes the eighth bit from all data, a compressed batch may be protected using what is called c7-encoding; these batches will be marked by c7unbatch.

When a batch is fed to **rnews** on the remote site, it checks for these markers and processes the batch appropriately. Some sites also use other compression tools, like gzip, and precede their gzipped files with zunbatch instead. C-News does not recognize nonstandard headers like these; you have to modify the source to support them.

In C-News, article batching is performed by /usr/lib/news/bin/batch/sendbatches, which takes a list of articles from the site/togo file and puts them into several news batches. It should be executed once per hour or even more frequently, depending on the volume of traffic.

Its operation is controlled by the batchparms file in /usr/lib/news. This file describes the maximum batch size allowed for each site, the batching and optional compression program to be used, and the transport for delivering it to the remote site. You may specify batching parameters on a per-site basis, as well as a set of default parameters for sites not explicitly mentioned.

To perform batching for a specific site, you invoke it as

```
# su news -c "/usr/lib/news/bin/batch/sendbatches site"
```

When invoked without arguments, sendbatches handles all batch queues. The interpretation of "all" depends on the presence of a default entry in batchparms. If one is found, all directories in /var/spool/news/out.going are checked, otherwise, it cycles through all entries in batchparms. Note that sendbatches, when scanning the out.going directory, takes only those directories that contain no dot or at sign (@) as site names.

When installing C-News, you will most likely find a batchparms file in your distribution which contains a reasonable default entry, so there's a good chance that you wouldn't have to touch the file. Just in case, we describe its format nevertheless. Each line consists of six fields, separated by spaces or tabs:

```
site size max batcher muncher transport
```

The meaning of these fields is as follows:

♦ **site**—is the name of the site the entry applies to. The togo file for this site must reside in out.going/togo below the news spool. A site name of /default/ denotes the default entry.

♦ **size**—is the maximum size of article batches created (before compression). For single articles larger than this, C-News makes an exception and puts them in a single batch by themselves.

♦ **max**—is the maximum number of batches created and scheduled for transfer before batching stalls for this particular site. This is useful in case the remote site should be down for a long time, because it prevents C-News from cluttering your UUCP spool directories with zillions of newsbatches.

C-News determines the number of queued batches using the queulen script in /usr/lib/news/bin. Vince Skahan's newspak release should contain a script for BNU-compatible UUCPs. If you use a different flavor of spool directories, for example, Taylor UUCP, you might have to write your own. If you don't care about the number of spool files (because you're the only person using your computer, and you don't write articles by the megabyte), you may replace the script's contents by a simple exit 0 statement.

The batcher field contains the command used for producing a batch from the list of articles in the togo file. For regular feeds, this is usually **batcher**. For other purposes, alternative batchers may be provided. For instance, the ihave/sendme protocol requires the article list to be turned into ihave or sendme control messages, which are posted to the newsgroup to.site. This is performed by batchih and batchsm.

The muncher field specifies the command used for compression. Usually, this is **compcun**, a script that produces a compressed batch. (As shipped with C-News, **compcun** uses compress with the 12-bit option, since this is the least common denominator for most sites. You may produce a copy of it, say compcun16, where you use 16-bit compression. The improvement is not too impressive, though.) Alternatively, you might provide a muncher that uses gzip, say gzipcun (to be clear: you have to write it yourself). You have to make sure that uncompress on the remote site is patched to recognize files compressed with gzip.

If the remote site does not have an uncompress command, you may specify nocomp, which does not do any compression.

The last field, transport, describes the transport to be used. A number of standard commands for different transports are available whose names begin with via. sendbatches passes them the destination site name on the command line. If the batchparms entry was not /default/, it derives the site name from the site field by stripping of anything after and including the first dot or slash. If entry was /default/, the directory names in out.going are used.

There are two commands that use uux to execute **rnews** on the remote system: **viauux** and **viauuxz**. The latter sets the -z flag for (older versions of) uux to keep it from returning success messages for each article delivered. Another command, **viamail**, sends article batches to the user rnews on the remote system via mail. Of course, this requires that the remote system somehow feeds all mail for rnews to their local news system. For a complete list of these transports, refer to the newsbatch(8) manual page.

All commands from the last three fields must be located in either of out.going/site or /usr/lib/news/bin/batch. Most of them are scripts, so that you may easily tailor new tools for your personal needs. They are invoked as a pipe. The list of articles is fed to the batcher on standard input, which produces the batch on standard output. This is piped into the muncher, and so on.

A sample file is given below.

```
# batchparms file for the brewery
# site        | size  |max  |batcher  |muncher   |transport
#-------+----+---+----+------+-----
/default/       100000 22      batcher   compcun    viauux
swim            10000  10      batcher   nocomp     viauux
```

Expiring News

In Bnews, expiring used to be performed by a program called expire, which took a list of newsgroups as arguments, along with a time specification after which articles had to be expired. To have different hierarchies expired at different times, you had to write a script that invoked expire for each of them separately. C-News offers a more convenient solution to this: In a file called explist, you may specify newsgroups and expiration intervals. A command called **doexpire** is usually run once a day from **cron**, and processes all groups according to this list.

Occasionally, you may want to retain articles from certain groups even after they have been expired; for example, you might want to keep programs posted to comp.sources.unix. This is called archiving. explist permits you to mark groups for archiving.

An entry in explist looks like this:

```
grouplist perm times archive
```

Grouplist is a comma-separated list of newsgroups to which the entry applies. Hierarchies may be specified by giving the group name prefix, optionally appended with all. For example, for an entry applying to all groups below comp.os, you might either enter comp.os or comp.os.all in grouplist.

When expiring news from a group, the name is checked against all entries in explist in the order given. The first matching entry applies. For example, to throw away the majority of comp after four days, except for comp.os.linux.announce which you want to keep for a week, you simply have an entry for the latter, which specifies a seven-day expiration period, followed by that for comp, which specifies four days.

The perm field details if the entry applies to moderated, unmoderated, or any groups. It may take the values m, u, or x, which denote moderated, unmoderated, or any type.

The third field, times, usually contains only a single number. This is the number of days after which articles will be expired if they haven't been assigned an artificial expiration date in an Expires: field in the article header. Note that this is the number of days counting from its arrival at your site, not the date of posting.

The times field may, however, be more complex than that. It may be a combination of up to three numbers, separated from one another by a dash. The first denotes the number of days that have to pass before the article is considered a candidate for expiration. It is rarely useful to use a value other than zero. The second field is the above-mentioned default number of days after which it will be expired. The third is the number of days after which an article will be expired unconditionally, regardless of whether it has an Expires: field or not. If only the middle number is given, the other two take default values. These may be specified using the special entry /bounds/, which is described below.

The fourth field, archive, denotes whether the newsgroup is to be archived and where. If no archiving is intended, a dash should be used. Otherwise, you either use a full path name (pointing to a directory), or an at sign (@). The at sign denotes the default archive directory which must then be given to doexpire by using the **-a** flag on the command line. An archive directory should be owned by news. When **doexpire** archives an article from, say, comp.sources.unix, it stores it in the directory comp/sources/unix below the archive directory, creating it if not existent. The archive directory itself, however, will not be created.

There are two special entries in your explist file that **doexpire** relies on. Instead of a list of newsgroups, they have the keywords /bounds/ and /expired/. The /bounds/ entry contains the default values for the three values of the times field described above.

The /expired/ field determines how long C-News will hold on to lines in the history file. This is needed because C-News will not remove a line from the history file once the corresponding article(s) have been expired, but will hold on to it in case a duplicate should arrive after this date. If you are fed by only one site, you can keep this value small. Otherwise, a couple of weeks is advisable on UUCP networks, depending on the delays you experience with articles from these sites.

A sample explist file with rather tight expiry intervals is reproduced below:

```
# keep history lines for two weeks. Nobody gets more than three mont
/expired/                     x      14       -
/bounds/                      x      0-1-90   -

# groups we want to keep longer than the rest
comp.os.linux.announce        m      10       -
comp.os.linux                 x      5        -
alt.folklore.computers        u      10       -
rec.humor.oracle              m      10       -
soc.feminism                  m      10       -

# Archive *.sources groups
comp.sources,alt.sources      x      5        @

# defaults for tech groups
comp,sci                      x      7        -

# enough for a long weekend
misc,talk                     x      4        -

# throw away junk quickly
junk                          x      1        -

# Archive *.sources groups
comp.sources,alt.sources      x      5        @
```

```
# defaults for tech groups
comp,sci                        x       7       -

# enough for a long weekend
misc,talk                       x       4       -

# throw away junk quickly
junk                            x       1       -

# control messages are of scant interest, too
control                         x       1       -

# catch-all entry for the rest of it
all                             x       2       -
```

With expiring in C-News, there are a number of potential troubles looming. One is that your newsreader might rely on the third field of the active file, which contains the number of the lowest article online. When expiring articles, C-News does not update this field. If you need (or want) to have this field represent the real situation, you need to run a program called updatemiin after each run of **doexpire**. (In older versions of C-News, this was done by a script called upact.)

Second, C-News does not expire by scanning the newsgroup's directory, but simply checks the history file if the article is due for expiration. (The article's date of arrival is kept in the middle field of the history line, given in seconds since January 1, 1970.) If your history file somehow gets out of sync, articles may be around on your disk forever, because C-News has literally forgotten them. (I don't know why this happens, but for me, it does from time to time.) You can repair this using the addmissing script in /usr/lib/news/bin/maint, which will add missing articles to the history file, or mkhistory, which rebuilds the entire file from scratch. Don't forget to become news before invoking it, else you will wind up with a history file unreadable by C-News.

Miscellaneous Files

There are a number of files that control C-News's behavior, but are not essential to its functioning. All of them reside in /usr/lib/news. We will describe them briefly.

- **newsgroups**—This is a companion file of active which contains a list of newsgroup names, along with a one-line description of its main topic. This file is automatically updated when C-News receives a check-news control message (see section 18.8).

- **localgroups**—If you have a number of local groups that you don't want C-News to complain about every time you receive a checknews message, put their names and descriptions in this file, just like they would appear in newsgroups.

♦ **Mailpaths**—This file contains the moderator's address for each moderated group. Each line contains the group name, followed by the moderator's email address (offset by a tab).

Two special entries are provided as default. These are backbone and Internet. Both provide—in bang-path notation—the path to the nearest backbone site, and the site that understands RFC 822-style addresses (**user@host**). The default entries are

```
internet          backbone
```

You will not have to change the Internet entry if you have smail or sendmail installed, because they understand RFC 822-addressing.

The backbone entry is used whenever a user posts to a moderated group whose moderator is not listed explicitly. If the newsgroup's name is alt.sewer, and the backbone entry contains path!%s, C-News will mail the article to path!alt-sewer, hoping that the backbone machine is able to forward the article. To find out which path to use, ask the news admins at the site that feeds you. As a last resort, you can also use uunet.uu.net!%s.

♦ **distributions**—This file is not really a C-News file, but it is used by some newsreaders, and nntpd. It contains the list of distributions recognized by your site, and a description of its (intended) effect. For example, Virtual Brewery has the following file:

   ♦ world
   ♦ everywhere in the world
   ♦ local
   ♦ Only local to this site
   ♦ nl
   ♦ Netherlands only
   ♦ mugnet
   ♦ MUGNET only
   ♦ fr
   ♦ France only
   ♦ de
   ♦ Germany only
   ♦ brewery
   ♦ Virtual Brewery only

♦ **log**—This file contains a log of all C-News activities. It is culled regularly by running newsdaily; copies of the old logfiles are kept in log.o, log.oo, and so on.

♦ **errlog**—This is a log of all error messages created by C-News. These do not include articles junked due to wrong group, etc. This file is mailed to the newsmaster (usenet by default) automatically by newsdaily if it is found to be non-empty. errlog is cleared by newsdaily. Old copies are kept in errlog.o and companions.

♦ **batchlog**—This logs all runs of sendbatches. It is usually of scant interest only. It is also attended by newsdaily.

♦ **watchtime**—This is an empty file created each time newswatch is run.

Control Messages

The Usenet news protocol knows a special category of articles which evoke certain responses or actions by the news system. These are called *control messages*. They are recognized by the presence of a Control: field in the article header, which contains the name of the control operation to be performed. There are several types of them, all of which are handled by shell scripts located in /usr/lib/news/ctl.

Most of these will perform their action automatically at the time the article is processed by C-News, without notifying the newsmaster. By default, only checkgroups messages will be handed to the newsmaster (there's a funny typo in RFC-1036 (p. 12): "Implementers and administrators may choose to allow control messages to be carried out automatically, or to queue them for annual processing"), but you may change this by editing the scripts.

The cancel Message

The most widely known message is cancel, with which a user may cancel an article sent earlier. This effectively removes the article from the spool directories, if it exists. The cancel message is forwarded to all sites that receive news from the groups affected, regardless of whether the article has been seen already or not. This is to take into account the possibility that the original article has been delayed over the cancellation message. Some news systems allow users to cancel other person's messages; this is of course a definite no-no.

newgroup And rmgroup

Two messages dealing with creation or removal of newsgroups are the newgroup and rmgroup message. Newsgroups below the "usual" hierarchies may be created only after a discussion and voting has been held among Usenet readers. The rules applying to the alt hierarchy allow for something close to anarchy. For more information, see the regular postings in news.announce.newusers and news.announce.newgroups. Never send a newgroup or rmgroup message yourself unless you definitely know that you are allowed to.

The checkgroups Message

checkgroups messages are sent by news administrators to make all sites within a network synchronize their active files with the realities of Usenet. For example, commercial Internet service providers might send out such a message to their customers' sites. Once a month,

the "official" checkgroups message for the major hierarchies is posted to comp.
announce.newgroups by its moderator. However, it is posted as an ordinary article, not as a
control message. To perform the checkgroups operation, save this article to a file, say /tmp/
check, remove everything up to the beginning of the control message itself, and feed it to
the checkgroups script using the following command:

```
#  su   news  -c  "/usr/lib/news/bin/ctl/checkgroups"  <        /tmp/check
```

This will update your newsgroups file, adding the groups listed in localgroups. The old
newsgroups file will be moved to newsgroups.bac. Note that posting the message locally will
rarely work, because inews refuses to accept that large an article.

If C-News finds mismatches between the checkgroups list and the active file, it will produce
a list of commands that would bring your site up to date and mail it to the news administrator. The output typically looks like this:

```
From news Sun Jan 30 16:18:11 1994
Date: Sun, 30 Jan 94 16:18 MET
From: news (News Subsystem)
To: usenet
Subject: Problems with your active file
The following newsgroups are not valid and should be removed.
alt.ascii-art
bionet.molbio.gene-org
comp.windows.x.intrisics
de.answers

You can do this by executing the commands:
/usr/lib/news/bin/maint/delgroup alt.ascii-art
/usr/lib/news/bin/maint/delgroup bionet.molbio.gene-org
/usr/lib/news/bin/maint/delgroup comp.windows.x.intrisics
/usr/lib/news/bin/maint/delgroup de.answers

The following newsgroups were missing.
comp.binaries.cbm
comp.databases.rdb
comp.os.geos
comp.os.qnx
comp.unix.user-friendly
misc.legal.moderated
news.newsites
soc.culture.scientists
talk.politics.crypto
talk.politics.tibet
```

When you receive a message like this from your news system, don't believe it blindly. Depending on who sent the checkgroups message, it may lack a few groups or even entire hierarchies; so you should be careful about removing any groups. If you find groups are listed as missing that you want to carry at your site, you have to add them using the addgroup script. Save the list of missing groups to a file and feed it to the following little script:

```
#!/bin/sh
cd /usr/lib/news

while read group; do
    if grep -si "^$group[[:space:]].*moderated" newsgroup; then
        mod=m
    else
        mod=y
    fi
    /usr/lib/news/bin/maint/addgroup $group $mod
done
```

sendsys, version, And senduuname

Finally, there are three messages that may be used to find out about the network's topology. These are sendsys, version, and senduuname. They cause C-News to return to the sender the sys file, a software version string, and the output of uuname(1), respectively. C-News is very laconic about version messages; it returns a simple, unadorned "C".

Again, you should never issue such a message, unless you have made sure that it cannot leave a your (regional) network. Replies to sendsys messages can quickly bring down a UUCP network. (I wouldn't try this on the Internet, either.)

C-News In An NFS Environment

A simple way to distribute news within a local network is to keep all news on a central host, and export the relevant directories via NFS, so that newsreaders may scan the articles directly. The advantage of this method over NNTP is that the overhead involved in retrieving and threading articles is significantly lower. NNTP, on the other hand, wins in a heterogeneous network where equipment varies widely among hosts, or where users don't have equivalent accounts on the server machine.

When using NFS, articles posted on a local host have to be forwarded to the central machine, because accessing administrative files might otherwise expose the system to race conditions that leave the files inconsistent. Also, you might want to protect your news spool area by exporting it read-only, which requires forwarding to the central machine, too.

C-News handles this transparently. When you post an article, your newsreader usually invokes **inews** to inject the article into the news system. This command runs a number of checks on the article, completes the header, and checks the file server in /usr/lib/news. If this file exists and contains a hostname different from the local host's name, **inews** is invoked on that server host via rsh. Since the inews script uses a number of binary commands and support files from C-News, you have to either have C-News installed locally or mount the news software from the server.

For the rsh invocation to work properly, each user must have an equivalent account on the server system, i.e., one to which she can log in without being asked for a password.

Make sure that the hostname given in server literally matches the output of the **hostname(1)** command on the server machine, else C-News will loop forever when trying to deliver the article.

Maintenance Tools And Tasks

Despite the complexity of C-News, a news administrator's life can be fairly easy, because C-News provides you with a wide variety of maintenance tools. Some of these are intended to be run regularly from **cron**, like newsdaily. Using these scripts reduces daily care and feeding requirements of your C-News installation greatly.

Unless stated otherwise, these commands are located in /usr/lib/news/bin/maint. Note that you must become user news before invoking these commands. Running them as super-user may render these files inaccessible to C-News.

♦ **newsdaily**—The name already says it: runs this once a day. It is an important script that helps you keep log files small, retaining copies of each from the last three runs. It also tries to sense any anomalies, like stale batches in the incoming and outgoing directories, postings to unknown or moderated newsgroups, and so on. Resulting error messages will be mailed to the newsmaster.

♦ **newswatch**—This is a script that should be run regularly to look for anomalies in the news system, once an hour or so. It is intended to detect problems that will have immediate effect on the operability of your news system and mail a trouble report to the newsmaster. Things checked include stale lock files that don't get removed, unattended input batches, and disk space shortage.

♦ **addgroup**—Adds a group to your site locally. The proper invocation is

```
addgroup groupname y|n|m|=realgroup
```

The second argument has the same meaning as the flag in the active file, meaning that anyone may post to the group (y), that no one may post (n), that it is moderated (m), or that it is an alias for another group (=realgroup).

You might also want to use addgroup when the first articles in a newly created group arrive earlier than the newgroup control message that is intended to create it.

- **delgroup**—Allows you to delete a group locally. Invoke it as

```
delgroup groupname
```

You still have to delete the articles that remain in the newsgroup's spool directory. Alternatively, you might leave it to the natural course of events (a.k.a. expire) to make them go away.

- **addmissing**—Adds missing articles to the history file. Run this script when there are articles that seem to hang around forever.
- **newsboot**—This script should be run at system boot time. It removes any lock files left over when news processes were killed at shutdown, and closes and executes any batches left over from NNTP connections that were terminated when shutting down the system.
- **newsrunning**—This resides in /usr/lib/news/bin/input, and may be used to disable un-batching of incoming news, for instance during work hours. You may turn off un-batching by invoking

```
/usr/lib/news/bin/input/newsrunning off
```

Chapter 17
A Description Of NNTP

D ue to the different network transport used, NNTP provides for a vastly different approach to news exchange from C-news. NNTP stands for "Network News Transfer Protocol," and is not a particular software package but an Internet Standard (formally specified in RFC-977). It is based on a stream-oriented connection—usually over TCP—between a client anywhere in the network, and a server on a host that keeps netnews on disk storage. The stream connection allows the client and server to interactively negotiate article transfer with nearly no turnaround delay, thus keeping the number of duplicate articles low. Together with the Internet's high transfer rates, this adds up to a news transport that surpasses the original UUCP networks by far. Although some years ago it was not uncommon for an article to take two weeks or more before it arrived in the last corner of Usenet, this is now often less than two days; on the Internet itself, it is even within the range of minutes.

Various commands allow clients to retrieve, send, and post articles. The difference between sending and posting is that the latter may involve articles with incomplete header information. (When posting an article over NNTP, the server always adds at least one header field, which is Nntp-Posting-Host:. It contains the client's hostname.) Article retrieval may be used by news transfer clients as well as newsreaders. This makes NNTP an excellent tool for providing news access to many clients on a local network without going through the contortions that are necessary when using NFS.

NNTP also provides for an active and a passive way of news transfer, colloquially called "pushing" and "pulling." Pushing is basically the same as the C-News ihave/sendme protocol. The client offers an article to the server through the **IHAVE <varmsgid>** command, and the server returns a response code that indicates whether it already has the article, or if it wants it. If so, the client sends the article, terminated by a single dot on a separate line.

Pushing news has the single disadvantage that it places a heavy load on the server system, since it has to search its history database for every single article.

The opposite technique is pulling news, in which the client requests a list of all (available) articles from a group that have arrived after a specified date. This query is performed by the **NEWNEWS** command. From the returned list of message IDs, the client selects those articles it does not yet have, using the **ARTICLE** command for each of them in turn.

The problem with pulling news is that it needs tight control by the server over which groups and distributions it allows a client to request. For example, it has to make sure that no confidential material from newsgroups local to the site are sent to unauthorized clients.

There are also a number of convenience commands for newsreaders that permit them to retrieve the article header and body separately, or even single header lines from a range of articles. This lets you keep all news on a central host, with all users on the (presumably local) network using NNTP-based client programs for reading and posting. This is an alternative to exporting the news directories via NFS, which is described in Chapter 16.

An overall problem of NNTP is that it allows the knowledgeable to insert articles into the news stream with false sender specification. This is called *news faking*. (The same problem exists with SMTP, the Simple Mail Transfer Protocol.) An extension to NNTP allows to require a user authentication for certain commands.

There are a number of NNTP packages available. One of the more widely known is the NNTP daemon, also known as the reference implementation. Originally, it was written by Stan Barber and Phil Lapsley to illustrate the details of RFC-977. Its most recent version is nntpd 1.5.11, which will be described below. You may either get the sources and compile it yourself, or use the nntpd from Fred van Kempen's net-std binary package. No ready-to-go binaries of nntpd are provided, because of various site-specific values that must be compiled in.

Note

*Since the time of this writing, things have evolved. The INN package, mentioned below, is now maintained by the ISC (Internet Software Consortium) and is considered the current "reference" implementation. The current version number for INN is 2.2. Please look here for more information: **http://www.isc.org/view.cgi?/products/ INN/index.phtml**.*

The nntpd package consists of a server and two clients for pulling and pushing news, respectively, as well as an inews replacement. They live in a Bnews environment, but with a little tweaking, they will be happy with C-News, too. However if you plan to use NNTP for more than offering newsreaders access to your news server, the reference implementation is not really an option. We will therefore discuss only the NNTP daemon contained in the nntpd package, and leave out the client programs.

Installing The NNTP Server

The NNTP server is called nntpd and may be compiled in two ways, depending on the expected load on the news system. There are no compiled versions available, because of some site-specific defaults that are hard-coded into the executable. All configuration is done through macro definitions in common/conf.h.

nntpd may be configured as either a standalone server that is started at system boot time from rc.inet2, or a daemon managed by inetd. In the latter case you have to have the following entry in /etc/inetd.conf:

```
nntp    stream  tcp nowait      news    /usr/etc/in.nntpd    nntpd
```

If you configure nntpd as standalone, make sure that any such line in inetd.conf is commented out. In either case, you have to make sure there's the following line in /etc/services:

```
nntp    119/tcp    readnews untp    # Network News Transfer Protocol
```

To temporarily store any incoming articles and so on, nntpd also needs a .tmp directory in your news spool. You should create it using

```
# mkdir /var/spool/news/.tmp
# chown news.news /var/spool/news/.tmp
```

Restricting NNTP Access

Access to NNTP resources is governed by the file nntp_access in /usr/lib/news. Lines in the file describe the access rights granted to foreign hosts. Each line has the following format:

```
site    read|xfer|both|no    post|no      [!exceptgroups]
```

If a client connects to the NNTP port, nntpd attempts to obtain the host's fully qualified domain name from its IP address by reverse lookup. The client's hostname and IP address are checked against the site field of each entry in the order in which they appear in the file. Matches may be either partial or exact. If an entry matches exactly, it applies; if the match is partial, it only applies if there is no other match following which is at least as good. The site may be specified in one of the following ways:

♦ **Hostname**—This is a fully qualified domain name of a host. If this matches the client's canonical hostname literally, the entry applies, and all following entries are ignored.

♦ **IP address**—This is an IP address in dotted quad notation. If the client's IP address matches this, the entry applies, and all following entries are ignored.

♦ **Domain name**—This is a domain name, specified as *.domain. If the client's hostname matches the domain name, the entry matches.

♦ **Network name**—This is the name of a network as specified in /etc/networks. If the network number of the client's IP address matches the network number associated with the network name, the entry matches.

♦ **Default**—The default matches any client.

Entries with a more general site specification should be specified earlier, because any matches by these will be overridden by later, more exact matches.

The second and third field describe the access rights granted to the client. The second details the permissions to retrieve news by pulling (read), and transmit news by pushing (xfer). A value of both enables both, no denies access altogether. The third field grants the client the right to post articles, that is, deliver articles with incomplete header information which is completed by the news software. If the second field contains no, the third field is ignored.

The fourth field is optional, and contains a comma-separated list of groups the client is denied access to.

A sample nntp_access file is shown below:

```
#
# by default, anyone may transfer news, but not read or post
default                 xfer            no
#
# public.vbrew.com offers public access via modem, we allow
# them to read and post to any but the local.* groups
public.vbrew.com        read            post    !local
#
# all other hosts at the brewery may read and post
*.vbrew.com             read            post
```

NNTP Authorization

When capitalizing the access tokens like xfer or read in the nntp_acces file, nntpd requires the authorization from the client for the respective operations. For instance, when specifying a permission of Xfer or XFER, nntpd will not let the client transfer articles to your site unless it passes authorization.

The authorization procedure is implemented by means of a new NNTP command named **AUTHINFO**. Using this command, the client transmits a username and a password to the NNTP server. nntpd will validate them by checking them against the /etc/passwd database and verify that the user belongs to the nntp group.

The current implementation of NNTP authorization is only experimental, and has therefore not been implemented very portably. The result of this is that it works only with plain-style password databases; shadow passwords will not be recognized.

nntpd Interaction With C-News

When receiving an article, nntpd has to deliver it to the news subsystem. Depending on whether it was received as a result of an **IHAVE** or **POST** command, the article is handed to rnews or inews, respectively. Instead of invoking rnews, you may also configure it (at compile time) to batch the incoming articles and move the resulting batches to /var/spool/news/in.coming, where they are left for relaynews to pick them up at the next queue run.

To be able to properly perform the ihave/sendme protocol, nntpd has to be able to access the history file. At compile time, you therefore have to make sure the path is set correctly. You should also make sure that C-News and nntpd agree on the format of your history file. C-News uses dbm hashing functions to access it; however, there are quite a number of different and slightly incompatible implementations of the dbm library. If C-News has been linked with the a different dbm library than you have in your standard libc, you have to link nntpd with this library, too.

A typical symptom of nntpd and C-News disagreeing on the database format are error messages in the system log that nntpd could not open it properly, or duplicate articles received via NNTP. A good test is to pick an article from your spool area, telnet to the nntp port, and offer it to nntpd as shown in the example below (your input is marked like this). Of course, you have to replace <msg@id> with the message ID of the article you want to feed to nntpd again.

```
$ telnet localhost nntp
Trying 127.0.0.1...
Connected to localhost
Escape characters is '^]'.
201 vstout NNTP[auth] server version 1.5.11t (16 November
1991) ready at Sun Feb 6 16:02:32 1194 (no posting)
IHAVE <msg@id>
```

```
435 Got it.
QUIT
```

This conversation shows the proper reaction of nntpd; the message "Got it" tells you that it already has this article. If you get a message of "335 Ok" instead, the lookup in the history file failed for some reason. Terminate the conversation by typing Ctrl+D. You can check what has gone wrong by checking the system log; nntpd logs all kinds of messages to the daemon facility of syslog. An incompatible dbm library usually manifests itself in a message complaining that dbminit failed.

Chapter 18
Newsreader Configuration

Newsreaders are intended to offer the user functionality that allows him or her to access the functions of the news system easily, like posting articles or skimming the contents of a newsgroup in a comfortable way. The quality of this interface is subject of endless flame wars.

There are a couple of newsreaders available that have been ported to Linux. Below I will describe the basic setup for the three most popular ones, namely tin, trn, and nn.

One of the most effective newsreaders is

```
        $ find /var/spool/news -name '[0-9]*' -exec
cat {} \; | more
```

This is the way die-hards read their news.

The majority of newsreaders, however, are much more sophisticated. They usually offer a full-screen interface with separate levels for displaying all groups the user has subscribed to, for displaying an overview of all articles in one group and for individual articles.

At the newsgroup level, most newsreaders display a list of articles, showing their subject line and the author. In big groups, it is impossible for the user to keep track of articles relating to each other, although it is possible to identify responses to earlier articles.

A response usually repeats the original article's subject, prepending it with "Re:." Additionally, the message ID of the article it is a direct follow-up to may be given in the References: header line. Sorting articles by these two criteria generates small clusters (in fact, trees) of articles, which are called threads. One of the tasks in writing a newsreader is devising an efficient scheme of threading, because the time required for this is proportional to the square of the number of articles.

Here, we will not dig any further into how the user interfaces are built. All newsreaders currently available for Linux have a good help function, so you ought to get along.

In the following, we will only deal with administrative tasks. Most of these relate to the creation of threads databases and accounting.

tin Configuration

The most versatile newsreader with respect to threading is tin. It was written by Iain Lea and is loosely modeled on an older newsreader named tass (written by Rich Skrenta). It does its threading when the user enters the newsgroup, and it is pretty fast at this unless you're doing this via NNTP.

On an 486DX50, it takes roughly 30 seconds to thread 1,000 articles when reading directly from disk. Over NNTP to a loaded news server, this would be somewhere above five minutes.

Note

Things improve drastically if the NNTP server does the threading itself and lets the client retrieve the threads databases; INN-1.4 does this, for instance.

You may improve this by regularly updating your index file with the -u option, or by invoking tin with the -U option.

Usually, tin dumps its threading databases in the user's home directory below .tin/index. This may however be costly in terms of resources, so that you should want to keep a single copy of them in a central location. This may be achieved by making tin setuid to news, for example, or some entirely unprivileged account. (However, do not use nobody for this. As a rule, no files or commands whatsoever should be associated with this user.)

tin will then keep all thread databases below /var/spool/news/.index. For any file access or shell escape, it will reset its effective uid to the real uid of the user who invoked it. (This is the reason why you will get ugly error messages when invoking it as super-user. But then, you shouldn't work as root, anyway.)

A better solution is to install the tind indexing daemon that runs as a daemon and regularly updates the index files. This daemon is, however, not included, so you would have to compile it yourself. If you are running a LAN with a central news server, you may even run tind on the server and have all clients retrieve the index files via NNTP. This, of course, requires an extension to NNTP. Patches for nntpd that implement this extension are included in the tin source.

The version of tin included in some distributions has no NNTP support compiled in, but most do have it now. When invoked as rtin or with the -r option, tin tries to connect to the NNTP server specified in the file /etc/nntpserver or in the NNTPSERVER environment variable. The nntpserver file simply contains the server's name on a single line.

trn Configuration

trn is the successor to an older newsreader, too, namely rn (which means read news). The "t" in its name stands for "threaded." It was written by Wayne Davidson.

Unlike tin, trn has no provision for generating its threading database at run-time. Instead, it uses those prepared by a program called mthreads that has to be invoked regularly from cron to update the index files.

Not running mthreads, however, doesn't mean you cannot access new articles; it only means you will have all those "Novell buys out Linux!!" articles scattered across your article selection menu, instead of a single thread you may easily skip.

To turn on threading for particular newsgroups, mthreads is invoked with the list of newsgroups on the command line. The list is made up in exactly the same fashion as the one in the sys file:

```
mthreads comp,rec,!rec.games.go
```

will enable threading for all of comp and rec, except for rec.games.go (people who play Go don't need fancy threads). After that, you simply invoke it without any option at all to make it thread any newly arrived articles. Threading of all groups found in your active file can be turned on by invoking mthreads with a group list of all.

If you're receiving news during the night, you will customarily run mthreads once in the morning, but you can also to do so more frequently if needed. Sites that have very heavy traffic may want to run mthreads in daemon mode. When it is started at boot time using the -d option, it puts itself in the background, and wakes up every 10 minutes to check if there are any newly arrived articles, and threads them. To run mthreads in daemon mode, put the following line in your rc.news script:

```
/usr/local/bin/rn/mthreads -deav
```

The -a option makes mthreads automatically turn on threading for new groups as they are created; -v enables verbose log messages to mthreads's log file, mt.log in the directory where you have trn installed.

Old articles no longer available must be removed from the index files regularly. By default, only articles whose number is below the low water mark will be removed.

> ### Note
> *C-News doesn't update this low water mark automatically; you have to run updatemin to do so. Please refer to Chapter 16.*

Articles above this number who have been expired nevertheless (because the oldest article has been assigned an long expiry date by an Expires: header field) may be removed by giving mthreads the -e option to force an "enhanced" expiry run. When mthreads is running in daemon mode, the -e option makes it put in such an enhanced expiry run once a day, shortly after midnight.

nn Configuration

nn, written by Kim F. Storm, claims to be a newsreader whose ultimate goal is not to read news. Its name stands for "no news," and its motto is "No news is good news. nn is better."

To achieve this ambitious goal, nn comes along with a large assortment of maintenance tools that not only allow generation of threads, but also extensive checks on the consistency of these databases, accounting, gathering of usage statistics, and access restrictions. There is also an administration program called nnadmin, which allows you to perform these tasks interactively. It is very intuitive; hence, we will not dwell on these aspects, and only deal with the generation of the index files.

The nn threads database manager is called nnmaster. It is usually run as a daemon, started from the rc.news or rc.inet2 script. It is invoked as

```
/usr/local/lib/nn/nnmaster -l -r -C
```

This enables threading for all newsgroups present in your active file.

Equivalently, you may invoke nnmaster periodically from cron, giving it a list of groups to act upon. This list is very similar to the subscription list in the sys file, except that it uses blanks instead of commas. Instead of the fake group name all, an empty argument of should be used to denote all groups. A sample invocation is

```
# /usr/local/lib/nn/nnmaster !rec.games.go rec comp
```

Note that the order is significant here: The leftmost group specification that matches always wins. Thus, if we had put !rec.games.go after rec, all articles from this group had been threaded nevertheless.

Nn offers several methods to remove expired articles from its databases. The first is to update the database by scanning the newsgroup directories and discarding the entries whose corresponding article is no longer available. This is the default operation obtained by invoking nnmaster with the -E option. It is reasonably fast unless you're doing this via NNTP.

Method 2 behaves exactly like a default expiry run of mthreads, in that it only removes those entries that refer to articles whose number is below the low water mark in the active file. It may be enabled using the -e option.

Finally, a third strategy is to discard the entire database and recollect all articles. This may be done by giving -E3 to nnmaster.

The list of groups to be expired is given by the -F option in the same fashion as above. However, if you have nnmaster running as daemon, you must kill it (using -k) before expiry can take place, and to restart it with the original options afterward. Thus the proper command to run expire on all groups using method-1 is:

```
# nnmaster -kF ""
# nnmaster -lrC
```

There are many more flags that may be used to fine-tune the behavior of nn. If you are concerned about removing bad articles or digestifying article digests, read the nnmaster manual page.

nnmaster relies on a file named GROUPS, which is located in /usr/local/lib/nn. If it does not exist initially, it is created. For each newsgroup, it contains a line that begins with the group's name, optionally followed by a time stamp and flags. You may edit these flags to enable certain behavior for the group in question, but you may not change the order in which the groups appear. (This is because their order has to agree with that of the entries in the (binary) MASTER file.) The flags allowed and their effects are detailed in the nnmaster manual page, too.

Chapter 19
A Null Printer Cable For PLIP

To make a Null Printer Cable for use with a PLIP connection, you need two 25-pin connectors (called DB-25) and some 11-conductor cable. The cable must be at most 15 meters long.

If you look at the connector, you should be able to read tiny numbers at the base of each pin, from 1 for the pin top left (if you hold the broader side up) to 25 for the pin bottom right. For the Null Printer Cable, you have to connect the following pins of both connectors with each other:

```
D0       2  -  15   ERROR
D1       3  -  13   SLCT
D2       4  -  12   PAPOUT
D3       5  -  10   ACK
D4       6  -  11   BUSY
GROUND  25  -  25   GROUND
ERROR   15  -   2   D0
SLCT    13  -   3   D1
PAPOUT  12  -   4   D2
ACK     10  -   5   D3
BUSY    11  -   6   D4
```

All remaining pins remain unconnected. If the cable is shielded, the shield should be connected to the DB-25's metallic shell on one end only.

Chapter 20
Sample smail Configuration Files

This section shows sample configuration files for a UUCP leaf site on a local area network. They are based on the sample files included in the source distribution of smail-3.1.28. Although I make a feeble attempt to explain how these files work, you are advised to read the very fine smail manual page, which discusses these files in great length. Once you've understood the basic idea behind smail configuration, it's worthwhile reading. It's easy!

The first file shown is the routers file, which describes a set of routers to smail. When smail has to deliver a message to a given address, it hands the address to all routers in turn, until one of them matches it. Matching here means that the router finds the destination host in its database, be it the paths file, /etc/hosts, or whatever routing mechanism the router interfaces to.

Entries in smail configuration files always begin with a unique name identifying the router, transport, or director. They are followed by a list of attributes that define its behavior. This list consists of a set of global attributes, such as the driver used and private attributes that are only understood by that particular driver. Attributes are separated by commas, while the sets of global and private attributes are separated from each other using a semicolon.

To make these fine distinctions clear, assume you want to maintain two separate pathalias files; one containing the routing information for your domain, and a second one containing global routing information, probably generated from the UUCP maps. With smail, you can now specify two routers in the routers file, both of which use the pathalias driver. This driver looks up hostnames in a pathalias database. It expects to be given the name of the file in a private attribute.

The second global attribute given in each of the two routers entries above defines the transport that should be used when the router matches the address. In our case, the message will be delivered using the uux transport. Transports are defined in the transports file, which is explained below.

You can fine-tune by which transport a message will be delivered if you specify *a method file* instead of the transports attribute. Method files provide a mapping from target hostnames to transports. We won't deal with them here.

In an environment that mixes UUCP and TCP/IP, you may encounter the problem that you have hosts in your /etc/hosts file that you have only occasional SLIP or PPP contact with. Usually, you would still want to send any mail for them over UUCP. To prevent the inet_hosts driver from matching these hosts, you have to put them into the paths/force file. This is another pathalias-style database, and is consulted before smail queries the resolver.

The handling of mail for local addresses is configured in the directors file. It is made up just like the routers file, with a list of entries that define a director each. Directors do not deliver a message; they merely perform all the redirection that is possible, for instance through aliases, mail forwarding, and the like.

When delivering mail to a local address, such as janet, smail passes the username to all directors in turn. If a director matches, it either specifies a transport the message should be delivered by (for instance, to the user's mailbox file) or generates a new address (for instance, after evaluating an alias).

Because of the security issues involved, directors usually do a lot of checking of whether the files they use may be compromised or not. Addresses obtained in a somewhat dubious way (for instance from a world-writable aliases file) are flagged as insecure. Some transport drivers will turn down such addresses, for instance, the transport that delivers a message to a file.

Apart from this, smail also associates a user with each address. Any write or read operations are performed as the user. For delivery to, say, janet's mailbox, the address is of course associated with janet. Other addresses, such as those obtained from the aliases file, have other users associated from them, for instance, the nobody user.

For details of these features, please refer to the smail manpage.

Note

The smail manpage is in Section 8 of the online manual (system administration commands) of the Linux Documentation Project.

After successfully routing or directing a message, smail hands the message to the transport specified by the router or director that matched the address. These transports are defined in the transports file. Again, a transport is defined by a set of global and private options.

The most important option defined by each entry is driver that handles the transport, for instance the pipe driver, which invokes the command specified in the cmd attribute. Apart from this, there are a number of global attributes a transport may use, that perform various transformations on the message header, and possibly message body. The return_path attribute, for instance, makes the transport insert a return_path field in the message header. The unix_from_hack attribute makes it precede every occurrence of the word "From" at the beginning of a line with a > sign. A sample /usr/lib/smail/transports file is shown in Listing 20.1.

Listing 20.1 A sample /usr/lib/smail/transports file.

```
# A sample /usr/lib/smail/transports file

# local - deliver mail to local users
local:   driver=appendfile,        # append message to a file
         return_path,               # include a Return-Path: field
         from,                      # supply a From_ envelope line
         unix_from_hack,            # insert > before From in body
         local;                     # use local forms for delivery

         file=/var/spool/mail/${lc:user}, # location of mailbox files
         group=mail,                # group to own file for System V
         mode=0660,                 # group mail can access
         suffix="\n",               # append an extra newline

# pipe - deliver mail to shell commands
pipe:    driver=pipe,              # pipe message to another program
         return_path,               # include a Return-Path: field
         from,                      # supply a From_ envelope line
         unix_from_hack,            # insert > before From in body
         local;                     # use local forms for delivery

         cmd="/bin/sh -c $user",   # send address to the Bourne Shell
         parent_env,                # environment info from parent addr
         pipe_as_user,              # use user-id associated with address
         ignore_status,             # ignore a non-zero exit status
         ignore_write_errors,       # ignore write errors, i.e., broken pipe
         umask=0022,                # umask for child process
         -log_output,               # do not log stdout/stderr

# file - deliver mail to files
file:    driver=appendfile,
         return_path,               # include a Return-Path: field
         from,                      # supply a From_ envelope line
         unix_from_hack,            # insert > before From in body
         local;                     # use local forms for delivery
```

```
            file=$user,                 # file is taken from address
            append_as_user,             # use user-id associated with address
            expand_user,                # expand ~ and $ within address
            suffix="\n",                # append an extra newline
            mode=0600,                  # set permissions to 600

# uux - deliver to the rmail program on a remote UUCP site
uux:    driver=pipe,
        uucp,                           # use UUCP-style addressing forms
        from,                           # supply a From_ envelope line
        max_addrs=5,                    # at most 5 addresses per invocation
        max_chars=200;                  # at most 200 chars of addresses

        cmd="/usr/bin/uux - -r -a$sender -g$grade $host!rmail $(($user)$)",
        pipe_as_sender,                 # have uucp logs contain caller
        log_output,                     # save error output for bounce messages
#       defer_child_errors,             # retry if uux returns an error

# demand - deliver to a remote rmail program, polling immediately
demand: driver=pipe,
        uucp,                           # use UUCP-style addressing forms
        from,                           # supply a From_ envelope line
        max_addrs=5,                    # at most 5 addresses per invocation
        max_chars=200;                  # at most 200 chars of addresses

        cmd="/usr/bin/uux - -a$sender -g$grade $host!rmail $(($user)$)",
        pipe_as_sender,                 # have uucp logs contain caller
        log_output,                     # save error output for bounce messages
#       defer_child_errors,             # retry if uux returns an error

# hbsmtp - half-baked BSMTP. The output files must
#          be processed regularly and sent out via UUCP.
hbsmtp: driver=appendfile,
        inet,                           # use RFC 822-addressing
        hbsmtp,                         # batched SMTP w/o HELO and QUIT
        -max_addrs, -max_chars;         # no limit on number of addresses

        file="/var/spool/smail/hbsmtp/$host",
        user=root,                      # file is owned by root
        mode=0600,                      # only read-/writable by root.

# smtp - deliver using SMTP over TCP/IP
smtp:   driver=tcpsmtp,
        inet,
        -max_addrs, -max_chars;         # no limit on number of addresses
```

```
            short_timeout=5m,          # timeout for short operations
            long_timeout=2h,           # timeout for longer SMTP operations
            service=smtp,              # connect to this service port
# For internet use: uncomment the below 4 lines
#           use_bind,                  # resolve MX and multiple A records
#           defnames,                  # use standard domain searching
#           defer_no_connect,          # try again if the nameserver is down
#           -local_mx_okay,            # fail an MX to the local host
```

Part II

The Linux System
Administrators' Guide

by Lars Wirzenius

Version 0.6.1

Lars Wirzenius

An introduction to system administration of a Linux system for novices.

Copyright 1993–1998 Lars Wirzenius.

Trademarks are owned by their owners.

About The Author

Lars Wirzenius has been involved with Linux almost from the beginning, being the second person to have Linux running on his computer. Not having the patience for kernel programming, he has concentrated on higher-level issues, such as moderating the comp.os.linux.announce newsgroup. In 1992, he helped co-found the Linux Documentation Project with Michael K. Johnson and Matt Welsh. The LDP set out to produce a complete and free set of documentation for Linux users, programmers, and system administrators. It has mostly succeeded. Lars wrote *The Linux System Administrators' Guide* for the LDP.

Lars continues to doodle with the LDP, and is a developer for the Debian Project, one of the Linux distributions. Mostly, he tries to finish even one of his eternal hobby projects. For more information, see his home page at **http://www.iki.fi/liw**. He can be reached at **http://liw@iki.fi**. (Unfortunately, to preserve his free time, Lars usually can't answer generic Linux questions. Questions and suggestions directly related to his book or other things he is working on are welcome, however.)

About This Book

Source And Preformatted Versions Available

The source code and other machine-readable formats of this book can be found on the Internet via anonymous FTP at the Linux Documentation Project home page at **http://sunsite.unc.edu/LDP/**, or at the home page of this book at **http://www.iki.fi/liw.linux/sag/**. Available are at least PostScript and TeX .DVI formats.

Introduction

*"In the beginning,
the file was without
form, and void; and
emptiness was upon
the face of the bits.
And the Fingers of
the Author moved
upon the face of the
keyboard. And the
Author said, 'Let
there be words,' and
there were words."*

This manual, *The Linux System Administrators' Guide*, describes the system administration aspects of using Linux. It is intended for people who know next to nothing about system administration (as in "what is it?"), but who have already mastered at least the basics of normal usage. This manual also doesn't tell you how to install Linux; that is described in the Installation and Getting Started document. See below for more information about Linux manuals.

System administration is all the things that one has to do to keep a computer system in a usable shape. It includes things like backing up files (and restoring them if necessary), installing new programs, creating accounts for users (and deleting them when no longer needed), making certain that the filesystem is not corrupted, and so on. If a computer were, say, a house, system administration would be called maintenance and would include cleaning, fixing broken windows, and other such things. System administration is not called maintenance, because that would be too simple. (There are some people who do call it that, but that's just because they have never read this manual, poor things.)

The structure of this manual is such that many of the chapters should be usable independently, so that if you need information about, say, backups, you can read just that chapter. This hopefully makes the book easier to use as a reference manual, and makes it possible to read just a small part when needed, instead of having to read everything. However, this manual is first and foremost a tutorial, and a reference manual only as a lucky coincidence.

This manual is not intended to be used completely by itself. Plenty of the rest of the Linux documentation is also important for system administrators. After all, a system administrator is just a user with special privileges and duties. A very important resource are the manual pages, which should always be consulted when a command is not familiar.

While this manual is targeted at Linux, a general principle has been that it should be useful with other Unix-based operating systems as well. Unfortunately, since there is so much variance between different versions of Unix in general, and in system administration in particular, there is little hope to cover all variants. Even covering all possibilities for Linux is difficult, due to the nature of its development.

There is no one official Linux distribution, so different people have different setups, and many people have a setup they have built up themselves. This book is not targeted at any one distribution, even though I use the Debian GNU/Linux system almost exclusively. When possible, I have tried to point out differences and explain several alternatives.

I have tried to describe how things work, rather than just listing "five easy steps" for each task. This means that there is much information here that is not necessary for everyone, but those parts are marked as such and can be skipped if you use a pre-configured system. Reading everything will, naturally, increase your understanding of the system and should make using and administering it more pleasant.

Like all other Linux-related development, the work was done on a volunteer basis: I did it because I thought it might be fun and because I felt it should be done. However, like all volunteer work, there is a limit to how much effort I have been able to spend, and also on how much knowledge and experience I have. This means that the manual is not necessarily as good as it would be if a wizard had been paid handsomely to write it and had spent a few years to perfect it. I think, of course, that it is pretty nice, but be warned.

One particular point where I have cut corners is that I have not covered very thoroughly many things that are already well documented in other freely available manuals. This applies especially to program specific documentation, such as all the details of using **mkfs**. I only describe the purpose of the program, and as much of its usage as is necessary for the purposes of this manual. For further information, I refer the gentle reader to these other manuals. Usually, all of the referred to documentation is part of the full Linux documentation set.

Although I have tried to make this manual as good as possible, I would really like to hear from you if you have any ideas on how to make it better. Bad language, factual errors, ideas for new areas to cover, rewritten sections, information about how various Unix versions do things, I am interested in all of it. My contact information is available via the World Wide Web at **http://www.iki.fi/liw/mail-to-lasu.html**.

Many people have helped me with this book, directly or indirectly. I would like to especially thank Matt Welsh for inspiration and LDP leadership, Andy Oram for getting me to work again with much-valued feedback, Olaf Kirch for showing me that it can be done, and Adam Richter at Yggdrasil and others for showing me that other people can find it interesting as well.

Stephen Tweedie, H. Peter Anvin, R'emy Card, and Theodore Ts'o have let me borrow their work (and thus make the book look thicker and much more impressive): a comparison between the xia and ext2 filesystems, the device list and a description of the ext2 filesystem. These aren't part of the book any more. I am most grateful for this, and very apologetic for the earlier versions that sometimes lacked proper attribution.

In addition, I would like to thank Mark Komarinski for sending his material in 1993 and the many system administration columns in *Linux Journal*. They are quite informative and inspirational.

Many useful comments have been sent by a large number of people. My miniature black hole of an archive doesn't let me find all their names, but some of them are, in alphabetical order: Paul Caprioli, Ales Cepek, Marie-France Declerfayt, Dave Dobson, Olaf Flebbe, Helmut Geyer, Larry Greenfield and his father, Stephen Harris, Jyrki Havia, Jim Haynes, York Lam, Timothy Andrew Lister, Jim Lynch, Michael J. Micek, Jacob Navia, Dan Poirier, Daniel Quinlan, Jouni K Seppänen, Philippe Steindl, and G.B. Stotte. My apologies to anyone I have forgotten.

The Linux Documentation Project

The Linux Documentation Project, or LDP, is a loose team of writers, proofreaders, and editors who are working together to provide complete documentation for the Linux operating system. The overall coordinator of the project is Greg Hankins.

This manual is one in a set of several being distributed by the LDP, including a *Linux Users' Guide, System Administrators' Guide, Network Administrators' Guide*, and *Kernel Hackers' Guide*. These manuals are all available in source format, .dvi format, and PostScript output by anonymous FTP from **sunsite.unc.edu**, in the directory **/pub/Linux/docs/LDP**.

We encourage anyone with a penchant for writing or editing to join us in improving Linux documentation. If you have Internet email access, you can contact Greg Hankins at **gregh@sunsite.unc.edu**.

Chapter 1
Overview Of A Linux System

"God looked over everything he had made, and saw that it was very good."

—Genesis 1:31

This chapter gives an overview of a Linux system. First, the major services provided by the operating system are described. Then, the programs that implement these services are described with a considerable lack of detail. The purpose of this chapter is to give an understanding of the system as a whole, so that each part is described in detail elsewhere.

Various Parts Of An Operating System

A Unix operating system consists of a kernel and some system programs. There are also some application programs for doing work. The *kernel* is the heart of the operating system. (In fact, it is often mistakenly considered to be the operating system itself, but it is not. An operating system provides many more services than a plain kernel.) It keeps track of files on the disk, starts programs and runs them concurrently, assigns memory and other resources to various processes, receives packets from and sends packets to the network, and so on. The kernel does very little by itself, but it provides tools with which all services can be built. It also prevents anyone from accessing the hardware directly, forcing everyone to use the tools it provides. This way the kernel provides some protection for users from each other. The tools provided by the kernel are used via system calls; see manual page section 2 for more information on these.

The system programs use the tools provided by the kernel to implement the various services required from an operating system. System programs, and all other programs, run "on top of the kernel," in what is called the *user mode*. The difference between system and application programs is one of intent: Applications are intended for getting useful things done (or for playing, if it happens to be a game), whereas system programs are needed to get the system working. A word processor is an application; Telnet is a system program. The difference is often somewhat blurry, however, and is important only to compulsive categorizers.

An operating system can also contain compilers and their corresponding libraries (GCC and the C library in particular under Linux), although not all programming languages need be part of the operating system. Documentation, and sometimes even games, can also be part of it. Traditionally, the operating system has been defined by the contents of the installation tape or disks; with Linux it is not as clear since it is spread all over the FTP sites of the world.

Important Parts Of The Kernel

The Linux kernel consists of several important parts: process management, memory management, hardware device drivers, filesystem drivers, network management, and various other bits and pieces. Figure 1.1 shows some of them.

Probably the most important parts of the kernel (nothing else works without them) are memory management and process management. Memory management takes care of assigning memory areas and swap space areas to processes, parts of the kernel, and for the

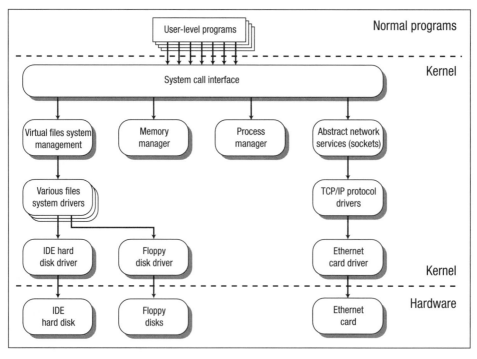

Figure 1.1
Some of the more important parts of the Linux kernel.

buffer cache. Process management creates processes and implements multitasking by switching the active process on the processor.

At the lowest level, the kernel contains a hardware device driver for each kind of hardware it supports. Since the world is full of different kinds of hardware, the number of hardware device drivers is large. There are often many otherwise similar pieces of hardware that differ in how they are controlled by software. The similarities make it possible to have general *classes* of drivers that support similar operations; each member of the class has the same interface to the rest of the kernel, but differs in what it needs to do to implement them. For example, all disk drivers look alike to the rest of the kernel, i.e., they all have operations like "initialize the drive," "read sector N," and "write sector N."

Some software services provided by the kernel itself have similar properties, and can therefore be abstracted into classes. For example, the various network protocols have been abstracted into one programming interface, the BSD socket library. Another example is the virtual filesystem (VFS) layer that abstracts the filesystem operations away from their implementation. Each filesystem type provides an implementation of each filesystem operation. When some entity tries to use a filesystem, the request goes via the VFS, which routes the request to the proper filesystem driver.

Major Services In A Unix System

This section describes some of the more important Unix services, but without much detail. They are described more thoroughly in later chapters.

init

The single most important service in a Unix system is provided by init. init is started as the first process of every Unix system, as the last thing the kernel does when it boots. When init starts, it continues the boot process by doing various startup chores (checking and mounting filesystems, starting daemons, and so on).

The exact list of things that init does depends on which flavor it is; there are several to choose from. init usually provides the concept of single user mode, in which no one can log in and root uses a shell at the console; the usual mode is called *multiuser mode*. Some flavors generalize this as run levels; single and multiuser modes are considered to be two run levels, and there can be additional ones as well, for example, to run X on the console.

In normal operation, init makes sure getty is working (to allow users to log in) and to adopt orphan processes (processes whose parent has died; in Unix all processes must be in a single tree, so orphans must be adopted).

When the system is shut down, it is init that is in charge of killing all other processes, unmounting all filesystems and stopping the processor, along with anything else it has been configured to do.

Logins From Terminals

Logins from terminals (via serial lines) and the console (when not running X) are provided by the getty program. init starts a separate instance of getty for each terminal for which logins are to be allowed. getty reads the username and runs the login program, which reads the password. If the username and password are correct, login runs the shell. When the shell terminates, i.e., the user logs out, or when login terminated because the username and password didn't match, init notices this and starts a new instance of getty. The kernel has no notion of logins, this is all handled by the system programs.

syslog

The kernel and many system programs produce error, warning, and other messages. It is often important that these messages can be viewed later, even much later, so they should be written to a file. The program doing this is syslog. It can be configured to sort the messages to different files according to writer or degree of importance. For example, kernel messages are often directed to a separate file from the others, since kernel messages are often more important and need to be read regularly to spot problems.

Periodic Command Execution: **cron** And **at**

Both users and system administrators often need to run commands periodically. For example, the system administrator might want to run a command to clean the directories with temporary files (/tmp and /var/tmp) from old files, to keep the disks from filling up, since not all programs clean up after themselves correctly.

The **cron** service is set up to do this. Each user has a crontab file, where he lists the commands he wants to execute and the times they should be executed. The cron daemon takes care of starting the commands when specified. The **at** service is similar to **cron**, but it is once only: The command is executed at the given time, but it is not repeated.

Graphical User Interface

Unix and Linux don't incorporate the user interface into the kernel; instead, they let it be implemented by user-level programs. This applies for both text mode and graphical environments.

This arrangement makes the system more flexible, but has the disadvantage that it is simple to implement a different user interface for each program, making the system harder to learn.

The graphical environment primarily used with Linux is called the X Window System (X for short). X also does not implement a user interface; it only implements a window system, i.e., tools with which a graphical user interface can be implemented. The three most popular user interface styles implemented over X are Athena, Motif, and Open Look. (More recently there are KDE and Gnome, both of which are user environments built on top of X.)

Networking

Networking is the act of connecting two or more computers so that they can communicate with each other. The actual methods of connecting and communicating are slightly complicated, but the end result is very useful.

Unix operating systems have many networking features. Most basic services (filesystems, printing, backups, and so on) can be done over the network. This can make system administration easier, since it allows centralized administration, while still reaping in the benefits of microcomputing and distributed computing, such as lower costs and better fault tolerance.

However, this book merely glances at networking; see the *Linux Network Administrators' Guide* for more information, including a basic description of how networks operate.

Network Logins

Network logins work a little differently than normal logins. There is a separate physical serial line for each terminal via which it is possible to log in. For each person logging in via the network, there is a separate virtual network connection, and there can be any number of these. (Well, at least there can be many. Network bandwidth still being a scarce resource, there is still some practical upper limit to the number of concurrent logins via one network connection.) It is therefore not possible to run a separate getty for each possible virtual connection. There are also several different ways to log in via a network, telnet and rlogin being the major ones in TCP/IP networks.

Network logins have, instead of a herd of gettys, a single daemon per way of logging in (telnet and rlogin have separate daemons) that listens for all incoming login attempts. When it notices one, it starts a new instance of itself to handle that single attempt; the original instance continues to listen for other attempts. The new instance works similarly to getty.

Network Filesystems

One of the more useful things that can be done with networking services is sharing files via a network filesystem. The one usually used is called the *network filesystem*, or NFS, developed by Sun.

With a network filesystem, any file operations done by a program on one machine are sent over the network to another computer. This fools the program to think that all the files on the other computer are actually on the computer the program is running on. This makes information sharing extremely simple, since it requires no modifications to programs.

Mail

Electronic mail is usually the most important method for communicating via computer. An electronic letter is stored in a file using a special format, and special mail programs are used to send and read the letters.

Each user has an incoming mailbox (a file in the special format), where all new mail is stored. When someone sends mail, the mail program locates the receiver's mailbox and appends the letter to the mailbox file. If the receiver's mailbox is in another machine, the letter is sent to the other machine, which delivers it to the mailbox as it best sees fit.

The mail system consists of many programs. The delivery of mail to local or remote mailboxes is done by one program (the mail transfer agent or MTA, e.g., sendmail or smail), while the programs users use are many and varied (mail user agent or MUA, e.g., pine or elm). The mailboxes are usually stored in /var/spool/mail.

Printing

Only one person can use a printer at one time, but it is uneconomical not to share printers between users. The printer is therefore managed by software that implements a print queue: All print jobs are put into a queue and whenever the printer is done with one job, the next one is sent to it automatically. This relieves the users from organizing the print queue and fighting over control of the printer. (Instead, they form a new queue at the printer, waiting for their printouts, since no one ever seems to be able to get the queue software to know exactly when anyone's printout is really finished. This is a great boost to intra-office social relations.)

The print queue software also spools the printouts on disk, i.e., the text is kept in a file while the job is in the queue. This allows an application program to spit out the print jobs quickly to the print queue software; the application does not have to wait until the job is actually printed to continue. This is really convenient, since it allows one to print out one version, and not have to wait for it to be printed before one can make a completely revised new version.

The Filesystem Layout

The filesystem is divided into many parts; usually along the lines of a root filesystem with /bin, /lib, /etc, /dev, and a few others; a /usr filesystem with programs and unchanging data; a /var filesystem with changing data (such as log files); and a /home filesystem for everyone's personal files. Depending on the hardware configuration and the decisions of the system administrator, the division can be different; it can even be all in one filesystem.

Chapter 3 describes the filesystem layout in some detail; the Linux Filesystem Standard covers it in somewhat more detail.

Chapter 2
Overview Of The Directory Tree

This chapter describes the important parts of a standard Linux directory tree, based on the FSSTND filesystem standard. (Superceded by the Filesystem Hierarchy Standard [fhs] **http://www.pathname.com/fhs/**. See also: Linux Standard Base (**http://www.linuxbase.org/**.) It outlines the normal way of breaking the directory tree into separate filesystems with different purposes and gives the motivation behind this particular split. Some alternative ways of splitting are also described.

Background

This chapter is loosely based on the Linux filesystem standard, FSSTND version 1.2 (see the bibliography), which attempts to set a standard for how the directory tree in a Linux system is organized. Such a standard has the advantage that it will be easier to write or port software for Linux and to administer Linux machines, since everything will be in their usual places. There is no authority behind the standard that forces anyone to comply with it, but it has got the support of most, if not all, Linux distributions. It is not a good idea to break with the FSSTND without very compelling reasons. The FSSTND attempts to follow Unix tradition and current trends, making Linux systems familiar to those with experience with other Unix systems, and vice versa.

This chapter is not as detailed as the FSSTND. A system administrator should also read the FSSTND for a complete understanding.

This chapter does not explain all files in detail. The intention is not to describe every file, but to give an overview of the system

271

from a filesystem point of view. Further information on each file is available elsewhere in this book or the manual pages.

The full directory tree is intended to be breakable into smaller parts, each on its own disk or partition, to accommodate to disk size limits and to ease backup and other system administration. The major parts are the root, /usr, /var, and /home filesystems (see Figure 2.1). Each part has a different purpose. The directory tree has been designed so that it works well in a network of Linux machines which may share some parts of the filesystems over a read-only device (e.g., a CD-ROM), or over the network with NFS.

The roles of the different parts of the directory tree are described below.

◆ The root filesystem is specific for each machine (it is generally stored on a local disk, although it could be a RAM disk or network drive as well) and contains the files that are necessary for booting the system up and bringing it up to such a state that the other filesystems may be mounted. The contents of the root filesystem will therefore be sufficient for the single-user state. It will also contain tools for fixing a broken system, and for recovering lost files from backups.

◆ The /usr filesystem contains all commands, libraries, manual pages, and other unchanging files needed during normal operation. No files in /usr should be specific for any given machine, nor should they be modified during normal use. This allows the files to be shared over the network, which can be cost-effective since it saves disk space (there can easily be hundreds of megabytes in /usr) and can make administration easier (only the master /usr needs to be changed when updating an application, not each machine separately). Even if the filesystem is on a local disk, it could be mounted read-only, to lessen the chance of filesystem corruption during a crash.

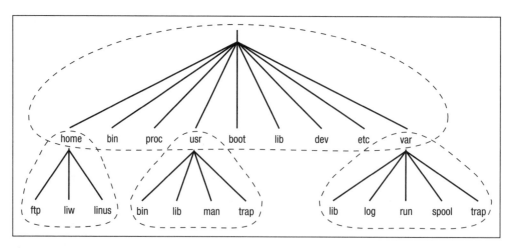

Figure 2.1
Parts of a Unix directory tree. Dashed lines indicate partition limits.

♦ The /var filesystem contains files that change, such as spool directories (for mail, news, printers, and so on), log files, formatted manual pages, and temporary files. Traditionally everything in /var has been somewhere below /usr, but that made it impossible to mount /usr read-only.

♦ The /home filesystem contains the users' home directories, i.e., all the real data on the system. Separating home directories to their own directory tree or filesystem makes backups easier; the other parts often do not have to be backed up, or at least not as often (they seldom change). A big /home might have to be broken on several filesystems, which requires adding an extra naming level below /home, e.g., /home/students and /home/staff.

Although the different parts have been called filesystems above, there is no requirement that they actually be on separate filesystems. They could easily be kept in a single one if the system is a small single-user system and the user wants to keep things simple. The directory tree might also be divided into filesystems differently, depending on how large the disks are, and how space is allocated for various purposes. The important part, though, is that all the standard names work; even if, say, /var and /usr are actually on the same partition, the names /usr/lib/libc.a and /var/log/messages must work, for example by moving files below /var into /usr/var, and making /var a symlink to /usr/var.

The Unix filesystem structure groups files according to purpose, i.e., all commands are in one place, all data files in another, documentation in a third, and so on. An alternative would be to group files files according to the program they belong to, i.e., all Emacs files would be in one directory, all TeX in another, and so on. The problem with the latter approach is that it makes it difficult to share files (the program directory often contains both static and shareable and changing and nonshareable files), and sometimes to even find the files (e.g., manual pages in a huge number of places, and making the manual page programs find all of them is a maintenance nightmare).

The root Filesystem

The root filesystem should generally be small, since it contains very critical files and a small, infrequently modified filesystem has a better chance of not getting corrupted. A corrupted root filesystem will generally mean that the system becomes unbootable except with special measures (e.g., from a floppy), so you don't want to risk it.

The root directory generally doesn't contain any files, except perhaps the standard boot image for the system, usually called /vmlinuz. All other files are in subdirectories in the root filesystems:

/bin

Commands needed during bootup that might be used by normal users (probably after bootup).

/sbin

Like /bin, but the commands are not intended for normal users, although they may use them if necessary and allowed.

/etc

Configuration files specific to the machine.

/root

The home directory for user \texttt{root}.

/lib

Shared libraries needed by the programs on the root filesystem.

/lib/modules

Loadable kernel modules, especially those that are needed to boot the system when recovering from disasters (e.g., network and filesystem drivers).

/dev

Device files.

/tmp

Temporary files. Programs running after bootup should use /var/tmp, not /tmp, since the former is probably on a disk with more space.

/boot

Files used by the bootstrap loader, e.g., LILO. Kernel images are often kept here instead of in the root directory. If there are many kernel images, the directory can easily grow rather big, and it might be better to keep it in a separate filesystem. Another reason would be to make sure the kernel images are within the first 1,024 cylinders of an IDE disk.

/mnt

Mount point for temporary mounts by the system administrator. Programs aren't supposed to mount on /mnt automatically. /mnt might be divided into subdirectories (e.g., /mnt/dosa might be the floppy drive using an MS-DOS filesystem, and /mnt/exta might be the same with an ext2 filesystem).

/proc, /usr, /var, /home

Mount points for the other filesystems.

The /etc Directory

The /etc directory contains a lot of files. Some of them are described below. For others, you should determine which program they belong to and read the manual page for that program. Many networking configuration files are in /etc as well and are described in the *Networking Administrators' Guide*.

/etc/rc Or /etc/rc.d Or /etc/rc?.d

Scripts or directories of scripts to run at startup or when changing the run level. See the chapter on init for further information.

/etc/passwd

The user database, with fields giving the username, real name, home directory, encrypted password, and other information about each user. The format is documented in the \man{passwd} manual page.

/etc/fdprm

Floppy disk parameter table. Describes what different floppy disk formats look like. Used by setfdprm. See the setfdprm manual page for more information.

/etc/fstab

Lists the filesystems mounted automatically at startup by the **mount -a** command (in /etc/rc or equivalent startup file). Under Linux, also contains information about swap areas used automatically by **swapon -a**. See the section called "Mounting And Unmounting" in Chapter 3 and the mount manual page for more information.

/etc/group

Similar to /etc/passwd, but describes groups instead of users. See the group manual page for more information.

/etc/inittab

Configuration file for init.

/etc/issue

Output by getty before the login prompt. Usually contains a short description or welcoming message to the system. The contents are up to the system administrator.

/etc/magic

The configuration file for file. Contains the descriptions of various file formats based on which file guesses the type of the file. See the magic and file manual pages for more information.

/etc/motd

The message of the day, automatically output after a successful login. Contents are up to the system administrator. Often used for getting information to every user, such as warnings about planned downtimes.

/etc/mtab

List of currently mounted filesystems. Initially set up by the bootup scripts, and updated automatically by the **mount** command. Used when a list of mounted filesystems is needed, e.g., by the **df** command.

/etc/shadow

Shadow password file on systems with shadow password software installed. Shadow passwords move the encrypted password from /etc/passwd into /etc/shadow; the latter is not readable by anyone except root. This makes it harder to crack passwords.

/etc/login.defs

Configuration file for the **login** command.

/etc/printcap

Like /etc/termcap, but intended for printers. Different syntax.

/etc/profile, /etc/csh.login, /etc/csh.cshrc

Files executed at login or startup time by the Bourne or C shells. These allow the system administrator to set global defaults for all users. See the manual pages for the respective shells.

/etc/securetty

Identifies secure terminals, i.e., the terminals from which root is allowed to log in. Typically only the virtual consoles are listed, so that it becomes impossible (or at least harder) to gain superuser privileges by breaking into a system over a modem or a network.

/etc/shells

Lists trusted shells. The **chsh** command allows users to change their login shell only to shells listed in this file. ftpd, the server process that provides FTP services for a machine, will check that the user's shell is listed in /etc/shells and will not let people log in unless the shell is listed there.

/etc/termcap

The terminal capability database. Describes by what "escape sequences" various terminals can be controlled. Programs are written so that instead of directly outputting an escape sequence that only works on a particular brand of terminal, they look up the correct sequence to do whatever it is they want to do in /etc/termcap. As a result, most programs work with most kinds of terminals. See the termcap, curs_termcap, and terminfo manual pages for more information.

The /dev Directory

The /dev directory contains the special device files for all the devices. The device files are named using special conventions; these are described in the Device list. The device files are created during installation, and later with the /dev/MAKEDEV script. The /dev/ MAKEDEV.local is a script written by the system administrator that creates local-only device files or links (i.e. those that are not part of the standard MAKEDEV, such as device files for some nonstandard device driver).

The /usr Filesystem

The /usr filesystem is often large, since all programs are installed there. All files in /usr usually come from a Linux distribution; locally installed programs and other stuff goes below /usr/local. This makes it possible to update the system from a new version of the distribution, or even a completely new distribution, without having to install all programs again. Some of the subdirectories of /usr are listed below (some of the less important directories have been dropped; see the FSSTND for more information).

/usr/X11R6

The X Window System, all files. To simplify the development and installation of X, the X files have not been integrated into the rest of the system. There is a directory tree below /usr/X11R6 similar to that below /usr itself.

/usr/X386

Similar to /usr/X11R6, but for X11 release 5.

/usr/bin

Almost all user commands. Some commands are in /bin or in /usr/local/bin.

/usr/sbin

System administration commands that are not needed on the root filesystem, e.g., most server programs.

/usr/man, /usr/info, /usr/doc

Manual pages, GNU Info documents, and miscellaneous other documentation files, respectively.

/usr/include

Header files for the C programming language. This should actually be below /usr/lib for consistency, but the tradition is overwhelmingly in support for this name.

/usr/lib

Unchanging data files for programs and subsystems, including some sitewide configuration files. The name lib comes from library; originally libraries of programming subroutines were stored in /usr/lib.

/usr/local

The place for locally installed software and other files.

The /var Filesystem

The /var contains data that is changed when the system is running normally. It is specific for each system, i.e., not shared over the network with other computers.

/var/catman

A cache for man pages that are formatted on demand. The source for manual pages is usually stored in /usr/man/man*; some manual pages might come with a preformatted version, which is stored in /usr/man/cat*. Other manual pages need to be formatted when they are first viewed; the formatted version is then stored in /var/man so that the next person to view the same page won't have to wait for it to be formatted. (/var/catman is often cleaned in the same way temporary directories are cleaned.)

/var/lib

Files that change while the system is running normally.

/var/local

Variable data for programs that are installed in /usr/local (i.e., programs that have been installed by the system administrator). Note that even locally installed programs should use the other /var directories if they are appropriate, e.g., /var/lock.

/var/lock

Lock files. Many programs follow a convention to create a lock file in /var/lock to indicate that they are using a particular device or file. Other programs will notice the lock file and won't attempt to use the device or file.

/var/log

Log files from various programs, especially login (/var/log/wtmp, which logs all logins and logouts into the system) and syslog (/var/log/messages, where all kernel and system program message are usually stored). Files in /var/log can often grow indefinitely and may require cleaning at regular intervals.

/var/run

Files that contain information about the system that is valid until the system is next booted. For example, /var/run/utmp contains information about people currently logged in.

/var/spool

Directories for mail, news, printer queues, and other queued work. Each different spool has its own subdirectory below /var/spool, e.g., the mailboxes of the users are in /var/spool/mail.

/var/tmp

Temporary files that are large or that need to exist for a longer time than what is allowed for /tmp. (Although the system administrator might not allow very old files in /var/tmp either.)

The /proc Filesystem

The /proc filesystem contains a illusionary filesystem. It does not exist on a disk. Instead, the kernel creates it in memory. It is used to provide information about the system (originally about processes, hence the name). Some of the more important files and directories are explained below. The /proc filesystem is described in more detail in the proc manual page.

/proc/1

A directory with information about process number 1. Each process has a directory below /proc with the name being its process identification number.

/proc/cpuinfo

Information about the processor, such as its type, make, model, and performance.

/proc/devices

List of device drivers configured into the currently running kernel.

/proc/dma

Shows which DMA channels are being used at the moment.

/proc/filesystems

Filesystems configured into the kernel.

/proc/interrupts

Shows which interrupts are in use and how many of each there have been.

/proc/ioports

Which I/O ports are in use at the moment.

/proc/kcore

An image of the physical memory of the system. This is exactly the same size as your physical memory, but does not really take up that much memory; it is generated on the fly as programs access it. (Remember: unless you copy it elsewhere, nothing under /proc takes up any disk space at all.)

/proc/kmsg

Messages output by the kernel. These are also routed to syslog.

/proc/ksyms

Symbol table for the kernel.

/proc/loadavg

The "load average" of the system; three meaningless indicators of how much work the system has to do at the moment.

/proc/meminfo

Information about memory usage, both physical and swap.

/proc/modules

Which kernel modules are loaded at the moment.

/proc/net
Status information about network protocols.

/proc/self
A symbolic link to the process directory of the program that is looking at /proc. When two processes look at /proc, they get different links. This is mainly a convenience to make it easier for programs to get at their process directory.

/proc/stat
Various statistics about the system, such as the number of page faults since the system was booted.

/proc/uptime
The time the system has been up.

/proc/version
The kernel version.

Note that while the above files tend to be easily readable text files, they can sometimes be formatted in a way that is not easily digestible. There are many commands that do little more than read the above files and format them for easier understanding. For example, the free program reads /proc/meminfo and converts the amounts given in bytes to kilobytes (and adds a little more information, as well).

Chapter 3
Using Disks And Other Storage Media

"On a clear disk you can seek forever."

When you install or upgrade your system, you need to do a fair amount of work on your disks. You have to make filesystems on your disks so that files can be stored on them and reserve space for the different parts of your system.

This chapter explains all these initial activities. Usually, once you get your system set up, you won't have to go through the work again, except for using floppies. You'll need to come back to this chapter if you add a new disk or want to fine-tune your disk usage.

The basic tasks in administering disks are:

♦ Format your disk. This does various things to prepare it for use, such as checking for bad sectors. (Formatting is nowadays not necessary for most hard disks.)

♦ Partition a hard disk, if you want to use it for several activities that aren't supposed to interfere with one another. One reason for partitioning is to store different operating systems on the same disk. Another reason is to keep user files separate from system files, which simplifies backups and helps protect the system files from corruption.

♦ Make a filesystem (of a suitable type) on each disk or partition. The disk means nothing to Linux until you make a filesystem; then files can be created and accessed on it.

♦ Mount different filesystems to form a single tree structure, either automatically, or manually as needed. (Manually mounted filesystems usually need to be unmounted manually as well.)

Chapter 4 contains information about virtual memory and disk caching, of which you also need to be aware when using disks.

Two Kinds Of Devices

Unix, and therefore Linux, recognizes two different kinds of device: random-access block devices (such as disks) and character devices (such as tapes and serial lines), some of which may be serial and some random-access. Each supported device is represented in the filesystem as a device file. When you read or write a device file, the data comes from or goes to the device it represents. This way no special programs (and no special application programming methodology, such as catching interrupts or polling a serial port) are necessary to access devices; for example, to send a file to the printer, one could just say

```
$ cat filename > /dev/lp1
$
```

and the contents of the file are printed (the file must, of course, be in a form that the printer understands). However, since it is not a good idea to have several people cat their files to the printer at the same time, one usually uses a special program to send the files to be printed (usually lpr). This program makes sure that only one file is being printed at a time, and will automatically send files to the printer as soon as it finishes with the previous file. Something similar is needed for most devices. In fact, one seldom needs to worry about device files at all.

Since devices show up as files in the filesystem (in the /dev directory), it is easy to see just what device files exist, using **ls** or another suitable command. In the output of **ls -l**, the first column contains the type of the file and its permissions. For example, inspecting a serial device gives on my system

```
$ ls -l /dev/cua0
crw-rw-rw-    1 root        uucp        5,  64 Nov 30  1993 /dev/cua0
$
```

The first character in the first column, i.e., "c" in crw-rw-rw- above, tells an informed user the type of the file, in this case a character device. For ordinary files, the first character is "-", for directories it is "d", and for block devices "b"; see the ls man page for further information.

Note that usually all device files exist even though the device itself might be not be installed. So just because you have a file /dev/sda, it doesn't mean that you really do have an SCSI hard disk. Having all the device files makes the installation programs simpler, and makes it easier to add new hardware (there is no need to find out the correct parameters for and create the device files for the new device).

Hard Disks

This subsection introduces terminology related to hard disks. If you already know the terms and concepts, you can skip this subsection.

See Figure 3.1 for a schematic picture of the important parts in a hard disk. A hard disk consists of one or more circular *platters* (the platters are made of a hard substance, e.g., aluminum, which gives the hard disk its name), of which either or both surfaces are coated with a magnetic substance used for recording the data. For each surface, there is a *read-write head* that examines or alters the recorded data. The platters rotate on a common axis; a typical rotation speed is 3,600 rotations per minute, although high-performance hard disks have higher speeds. The heads move along the radius of the platters; this movement combined with the rotation of the platters allows the head to access all parts of the surfaces.

The processor (CPU) and the actual disk communicate through a *disk controller*. This relieves the rest of the computer from knowing how to use the drive, since the controllers for different types of disks can be made to use the same interface toward the rest of the computer. Therefore, the computer can say just "hey disk, gimme what I want," instead of a long and complex series of electric signals to move the head to the proper location and waiting for the correct position to come under the head and doing all the other unpleasant necessary stuff. (In reality, the interface to the controller is still complex, but much less so than it would otherwise be.) The controller can also do some other stuff, such as caching or automatic bad sector replacement.

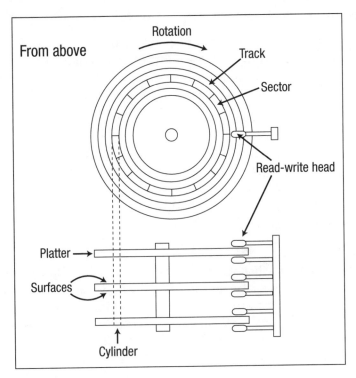

Figure 3.1
A schematic picture of a hard disk.

The above is usually all one needs to understand about the hardware. There is also a bunch of other stuff, such as the motor that rotates the platters and moves the heads, and the electronics that control the operation of the mechanical parts, but that is mostly not relevant for understanding the working principle of a hard disk.

The surfaces are usually divided into concentric rings, called *tracks*, and these in turn are divided into *sectors*. This division is used to specify locations on the hard disk and to allocate disk space to files. To find a given place on the hard disk, one might say "surface 3, track 5, sector 7." Usually the number of sectors is the same for all tracks, but some hard disks put more sectors in outer tracks (all sectors are of the same physical size, so more of them fit in the longer outer tracks). Typically, a sector will hold 512 bytes of data. The disk itself can't handle smaller amounts of data than one sector.

Each surface is divided into tracks (and sectors) in the same way. This means that when the head for one surface is on a track, the heads for the other surfaces are also on the corresponding tracks. All the corresponding tracks taken together are called a cylinder. It takes time to move the heads from one track (cylinder) to another, so by placing the data that is often accessed together (say, a file) so that it is within one cylinder, it is not necessary to move the heads to read all of it. This improves performance. It is not always possible to place files like this; files that are stored in several places on the disk are called *fragmented*.

The number of surfaces (or heads, which is the same thing), cylinders, and sectors vary a lot; the specification of the number of each is called the *geometry* of a hard disk. The geometry is usually stored in a special, battery-powered memory location called the CMOS RAM, from where the operating system can fetch it during bootup or driver initialization.

Unfortunately, the BIOS (the BIOS is some built-in software stored on ROM chips; it takes care, among other things, of the initial stages of booting) has a design limitation, which makes it impossible to specify a track number that is larger than 1,024 in the CMOS RAM, which is too little for a large hard disk. To overcome this, the hard disk controller lies about the geometry and translates the addresses given by the computer into something that fits reality. For example, a hard disk might have 8 heads, 2,048 tracks, and 35 sectors per track. (The numbers are completely imaginary.)

Its controller could lie to the computer and claim that it has 16 heads, 1,024 tracks, and 35 sectors per track, thus not exceeding the limit on tracks, and translates the address that the computer gives it by halving the head number and doubling the track number. The math can be more complicated in reality, because the numbers are not as nice as here (but again, the details are not relevant for understanding the principle). This translation distorts the operating system's view of how the disk is organized, thus making it impractical to use the all-data-on-one-cylinder trick to boost performance.

The translation is only a problem for IDE disks. SCSI disks use a sequential sector number (i.e., the controller translates a sequential sector number to a head, cylinder, and sector triplet), and a completely different method for the CPU to talk with the controller, so they are insulated from the problem. Note, however, that the computer might not know the real geometry of an SCSI disk either.

Since Linux often will not know the real geometry of a disk, its filesystems don't even try to keep files within a single cylinder. Instead, it tries to assign sequentially numbered sectors to files, which almost always gives similar performance. The issue is further complicated by on-controller caches and automatic prefetches done by the controller.

Each hard disk is represented by a separate device file. There can (usually) be only two or four IDE hard disks. These are known as /dev/hda, /dev/hdb, /dev/hdc, and /dev/hdd, respectively. SCSI hard disks are known as /dev/sda, /dev/sdb, and so on. Similar naming conventions exist for other hard disk types. Note that the device files for the hard disks give access to the entire disk, with no regard to partitions (which will be discussed below), and it's easy to mess up the partitions or the data in them if you aren't careful. The disks' device files are usually used only to get access to the master boot record (which will also be discussed below).

Floppies

A floppy disk consists of a flexible membrane covered on one or both sides with similar magnetic substance as a hard disk. The floppy disk itself doesn't have a read-write head, that is included in the drive. A floppy corresponds to one platter in a hard disk, but is removable and one drive can be used to access different floppies, whereas the hard disk is one indivisible unit.

Like a hard disk, a floppy is divided into tracks and sectors (and the two corresponding tracks on either side of a floppy form a cylinder), but there are fewer of them than on a hard disk.

A floppy drive can usually use several different types of disks; for example, a 3.5-inch drive can use both 720K and 1.44MB disks. Since the drive has to operate a bit differently and the operating system must know how big the disk is, there are many device files for floppy drives, one per combination of drive and disk type. Therefore, /dev/fd0H1440 is the first floppy drive (fd0), which must be a 3.5-inch drive, using a 3.5-inch, high-density disk (H) of size 1440K (1440), i.e., a normal 3.5-inch HD floppy

The names for floppy drives are complex, however, and Linux therefore has a special floppy device type that automatically detects the type of the disk in the drive. It works by trying to read the first sector of a newly inserted floppy using different floppy types until it finds the correct one. This naturally requires that the floppy is formatted first. The automatic devices are called /dev/fd0, /dev/fd1, and so on.

The parameters the automatic device uses to access a disk can also be set using the program \cmd{setfdprm}. This can be useful if you need to use disks that do not follow any usual floppy sizes, e.g., if they have an unusual number of sectors, or if the autodetecting for some reason fails and the proper device file is missing.

Linux can handle many nonstandard floppy disk formats in addition to all the standard ones. Some of these require using special formatting programs. We'll skip these disk types for now, but in the meantime you can examine the /etc/fdprm file. It specifies the settings that setfdprm recognizes.

The operating system must know when a disk has been changed in a floppy drive, for example, in order to avoid using cached data from the previous disk. Unfortunately, the signal line that is used for this is sometimes broken, and worse, this won't always be noticeable when using the drive from within MS-DOS. If you are experiencing weird problems using floppies, this might be the reason. The only way to correct it is to repair the floppy drive.

CD-ROMs

A CD-ROM drive uses an optically read, plastic-coated disk. The information is recorded on the surface of the disk (that is, the surface of the disk, on the metal disk inside the plastic coating) in small "holes" aligned along a spiral from the center to the edge. The drive directs a laser beam along the spiral to read the disk. When the laser hits a hole, the laser is reflected in one way; when it hits smooth surface, it is reflected in another way. This makes it easy to code bits, and therefore information. The rest is easy, mere mechanics.

CD-ROM drives are slow compared to hard disks. Whereas a typical hard disk will have an average seek time less than 15 milliseconds, a fast CD-ROM drive can use tenths of a second for seeks. The actual data transfer rate is fairly high at hundreds of kilobytes per second. The slowness means that CD-ROM drives are not as pleasant to use instead of hard disks (some Linux distributions provide "live" filesystems on CD-ROMs, making it unnecessary to copy the files to the hard disk, making installation easier and saving a lot of hard disk space), although it is still possible. For installing new software, CD-ROMs are very good, since maximum speed is not essential during installation.

There are several ways to arrange data on a CD-ROM. The most popular one is specified by the international standard ISO 9660. This standard specifies a very minimal filesystem, which is even more crude than the one MS-DOS uses. On the other hand, it is so minimal that every operating system should be able to map it to its native system.

For normal Unix use, the ISO 9660 filesystem is not usable, so an extension to the standard has been developed, called the Rock Ridge extension. Rock Ridge allows longer file names, symbolic links, and a lot of other goodies, making a CD-ROM look more or less like any contemporary Unix filesystem. Even better, a Rock Ridge filesystem is still a valid ISO 9660 filesystem, making it usable by non-Unix systems as well. Linux supports both ISO 9660 and the Rock Ridge extensions; the extensions are recognized and used automatically.

The filesystem is only half the battle, however. Most CD-ROMs contain data that requires a special program to access, and most of these programs do not run under Linux (except, possibly, under dosemu, the Linux MS-DOS emulator).

A CD-ROM drive is accessed via the corresponding device file. There are several ways to connect a CD-ROM drive to the computer: via SCSI, via a sound card, or via EIDE. The hardware hacking needed to do this is outside the scope of this book, but the type of connection decides the device file.

Tapes

A tape drive uses a tape, similar (but completely different, of course) to cassettes used for music. A tape is serial in nature, which means that in order to get to any given part of it, you first have to go through all the parts in between. A disk can be accessed randomly, i.e., you can jump directly to any place on the disk. The serial access of tapes makes them slow.

On the other hand, tapes are relatively cheap to make, since they do not need to be fast. They can also easily be made quite long, and can therefore contain a large amount of data. This makes tapes very suitable for things like archiving and backups, which do not require large speeds, but benefit from low costs and large storage capacities.

Formatting

Formatting is the process of writing marks on the magnetic media that are used to mark tracks and sectors. Before a disk is formatted, its magnetic surface is a complete mess of magnetic signals. When it is formatted, some order is brought into the chaos by essentially drawing lines where the tracks go, and where they are divided into sectors. The actual details are not quite exactly like this, but that is irrelevant. What is important is that a disk cannot be used unless it has been formatted.

The terminology is a bit confusing here: In MS-DOS, the word *formatting* is used to cover also the process of creating a filesystem (which will be discussed below). There, the two processes are often combined, especially for floppies. When the distinction needs to be made, the real formatting is called *low-level formatting*, while making the filesystem is called *high-level formatting*. In Unix circles, the two are called formatting and making a filesystem, so that's what is used in this book as well.

For IDE and some SCSI disks the formatting is actually done at the factory and doesn't need to be repeated; hence, most people rarely need to worry about it. In fact, formatting a hard disk can cause it to work less well, for example because a disk might need to be formatted in some very special way to allow automatic bad sector replacement to work.

Disks that need to be or can be formatted often require a special program anyway, because the interface to the formatting logic inside the drive is different from drive to drive. The formatting program is often either on the controller BIOS, or is supplied as an MS-DOS program; neither of these can easily be used from within Linux.

During formatting one might encounter bad spots on the disk, called *bad blocks* or *bad sectors*. These are sometimes handled by the drive itself, but even then, if more of them develop, something needs to be done to avoid using those parts of the disk. The logic to do this is built into the filesystem; how to add the information into the filesystem is described below. Alternatively, one might create a small partition that covers just the bad part of the disk; this approach might be a good idea if the bad spot is very large, since filesystems can sometimes have trouble with very large bad areas.

Floppies are formatted with **fdformat**. The floppy device file to use is given as the parameter. For example, the following command would format a high-density, 3.5-inch floppy in the first floppy drive:

```
$ fdformat /dev/fd0H1440
Double-sided, 80 tracks, 18 sec/track. Total capacity 1440 kB.
Formatting ... done
Verifying ... done
$
```

Note that if you want to use an autodetecting device (e.g., /dev/fd0), you must set the parameters of the device with **setfdprm** first. To achieve the same effect as above, one would have to do the following:

```
$ setfdprm /dev/fd0 1440/1440
$ fdformat /dev/fd0
Double-sided, 80 tracks, 18 sec/track. Total capacity 1440 kB.
Formatting ... done
Verifying ... done
$
```

It is usually more convenient to choose the correct device file that matches the type of the floppy. Note that it is unwise to format floppies to contain more information than what they are designed for.

fdformat will also validate the floppy, i.e., check it for bad blocks. It will try a bad block several times (you can usually hear this, the drive noise changes dramatically). If the floppy is only marginally bad (due to dirt on the read-write head, some errors are false signals), **fdformat** won't complain, but a real error will abort the validation process. The kernel will print log messages for each I/O error it finds; these will go to the console or, if syslog is being used, to the file /usr/log/messages. **fdformat** itself won't tell where the error is (one usually doesn't care; floppies are cheap enough that a bad one is automatically thrown away).

```
$ fdformat /dev/fd0H1440
Double-sided, 80 tracks, 18 sec/track. Total capacity 1440 kB.
Formatting ... done
Verifying ... read: Unknown error
$
```

The **badblocks** command can be used to search any disk or partition for bad blocks (including a floppy). It does not format the disk, so it can be used to check even existing filesystems. The example below checks a 3.5-inch floppy with two bad blocks.

```
$ badblocks /dev/fd0H1440 1440
718
719
$
```

badblocks outputs the block numbers of the bad blocks it finds. Most filesystems can avoid such bad blocks. They maintain a list of known bad blocks, which is initialized when the filesystem is made, and can be modified later. The initial search for bad blocks can be done by the **mkfs** command (which initializes the filesystem), but later checks should be done with **badblocks** and the new blocks should be added with **fsck**. We'll describe \cmd{mkfs} and **fsck** later.

Many modern disks automatically notice bad blocks and attempt to fix them by using a special, reserved good block instead. This is invisible to the operating system. This feature should be documented in the disk's manual, if you're curious if it is happening. Even such disks can fail, if the number of bad blocks grows too large, although chances are that by then the disk will be so rotten as to be unusable.

Partitions

A hard disk can be divided into several partitions. Each partition functions as if it were a separate hard disk. The idea is that if you have one hard disk, and want to have, say, two operating systems on it, you can divide the disk into two partitions. Each operating system uses its partition as it wishes and doesn't touch the other one's. This way the two operating systems can coexist peacefully on the same hard disk. Without partitions one would have to buy a hard disk for each operating system.

Floppies are not partitioned. There is no technical reason against this, but since they're so small, partitions would be useful only very rarely. CD-ROMs are usually also not partitioned, since it's easier to use them as one big disk, and there is seldom a need to have several operating systems on one.

The MBR, Boot Sectors, And Partition Table

The information about how a hard disk has been partitioned is stored in its first sector (that is, the first sector of the first track on the first disk surface). The first sector is the *master boot record* (MBR) of the disk; this is the sector that the BIOS reads in and starts when the machine is first booted. The master boot record contains a small program that reads the partition table, checks which partition is active (that is, marked bootable), and reads the first sector of that partition, the partition's boot sector (the MBR is also a boot sector, but it has a special status and therefore a special name). This boot sector contains another small program that reads the first part of the operating system stored on that partition (assuming it is bootable) and then starts it.

The partitioning scheme is not built into the hardware, or even into the BIOS. It is only a convention that many operating systems follow. Not all operating systems do follow it, but they are the exceptions. Some operating systems support partitions, but they occupy one partition on the hard disk, and use their internal partitioning method within that partition. The latter type exists peacefully with other operating systems (including Linux), and does not require any special measures, but an operating system that doesn't support partitions cannot coexist on the same disk with any other operating system.

As a safety precaution, it is a good idea to write down the partition table on a piece of paper, so that if it ever corrupts you don't have to lose all your files. (A bad partition table can be fixed with **fdisk**). The relevant information is given by the **fdisk -l** command:

```
$ fdisk -l /dev/hda

Disk /dev/hda: 15 heads, 57 sectors, 790 cylinders
Units = cylinders of 855 * 512 bytes

    Device Boot   Begin   Start    End   Blocks    Id  System
/dev/hda1             1       1     24   10231+    82  Linux swap
/dev/hda2            25      25     48   10260     83  Linux native
/dev/hda3            49      49    408   153900    83  Linux native
/dev/hda4           409     409    790   163305     5  Extended
/dev/hda5           409     409    744   143611+   83  Linux native
/dev/hda6           745     745    790   19636+    83  Linux native
$
```

Extended And Logical Partitions

The original partitioning scheme for PC hard disks allowed only four partitions. This quickly turned out to be too little in real life, partly because some people want more than four operating systems (Linux, MS-DOS, OS/2, Minix, FreeBSD, NetBSD, or Windows/NT, to name a few), but primarily because sometimes it is a good idea to have several partitions for one operating system. For example, swap space is usually best put in its own partition for Linux instead of in the main Linux partition for reasons of speed (see below).

To overcome this design problem, extended partitions were invented. This trick allows partitioning a primary partition into subpartitions. The primary partition thus subdivided is the extended partition; the subpartitions are logical partitions. They behave like primary (illogical?) partitions, but are created differently. There is no speed difference between them.

The partition structure of a hard disk might look like that in Figure 3.2. The disk is divided into three primary partitions, the second of which is divided into two logical partitions. Part of the disk is not partitioned at all. The disk as a whole and each primary partition has a boot sector.

Partition Types

The partition tables (the one in the MBR and the ones for extended partitions) contain one byte per partition that identifies the type of that partition. This attempts to identify the operating system that uses the partition, or what it uses it for. The purpose is to make it possible to avoid having two operating systems accidentally using the same partition. However, in reality, operating systems do not really care about the partition type byte; e.g., Linux doesn't care at all what it is. Worse, some of them use it incorrectly; e.g., at least some versions of DR-DOS ignore the most significant bit of the byte, while others don't.

There is no standardization agency to specify what each byte value means, but some commonly accepted ones are included in Table 3.1. The same list is available in the Linux **fdisk** program.

Partitioning A Hard Disk

There are many programs for creating and removing partitions. Most operating systems have their own, and it can be a good idea to use each operating system's own, just in case it does something unusual that the others can't. Many of the programs are called **fdisk**, including the

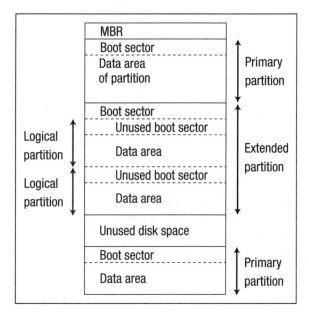

Figure 3.2
A sample hard disk partitioning.

Table 3.1 Partition types (from the Linux fdisk program).

0	Empty	40	Venix 80286	94	Amoeba BBT
1	DOS 12-bit FAT	51	Novell?	a5	BSD/386
2	XENIX root	52	Microport	b7	BSDI fs
3	XENIX usr	63	GNU HURD	b8	BSDI swap
4	DOS 16-bitf <32M	64	Novell	c7	Syrinx
5	Extended	75	PC/IX	Db	CP/M
6	DOS 16-bit >=32M	80	Old MINIX	e1	DOS access
7	OS/2 HPFS	81	Linux/MINIX	e3	DOS R/O
8	AIX	82	Linux swap	f2	DOS secondary
9	AIX bootable	83	Linux native	Ff	BBT
a	OS/2 Boot Manag	93	Amoeba		

Linux one, or variations thereof. Details on using the Linux **fdisk** are given on its man page. The **cfdisk** command is similar to **fdisk**, but has a nicer (full screen) user interface.

When using IDE disks, the boot partition (the partition with the bootable kernel image files) must be completely within the first 1,024 cylinders. This is because the disk is used via the BIOS during boot (before the system goes into protected mode), and BIOS can't handle more than 1,024 cylinders. It is sometimes possible to use a boot partition that is only partly within the first 1,024 cylinders. This works as long as all the files that are read with the BIOS are within the first 1,024 cylinders. Because this is difficult to arrange, it is a very bad idea to do it; you never know when a kernel update or disk defragmentation will result in an unbootable system. Therefore, make sure your boot partition is completely within the first 1,024 cylinders.

Some newer versions of the BIOS and IDE disks can, in fact, handle disks with more than 1,024 cylinders. If you have such a system, you can forget about the problem; if you aren't quite sure of it, put it within the first 1,024 cylinders.

Each partition should have an even number of sectors, since the Linux filesystems use a 1K block size, i.e., two sectors. An odd number of sectors will result in the last sector being unused. This won't result in any problems, but it is ugly, and some versions of **fdisk** will warn about it.

Changing a partition's size usually requires first backing up everything you want to save from that partition (preferably the whole disk, just in case), deleting the partition, creating new partition, then restoring everything to the new partition. If the partition is growing, you may need to adjust the sizes (and back up and restore) of the adjoining partitions as well.

Because changing partition sizes is painful, it is preferable to get the partitions right the first time, or have an effective and easy to use backup system. If you're installing from a media that does not require much human intervention (say, from CD-ROM, as opposed to floppies), it is often easy to play with different configuration at first. Since you don't already have data to back up, it is not so painful to modify partition sizes several times.

There is a program for MS-DOS, called fips, which resizes an MS-DOS partition without requiring the backup and restore, but for other filesystems it is still necessary.

Device Files And Partitions

Each partition and extended partition has its own device file. The naming convention for these files is that a partition's number is appended after the name of the whole disk, with the convention that 1–4 are primary partitions (regardless of how many primary partitions there are) and 5–8 are logical partitions (regardless of within which primary partition they reside). For example, /dev/hda1 is the first primary partition on the first IDE hard disk, and /dev/sdb7 is the third extended partition on the second SCSI hard disk.

Filesystems

What Are Filesystems?

A filesystem is the methods and data structures that an operating system uses to keep track of files on a disk or partition; that is, the way the files are organized on the disk. The word is also used to refer to a partition or disk that is used to store the files or the type of the filesystem. Thus, one might say "I have two filesystems," meaning one has two partitions on which one stores files, or that one is using the "extended filesystem," meaning the type of the filesystem.

The difference between a disk or partition and the filesystem it contains is important. A few programs (including, reasonably enough, programs that create filesystems) operate directly on the raw sectors of a disk or partition; if there is an existing filesystem there it will be destroyed or seriously corrupted. Most programs operate on a filesystem, and therefore won't work on a partition that doesn't contain one (or that contains one of the wrong type).

Before a partition or disk can be used as a filesystem, it needs to be initialized, and the bookkeeping data structures need to be written to the disk. This process is called making a filesystem.

Most Unix filesystem types have a similar general structure, although the exact details vary quite a bit. The central concepts are superblock, *inode*, data block, directory block, and indirection block. The superblock contains information about the filesystem as a whole, such as its size (the exact information here depends on the filesystem). An *inode* contains all information about a file, except its name. The name is stored in the directory, together with the number of the inode. A directory entry consists of a file name and the number of the inode which represents the file. The inode contains the numbers of several data blocks, which are used to store the data in the file. There is space only for a few data block numbers in the inode, however, and if more are needed, more space for pointers to the data blocks is allocated dynamically. These dynamically allocated blocks are *indirect blocks*; the name indicates that in order to find the data block, one has to find its number in the indirect block first.

Unix filesystems usually allow one to create a hole in a file (this is done with **lseek**; check the manual page), which means that the filesystem just pretends that at a particular place in the file there is just zero bytes, but no actual disk sectors are reserved for that place in the file (this means that the file will use a bit less disk space). This happens especially often for small binaries, Linux shared libraries, some databases, and a few other special cases. (Holes are implemented by storing a special value as the address of the data block in the indirect block or inode. This special address means that no data block is allocated for that part of the file, ergo, there is a hole in the file.)

Holes are moderately useful. On the author's system, a simple measurement showed a potential for about 4MB of savings through holes of about 200MB total used disk space. That system, however, contains relatively few programs and no database files.

Filesystems Galore

Linux supports several types of filesystems. As of this writing the most important ones are:

minix

The oldest, presumed to be the most reliable, but quite limited in features (some time stamps are missing, at most 30-character file names) and restricted in capabilities (at most 64MB per filesystem).

xia

A modified version of the minix filesystem that lifts the limits on the file names and filesystem sizes, but does not otherwise introduce new features. It is not very popular, but is reported to work very well.

ext2

The most featureful of the native Linux filesystems, currently also the most popular one. It is designed to be easily upward compatible, so that new versions of the filesystem code do not require remaking the existing filesystems.

ext

An older version of ext2 that wasn't upward compatible. It is hardly ever used in new installations any more, and most people have converted to ext2.

In addition, support for several foreign filesystems exists, to make it easier to exchange files with other operating systems. These foreign filesystems work just like native ones, except that they may be lacking in some usual Unix features, or have curious limitations, or other oddities.

msdos

Compatibility with MS-DOS (and OS/2 and Windows NT) FAT filesystems.

umsdos

Extends the msdos filesystem driver under Linux to get long filenames, owners, permissions, links, and device files. This allows a normal msdos filesystem to be used as if it were a Linux one, thus removing the need for a separate partition for Linux.

iso9660

The standard CD-ROM filesystem; the popular Rock Ridge extension to the CD-ROM standard that allows longer file names is supported automatically.

nfs

A networked filesystem that allows sharing a filesystem between many computers to allow easy access to the files from all of them.

hpfs

The OS/2 filesystem.

sysv

SystemV/386, Coherent, and Xenix filesystems.

The choice of filesystem to use depends on the situation. If compatibility or other reasons make one of the non-native filesystems necessary, then that one must be used. If one can choose freely, then it is probably wisest to use ext2, since it has all the features but does not suffer from lack of performance.

There is also the proc filesystem, usually accessible as the /proc directory, which is not really a filesystem at all, even though it looks like one. The proc filesystem makes it easy to access certain kernel data structures, such as the process list (hence the name). It makes these data structures look like a filesystem, and that filesystem can be manipulated with all the usual file tools. For example, to get a listing of all processes one might use the command

```
$ ls -l /proc
total 0
dr-xr-xr-x   4 root      root           0 Jan 31 20:37 1
dr-xr-xr-x   4 liw       users          0 Jan 31 20:37 63
dr-xr-xr-x   4 liw       users          0 Jan 31 20:37 94
dr-xr-xr-x   4 liw       users          0 Jan 31 20:37 95
dr-xr-xr-x   4 root      users          0 Jan 31 20:37 98
dr-xr-xr-x   4 liw       users          0 Jan 31 20:37 99
-r-r-r-   1 root      root        0 Jan 31 20:37 devices
-r-r-r-   1 root      root        0 Jan 31 20:37 dma
-r-r-r-   1 root      root        0 Jan 31 20:37 filesystems
-r-r-r-   1 root      root        0 Jan 31 20:37 interrupts
-r------   1 root      root  8654848 Jan 31 20:37 kcore
```

```
-r-r-r-    1 root     root         0 Jan 31 11:50 kmsg
-r-r-r-    1 root     root         0 Jan 31 20:37 ksyms
-r-r-r-    1 root     root         0 Jan 31 11:51 loadavg
-r-r-r-    1 root     root         0 Jan 31 20:37 meminfo
-r-r-r-    1 root     root         0 Jan 31 20:37 modules
dr-xr-xr-x 2 root     root         0 Jan 31 20:37 net
dr-xr-xr-x 4 root     root         0 Jan 31 20:37 self
-r-r-r-    1 root     root         0 Jan 31 20:37 stat
-r-r-r-    1 root     root         0 Jan 31 20:37 uptime
-r-r-r-    1 root     root         0 Jan 31 20:37 version
$
```

(There will be a few extra files that don't correspond to processes, though. The above example has been shortened.)

Note that even though it is called a filesystem, no part of the proc filesystem touches any disk. It exists only in the kernel's imagination. Whenever anyone tries to look at any part of the proc filesystem, the kernel makes it look as if the part existed somewhere, even though it doesn't. So, even though there is a multimegabyte /proc/kcore file, it doesn't take any disk space.

Which Filesystem Should Be Used?

There is usually little point in using many different filesystems. Currently, ext2fs is the most popular one, and it is probably the wisest choice. Depending on the overhead for bookkeeping structures, speed, (perceived) reliability, compatibility, and various other reasons, it may be advisable to use another filesystem. This needs to be decided on a case-by-case basis.

Creating A Filesystem

Filesystems are created, i.e., initialized, with the **mkfs** command. There is actually a separate program for each filesystem type. **mkfs** is just a front end that runs the appropriate program depending on the desired filesystem type. The type is selected with the **-t fstype** option.

The programs called by **mkfs** have slightly different command line interfaces. The common and most important options are summarized below; see the manual pages for more.

-t fstype-
Select the type of the filesystem.

-c
Search for bad blocks and initialize the bad block list accordingly.

-l filename
Read the initial bad block list from the name file.

To create an ext2 filesystem on a floppy, one would give the following commands:

```
$ fdformat -n /dev/fd0H1440
Double-sided, 80 tracks, 18 sec/track. Total capacity 1440 kB.
Formatting ... done
$ badblocks /dev/fd0H1440 1440 $>$ bad-blocks
$ mkfs -t ext2 -l bad-blocks /dev/fd0H1440
mke2fs 0.5a, 5-Apr-94 for EXT2 FS 0.5, 94/03/10
360 inodes, 1440 blocks
72 blocks (5.00%) reserved for the super user
First data block=1
Block size=1024 (log=0)
Fragment size=1024 (log=0)
1 block group
8192 blocks per group, 8192 fragments per group
360 inodes per group

Writing inode tables: done
Writing superblocks and filesystem accounting information: done
$
```

First, the floppy was formatted (the **-n** option prevents validation, i.e., bad block checking). Then bad blocks were searched with **badblocks**, with the output redirected to a file, bad-blocks. Finally, the filesystem was created, with the bad block list initialized by whatever **badblocks** found.

The **-c** option could have been used with **mkfs** instead of **badblocks** and a separate file. The example below does that.

```
$ mkfs -t ext2 -c /dev/fd0H1440
mke2fs 0.5a, 5-Apr-94 for EXT2 FS 0.5, 94/03/10
360 inodes, 1440 blocks
72 blocks (5.00%) reserved for the super user
First data block=1
Block size=1024 (log=0)
Fragment size=1024 (log=0)
1 block group
8192 blocks per group, 8192 fragments per group
360 inodes per group

Checking for bad blocks (read-only test): done
Writing inode tables: done
Writing superblocks and filesystem accounting information: done
$
```

The **-c** option is more convenient than a separate use of **badblocks**, but **badblocks** is necessary for checking after the filesystem has been created.

The process to prepare filesystems on hard disks or partitions is the same as for floppies, except that the formatting isn't needed.

Mounting And Unmounting

Before one can use a filesystem, it has to be mounted. The operating system then does various bookkeeping things to make sure that everything works. Since all files in Unix are in a single directory tree, the mount operation will make it look like the contents of the new filesystem are the contents of an existing subdirectory in some already mounted filesystem.

For example, Figure 3.3 shows three separate filesystems, each with their own root directory. When the last two filesystems are mounted below /home and /usr, respectively, on the first filesystem, we can get a single directory tree, as in Figure 3.4.

The mounts could be done as in the following example:

```
$ mount /dev/hda2 /home
$ mount /dev/hda3 /usr
$
```

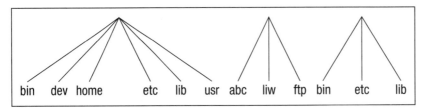

Figure 3.3
Three separate filesystems.

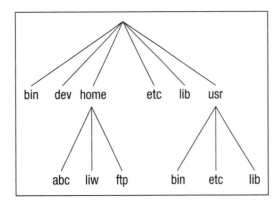

Figure 3.4
/home and /usr have been mounted.

The **mount** command takes two arguments. The first one is the device file corresponding to the disk or partition containing the filesystem. The second one is the directory below which it will be mounted. After these commands the contents of the two filesystems look just like the contents of the /home and /usr directories, respectively. One would then say that "/dev/hda2 is mounted on /home," and similarly for /usr. To look at either filesystem, one would look at the contents of the directory on which it has been mounted, just as if it were any other directory. Note the difference between the device file, /dev/hda2, and the mounted-on directory, /home. The device file gives access to the raw contents of the disk, the mounted-on directory gives access to the files on the disk. The mounted-on directory is called the *mount point*.

Linux supports many filesystem types. **mount** tries to guess the type of the filesystem. You can also use the **-t fstype** option to specify the type directly; this is sometimes necessary, since the heuristics **mount** uses do not always work. For example, to mount an MS-DOS floppy, you could use the following command:

```
$ mount -t msdos /dev/fd0 /floppy
$
```

The mounted-on directory need not be empty, although it must exist. Any files in it, however, will be inaccessible by name while the filesystem is mounted. (Any files that have already been opened will still be accessible. Files that have hard links from other directories can be accessed using those names.) There is no harm done with this, and it can even be useful. For instance, some people like to have /tmp and /var/tmp synonymous, and make /tmp be a symbolic link to /var/tmp. When the system is booted, before the /var filesystem is mounted, a /var/tmp directory residing on the root filesystem is used instead. When /var is mounted, it will make the /var/tmp directory on the root filesystem inaccessible. If /var/tmp didn't exist on the root filesystem, it would be impossible to use temporary files before mounting /var.

If you don't intend to write anything to the filesystem, use the **-r** switch for **mount** to do a read-only mount. This will make the kernel stop any attempts at writing to the filesystem, and will also stop the kernel from updating file access times in the inodes. Read-only mounts are necessary for unwritable media, e.g., CD-ROMs.

The alert reader has already noticed a slight logistical problem. How is the first filesystem (called the root filesystem, because it contains the root directory) mounted, since it obviously can't be mounted on another filesystem? Well, the answer is that it is done by magic. (For more information, see the kernel source or the Kernel Hackers' Guide.) The root filesystem is magically mounted at boot time, and one can rely on it to always be mounted. If the root filesystem can't be mounted, the system does not boot. The name of the filesystem that is magically mounted as root is either compiled into the kernel, or set using LILO or rdev.

The root filesystem is usually first mounted readonly. The startup scripts will then run **fsck** to verify its validity, and if there are no problems, they will remount it so that writes will also be allowed. **fsck** must not be run on a mounted filesystem, since any changes to the filesystem while **fsck** is running will cause trouble. Since the root filesystem is mounted readonly while it is being checked, **fsck** can fix any problems without worry, since the remount operation will flush any metadata that the filesystem keeps in memory.

On many systems there are other filesystems that should also be mounted automatically at boot time. These are specified in the /etc/fstab file; see the fstab man page for details on the format. The details of exactly when the extra filesystems are mounted depend on many factors, and can be configured by each administrator if need be; see Chapter 5..

When a filesystem no longer needs to be mounted, it can be unmounted with **umount**. (It should of course be unmount, but the "n" mysteriously disappeared in the 1970s, and hasn't been seen since.) **umount** takes one argument: either the device file or the mount point. For example, to unmount the directories of the previous example, one could use the commands

```
$ umount /dev/hda2
$ umount /usr
$
```

See the man page for further instructions on how to use the command. It is imperative that you always unmount a mounted floppy. Don't just pop the floppy out of the drive! Because of disk caching, the data is not necessarily written to the floppy until you unmount it, so removing the floppy from the drive too early might cause the contents to become garbled. If you only read from the floppy, this is not very likely, but if you write, even accidentally, the result may be catastrophic.

Mounting and unmounting requires super-user privileges, i.e., only root can do it. The reason for this is that if any user can mount a floppy on any directory, then it is rather easy to create a floppy with, say, a Trojan horse disguised as /bin/sh, or any other often used program. However, it is often necessary to allow users to use floppies, and there are several ways to do this:

♦ Give the users the root password. This is obviously bad security, but is the easiest solution. It works well if there is no need for security anyway, which is the case on many non-networked, personal systems.

♦ Use a program such as sudo to allow users to use mount. This is still bad security, but doesn't directly give super-user privileges to everyone. (It requires several seconds of hard thinking on the users' behalf.)

♦ Make the users use mtools, a package for manipulating MS-DOS filesystems, without mounting them. This works well if MS-DOS floppies are all that is needed, but is rather awkward otherwise.

♦ List the floppy devices and their allowable mount points together with the suitable options in /etc/fstab.

The last alternative can be implemented by adding a line like the following to the \fn{/etc/ fstab} file:

```
/dev/fd0              /floppy       msdos    user,noauto      0    0
```

The columns are: device file to mount, directory to mount on, filesystem type, options, backup frequency (used by dump), and **fsck** pass number (to specify the order in which filesystems should be checked upon boot; 0 means no check).

The noauto option stops this mount to be done automatically when the system is started (i.e., it stops **mount -a** from mounting it). The user option allows any user to mount the filesystem, and, because of security reasons, disallows execution of programs (normal or setuid) and interpretation of device files from the mounted filesystem. After this, any user can mount a floppy with an msdos filesystem with the following command:

```
$ mount /floppy
$
```

The floppy can (and needs to, of course) be unmounted with the corresponding \cmd{umount} command.

If you want to provide access to several types of floppies, you need to give several mount points. The settings can be different for each mount point. For example, to give access to both MS-DOS and ext2 floppies, you could have the following to lines in /etc/fstab:

```
/dev/fd0    /dosfloppy    msdos    user,noauto 0 0
/dev/fd0    /ext2floppy   ext2     user,noauto 0 0
```

For MS-DOS filesystems (not just floppies), you probably want to restrict access to it by using the uid, gid, and umask filesystem options, described in detail on the **mount** manual page. If you aren't careful, mounting an MS-DOS filesystem gives everyone at least read access to the files in it, which is not a good idea.

Checking Filesystem Integrity With **fsck**

Filesystems are complex creatures, and as such, they tend to be somewhat error-prone. A filesystem's correctness and validity can be checked using the **fsck** command. It can be instructed to repair any minor problems it finds, and to alert the user if there any unrepairable problems. Fortunately, the code to implement filesystems is debugged quite effectively, so there are seldom any problems at all, and they are usually caused by power failures, failing hardware, or operator errors; for example, by not shutting down the system properly.

Most systems are setup to run **fsck** automatically at boot time, so that any errors are detected (and hopefully corrected) before the system is used. Use of a corrupted filesystem tends to make things worse: If the data structures are messed up, using the filesystem will probably mess them up even more, resulting in more data loss. However, **fsck** can take a while to run on big filesystems, and because errors almost never occur if the system has been shut down properly, a couple of tricks are used to avoid doing the checks in such cases. The first is that if the file /etc/fastboot exists, no checks are made. The second is that the ext2 filesystem has a special marker in its superblock that tells whether the filesystem was un-mounted properly after the previous mount. This allows **e2fsck** (the version of **fsck** for the ext2 filesystem) to avoid checking the filesystem if the flag indicates that the unmount was done (the assumption being that a proper unmount indicates no problems). Whether the /etc/fastboot trick works on your system depends on your startup scripts, but the ext2 trick works every time you use **e2fsck**. It has to be explicitly bypassed with an option to **e2fsck** to be avoided. (See the **e2fsck** man page for details on how.)

The automatic checking only works for the filesystems that are mounted automatically at boot time. Use **fsck** manually to check other filesystems, e.g., floppies.

If **fsck** finds unrepairable problems, you need either in-depth knowledge of how filesystems work in general, and the type of the corrupt filesystem in particular, or good backups. The latter is easy (although sometimes tedious) to arrange, the former can sometimes be ar-ranged via a friend, the Linux newsgroups and mailing lists, or some other source of support, if you don't have the know-how yourself. I'd like to tell you more about it, but my lack of education and experience in this regard hinders me. The debugfs program by Theodore Ts'o should be useful.

fsck must only be run on unmounted filesystems, never on mounted filesystems (with the exception of the read-only root during startup). This is because it accesses the raw disk, and can therefore modify the filesystem without the operating system realizing it. There will be trouble if the operating system is confused.

Checking For Disk Errors With **badblocks**

It can be a good idea to periodically check for bad blocks. This is done with the **badblocks** command. It outputs a list of the numbers of all bad blocks it can find. This list can be fed to **fsck** to be recorded in the filesystem data structures so that the operating system won't try to use the bad blocks for storing data. The following example will show how this could be done.

```
$ badblocks /dev/fd0H1440 1440 > bad-blocks
$ fsck -t ext2 -l bad-blocks /dev/fd0H1440
Parallelizing fsck version 0.5a (5-Apr-94)
e2fsck 0.5a, 5-Apr-94 for EXT2 FS 0.5, 94/03/10
Pass 1: Checking inodes, blocks, and sizes
Pass 2: Checking directory structure
Pass 3: Checking directory connectivity
Pass 4: Check reference counts.
Pass 5: Checking group summary information.
```

```
/dev/fd0H1440: ***** FILESYSTEM WAS MODIFIED *****
/dev/fd0H1440: 11/360 files, 63/1440 blocks
$
```

If **badblocks** reports a block that was already used, **e2fsck** will try to move the block to another place. If the block was really bad, not just marginal, the contents of the file may be corrupted.

Fighting Fragmentation

When a file is written to disk, it can't always be written in consecutive blocks. A file that is not stored in consecutive blocks is fragmented. It takes longer to read a fragmented file, since the disk's read-write head will have to move more. It is desirable to avoid fragmentation, although it is less of a problem in a system with a good buffer cache with read-ahead.

The ext2 filesystem attempts to keep fragmentation at a minimum, by keeping all blocks in a file close together, even if they can't be stored in consecutive sectors. ext2 effectively always allocates the free block that is nearest to other blocks in a file. For ext2, it is therefore seldom necessary to worry about fragmentation. There is a program for defragmenting an ext2 filesystem, see **ftp://tsx-11.mit.edu/pub/linux/packages/ext2fs/defrag-0.70.lsm** and **ftp://tsx-11.mit.edu/pub/linux/packages/ext2fs/defrag-0.70.tar.gz**.

There are many MS-DOS defragmentation programs that move blocks around in the filesystem to remove fragmentation. For other filesystems, defragmentation must be done by backing up the filesystem, re-creating it, and restoring the files from backups. Backing up a filesystem before defragmenting is a good idea for all filesystems, since many things can go wrong during the defragmentation.

Other Tools For All Filesystems

Some other tools are also useful for managing filesystems. **df** shows the free disk space on one or more filesystems; **du** shows how much disk space a directory and all its files contain. These can be used to hunt down disk space wasters.

sync forces all unwritten blocks in the buffer cache (see the section called "The Buffer Cache" in Chapter 4) to be written to disk. It is seldom necessary to do this by hand; the daemon process update does this automatically. It can be useful in catastrophes, for example if update or its helper process bdflush dies, or if you must turn off power now and can't wait for update to run.

Other Tools For The ext2 Filesystem

In addition to the filesystem creator (**mke2fs**) and checker (**e2fsck**) accessible directly or via the filesystem type independent front ends, the ext2 filesystem has some additional tools that can be useful.

tune2fs adjusts filesystem parameters. Some of the more interesting parameters are:

♦ A maximal mount count. **e2fsck** enforces a check when filesystem has been mounted too many times, even if the clean flag is set. For a system that is used for developing or testing the system, it might be a good idea to reduce this limit.

♦ A maximal time between checks. **e2fsck** can also enforce a maximal time between two checks, even if the clean flag is set, and the filesystem hasn't been mounted very often. This can be disabled, however.

♦ Number of blocks reserved for root. ext2 reserves some blocks for root so that if the filesystem fills up, it is still possible to do system administration without having to delete anything. The reserved amount is by default 5 percent, which on most disks isn't enough to be wasteful. However, for floppies there is no point in reserving any blocks.

See the **tune2fs** manual page for more information.

dumpe2fs shows information about an ext2 filesystem, mostly from the superblock. The code listing below shows a sample output. Some of the information in the output is technical and requires understanding of how the filesystem works, but much of it is readily understandable even for lay admins.

```
dumpe2fs 0.5b, 11-Mar-95 for EXT2 FS 0.5a, 94/10/23
Filesystem magic number:  0xEF53
Filesystem state:         clean
Errors behavior:          Continue
Inode count:              360
Block count:              1440
Reserved block count:     72
Free blocks:              1133
Free inodes:              326
First block:              1
Block size:               1024
Fragment size:            1024
Blocks per group:         8192
Fragments per group:      8192
Inodes per group:         360
Last mount time:          Tue Aug  8 01:52:52 1995
Last write time:          Tue Aug  8 01:53:28 1995
Mount count:              3
Maximum mount count:      20
Last checked:             Tue Aug  8 01:06:31 1995
Check interval:           0
Reserved blocks uid:      0 (user root)
Reserved blocks gid:      0 (group root)

Group 0:
  Block bitmap at 3, Inode bitmap at 4, Inode table at 5
  1133 free blocks, 326 free inodes, 2 directories
  Free blocks: 307-1439
  Free inodes: 35-360
```

debugfs is a filesystem debugger. It allows direct access to the filesystem data structures stored on disk and can thus be used to repair a disk that is so broken that **fsck** can't fix it automatically. It has also been known to be used to recover deleted files. However, **debugfs** very much requires that you understand what you're doing; a failure to understand can destroy all your data.

Dump and restore can be used to back up an ext2 filesystem. They are ext2-specific versions of the traditional Unix backup tools. See Chapter 9 for more information on backups.

Disks Without Filesystems

Not all disks or partitions are used as filesystems. A swap partition, for example, will not have a filesystem on it. Many floppies are used in a tape-drive emulating fashion, so that a tar or other file is written directly on the raw disk, without a filesystem. Linux boot floppies don't contain a filesystem, only the raw kernel.

Avoiding a filesystem has the advantage of making more of the disk usable, since a filesystem always has some bookkeeping overhead. It also makes the disks more easily compatible with other systems: for example, the tar file format is the same on all systems, while filesystems are different on most systems. You will quickly get used to disks without filesystems if you need them. Bootable Linux floppies also do not necessarily have a filesystem, although that is also possible.

One reason to use raw disks is to make image copies of them. For instance, if the disk contains a partially damaged filesystem, it is a good idea to make an exact copy of it before trying to fix it, since then you can start again if your fixing breaks things even more. One way to do this is to use **dd**:

```
$ dd if=/dev/fd0H1440 of=floppy-image
2880+0 records in
2880+0 records out
$ dd if=floppy-image of=/dev/fd0H1440
2880+0 records in
2880+0 records out
$
```

The first **dd** makes an exact image of the floppy to the file floppy-image, the second one writes the image to the floppy. (The user has presumably switched the floppy before the second command. Otherwise the command pair is of doubtful usefulness.)

Allocating Disk Space
Partitioning Schemes

It is not easy to partition a disk in the best possible way. Worse, there is no universally correct way to do it; there are too many factors involved.

The traditional way is to have a (relatively) small root filesystem, which contains /bin, /etc, /dev, /lib, /tmp, and other stuff that is needed to get the system up and running. This way, the root filesystem (in its own partition or on its own disk) is all that is needed to bring up the system. The reasoning is that if the root filesystem is small and is not heavily used, it is less likely to become corrupt when the system crashes, and you will therefore find it easier to fix any problems caused by the crash. Then you create separate partitions or use separate disks for the directory tree below /usr, the users' home directories (often under /home), and the swap space. Separating the home directories (with the users' files) in their own partition makes backups easier, since it is usually not necessary to back up programs (which reside below /usr). In a networked environment it is also possible to share /usr among several machines (e.g., by using NFS), thereby reducing the total disk space required by several tens or hundreds of megabytes times the number of machines.

The problem with having many partitions is that it splits the total amount of free disk space into many small pieces. Nowadays, when disks and (hopefully) operating systems are more reliable, many people prefer to have just one partition that holds all their files. On the other hand, it can be less painful to back up (and restore) a small partition.

For a small hard disk (assuming you don't do kernel development), the best way to go is probably to have just one partition. For large hard disks, it is probably better to have a few large partitions, just in case something does go wrong. (Note that "small" and "large" are used in a relative sense here; your needs for disk space decide what the threshold is.)

If you have several disks, you might wish to have the root filesystem (including /usr) on one, and the users' home directories on another.

It is a good idea to be prepared to experiment a bit with different partitioning schemes (over time, not just while first installing the system). This is a bit of work, since it essentially requires you to install the system from scratch several times, but it is the only way to be sure you do it right.

Space Requirements

The Linux distribution you install will give some indication of how much disk space you need for various configurations. Programs installed separately may also do the same. This will help you plan your disk space usage, but you should prepare for the future and reserve some extra space for things you will notice later that you need.

The amount you need for user files depends on what your users wish to do. Most people seem to need as much space for their files as possible, but the amount they will live happily with varies a lot. Some people do only light text processing and will survive nicely with a few megabytes, others do heavy image processing and will need gigabytes.

By the way, when comparing file sizes given in kilobytes or megabytes and disk space given in megabytes, it can be important to know that the two units can be different. Some disk manufacturers like to pretend that a kilobyte is 1,000 bytes and a megabyte is 1,000 kilobytes, while all the rest of the computing world uses 1,024 for both factors. Therefore, my 345MB hard disk was really a 330MB hard disk. (Sic transit discus mundi.)

Swap space allocation is discussed in the section called "Allocating Swap Space" in Chapter 4.

Examples Of Hard Disk Allocation

I used to have a 109MB hard disk. Now I am using a 330MB hard disk. I'll explain how and why I partitioned these disks.

The 109MB disk I partitioned in a lot of ways, when my needs and the operating systems I used changed; I'll explain two typical scenarios. First, I used to run MS-DOS together with Linux. For that, I needed about 20MB of hard disk, or just enough to have MS-DOS, a C compiler, an editor, a few other utilities, the program I was working on, and enough free disk space to not feel claustrophobic. For Linux, I had a 10MB swap partition, and the rest, or 79 MB, was a single partition with all the files I had under Linux. I experimented with having separate root, /usr, and /home partitions, but there was never enough free disk space in one piece to do anything interesting.

When I didn't need MS-DOS anymore, I repartitioned the disk so that I had a 12MB swap partition, and again had the rest as a single filesystem.

The 330MB disk is partitioned into several partitions, like this:

5MB   root <u>filesystem</u>

10MB   swap partition

180MB   \fn{/usr} <u>filesystem</u>

120MB   \fn{/home} <u>filesystem</u>

15MB   scratch partition

The scratch partition is for playing around with things that require their own partition, e.g., trying different Linux distributions, or comparing speeds of filesystems. When not needed for anything else, it is used as swap space (I like to have a lot of open windows).

Adding More Disk Space For Linux

Adding more disk space for Linux is easy, at least after the hardware has been properly installed (the hardware installation is outside the scope of this book). You format it if necessary, then create the partitions and filesystem as described above, and add the proper lines to /etc/fstab so that it is mounted automatically.

Tips For Saving Disk Space

The best tip for saving disk space is to avoid installing unnecessary programs. Most Linux distributions have an option to install only part of the packages they contain, and by analyzing your needs you might notice that you don't need most of them. This will help save a lot of disk space, since many programs are quite large. Even if you do need a particular package or program, you might not need all of it. For example, some online documentation might be unnecessary, as might some of the Elisp files for GNU Emacs, some of the fonts for X11, or some of the libraries for programming.

If you cannot uninstall packages, you might look into compression. Compression programs such as gzip or zip will compress (and uncompress) individual files or groups of files. The gzexe system will compress and uncompress programs invisibly to the user (unused programs are compressed, then uncompressed as they are used). The experimental DouBle system will compress all files in a filesystem, invisibly to the programs that use them. (If you are familiar with products such as Stacker for MS-DOS, the principle is the same.)

Chapter 4

Memory Management

*"Minnet, jag har
tappat mitt minne, är
jag svensk eller finne,
kommer inte ihåg."*

—*Bosse Österberg*

This section describes the Linux memory management features, i.e., virtual memory and the disk buffer cache. The purpose and workings and the things the system administrator needs to take into consideration are described.

What Is Virtual Memory?

Linux supports *virtual memory*, that is, using a disk as an extension of RAM so that the effective size of usable memory grows correspondingly. The kernel will write the contents of a currently unused block of memory to the hard disk so that the memory can be used for another purpose. When the original contents are needed again, they are read back into memory. This is all made completely transparent to the user; programs running under Linux only see the larger amount of memory available and don't notice that parts of them reside on the disk from time to time. Of course, reading and writing the hard disk is slower (on the order of a thousand times slower) than using real memory, so the programs don't run as fast. The part of the hard disk that is used as virtual memory is called the *swap space*.

Linux can use either a normal file in the filesystem or a separate partition for swap space. A swap partition is faster, but it is easier to change the size of a swap file (there's no need to repartition the whole hard disk and possibly install everything from scratch). When you know how much swap space you need, you should go for a swap partition, but if you are uncertain, you can use a swap file first, use the system for a while so that you can get a feel for how much swap you need, and then make a swap partition when you're confident about its size.

311

You should also know that Linux allows one to use several swap partitions and/or swap files at the same time. This means that if you only occasionally need an unusual amount of swap space, you can set up an extra swap file at such times, instead of keeping the whole amount allocated all the time.

A note on operating system terminology: Computer science usually distinguishes between swapping (writing the whole process out to swap space) and *paging* (writing only fixed-size parts, usually a few kilobytes, at a time). Paging is usually more efficient, and that's what Linux does, but traditional Linux terminology talks about swapping anyway. (Thus quite needlessly annoying a number of computer scientists something horrible.)

Creating A Swap Space

A swap file is an ordinary file; it is in no way special to the kernel. The only thing that matters to the kernel is that it has no holes, and that it is prepared for use with **mkswap**. It must reside on a local disk, however; it can't reside in a filesystem that has been mounted over NFS due to implementation reasons.

The bit about holes is important. The swap file reserves the disk space so that the kernel can quickly swap out a page without having to go through all the things that are necessary when allocating a disk sector to a file. The kernel merely uses any sectors that have already been allocated to the file. Because a hole in a file means that there are no disk sectors allocated (for that place in the file), it is not good for the kernel to try to use them.

One good way to create the swap file without holes is through the following command:

```
$ dd if=/dev/zero of=/extra-swap bs=1024 count=1024
1024+0 records in
1024+0 records out
$
```

where /extra-swap is the name of the swap file and the size of is given after the count =. It is best for the size to be a multiple of 4, because the kernel writes out memory pages, which are 4K in size. If the size is not a multiple of 4, the last couple of kilobytes may be unused.

A swap partition is also not special in any way. You create it just like any other partition; the only difference is that it is used as a raw partition, that is, it will not contain any filesystem at all. It is a good idea to mark swap partitions as type 82 (Linux swap); this will the make partition listings clearer, even though it is not strictly necessary to the kernel.

After you have created a swap file or a swap partition, you need to write a signature to its beginning; this contains some administrative information and is used by the kernel. The command to do this is \cmd{mkswap}, used like this:

```
$ mkswap /extra-swap 1024
Setting up swapspace, size = 1044480 bytes
$
```

Note that the swap space is still not in use yet: it exists, but the kernel does not use it to provide virtual memory.

You should be very careful when using **mkswap**, since it does not check that the file or partition isn't used for anything else. You can easily overwrite important files and partitions with **mkswap**! Fortunately, you should only need to use **mkswap** when you install your system.

The Linux memory manager limits the size of each swap space to about 127MB (for various technical reasons, the actual limit is (4096-10) * 8 * 4096 = 133890048$ bytes, or 127.6875MB). You can, however, use up to 16 swap spaces simultaneously, for a total of almost 2GB. (A gigabyte here, a gigabyte there, pretty soon we start talking about real memory.)

Using A Swap Space

An initialized swap space is taken into use with **swapon**. This command tells the kernel that the swap space can be used. The path to the swap space is given as the argument, so to start swapping on a temporary swap file one might use the following command.

```
$ swapon /extra-swap
$
```

Swap spaces can be used automatically by listing them in the /etc/fstab file.

```
/dev/hda8        none        swap        sw      0    0
/swapfile        none        swap        sw      0    0
```

The startup scripts will run the command **swapon -a**, which will start swapping on all the swap spaces listed in /etc/fstab. Therefore, the **swapon** command is usually used only when extra swap is needed.

You can monitor the use of swap spaces with **free**. It will tell the total amount of swap space used.

```
$ free
              total        used        free      shared     buffers
Mem:          15152       14896         256       12404        2528
-/+ buffers:              12368        2784
Swap:         32452        6684       25768
$
```

The first line of output (Mem:) shows the physical memory. The total column does not show the physical memory used by the kernel, which is usually about a megabyte. The used column shows the amount of memory used (the second line does not count buffers). The free column shows completely unused memory. The shared column shows the amount of memory shared by several processes; the more, the merrier. The buffers column shows the current size of the disk buffer cache.

That last line (Swap:) shows similar information for the swap spaces. If this line is all zeroes, your swap space is not activated.

The same information is available via top, or using the proc filesystem in file /proc/meminfo. It is currently difficult to get information on the use of a specific swap space.

A swap space can be removed from use with **swapoff**. It is usually not necessary to do it, except for temporary swap spaces. Any pages in use in the swap space are swapped in first; if there is not sufficient physical memory to hold them, they will then be swapped out (to some other swap space). If there is not enough virtual memory to hold all of the pages Linux will start to thrash; after a long while it should recover, but meanwhile the system is unusable. You should check (e.g., with **free**) that there is enough free memory before removing a swap space from use.

All the swap spaces that are used automatically with **swapon -a** can be removed from use with **swapoff -a**; it looks at the file /etc/fstab to find what to remove. Any manually used swap spaces will remain in use.

Sometimes a lot of swap space can be in use even though there is a lot of free physical memory. This can happen for instance if at one point there is need to swap, but later a big process that occupied much of the physical memory terminates and frees the memory. The swapped-out data is not automatically swapped in until it is needed, so the physical memory may remain free for a long time. There is no need to worry about this, but it can be comforting to know what is happening.

Sharing Swap Spaces With Other Operating Systems

Virtual memory is built into many operating systems. Because they each need it only when they are running, that is, never at the same time, the swap spaces of all but the currently running one are being wasted. It would be more efficient for them to share a single swap space. This is possible, but can require a bit of hacking. The Tips-HOWTO contains some advice on how to implement this.

Allocating Swap Space

Some people will tell you that you should allocate twice as much swap space as you have physical memory, but this is a bogus rule. Here's how to do it properly:

1. Estimate your total memory needs. This is the largest amount of memory you'll probably need at a time, that is the sum of the memory requirements of all the programs you want to run at the same time. This can be done by running at the same time all the programs you are likely to ever be running at the same time.

   For instance, if you want to run X, you should allocate about 8MB for it, gcc wants several megabytes (some files need an unusually large amount, up to tens of megabytes, but usually about four should do), and so on. The kernel will use about a megabyte by itself, and the usual shells and other small utilities perhaps a few hundred kilobytes (say a megabyte together). There is no need to try to be exact, rough estimates are fine, but you might want to be on the pessimistic side.

   Remember that if there are going to be several people using the system at the same time, they are all going to consume memory. However, if two people run the same program at the same time, the total memory consumption is usually not double, since code pages and shared libraries exist only once.

   The **free** and **ps** commands are useful for estimating the memory needs.

2. Add some security to the estimate in Step 1. This is because estimates of program sizes will probably be wrong, because you'll probably forget some programs you want to run, and to make certain that you have some extra space just in case. A couple of megabytes should be fine. (It is better to allocate too much than too little swap space, but there's no need to overdo it and allocate the whole disk, since unused swap space is wasted space; see later about adding more swap.) Also, since it is nicer to deal with even numbers, you can round the value up to the next full megabyte.

3. Based on the computations above, you know how much memory you'll be needing in total. So, in order to allocate swap space, you just need to subtract the size of your physical memory from the total memory needed, and you know how much swap space you need. (On some versions of Unix, you need to allocate space for an image of the physical memory as well, so the amount computed in Step 2 is what you need and you shouldn't do the subtraction.)

4. If your calculated swap space is very much larger than your physical memory (more than a couple times larger), you should probably invest in more physical memory, otherwise performance will be too low.

It's a good idea to have at least some swap space, even if your calculations indicate that you need none. Linux uses swap space somewhat aggressively, so that as much physical memory as possible can be kept free. Linux will swap out memory pages that have not been used, even if the memory is not yet needed for anything. This avoids waiting for swapping when it is needed: The swapping can be done earlier, when the disk is otherwise idle.

Swap space can be divided among several disks. This can sometimes improve performance, depending on the relative speeds of the disks and the access patterns of the disks. You might want to experiment with a few schemes, but be aware that doing the experiments properly is quite difficult. You should not believe claims that any one scheme is superior to any other, because it won't always be true.

The Buffer Cache

Reading from a disk (except a RAM disk, for obvious reasons) is very slow compared to accessing (real) memory. In addition, it is common to read the same part of a disk several times during relatively short periods of time. For example, one might first read an email message, then read the letter into an editor when replying to it, then make the mail program read it again when copying it to a folder. Or, consider how often the command **ls** might be run on a system with many users. By reading the information from disk only once and then keeping it in memory until no longer needed, one can speed up all but the first read. This is called *disk buffering*, and the memory used for the purpose is called the *buffer cache*.

Because memory is, unfortunately, a finite, nay, scarce resource, the buffer cache usually cannot be big enough (it can't hold all the data one ever wants to use). When the cache fills up, the data that has been unused for the longest time is discarded and the memory thus freed is used for the new data.

Disk buffering works for writes as well. On the one hand, data that is written is often soon read again (e.g., a source code file is saved to a file, then read by the compiler), so putting data that is written in the cache is a good idea. On the other hand, by only putting the data into the cache, not writing it to disk at once, the program that writes runs quicker. The writes can then be done in the background, without slowing down the other programs.

Most operating systems have buffer caches (although they might be called something else), but not all of them work according to the above principles. Some are write-through: the data is written to disk at once (it is kept in the cache as well, of course). The cache is called *write-back* if the writes are done at a later time. Write-back is more efficient than write-through, but also a bit more prone to errors: If the machine crashes, or the power is cut at a bad moment, or the floppy is removed from the disk drive before the data in the cache waiting to be written gets written, the changes in the cache are usually lost. This might even mean that the file system (if there is one) is not in full working order, perhaps because the unwritten data held important changes to the bookkeeping information.

Because of this, you should never turn off the power without using a proper shutdown procedure (see Chapter 5), or remove a floppy from the disk drive until it has been unmounted (if it was mounted) or after whatever program is using it has signaled that it is finished and the floppy drive light doesn't shine anymore. The **sync** command flushes the buffer, that is, forces all unwritten data to be written to disk, and can be used when one wants to be sure that everything is safely written. In traditional Unix systems, there is a program called update running in the background which does a sync every 30 seconds, so it is usually not necessary to use **sync**. Linux has an additional daemon, bdflush, which does a more imperfect sync more frequently to avoid the sudden freeze due to heavy disk I/O that **sync** sometimes causes.

Under Linux, bdflush is started by update. There is usually no reason to worry about it, but if bdflush happens to die for some reason, the kernel will warn about this, and you should start it by hand (/sbin/update).

The cache does not actually buffer files, but blocks, which are the smallest units of disk I/O (under Linux, they are usually 1K). This way, also directories, super blocks, other file system bookkeeping data, and non-filesystem disks are cached.

The effectiveness of a cache is primarily decided by its size. A small cache is next to useless: it will hold so little data that all cached data is flushed from the cache before it is reused. The critical size depends on how much data is read and written and how often the same data is accessed. The only way to know is to experiment.

If the cache is of a fixed size, it is not very good to have it too big, either, because that might make the free memory too small and cause swapping (which is also slow). To make the most efficient use of real memory, Linux automatically uses all free RAM for buffer cache, but also automatically makes the cache smaller when programs need more memory.

Under Linux, you do not need to do anything to make use of the cache, it happens completely automatically. Except for following the proper procedures for shutdown and removing floppies, you do not need to worry about it.

Chapter 5
Boots And Shutdowns

This section explains what goes on when a Linux system is brought up and taken down, and how it should be done properly. If proper procedures are not followed, files might be corrupted or lost.

An Overview Of Boots And Shutdowns

The act of turning on a computer system and causing its operating system to be loaded is called *booting*. (On early computers, it wasn't enough to merely turn on the computer, you had to manually load the operating system as well. These newfangled thingamajigs do it all by themselves.) The name comes from an image of the computer pulling itself up from its bootstraps, but the act itself slightly more realistic.

During bootstrapping, the computer first loads a small piece of code called the *bootstrap loader*, which in turn loads and starts the *operating system*. The bootstrap loader is usually stored in a fixed location on a hard disk or a floppy. The reason for this two-step process is that the operating system is big and complicated, but the first piece of code that the computer loads must be very small (a few hundred bytes), to avoid making the firmware unnecessarily complicated.

Different computers do the bootstrapping differently. For PCs, the computer (its BIOS) reads in the first sector (called the *boot sector*) of a floppy or hard disk. The bootstrap loader is contained within this sector. It loads the operating system from elsewhere on the disk (or from some other place).

After Linux has been loaded, it initializes the hardware and device drivers, and then runs init. init starts other processes to allow users to log in and do things. The details of this part will be discussed below.

In order to shut down a Linux system, first all processes are told to terminate (this makes them close any files and do other necessary things to keep things tidy), then filesystems and swap areas are unmounted, and finally a message is printed to the console that the power can be turned off. If the proper procedure is not followed, terrible things can and will happen; most importantly, the filesystem buffer cache might not be flushed, which means that all data in it is lost and the filesystem on disk is inconsistent, and therefore possibly unusable.

The Boot Process In Closer Look

You can boot Linux either from a floppy or from the hard disk. The installation section in the Installation and Getting Started guide by Matt Welsh, et. al., of the Linux Documentation Project (**http://MetaLab.unc.edu/LDP/LDP/gs/gs.html**) tells you how to install Linux so you can boot it the way you want to.

When a PC is booted, the BIOS will do various tests to check that everything looks all right (this is called the power on self test, or POST for short) and will then start the actual booting. It will choose a disk drive (typically the first floppy drive, if there is a floppy inserted, otherwise the first hard disk, if one is installed in the computer; the order might be configurable, however) and will then read its very first sector. This is called the boot sector; for a hard disk, it is also called the *master boot record*, since a hard disk can contain several partitions, each with their own boot sectors.

The boot sector contains a small program (small enough to fit into one sector) whose responsibility is to read the actual operating system from the disk and start it. When booting Linux from a floppy disk, the boot sector contains code that just reads the first few hundred blocks (depending on the actual kernel size, of course) to a predetermined place in memory. On a Linux boot floppy, there is no filesystem, the kernel is just stored in consecutive sectors, since this simplifies the boot process. It is possible, however, to boot from a floppy with a filesystem, by using LILO, the LInux LOader.

When booting from the hard disk, the code in the master boot record will examine the partition table (also in the master boot record), identify the active partition (the partition that is marked to be bootable), read the boot sector from that partition, and then start the code in that boot sector. The code in the partition's boot sector does what a floppy disk's boot sector does: It will read in the kernel from the partition and start it. The details vary, however, since it is generally not useful to have a separate partition for just the kernel image, so the code in the partition's boot sector can't just read the disk in sequential order, it has to find the sectors wherever the filesystem has put them. There are several ways around this problem, but the most common way is to use LILO. (The details about how to do this are irrelevant for this discussion, however; see the LILO documentation for more information; it is most thorough.)

When booting with LILO, it will normally go right ahead and read in and boot the default kernel. It is also possible to configure LILO to be able to boot one of several kernels, or even other operating systems than Linux, and it is possible for the user to choose which kernel or operating system is to be booted at boot time. LILO can be configured so that if one holds down the Alt, Shift, or Ctrl key at boot time (when LILO is loaded), LILO will ask what is to be booted and not boot the default right away. Alternatively, LILO can be configured so that it will always ask, with an optional timeout that will cause the default kernel to be booted.

With LILO, it is also possible to give a kernel command line argument, after the name of the kernel or operating system.

Booting from floppy and from hard disk have both their advantages, but generally booting from the hard disk is nicer, since it avoids the hassle of playing around with floppies. It is also faster. However, it can be more troublesome to install the system to boot from the hard disk, so many people will first boot from floppy, then, when the system is otherwise installed and working well, will install LILO and start booting from the hard disk.

After the Linux kernel has been read into the memory, by whatever means, and is started for real, roughly the following things happen:

♦ The Linux kernel is installed compressed, so it will first uncompress itself. The beginning of the kernel image contains a small program that does this.

♦ If you have a super-VGA card that Linux recognizes and that has some special text modes (such as 100 columns by 40 rows), Linux asks you which mode you want to use. During the kernel compilation, it is possible to preset a video mode, so that this is never asked. This can also be done with LILO or rdev.

♦ After this, the kernel checks what other hardware there is (hard disks, floppies, network adapters, and so on), and configures some of its device drivers appropriately; while it does this, it outputs messages about its findings. For example, when I boot, it looks like this:

```
LILO boot:
Loading linux.
Console: colour EGA+ 80x25, 8 virtual consoles
Serial driver version 3.94 with no serial options enabled
tty00 at 0x03f8 (irq = 4) is a 16450
tty01 at 0x02f8 (irq = 3) is a 16450
lp_init: lp1 exists (0), using polling driver
Memory: 7332k/8192k available (300k kernel code, 384k reserved, 176k data)
Floppy drive(s): fd0 is 1.44M, fd1 is 1.2M
Loopback device init
Warning WD8013 board not found at i/o = 280.
Math coprocessor using irq13 error reporting.
Partition check:
  hda: hda1 hda2 hda3
VFS: Mounted root (ext filesystem).
Linux version 0.99.p19-1 (root@haven) 05/01/93 14:12:20
```

The exact texts are different on different systems, depending on the hardware, the version of Linux being used, and how it has been configured.

♦ Then the kernel will try to mount the root filesystem. The place is configurable at compilation time, or any time with rdev or LILO. The filesystem type is detected automatically. If the mounting of the root filesystem fails, for example because you didn't remember to include the corresponding filesystem driver in the kernel, the kernel panics and halts the system (there isn't much it can do, anyway).

♦ The root filesystem is usually mounted read-only (this can be set in the same way as the place). This makes it possible to check the filesystem while it is mounted; it is not a good idea to check a filesystem that is mounted read-write.

♦ After this, the kernel starts the program init (located in /sbin/init) in the background (this will always become process number 1). init does various startup chores. The exact things it does depends on how it is configured; see Chapter 6 for more information. It will at least start some essential background daemons.

♦ init then switches to multiuser mode, and starts a getty for virtual consoles and serial lines. getty is the program which lets people log in via virtual consoles and serial terminals. init may also start some other programs, depending on how it is configured.

♦ After this, the boot is complete, and the system is up and running normally.

More About Shutdowns

It is important to follow the correct procedures when you shut down a Linux system. If you fail do so, your filesystems probably will become trashed and the files probably will become scrambled. This is because Linux has a disk cache that won't write things to disk at once, but only at intervals. This greatly improves performance, but also means that if you just turn off the power at a whim the cache may hold a lot of data and that what is on the disk may not be a fully working filesystem (because only some things have been written to the disk).

Another reason against just flipping the power switch is that in a multitasking system there can be lots of things going on in the background, and shutting the power can be quite disastrous. By using the proper shutdown sequence, you ensure that all background processes can save their data.

The command for properly shutting down a Linux system is **shutdown**. It is usually used in one of two ways.

If you are running a system where you are the only user, the usual way of using **shutdown** is to quit all running programs, log out on all virtual consoles, log in as root on one of them (or stay logged in as root if you already are, but you should change to root's home directory or the root directory, to avoid problems with unmounting), then give the command **shutdown -h now** (substitute **now** with a plus sign and a number in minutes if you want a delay, though you usually don't on a single user system).

Alternatively, if your system has many users, use the command **shutdown -h +time message**, where **time** is the time in minutes until the system is halted, and **message** is a short explanation of why the system is shutting down.

```
# shutdown -h +10 'We will install a new disk.  System should
> be back on-line in three hours.'
#
```

This will warn everybody that the system will shut down in ten minutes, and that they'd better get lost or lose data. The warning is printed to every terminal on which someone is logged in, including all xterms:

```
Broadcast message from root (ttyp0) Wed Aug  2 01:03:25 1995...

We will install a new disk.  System should
be back on-line in three hours.
The system is going DOWN for system halt in 10 minutes !!
```

The warning is automatically repeated a few times before the boot, with shorter and shorter intervals as the time runs out.

When the real shutting down starts after any delays, all filesystems (except the root one) are unmounted, user processes (if anybody is still logged in) are killed, daemons are shut down, all filesystem are unmounted, and generally everything settles down. When that is done, init prints out a message that you can power down the machine. Then, and only then, should you move your fingers toward the power switch.

Sometimes, although rarely on any good system, it is impossible to shut down properly. For instance, if the kernel panics, crashes and burns, and generally misbehaves, it might be completely impossible to give any new commands; hence, shutting down properly is somewhat difficult, and just about everything you can do is hope that nothing has been too severely damaged and turn off the power. If the troubles are a bit less severe (say, somebody hit your keyboard with an ax), and the kernel and the update program still run normally, it is probably a good idea to wait a couple of minutes to give update a chance to flush the buffer cache, and only cut the power after that.

Some people like to shut down using the command **sync** (**sync** flushes the buffer cache.) three times, waiting for the disk I/O to stop, then turn off the power. If there are no running programs, this is about equivalent to using **shutdown**. However, it does not unmount any filesystems and this can lead to problems with the **ext2fs** "clean filesystem" flag. The triple-**sync** method is not recommended.

(In case you're wondering: the reason for three **sync**s is that in the early days of Unix, when the commands were typed separately, that usually gave sufficient time for most disk I/O to be finished.)

Rebooting

Rebooting means booting the system again. This can be accomplished by first shutting it down completely, turning power off, and then turning it back on. A simpler way is to ask shutdown to reboot the system, instead of merely halting it. This is accomplished by using the **-r** option to **shutdown**, for example, by giving the command **shutdown -r now**.

Most Linux systems run **shutdown -r now** when Ctrl+Alt+Del is pressed on the keyboard. This reboots the system. The action on Ctrl+Alt+Del is configurable, however, and it might be better to allow for some delay before the reboot on a multiuser machine. Systems that are physically accessible to anyone might even be configured to do nothing when Ctrl+Alt+Del is pressed.

Single User Mode

The **shutdown** command can also be used to bring the system down to single user mode, in which no one can log in, but root can use the console. This is useful for system administration tasks that can't be done while the system is running normally.

Emergency Boot Floppies

It is not always possible to boot a computer from the hard disk. For example, if you make a mistake in configuring LILO, you might make your system unbootable. For these situations, you need an alternative way of booting that will always work (as long as the hardware works). For typical PCs, this means booting from the floppy drive.

Most Linux distributions allow one to create an emergency boot floppy during installation. It is a good idea to do this. However, some such boot disks contain only the kernel, and assume you will be using the programs on the distribution's installation disks to fix whatever problem you have. Sometimes those programs aren't enough; for example, you might have to restore some files from backups made with software not on the installation disks.

Thus, it might be necessary to create a custom root floppy as well. *The Bootdisk HOWTO* by Graham Chapman (**http://MetaLab.unc.edu/LDP/HOWTO/Bootdisk-HOWTO.html**) contains instructions for doing this. You must, of course, remember to keep your emergency boot and root floppies up to date.

You can't use the floppy drive you use to mount the root floppy for anything else. This can be inconvenient if you only have one floppy drive. However, if you have enough memory, you can configure your boot floppy to load the root disk to a RAM disk (the boot floppy's kernel needs to be specially configured for this). Once the root floppy has been loaded into the ramdisk, the floppy drive is free to mount other disks.

Chapter 6
init

"Uuno on numero yksi."

—Slogan for a series of Finnish movies

This chapter describes the init process, which is the first user-level process started by the kernel. init has many important duties, such as starting getty (so that users can log in), implementing run levels, and taking care of orphaned processes. This chapter explains how init is configured and how you can make use of the different run levels.

init Comes First

init is one of those programs that are absolutely essential to the operation of a Linux system, but that you still can mostly ignore. A good Linux distribution will come with a configuration for init that will work for most systems, and on these systems there is nothing you need to do about init. Usually, you only need to worry about init if you hook up serial terminals, dial-in (not dial-out) modems, or if you want to change the default run level.

When the kernel has started itself (has been loaded into memory, has started running, and has initialized all device drivers and data structures and such), it finishes its own part of the boot process by starting a user-level program, init. Thus, init is always the first process (its process number is always 1).

The kernel looks for init in a few locations that have been historically used for it, but the proper location for it (on a Linux system) is /sbin/init. If the kernel can't find init, it tries to run /bin/sh, and if that also fails, the startup of the system fails.

When init starts, it finishes the boot process by doing a number of administrative tasks, such as checking filesystems, cleaning up

/tmp, starting various services, and starting a getty for each terminal and virtual console where users should be able to log in (see Chapter 7).

After the system is properly up, init restarts getty for each terminal after a user has logged out (so that the next user can log in). init also adopts orphan processes: When a process starts a child process and dies before its child, the child immediately becomes a child of init. This is important for various technical reasons, but it is good to know it, since it makes it easier to understand process lists and process tree graphs. (init itself is not allowed to die. You can't kill init even with SIGKILL.) There are a few variants of init available. Most Linux distributions use sysvinit (written by Miquel van Smoorenburg), which is based on the System V init design. The BSD versions of Unix have a different init. The primary difference is run levels: System V has them, BSD does not (at least traditionally). This difference is not essential. We'll look at sysvinit only.

Configuring init To Start getty: The /etc/inittab File

When it starts up, init reads the /etc/inittab configuration file. While the system is running, it will re-read it, if sent the HUP signal (using the command **kill -HUP 1 as root**, for example). This feature makes it unnecessary to boot the system to make changes to the init configuration take effect.

The /etc/inittab file is a bit complicated. We'll start with the simple case of configuring getty lines. Lines in /etc/inittab consist of four colon-delimited fields:

```
id:runlevels:action:process
```

The fields are described below. In addition, /etc/inittab can contain empty lines, and lines that begin with a number sign (#); these are both ignored.

id

This identifies the line in the file. For getty lines, it specifies the terminal it runs on (the characters after /dev/tty in the device file name). For other lines, it doesn't matter (except for length restrictions), but it should be unique.

runlevels

The run levels the line should be considered for. The run levels are given as single digits, without delimiters. (Run levels are described in the next section.)

action

What action should be taken by the line, e.g., respawn to run the command in the next field again, when it exits, or once to run it just once.

process
The command to run.

To start a getty on the first virtual terminal (/dev/tty1}), in all the normal multiuser run levels (2–5), one would write the following line:

```
1:2345:respawn:/sbin/getty 9600 tty1
```

The first field says that this is the line for /dev/tty1. The second field says that it applies to run levels 2, 3, 4, and 5. The third field means that the command should be run again, after it exits (so that one can log in, log out, and then log in again). The last field is the command that runs getty on the first virtual terminal. (Different versions of getty are run differently. Consult your manual page, and make sure it is the correct manual page.)

If you wanted to add terminals or dial-in modem lines to a system, you'd add more lines to /etc/inittab, one for each terminal or dial-in line. For more details, see the manual pages init, inittab, and getty.

If a command fails when it starts, and init is configured to restart it, it will use a lot of system resources: init starts it, it fails, init starts it, it fails, init starts it, it fails, and so on, ad infinitum. To prevent this, init will keep track of how often it restarts a command, and if the frequency grows to high, it will delay for five minutes before restarting again.

Run Levels

A run level is a state of init and the whole system that defines what system services are operating. Run levels are identified by numbers, see Table 6.1. There is no consensus of how to use the user-defined run levels (2 through 5). Some system administrators use run levels to define which subsystems are working, e.g., whether X is running, whether the network is operational, and so on. Others have all subsystems always running or start and stop them individually, without changing run levels, since run levels are too coarse for controlling their systems. You need to decide for yourself, but it might be easiest to follow the way your Linux distribution does things.

Table 6.1 Run level numbers.

0	Halt the system
1	Single-user mode (for special administration)
-2	Normal operation (user-defined)
6	Reboot

Run levels are configured in /etc/inittab by lines like the following:

```
l2:2:wait:/etc/init.d/rc 2
```

The first field is an arbitrary label, the second one means that this applies for run level 2. The third field means that init should run the command in the fourth field once, when the run level is entered, and that init should wait for it to complete. The /etc/init.d/rc command runs whatever commands are necessary to start and stop services to enter run level 2.

The command in the fourth field does all the hard work of setting up a run level. It starts services that aren't already running, and stops services that shouldn't be running in the new run level any more. Exactly what the command is, and how run levels are configured, depends on the Linux distribution.

When init starts, it looks for a line in /etc/inittab that specifies the default run level:

```
id:2:initdefault:
```

You can ask init to go to a nondefault run level at startup by giving the kernel a command line argument of single or emergency. Kernel command line arguments can be given via LILO, for example. This allows you to choose the single user mode (run level 1).

While the system is running, the **telinit** command can change the run level. When the run level is changed, init runs the relevant command from /etc/inittab.

Special Configuration In /etc/inittab

The /etc/inittab has some special features that allow init to react to special circumstances. These special features are marked by special keywords in the third field. Some examples:

powerwait
Allows init to shut the system down, when the power fails. This assumes the use of a UPS, and software that watches the UPS and informs init that the power is off.

ctrlaltdel
Allows init to reboot the system, when the user presses Ctrl+Alt+Del on the console keyboard. Note that the system administrator can configure the reaction to Ctrl+Alt+Del to be something else instead, e.g., to be ignored, if the system is in a public location (or to start nethack).

sysinit
Command to be run when the system is booted. This command usually cleans up /tmp, for example.

The list above is not exhaustive. See your inittab manual page for all possibilities, and for details on how to use the above ones.

Booting In Single User Mode

An important run level is single user mode (run level 1), in which only the system administrator is using the machine and as few system services, including logins, as possible are running. Single user mode is necessary for a few administrative tasks (it probably shouldn't be used for playing nethack), such as running **fsck** on a /usr partition, because this requires that the partition be unmounted, and that can't happen, unless just about all system services are killed.

A running system can be taken to single user mode by using **telinit** to request run level 1. At bootup, it can be entered by giving the word single or emergency on the kernel command line: The kernel gives the command line to init as well, and init understands from that word that it shouldn't use the default run level. (The kernel command line is entered in a way that depends on how you boot the system.)

Booting into single user mode is sometimes necessary so that one can run **fsck** by hand, before anything mounts or otherwise touches a broken /usr partition (any activity on a broken filesystem is likely to break it more, so **fsck** should be run as soon as possible).

The bootup scripts init runs will automatically enter single user mode, if the automatic **fsck** at bootup fails. This is an attempt to prevent the system from using a filesystem that is so broken that **fsck** can't fix it automatically. Such breakage is relatively rare, and usually involves a broken hard disk or an experimental kernel release, but it's good to be prepared.

As a security measure, a properly configured system will ask for the root password before starting the shell in single user mode. Otherwise, it would be simple to just enter a suitable line to LILO to get in as root. (This will break if /etc/passwd has been broken by filesystem problems, of course, and in that case you'd better have a boot floppy handy.)

Chapter 7
Logging In And Out

This section describes what happens when a user logs in or out. The various interactions of background processes, log files, configuration files, and so on are described in some detail.

Logins Via Terminals

Figure 7.1 shows how logins happen via terminals. First, init makes sure there is a getty program for the terminal connection (or console). getty listens at the terminal and waits for the user to notify that he is ready to login in (this usually means that the user must type something). When it notices a user, getty outputs a welcome message (stored in /etc/issue), prompts for the username, and finally runs the login program. login gets the username as a parameter, and prompts the user for the password. If these match, login starts the shell configured for the user; otherwise it just exits and terminates the process (perhaps after giving the user another chance at entering the username and password). init notices that the process terminated, and starts a new getty for the terminal.

Note that the only new process is the one created by init (using the fork system call); getty and login only replace the program running in the process (using the exec system call).

A separate program, for noticing the user, is needed for serial lines, since it can be (and traditionally was) complicated to notice when a terminal becomes active. getty also adapts to the speed and other settings of the connection, which is important especially for dial-in connections, where these parameters may change from call to call.

331

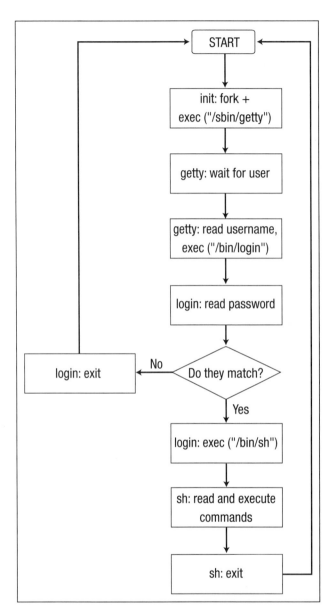

Figure 7.1
Logins via terminals: the interaction of init, getty, login, and the shell.

There are several versions of getty and init in use, all with their good and bad points. It is a good idea to learn about the versions on your system, and also about the other versions (you could use the Linux Software Map to search them). If you don't have dial-ins, you probably don't have to worry about getty, but init is still important.

Logins Via The Network

Two computers in the same network are usually linked via a single physical cable. When they communicate over the network, the programs in each computer that take part in the communication are linked via a virtual connection, a sort of imaginary cable. As far as the programs at either end of the virtual connection are concerned, they have a monopoly on their own cable. However, since the cable is not real, only imaginary, the operating systems of both computers can have several virtual connections share the same physical cable. This way, using just a single cable, several programs can communicate without having to know of or care about the other communications. It is even possible to have several computers use the same cable; the virtual connections exist between two computers, and the other computers ignore those connections that they don't take part in.

That's a complicated and over-abstracted description of the reality. It might, however, be good enough to understand the important reason why network logins are somewhat different from normal logins. The virtual connections are established when there are two programs on different computers that wish to communicate. Since it is in principle possible to log in from any computer in a network to any other computer, there is a huge number of potential virtual communications. Because of this, it is not practical to start a getty for each potential login.

There is a single process inetd (corresponding to getty) that handles all network logins. When it notices an incoming network login (i.e., it notices that it gets a new virtual connection to some other computer), it starts a new process to handle that single login. The original process remains and continues to listen for new logins.

To make things a bit more complicated, there is more than one communication protocol for network logins. The two most important ones are *telnet* and *rlogin*. In addition to logins, there are many other virtual connections that may be made (for FTP, Gopher, HTTP, and other network services). It would be ineffective to have a separate process listening for a particular type of connection, so instead there is only one listener that can recognize the type of the connection and can start the correct type of program to provide the service. This single listener is called **\cmd{inetd}**; see *The Linux Network Administrators' Guide* for more information.

What login Does

The login program takes care of authenticating the user (making sure that the username and password match), and of setting up an initial environment for the user by setting permissions for the serial line and starting the shell.

Part of the initial setup is outputting the contents of the file /etc/motd (short for message of the day) and checking for electronic mail. These can be disabled by creating a file called .hushlogin in the user's home directory.

If the file /etc/nologin exists, logins are disabled. That file is typically created by shutdown and relatives. login checks for this file and will refuse to accept a login if it exists. If it does exist, login outputs its contents to the terminal before it quits.

login logs all failed login attempts in a system log file (via syslog). It also logs all logins by root. Both of these can be useful when tracking down intruders.

Currently logged in people are listed in /var/run/utmp. This file is valid only until the system is next rebooted or shut down; it is cleared when the system is booted. It lists each user and the terminal (or network connection) he is using, along with some other useful information. The **who, w,** and other similar commands look in utmp to see who are logged in.

All successful logins are recorded into /var/log/wtmp. This file will grow without limit, so it must be cleaned regularly, for example by having a weekly **cron** job to clear it. (Good Linux distributions do this out of the box.) The last command browses wtmp.

Both utmp and wtmp are in a binary format (see the utmp manual page); it is unfortunately not convenient to examine them without special programs.

Access Control

The user database is traditionally contained in the /etc/passwd file. Some systems use shadow passwords, and have moved the passwords to /etc/shadow. Sites with many computers that share the accounts use NIS or some other method to store the user database; they might also automatically copy the database from one central location to all other computers.

The user database contains not only the passwords but also some additional information about the users, such as their real names, home directories, and login shells. This other information needs to be public, so that anyone can read it. Therefore the password is stored encrypted. This does have the drawback that anyone with access to the encrypted password can use various cryptographic methods to guess it, without trying to actually log into the computer. Shadow passwords try to avoid this by moving the password into another file, which only root can read (the password is still stored encrypted). However, installing shadow passwords later onto a system that does not support them can be difficult.

With or without passwords, it is important to make sure that all passwords in a system are good, that is, not easily guessable. The crack program can be used to crack passwords; any password it can find is by definition not a good one. While crack can be run by intruders, it can also be run by the system administrator to avoid bad passwords. Good passwords can also be enforced by the passwd program; this is in fact more effective in CPU cycles, since cracking passwords requires quite a lot of computation.

The user group database is kept in /etc/group; for systems with shadow passwords, there can be a /etc/shadow.group.

root usually can't login via most terminals or the network, only via terminals listed in the /etc/securetty file. This makes it necessary to get physical access to one of these terminals. It is, however, possible to log in via any terminal as any other user, and use the **su** command to become root.

Shell Startup

When an interactive login shell starts, it automatically executes one or more predefined files. Different shells execute different files; see the documentation of each shell for further information.

Most shells first run some global file, for example, the Bourne shell (/bin/sh) and its derivatives execute /etc/profile; in addition, they execute .profile in the user's home directory. /etc/profile allows the system administrator to have set up a common user environment, especially by setting the path to include local command directories in addition to the normal ones. On the other hand, .profile allows the user to customize the environment to his own tastes by overriding, if necessary, the default environment.

Chapter 8
Managing User Accounts

"The similarities of sysadmins and drug dealers: both measure stuff in K's, and both have users."

—Old, tired computer joke

This chapter explains how to create new user accounts, how to modify the properties of those accounts, and how to remove the accounts. Different Linux systems have different tools for doing this.

What's An Account?

When a computer is used by many people it is usually necessary to differentiate between the users, for example, so that their private files can be kept private. This is important even if the computer can only be used by a single person at a time, as with most microcomputers. (It might be quite embarrassing if my sister could read my love letters.) Thus, each user is given a unique username, and that name is used to log in.

There's more to a user than just a name, however. An account is all the files, resources, and information belonging to one user. The term hints at banks, and in a commercial system each account usually has some money attached to it, and that money vanishes at different speeds depending on how much the user stresses the system. For example, disk space might have a price per megabyte and day, and processing time might have a price per second.

Creating A User

The Linux kernel itself treats users are mere numbers. Each user is identified by a unique integer, the user ID or *uid*, because numbers are faster and easier for a computer to process than textual names.

A separate database outside the kernel assigns a textual name, the username, to each user ID. The database contains additional information as well.

To create a user, you need to add information about the user to the user database, and create a home directory for him. It may also be necessary to educate the user, and set up a suitable initial environment for him.

Most Linux distributions come with a program for creating accounts. There are several such programs available. Two command line alternatives are **adduser** and **useradd**; there may be a GUI tool as well. Whatever the program, the result is that there is little if any manual work to be done. Even if the details are many and intricate, these programs make everything seem trivial. However, the section called "Creating A User By Hand" describes how to do it by hand.

/etc/passwd And Other Informative Files

The basic user database in a Unix system is the text file, /etc/passwd (called the password file), which lists all valid usernames and their associated information. The file has one line per username, and is divided into seven colon-delimited fields:

- ♦ Username
- ♦ Password, in an encrypted form
- ♦ Numeric user ID
- ♦ Numeric group ID
- ♦ Full name or other description of account
- ♦ Home directory
- ♦ Login shell (program to run at login)

The format is explained in more detail on the passwd manual page.

Any user on the system may read the password file, so that they can, for example, learn the name of another user. This means that the password (the second field) is also available to everyone. The password file encrypts the password, so in theory there is no problem. However, the encryption is breakable, especially if the password is weak (that is, if it is short or it can be found in a dictionary). Therefore it is not a good idea to have the password in the password file.

Many Linux systems have shadow passwords. This is an alternative way of storing the password: The encrypted password is stored in a separate file, /etc/shadow, which only root can read. The /etc/passwd file only contains a special marker in the second field. Any program that needs to verify a user is setuid, and can therefore access the shadow password file. Normal programs, which only use the other fields in the password file, can't get at the password. (Yes, this means that the password file has all the information about a user except his password. The wonder of development.)

Picking Numeric User And Group IDs

On most systems it doesn't matter what the numeric user and group IDs are, but if you use the *Network Filesystem* (NFS), you need to have the same uid and gid on all systems. This is because NFS also identifies users with the numeric uids. If you aren't using NFS, you can let your account creation tool pick them automatically.

If you are using NFS, you'll have to be invent a mechanism for synchronizing account information. One alternative is to the NIS system (please refer to the network-admin-guide in the first part of this book).

However, you should try to avoid reusing numeric uids (and textual usernames), because the new owner of the uid (or username) may get access to the old owner's files (or mail, or whatever).

Initial Environment: /etc/skel

When the home directory for a new user is created, it is initialized with files from the /etc/skel directory. The system administrator can create files in /etc/skel that will provide a nice default environment for users. For example, he might create a /etc/skel/.profile that sets the EDITOR environment variable to some editor that is friendly toward new users.

However, it is usually best to try to keep /etc/skel as small as possible, since it will be next to impossible to update existing users' files. For example, if the name of the friendly editor changes, all existing users would have to edit their .profile. The system administrator could try to do it automatically, with a script, but that is almost certain going to break someone's file.

Whenever possible, it is better to put global configuration into global files, such as /etc/profile. This way it is possible to update it without breaking users' own setups.

Creating A User By Hand

To create a new account manually, follow these steps:

1. Edit /etc/passwd with **vipw** and add a new line for the new account. Be careful with the syntax. Do not edit directly with an editor! **vipw** locks the file, so that other commands won't try to update it at the same time. You should make the password field be "*", so that it is impossible to log in.

2. Similarly, edit /etc/group with **vigr**, if you need to create a new group as well.

3. Create the home directory of the user with **mkdir**.

4. Copy the files from /etc/skel to the new home directory.

5. Fix ownerships and permissions with **chown** and **chmod**. The **-R** option is most useful. The correct permissions vary a little from one site to another, but usually the following commands do the right thing:

```
cd /home/newusername
chown -R username.group .
chmod -R go=u,go-w .
chmod go= .
```

Set the password with **passwd**.

After you set the password in the last step, the account will work. You shouldn't set it until everything else has been done, otherwise the user may inadvertently log in while you're still copying the files.

It is sometimes necessary to create dummy accounts that are not used by people. For example, to set up an anonymous FTP server (so that anyone can download files from it, without having to get an account first), you need to create an account called ftp. In such cases, it is usually not necessary to set the password (last step above). Indeed, it is better not to, so that no one can use the account, unless they first become root, since root can become any user.

Changing User Properties

There are a few commands for changing various properties of an account (i.e., the relevant field in /etc/passwd):

♦ **chfn**—changes the full name field

♦ **chsh**—changes the login shell

♦ **passwd**—changes the password

The super-user may use these commands to change the properties of any account. Normal users can only change the properties of their own account. It may sometimes be necessary to disable these commands (with **chmod**) for normal users, for example in an environment with many novice users.

Other tasks need to be done by hand. For example, to change the username, you need to edit /etc/passwd directly (with **vipw**, remember). Likewise, to add or remove the user to more groups, you need to edit /etc/group (with **vigr**). Such tasks tend to be rare, however, and should be done with caution: For example, if you change the username, email will no longer reach the user, unless you also create a mail alias. (The user's name might change due to marriage, for example, and he might want to have his username reflect his new name.)

Removing A User

To remove a user, you first remove all his files, mailboxes, mail aliases, print jobs, cron and at jobs, and all other references to the user. Then you remove the relevant lines from /etc/

passwd and /etc/group (remember to remove the username from all groups it's been added to). It may be a good idea to first disable the account (see below), before you start removing stuff, to prevent the user from using the account while it is being removed.

Remember that users may have files outside their home directory. The **find** command can find them:

```
find / -user username
```

However, note that the above command will take a long time, if you have large disks. If you mount network disks, you need to be careful so that you won't trash the network or the server.

Some Linux distributions come with special commands to do this; look for **deluser** or **userdel**. However, it is easy to do it by hand as well, and the commands might not do everything.

Disabling A User Temporarily

It is sometimes necessary to temporarily disable an account, without removing it. For example, the user might not have paid his fees, or the system administrator may suspect that a cracker has got the password of that account.

The best way to disable an account is to change its shell into a special program that just prints a message. This way, whoever tries to log into the account will fail, and will know why. The message can tell the user to contact the system administrator so that any problems may be dealt with.

It would also be possible to change the username or password to something else, but then the user won't know what is going on. Confused users mean more work. (But they can be so fun, if you're a BOFH.)

A simple way to create the special programs is to write "tail scripts":

```
#!/usr/bin/tail +2
This account has been closed due to a security breach.
Please call 555-1234 and wait for the men in black to arrive.
```

The first two characters ("#!") tell the kernel that the rest of the line is a command that needs to be run to interpret this file. The **tail** command in this case outputs everything except the first line to the standard output.

If user billg is suspected of a security breach, the system administrator would do something like this:

```
# chsh -s /usr/local/lib/no-login/security billg
# su - tester
```

```
This account has been closed due to a security breach.
Please call 555-1234 and wait for the men in black to arrive.
#
```

The purpose of the **su** is to test that the change worked, of course.

Tail scripts should be kept in a separate directory, so that their names don't interfere with normal user commands.

Chapter 9
Backups

Hardware is indeterministically reliable. Software is deterministically unreliable. People are indeterministically unreliable. Nature is deterministically reliable.

This chapter explains about why, how, and when to make backups, and how to restore things from backups.

On The Importance Of Being Backed Up

Your data is valuable. It will cost you time and effort to re-create it, and that costs money or at least personal grief and tears; sometimes it can't even be re-created, that is, if it is the results of some experiments. Since it is an investment, you should protect it and take steps to avoid losing it.

There are basically four reasons why you might lose data: hardware failures, software bugs, human action, or natural disasters. (The fifth reason is "something else.") Although modern hardware tends to be quite reliable, it can still break seemingly spontaneously. The most critical piece of hardware for storing data is the hard disk, which relies on tiny magnetic fields remaining intact in a world filled with electromagnetic noise. Modern software doesn't even tend to be reliable; a rock-solid program is an exception, not a rule. Humans are quite unreliable; they will either make a mistake, or they will be malicious and destroy data on purpose. Nature might not be evil, but it can wreak havoc even when being good. All in all, it is a small miracle that anything works at all.

Backups are a way to protect the investment in data. By having several copies of the data, it does not matter as much if one is destroyed (the cost is only that of the restoration of the lost data from the backup).

It is important to do backups properly. Like everything else that is related to the physical world, backups will fail sooner or later. Part of doing backups well is to make sure they work; you don't want to notice that your backups didn't work. (Don't laugh. This has happened to several people.) Adding insult to injury, you might have a bad crash just as you're making the backup; if you have only one backup medium, it might be destroyed as well, leaving you with the smoking ashes of hard work. (Been there, done that....) Or you might notice, when trying to restore, that you forgot to back up something important, like the user database on a 15,000-user site. Best of all, all your backups might be working perfectly, but the last known tape drive reading the kind of tapes you used was the one that now has a bucketful of water in it.

When it comes to backups, paranoia is in the job description.

Selecting The Backup Medium

The most important decision regarding backups is the choice of backup medium. You need to consider cost, reliability, speed, availability, and usability.

Cost is important, since you should preferably have several times more backup storage than what you need for the data. A cheap medium is usually a must.

Reliability is extremely important, since a broken backup can make a grown man cry. A backup medium must be able to hold data without corruption for years. The way you use the medium affects it reliability as a backup medium. A hard disk is typically very reliable, but as a backup medium it is not very reliable, if it is in the same computer as the disk you are backing up.

Speed is usually not very important, if backups can be done without interaction. It doesn't matter if a backup takes two hours, as long as it needs no supervision. On the other hand, if the backup can't be done when the computer would otherwise be idle, then speed is an issue.

Availability is obviously necessary, since you can't use a backup medium if it doesn't exist. Less obvious is the need for the medium to be available even in the future, and on computers other than your own. Otherwise you may not be able to restore your backups after a disaster.

Usability is a large factor in how often backups are made. The easier it is to make backups, the better. A backup medium mustn't be hard or boring to use.

The typical alternatives are floppies and tapes. Floppies are very cheap, fairly reliable, not very fast, very available, but not very usable for large amounts of data. Tapes are cheap to somewhat expensive, fairly reliable, fairly fast, quite available, and, depending on the size of the tape, quite comfortable.

There are other alternatives. They are usually not very good on availability, but if that is not a problem, they can be better in other ways. For example, magneto-optical disks can have good sides of both floppies (they're random access, making restoration of a single file quick) and tapes (contain a lot of data).

Selecting The Backup Tool

There are many tools that can be used to make backups. The traditional Unix tools used for backups are tar, cpio, and dump. In addition, there are large number of third-party packages (both freeware and commercial) that can be used. The choice of backup medium can affect the choice of tool.

tar and cpio are similar, and mostly equivalent from a backup point of view. Both are capable of storing files on tapes, and retrieving files from them. Both are capable of using almost any media, since the kernel device drivers take care of the low-level device handling and the devices all tend to look alike to user-level programs. Some Unix versions of tar and cpio may have problems with unusual files (symbolic links, device files, files with very long path names, and so on), but the Linux versions should handle all files correctly.

dump is different in that it reads the filesystem directly and not via the filesystem. It is also written specifically for backups; tar and cpio are really for archiving files, although they work for backups as well.

Reading the filesystem directly has some advantages. It makes it possible to back files up without affecting their time stamps; for tar and cpio, you would have to mount the filesystem read-only first. Directly reading the filesystem is also more effective, if everything needs to be backed up, since it can be done with much less disk head movement. The major disadvantage is that it makes the backup program specific to one filesystem type; the Linux dump program understands the ext2 filesystem only.

dump also directly supports backup levels (which we'll be discussing below); with tar and cpio this has to be implemented with other tools.

A comparison of the third-party backup tools is beyond the scope of this book. The Linux Software Map lists many of the freeware ones.

Simple Backups

A simple backup scheme is to back up everything once, then back up everything that has been modified since the previous backup. The first backup is called a *full backup*, the subsequent ones are *incremental backups*. A full backup is often more laborious than incremental ones, since there is more data to write to the tape and a full backup might not fit onto one tape (or floppy). Restoring from incremental backups can be many times more work than from a full one. Restoration can be optimized so that you always back up everything since the previous full backup; this way, backups are a bit more work, but there should never be a need to restore more than a full backup and an incremental backup.

If you want to make backups every day and have six tapes, you could use tape 1 for the first full backup (say, on a Friday), and tapes 2 to 5 for the incremental backups (Monday through Thursday). Then you make a new full backup on tape 6 (second Friday), and start doing incremental ones with tapes 2 to 5 again. You don't want to overwrite tape 1 until you've got a new full backup, lest something happens while you're making the full backup. After you've made a full backup to tape 6, you want to keep tape 1 somewhere else, so that when your other backup tapes are destroyed in the fire, you still have at least something left. When you need to make the next full backup, you fetch tape 1 and leave tape 6 in its place.

If you have more than six tapes, you can use the extra ones for full backups. Each time you make a full backup, you use the oldest tape. This way you can have full backups from several previous weeks, which is good if you want to find an old, now deleted file, or an old version of a file.

Making Backups With **tar**

A full backup can easily be made with **tar**:

```
# tar —create —file /dev/ftape /usr/src
tar: Removing leading / from absolute path names in the archive
#
```

The example above uses the GNU version of **tar** and its long option names. The traditional version of **tar** only understands single character options. The GNU version can also handle backups that don't fit on one tape or floppy, and also very long paths; not all traditional versions can do these things. (Linux only uses GNU **tar**.)

If your backup doesn't fit on one tape, you need to use the multi-volume (**-M**) option:

```
# tar -cMf /dev/fd0H1440 /usr/src
tar: Removing leading / from absolute path names in the archive
Prepare volume \#2 for /dev/fd0H1440 and hit return:
#
```

Note that you should format the floppies before you begin the backup, or else use another window or virtual terminal and do it when **tar** asks for a new floppy.

After you've made a backup, you should check that it is OK, using the **-compare (d)** option:

```
# tar —compare —verbose -f /dev/ftape
usr/src/
usr/src/linux
usr/src/linux-1.2.10-includes/
....
#
```

Failing to check a backup means that you will not notice that your backups aren't working until after you've lost the original data.

An incremental backup can be done with tar using the **-newer** (**-N**) option:

```
# tar —create —newer '8 Sep 1995' —file /dev/ftape /usr/src —verbose
tar: Removing leading / from absolute path names in the archive
usr/src/
usr/src/linux-1.2.10-includes/
usr/src/linux-1.2.10-includes/include/
usr/src/linux-1.2.10-includes/include/linux/
usr/src/linux-1.2.10-includes/include/linux/modules/
usr/src/linux-1.2.10-includes/include/asm-generic/
usr/src/linux-1.2.10-includes/include/asm-i386/
usr/src/linux-1.2.10-includes/include/asm-mips/
usr/src/linux-1.2.10-includes/include/asm-alpha/
usr/src/linux-1.2.10-includes/include/asm-m68k/
usr/src/linux-1.2.10-includes/include/asm-sparc/
usr/src/patch-1.2.11.gz
#
```

Unfortunately, **tar** can't notice when a file's inode information has changed, for example, that its permission bits have been changed, or when its name has been changed. This can be worked around using find and comparing current filesystem state with lists of files that have been previously backed up. Scripts and programs for doing this can be found on Linux ftp sites.

Restoring Files With **tar**

The **-extract** (**-x**) option for tar extracts files:

```
# tar —extract —same-permissions —verbose —file /dev/fd0H1440
usr/src/
usr/src/linux
usr/src/linux-1.2.10-includes/
usr/src/linux-1.2.10-includes/include/
usr/src/linux-1.2.10-includes/include/linux/
usr/src/linux-1.2.10-includes/include/linux/hdreg.h
usr/src/linux-1.2.10-includes/include/linux/kernel.h
...
#
```

You also extract only specific files or directories (which includes all their files and subdirectories) by naming on the command line:

```
# tar xpvf /dev/fd0H1440 usr/src/linux-1.2.10-includes/include/linux/hdreg.h
usr/src/linux-1.2.10-includes/include/linux/hdreg.h
#
```

Use the **-list** (**-t**) option, if you just want to see what files are on a backup volume:

```
# tar —list —file /dev/fd0H1440
usr/src/
usr/src/linux
usr/src/linux-1.2.10-includes/
usr/src/linux-1.2.10-includes/include/
usr/src/linux-1.2.10-includes/include/linux/
usr/src/linux-1.2.10-includes/include/linux/hdreg.h
usr/src/linux-1.2.10-includes/include/linux/kernel.h
...
#
```

Note that **tar** always reads the backup volume sequentially, so for large volumes it is rather slow. It is not possible, however, to use random-access database techniques when using a tape drive or some other sequential medium.

tar doesn't handle deleted files properly. If you need to restore a file system from a full and an incremental backup, and you have deleted a file between the two backups, it will exist again after you have done the restore. This can be a big problem, if the file has sensitive data that should no longer be available.

Multilevel Backups

The simple backup method outlined in the previous section is often quite adequate for personal use or small sites. For more heavy duty use, multilevel backups are more appropriate.

The simple method has two backup levels: full and incremental backups. This can be generalized to any number of levels. A full backup would be level 0, and the different levels of incremental backups levels 1, 2, 3, and so on. At each incremental backup level you back up everything that has changed since the previous backup at the same or a previous level.

The purpose for doing this is that it allows a longer backup history cheaply. In the example in the previous section, the backup history went back to the previous full backup. This could be extended by having more tapes, but only a week per new tape, which might be too expensive. A longer backup history is useful, because deleted or corrupted files are often not noticed for a long time. Even a version of a file that is not very up to date is better than no file at all.

With multiple levels the backup history can be extended more cheaply. For example, if we buy ten tapes, we could use tapes 1 and 2 for monthly backups (first Friday each month), tapes 3 to 6 for weekly backups (other Fridays; note that there can be five Fridays in one month, so we need four more tapes), and tapes 7 to 10 for daily backups (Monday to Thursday). With only four more tapes, we've been able to extend the backup history from two weeks (after all daily tapes have been used) to two months. It is true that we can't restore every version of each file during those two months, but what we can restore is often good enough.

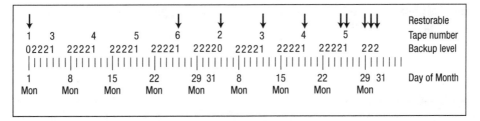

Figure 9.1
A sample multilevel backup schedule.

Figure 9.1 shows which backup level is used each day, and which backups can be restored from at the end of the month.

Backup levels can also be used to keep filesystem restoration time to a minimum. If you have many incremental backups with monotonously growing level numbers, you need to restore all of them if you need to rebuild the whole filesystem. Instead you can use level numbers that aren't monotonous, and keep down the number of backups to restore.

To minimize the number of tapes needed to restore, you could use a smaller level for each incremental tape. However, then the time to make the backups increases (each backup copies everything since the previous full backup). A better scheme is suggested by the dump manual page and described by the Table 9.1 (efficient backup levels). Use the following succession of backup levels: 3, 2, 5, 4, 7, 6, 9, 8, 9, and so forth. This keeps both the backup and restore times low. The most you have to backup is two days' worth of work. The number of tapes for a restore depends on how long you keep between full backups, but it is less than in the simple schemes.

A fancy scheme can reduce the amount of labor needed, but it does mean there are more things to keep track of. You must decide if it is worth it.

Table 9.1   Efficient backup scheme using many backup levels.

Tape	Level	Backup (days)	Restore tapes
1	0	n/a	1
2	3	1	1, 2
3	2	2	1, 3
4	5	1	1, 2, 4
5	4	2	1, 2, 5
6	7	1	1, 2, 5, 6
7	6	2	1, 2, 5, 7
8	9	1	1, 2, 5, 7, 8
9	8	2	1, 3, 5, 7, 9
10	9	1	1, 2, 5, 7, 9, 10
11	9	1	1, 2, 5, 7, 9, 10, 11
...	9	1	1, 2, 5, 7, 9, 10, 11

dump has built-in support for backup levels. For **tar** and **cpio** it must be implemented with shell scripts.

What To Back Up

You want to back up as much as possible. The major exception is software that can be easily reinstalled (you get to decide what's easy; some people consider installing from dozens of floppies easy), but even they may have configuration files that it is important to back up, lest you need to do all the work to configure them all over again. Another major exception is the /proc filesystem; since that only contains data that the kernel always generates automatically, it is never a good idea to back it up. Especially the /proc/kcore file is unnecessary, since it is just an image of your current physical memory; it's pretty large as well.

Gray areas include the news spool, log files, and many other things in /var. You must decide what you consider important.

The obvious things to back up are user files (/home) and system configuration files (/etc, but possibly other things scattered all over the filesystem).

Compressed Backups

Backups take a lot of space, which can cost quite a lot of money. To reduce the space needed, the backups can be compressed. There are several ways of doing this. Some programs have support for compression built in; for example, the **-gzip** (**-z**) option for GNU tar pipes the whole backup through the gzip compression program, before writing it to the backup medium.

Unfortunately, compressed backups can cause trouble. Due to the nature of how compression works, if a single bit is wrong, all the rest of the compressed data will be unusable. Some backup programs have some built-in error correction, but no method can handle a large number of errors. This means that if the backup is compressed the way GNU **tar** does it, with the whole output compressed as a unit, a single error makes all the rest of the backup lost. Backups must be reliable, and this method of compression is not a good idea.

An alternative way is to compress each file separately. This still means that the one file is lost, but all other files are unharmed. The lost file would have been corrupted anyway, so this situation is not much worse than not using compression at all. The afio program (a variant of **cpio**) can do this.

Compression takes some time, which may make the backup program unable to write data fast enough for a tape drive. (If a tape drive doesn't data fast enough, it has to stop; this makes backups even slower, and can be bad for the tape and the drive.) This can be avoided by buffering the output (either internally, if the backup program if smart enough, or by using another program), but even that might not work well enough. This should only be a problem on slow computers.

Chapter 10
Keeping Time

"Time is an illusion.
Lunchtime double so."

— Douglas Adams

This chapter explains how a Linux system keeps time, and what you need to do to avoid causing trouble. Usually, you don't need to do anything about time, but it is good to understand it.

Time Zones

Time measurement is based on mostly regular natural phenomena, such as alternating light and dark periods caused by the rotation of the planet. The total time taken by two successive periods is constant, but the lengths of the light and dark period vary. One simple constant is noon.

Noon is the time of the day when the sun is at its highest position. Since the earth is round (according to recent research), noon happens at different times in different places. This leads to the concept of *local time*. Humans measure time in many units, most of which are tied to natural phenomena like noon. As long as you stay in the same place, it doesn't matter that local times differ.

As soon as you need to communicate with distant places, you'll notice the need for a common time. In modern times, most of the places in the world communicate with most other places in the world, so a global standard for measuring time has been defined. This time is called universal time (UT or UTC, formerly known as Greenwich Mean Time or GMT, since it used to be local time in Greenwich, England). When people with different local times need to communicate, they can express times in universal time, so that there is no confusion about when things should happen.

Each local time is called a *time zone*. While geography would allow all places that have noon at the same time have the same time zone, politics makes it difficult. For various reasons, many countries use daylight savings time, that is, they move their clocks to have more natural light while they work, and then move the clocks back during winter. Other countries do not do this. Those that do, do not agree when the clocks should be moved, and they change the rules from year to year. This makes time zone conversions definitely nontrivial.

Time zones are best named by the location or by telling the difference between local and universal time. In the U.S. and some other countries, the local time zones have a name and a three-letter abbreviation. The abbreviations are not unique, however, and should not be used unless the country is also named. It is better to talk about the local time in, say, Helsinki, than about East European time, since not all countries in Eastern Europe follow the same rules.

Linux has a time zone package that knows about all existing time zones, and that can easily be updated when the rules change. All the system administrator needs to do is to select the appropriate time zone. Also, each user can set his own time zone; this is important since many people work with computers in different countries over the Internet. When the rules for daylight savings time change in your local time zone, make sure you'll upgrade at least that part of your Linux system. Other than setting the system time zone and upgrading the time zone data files, there is little need to bother about time.

The Hardware And Software Clocks

A personal computer has a battery-driven hardware clock. The battery ensures that the clock will work even if the rest of the computer is without electricity. The hardware clock can be set from the BIOS setup screen or from whatever operating system is running.

The Linux kernel keeps track of time independently from the hardware clock. During the boot, Linux sets its own clock to the same time as the hardware clock. After this, both clocks run independently. Linux maintains its own clock because looking at the hardware is slow and complicated.

The kernel clock always shows universal time. This way, the kernel does not need to know about time zones at all. The simplicity results in higher reliability and makes it easier to update the time zone information. Each process handles time zone conversions itself (using standard tools that are part of the time zone package).

The hardware clock can be in local time or in universal time. It is usually better to have it in universal time, because then you don't need to change the hardware clock when daylight savings time begins or ends (UTC does not have DST). Unfortunately, some PC operating systems, including MS-DOS, Windows, and OS/2, assume the hardware clock shows local time. Linux can handle either, but if the hardware clock shows local time, then it must be modified when daylight savings time begins or ends (otherwise it wouldn't show local time).

Showing And Setting Time

In the Debian system, the system time zone is determined by the symbolic link /etc/localtime. This link points at a time zone data file that describes the local time zone. The time zone data files are stored in /usr/lib/zoneinfo. Other Linux distributions may do this differently.

A user can change his private time zone by setting the TZ environment variable. If it is unset, the system time zone is assumed. The syntax of the TZ variable is described in the tzset manual page.

The **date** command shows the current date and time. (Beware of the **time** command, which does not show the current time.) For example:

```
$ date
Sun Jul 14 21:53:41 EET DST 1996
$
```

That time is Sunday, 14th of July, 1996, at about ten before ten at the evening, in the time zone called "EET DST" (which might be East European Daylight Savings Time). **date** can also show the universal time:

```
$ date -u
Sun Jul 14 18:53:42 UTC 1996
Sun Jul 14 18:53:42 UTC 1996
$
```

date is also used to set the kernel's software clock:

```
# date 07142157
Sun Jul 14 21:57:00 EET DST 1996
# date
Sun Jul 14 21:57:02 EET DST 1996
#
```

See the **date** manual page for more details; the syntax is a bit arcane. Only root can set the time. Although each user can have his own time zone, the clock is the same for everyone.

date only shows or sets the software clock. The **clock** command synchronizes the hardware and software clocks. It is used when the system boots to read the hardware clock and set the software clock. If you need to set both clocks, you first set the software clock with **date**, and then the hardware clock with **clock -w**.

The **-u** option to **clock** tells it that the hardware clock is in universal time. You must use the **-u** option correctly. If you don't, your computer will be quite confused about what the time is.

The clocks should be changed with care. Many parts of a Unix system require the clocks to work correctly. For example, the **cron** daemon runs commands periodically. If you change the clock, it can be confused of whether it needs to run the commands or not. On one early Unix system, someone set the clock 20 years into the future, and **cron** wanted to run all the periodic commands for 20 years all at once. Current versions of **cron** can handle this correctly, but you should still be careful. Big jumps or backward jumps are more dangerous than smaller or forward ones.

When The Clock Is Wrong

The Linux software clock is not always accurate. It is kept running by a periodic timer interrupt generated by PC hardware. If the system has too many processes running, it may take too long to service the timer interrupt, and the software clock starts slipping behind. The hardware clock runs independently and is usually more accurate. If you boot your computer often (as is the case for most systems that aren't servers), it will usually keep fairly accurate time.

If you need to adjust the hardware clock, it is usually simplest to reboot; go into the BIOS setup screen, and do it from there. This avoids all trouble that changing system time might cause. If doing it via BIOS is not an option, set the new time with **date** and **clock** (in that order), but be prepared to reboot, if some part of the system starts acting funny.

A networked computer (even if just over the modem) can check its own clock automatically, by comparing it to some other computer's time. If the other computer is known to keep very accurate time, then both computers will keep accurate time. This can be done by using the **rdate** and **netdate** commands. Both check the time of a remote computer (**netdate** can handle several remote computers), and set the local computer's time to that. By running one these commands regularly, your computer will keep as accurate time as the remote computer.

Glossary

This is a short list of word definitions for concepts relating to Linux and system administration.

ambition
The act of writing funny sentences in the hope of getting them into the Linux cookie file.

application program
Software that does something useful. The results of using an application program is what the computer was bought for. See also system program, operating system.

daemon
A process lurking in the background, usually unnoticed, until something triggers it into action. For example, the \cmd{update} daemon wakes up every 30 seconds or so to flush the buffer cache, and the \cmd{sendmail} daemon awakes whenever someone sends mail.

filesystem
The methods and data structures that an operating system uses to keep track of files on a disk or partition; the way the files are organized on the disk. Also used about a partition or disk that is used to store the files or the type of the filesystem.

glossary
A list of words and explanations of what they do. Not to be confused with a dictionary, which is also a list of words and explanations.

kernel

Part of an operating system that implements the interaction with hardware and the sharing of resources. See also system program.

operating system

Software that shares a computer system's resources (processor, memory, disk space, network bandwidth, and so on) between users and the application programs they run. Controls access to the system to provide security. See also kernel, system program, application program.

system call

The services provided by the kernel to application programs, and the way in which they are invoked. See section 2 of the manual pages.

system program

Programs that implement high-level functionality of an operating system, i.e., things that aren't directly dependent on the hardware. May sometimes require special privileges to run (that is, for delivering electronic mail), but often just commonly thought of as part of the system (e.g., a compiler). See also application program, kernel, operating system.

Part III

Appendixes

Appendix A
Linux Documentation Project Copying License

Last Modified 6 January 1997

The following copyright license applies to all works by the Linux Documentation Project.

Please read the license carefully—it is somewhat like the GNU General Public License, but there are several conditions in it that differ from what you may be used to. If you have any questions, please email the LDP coordinator at **mdw@metalab.unc.edu**.

The Linux Documentation Project manuals may be reproduced and distributed in whole or in part, subject to the following conditions.

All Linux Documentation Project manuals are copyrighted by their respective authors. THEY ARE NOT IN THE PUBLIC DOMAIN.

- The copyright notice above and this permission notice must be preserved complete on all complete or partial copies.
- Any translation or derivative work of Linux Installation and Getting Started must be approved by the author in writing before distribution.
- If you distribute Linux Installation and Getting Started in part, instructions for obtaining the complete version of this manual must be included, and a means for obtaining a complete version provided.
- Small portions may be reproduced as illustrations for reviews or quotes in other works without this permission notice if proper citation is given.
- The GNU General Public License referenced below may be reproduced under the conditions given within it.

Exceptions to these rules may be granted for academic purposes: Write to the author and ask. These restrictions are here to protect us as authors, not to restrict you as educators and learners. All source code in Linux Installation and Getting Started is placed under the GNU General Public License, available via anonymous FTP from the GNU archive site at **ftp://prep.ai.mit.edu:/pub/gnu/COPYING**.

Publishing LDP Manuals

If you're a publishing company interested in distributing any of the LDP manuals, read on.

By the license given in the previous section, anyone is allowed to publish and distribute verbatim copies of the Linux Documentation Project manuals. You don't need our explicit permission for this. However, if you would like to distribute a translation or derivative work based on any of the LDP manuals, you must obtain permission from the author, in writing, before doing so.

All translations and derivative works of LDP manuals must be placed under the Linux Documentation License given in the previous section. That is, if you plan to release a translation of one of the manuals, it must be freely distributable by the above terms.

You may, of course, sell the LDP manuals for profit. We encourage you to do so. Keep in mind, however, that because the LDP manuals are freely distributable, anyone may photocopy or distribute printed copies free of charge, if they wish to do so.

We do not require to be paid royalties for any profit earned from selling LDP manuals. However, we would like to suggest that if you do sell LDP manuals for profit, that you either offer the author royalties, or donate a portion of your earnings to the author, the LDP as a whole, or to the Linux development community. You may also wish to send one or more free copies of the LDP manual that you are distributing to the author. Your show of support for the LDP and the Linux community will be very appreciated.

We would like to be informed of any plans to publish or distribute LDP manuals, just so we know how they're becoming available. If you are publishing or planning to publish any LDP manuals, please send email to Matt Welsh at **mdw@metalab.unc.edu**.

We encourage Linux software distributors to distribute the LDP manuals (such as the Installation and Getting Started Guide) with their software. The LDP manuals are intended to be used as the "official" Linux documentation, and we'd like to see mail-order distributors bundling the LDP manuals with the software. As the LDP manuals mature, hopefully they will fulfill this goal more adequately.

Version 2, June 1991
Copyright © 1989, 1991 Free Software Foundation, Inc.
59 Temple Place—Suite 330, Boston, MA 02111-1307, USA

Appendix B
GNU General Public License

W e have included the GNU General Public License (GPL) for your reference as it applies to the software this book is about. However, the GPL does not apply to the text of this book.

Version 2, June 1991
Copyright © 1989, 1991 Free Software Foundation, Inc.
59 Temple Place—Suite 330, Boston, MA 02111-1307, USA

Preamble

The licenses for most software are designed to take away your freedom to share and change it. By contrast, the GNU General Public License is intended to guarantee your freedom to share and change free software—to make sure the software is free for all its users. This General Public License applies to most of the Free Software Foundation's software and to any other program whose authors commit to using it. (Some other Free Software Foundation software is covered by the GNU Library General Public License instead.) You can apply it to your programs, too.

When we speak of free software, we are referring to freedom, not price. Our General Public Licenses are designed to make sure that you have the freedom to distribute copies of free software (and charge for this service if you wish), that you receive source code or can get it if you want it, that you can change the software or use pieces of it in new free programs; and that you know you can do these things.

To protect your rights, we need to make restrictions that forbid anyone to deny you these rights or to ask you to surrender the rights. These restrictions translate to certain responsibilities for you if you distribute copies of the software, or if you modify it.

For example, if you distribute copies of such a program, whether gratis or for a fee, you must give the recipients all the rights that you have. You must make sure that they, too, receive or can get the source code. And you must show them these terms so they know their rights.

We protect your rights with two steps: (1) copyright the software, and (2) offer you this license which gives you legal permission to copy, distribute and/or modify the software.

Also, for each author's protection and ours, we want to make certain that everyone understands that there is no warranty for this free software. If the software is modified by someone else and passed on, we want its recipients to know that what they have is not the original, so that any problems introduced by others will not reflect on the original authors' reputations.

Finally, any free program is threatened constantly by software patents. We wish to avoid the danger that redistributors of a free program will individually obtain patent licenses, in effect making the program proprietary. To prevent this, we have made it clear that any patent must be licensed for everyone's free use or not licensed at all.

The precise terms and conditions for copying, distribution, and modification follow.

Terms And Conditions For Copying, Distribution, And Modification

This License applies to any program or other work which contains a notice placed by the copyright holder saying it may be distributed under the terms of this General Public License. The "Program", below, refers to any such program or work, and a "work based on the Program" means either the Program or any derivative work under copyright law: that is to say, a work containing the Program or a portion of it, either verbatim or with modifications and/or translated into another language. (Hereinafter, translation is included without limitation in the term "modification.") Each licensee is addressed as "you."

Activities other than copying, distribution, and modification are not covered by this License; they are outside its scope. The act of running the Program is not restricted, and the output from the Program is covered only if its contents constitute a work based on the Program (independent of having been made by running the Program). Whether that is true depends on what the Program does.

1. You may copy and distribute verbatim copies of the Program's source code as you receive it, in any medium, provided that you conspicuously and appropriately publish on each copy an appropriate copyright notice and disclaimer of warranty; keep intact all the notices that refer to this License and to the absence of any warranty; and give any other recipients of the Program a copy of this License along with the Program.

You may charge a fee for the physical act of transferring a copy, and you may at your option offer warranty protection in exchange for a fee.

2. You may modify your copy or copies of the Program or any portion of it, thus forming a work based on the Program, and copy and distribute such modifications or work under the terms of Section 1 above, provided that you also meet all of these conditions:

   a) You must cause the modified files to carry prominent notices stating that you changed the files and the date of any change.

   b) You must cause any work that you distribute or publish, that in whole or in part contains or is derived from the Program or any part thereof, to be licensed as a whole at no charge to all third parties under the terms of this License.

   c) If the modified program normally reads commands interactively when run, you must cause it, when started running for such interactive use in the most ordinary way, to print or display an announcement including an appropriate copyright notice and a notice that there is no warranty (or else, saying that you provide a warranty) and that users may redistribute the program under these conditions, and telling the user how to view a copy of this License. (Exception: if the Program itself is interactive but does not normally print such an announcement, your work based on the Program is not required to print an announcement.)

   These requirements apply to the modified work as a whole. If identifiable sections of that work are not derived from the Program, and can be reasonably considered independent and separate works in themselves, then this License, and its terms, do not apply to those sections when you distribute them as separate works. But when you distribute the same sections as part of a whole which is a work based on the Program, the distribution of the whole must be on the terms of this License, whose permissions for other licensees extend to the entire whole, and thus to each and every part regardless of who wrote it.

   Thus, it is not the intent of this section to claim rights or contest your rights to work written entirely by you; rather, the intent is to exercise the right to control the distribution of derivative or collective works based on the Program.

   In addition, mere aggregation of another work not based on the Program with the Program (or with a work based on the Program) on a volume of a storage or distribution medium does not bring the other work under the scope of this License.

3. You may copy and distribute the Program (or a work based on it, under Section 2) in object code or executable form under the terms of Sections 1 and 2 above provided that you also do one of the following:

   a) Accompany it with the complete corresponding machine-readable source code, which must be distributed under the terms of Sections 1 and 2 above on a medium customarily used for software interchange; or,

b) Accompany it with a written offer, valid for at least three years, to give any third party, for a charge no more than your cost of physically performing source distribution, a complete machine-readable copy of the corresponding source code, to be distributed under the terms of Sections 1 and 2 above on a medium customarily used for software interchange; or,

c) Accompany it with the information you received as to the offer to distribute corresponding source code. (This alternative is allowed only for noncommercial distribution and only if you received the program in object code or executable form with such an offer, in accord with Subsection b above.)

The source code for a work means the preferred form of the work for making modifications to it. For an executable work, complete source code means all the source code for all modules it contains, plus any associated interface definition files, plus the scripts used to control compilation and installation of the executable. However, as a special exception, the source code distributed need not include anything that is normally distributed (in either source or binary form) with the major components (compiler, kernel, and so on) of the operating system on which the executable runs, unless that component itself accompanies the executable.

If distribution of executable or object code is made by offering access to copy from a designated place, then offering equivalent access to copy the source code from the same place counts as distribution of the source code, even though third parties are not compelled to copy the source along with the object code.

4. You may not copy, modify, sublicense, or distribute the Program except as expressly provided under this License. Any attempt otherwise to copy, modify, sublicense, or distribute the Program is void, and will automatically terminate your rights under this License. However, parties who have received copies, or rights, from you under this License will not have their licenses terminated so long as such parties remain in full compliance.

5. You are not required to accept this License, since you have not signed it. However, nothing else grants you permission to modify or distribute the Program or its derivative works. These actions are prohibited by law if you do not accept this License. Therefore, by modifying or distributing the Program (or any work based on the Program), you indicate your acceptance of this License to do so, and all its terms and conditions for copying, distributing or modifying the Program or works based on it.

6. Each time you redistribute the Program (or any work based on the Program), the recipient automatically receives a license from the original licensor to copy, distribute or modify the Program subject to these terms and conditions. You may not impose any further restrictions on the recipients' exercise of the rights granted herein. You are not responsible for enforcing compliance by third parties to this License.

7. If, as a consequence of a court judgment or allegation of patent infringement or for any other reason (not limited to patent issues), conditions are imposed on you (whether by court order, agreement or otherwise) that contradict the conditions of this License,

they do not excuse you from the conditions of this License. If you cannot distribute so as to satisfy simultaneously your obligations under this License and any other pertinent obligations, then as a consequence you may not distribute the Program at all. For example, if a patent license would not permit royalty-free redistribution of the Program by all those who receive copies directly or indirectly through you, then the only way you could satisfy both it and this License would be to refrain entirely from distribution of the Program.

If any portion of this section is held invalid or unenforceable under any particular circumstance, the balance of the section is intended to apply and the section as a whole is intended to apply in other circumstances.

It is not the purpose of this section to induce you to infringe any patents or other property right claims or to contest validity of any such claims; this section has the sole purpose of protecting the integrity of the free software distribution system, which is implemented by public license practices. Many people have made generous contributions to the wide range of software distributed through that system in reliance on consistent application of that system; it is up to the author/donor to decide if he or she is willing to distribute software through any other system and a licensee cannot impose that choice.

This section is intended to make thoroughly clear what is believed to be a consequence of the rest of this License.

8. If the distribution and/or use of the Program is restricted in certain countries either by patents or by copyrighted interfaces, the original copyright holder who places the Program under this License may add an explicit geographical distribution limitation excluding those countries, so that distribution is permitted only in or among countries not thus excluded. In such case, this License incorporates the limitation as if written in the body of this License.

9. The Free Software Foundation may publish revised and/or new versions of the General Public License from time to time. Such new versions will be similar in spirit to the present version, but may differ in detail to address new problems or concerns.

   Each version is given a distinguishing version number. If the Program specifies a version number of this License which applies to it and "any later version", you have the option of following the terms and conditions either of that version or of any later version published by the Free Software Foundation. If the Program does not specify a version number of this License, you may choose any version ever published by the Free Software Foundation.

10. If you wish to incorporate parts of the Program into other free programs whose distribution conditions are different, write to the author to ask for permission. For software which is copyrighted by the Free Software Foundation, write to the Free Software Foundation; we sometimes make exceptions for this. Our decision will be guided by the two goals of preserving the free status of all derivatives of our free software and of promoting the sharing and reuse of software generally.

No Warranty

11. BECAUSE THE PROGRAM IS LICENSED FREE OF CHARGE, THERE IS NO WARRANTY FOR THE PROGRAM, TO THE EXTENT PERMITTED BY APPLICABLE LAW. EXCEPT WHEN OTHERWISE STATED IN WRITING THE COPYRIGHT HOLDERS AND/OR OTHER PARTIES PROVIDE THE PROGRAM "AS IS" WITHOUT WARRANTY OF ANY KIND, EITHER EXPRESSED OR IMPLIED, INCLUDING, BUT NOT LIMITED TO, THE IMPLIED WARRANTIES OF MERCHANTABILITY AND FITNESS FOR A PARTICULAR PURPOSE. THE ENTIRE RISK AS TO THE QUALITY AND PERFORMANCE OF THE PROGRAM IS WITH YOU. SHOULD THE PROGRAM PROVE DEFECTIVE, YOU ASSUME THE COST OF ALL NECESSARY SERVICING, REPAIR OR CORRECTION.

12. IN NO EVENT UNLESS REQUIRED BY APPLICABLE LAW OR AGREED TO IN WRITING WILL ANY COPYRIGHT HOLDER, OR ANY OTHER PARTY WHO MAY MODIFY AND/OR REDISTRIBUTE THE PROGRAM AS PERMITTED ABOVE, BE LIABLE TO YOU FOR DAMAGES, INCLUDING ANY GENERAL, SPECIAL, INCIDENTAL OR CONSEQUENTIAL DAMAGES ARISING OUT OF THE USE OR INABILITY TO USE THE PROGRAM (INCLUDING BUT NOT LIMITED TO LOSS OF DATA OR DATA BEING RENDERED INACCURATE OR LOSSES SUSTAINED BY YOU OR THIRD PARTIES OR A FAILURE OF THE PROGRAM TO OPERATE WITH ANY OTHER PROGRAMS), EVEN IF SUCH HOLDER OR OTHER PARTY HAS BEEN ADVISED OF THE POSSIBILITY OF SUCH DAMAGES.

How To Apply These Terms To Your New Programs

If you develop a new program, and you want it to be of the greatest possible use to the public, the best way to achieve this is to make it free software which everyone can redistribute and change under these terms.

To do so, attach the following notices to the program. It is safest to attach them to the start of each source file to most effectively convey the exclusion of warranty; and each file should have at least the "copyright" line and a pointer to where the full notice is found.

```
one line to give the program's name and an idea of what it does.
Copyright (C) yyyy  name of author

This program is free software; you can redistribute it and/or
modify it under the terms of the GNU General Public License as
published by the Free Software Foundation; either version 2 of
the License, or (at your option) any later version.

This program is distributed in the hope that it will be useful,
but WITHOUT ANY WARRANTY; without even the implied warranty of
```

```
MERCHANTABILITY or FITNESS FOR A PARTICULAR PURPOSE.
See the GNU General Public License for more details.

You should have received a copy of the GNU General Public License
along with this program; if not, write to the Free Software
Foundation, Inc., 59 Temple Place - Suite 330, Boston, MA
02111-1307, USA.
```

Also add information on how to contact you by electronic and paper mail.

If the program is interactive, make it output a short notice like this when it starts in an interactive mode:

```
Gnomovision version 69, Copyright (C) yyyy name of author
Gnomovision comes with ABSOLUTELY NO WARRANTY;
for details type 'show w'.
This is free software, and you are welcome to redistribute it
under certain conditions; type 'show c' for details.
```

The hypothetical commands 'show w' and 'show c' should show the appropriate parts of the General Public License. Of course, the commands you use may be called something other than 'show w' and 'show c'; they could even be mouse-clicks or menu items—whatever suits your program.

You should also get your employer (if you work as a programmer) or your school, if any, to sign a "copyright disclaimer" for the program, if necessary. Here is a sample; alter the names:

```
Yoyodyne, Inc., hereby disclaims all copyright interest
in the program 'Gnomovision' (which makes passes at compilers)
written by James Hacker.

signature of Ty Coon, 1 April 1989
Ty Coon, President of Vice
```

This General Public License does not permit incorporating your program into proprietary programs. If your program is a subroutine library, you may consider it more useful to permit linking proprietary applications with the library. If this is what you want to do, use the GNU Library General Public License instead of this License.

Index